THE FIRST 100 YEARS

A History of

𝕿𝖍𝖊 𝕾𝖆𝖑𝖙 𝕷𝖆𝖐𝖊 𝕿𝖗𝖎𝖇𝖚𝖓𝖊

1871-1971

by

O. N. Malmquist

O. N. Malmquist

UTAH STATE HISTORICAL SOCIETY

SALT LAKE CITY, UTAH

Acknowledgment

I am indebted to many colleagues on *The Salt Lake Tribune* for assistance in the preparation of this history. I thank them all, as a group.

Among those outside *The Tribune* organization to whom I owe special thanks are Dr. Leonard J. Arrington, editor of the Western Historical Quarterly and professor of economics, Utah State University; The Most Rev. Robert J. Dwyer, Roman Catholic Archbishop of Portland, Oregon; Dr. Charles S. Peterson, director of the Utah State Historical Society; and James D. Moyle, Salt Lake City. These individuals read all or virtually all the typescript and offered helpful suggestions and criticisms. I, however, am responsible for the ultimate treatment of all the material and any errors of commission or omission, or any conclusions with which any reader might disagree, are likewise my responsibility.

I owe special thanks also to James Ivers, an associate of the late Senator Thomas Kearns, for informational contributions; to Miriam B. Murphy for preparation of index, arrangement and checking of footnotes, editing assistance and proofreading; to Dee W. Crosby, composing room foreman for Newspaper Agency Corporation, for supervising the composition of this book; to Catherine Mary Drum, an employe of Newspaper Agency Corporation, for perceptive proofreading which diminished the number of errors; and finally, to my wife, whose determination to see the job finished sometimes exceeded my own.

O.N.M.

Malmquist Reports

Until 1952 the Kearns family corporation held working control of Park City's Silver King Coalition Mines which subsidized *The Salt Lake Tribune* through many years after the newspaper's acquisition by Thomas Kearns.

As the reader will learn, Senator Kearns maintained during his lifetime that "it takes a great mine to run a newspaper."

The Tribune once had an opportunity to substantially repay its debt to the Silver King, an opportunity that was thwarted by the author of this book.

O. N. Malmquist will be remembered so long as there is a *Tribune,* as a great political reporter and editor. His assignments outside of the political field, however, were many—as many as the publisher's need to know exactly what were the facts in any complicated problem or situation; particularly those involving the public welfare of the area served by *The Tribune.*

"If it's possible for any human being to be objective," John Fitzpatrick, the *Tribune's* late publisher, often said, "Malmquist is that one."

"Quist's" colleagues and readers unanimously agree, but in wonderment for O. N. Malmquist is as opinionated a man as one is apt to find in the ranks of the well-informed; and he is well-informed in many areas outside of politics. Historical, social, economic subjects never find Malmquist without a position. Additionally, he's been known to second guess more than one quarterback. Not that Malmquist is in any manner a contentious man, rather he is one made confident by careful examination and willing and anxious to to express his convictions.

In 1930, Malmquist was assigned by Fitzpatrick to discover the true worth to Salt Lake City of a substantial supply of water owned by the Silver King and flowing from its Spiro Tunnel. The city was seriously considering purchase of the water for a very considerable sum.

The sound of profit is pleasant. The perception of a lesser reporter might have been shaded by an instinctive urge to tell one's publisher what he wants to hear. But Malmquist is not that kind of reporter and Fitzpatrick was not that kind of publisher.

After typically intensive investigation, Malmquist reported to Fitzpatrick that this water purchase would be short-sighted and not in the best interests of the city.

Fitzpatrick's respect for this judgment caused *The Tribune* to crusade for the Deer Creek project alternative plan and the formation of the Metropolitan Water District which have been literally the fountainhead of Salt Lake Valley growth.

Many consider that campaign *The Tribune's* most valuable and far-reaching contribution of the Fitzpatrick years, the principal achievement of the Fitzpatrick dictated policy: If it's in the best interests of Utah and the Intermountain West, *The Tribune* is for it.

Malmquist's thoroughness, his informed objectivity greatly simplified in many instances the decision-making process for John Fitzpatrick and I must note for his successor.

This is a report of what happened during *The Tribune's* first 100 years. Read it with confidence. It bears the Malmquist by-line.

J. W. Gallivan, Publisher
The Salt Lake Tribune

This book was set in 10-point Century Schoolbook Roman by Newspaper Agency Corporation members of Salt Lake Typographical Union No. 115. Historical records indicate existence of the Typographical Society of Deseret prior to February 24, 1852, giving credence to the claim of being the oldest Utah labor union. Chartered nationally on August 17, 1868, as the Deseret Typographical Union; it was issued a duplicate charter on July 2, 1886, as the Salt Lake Typographical Union, Local No. 115. It is believed that type for the first *Tribune* was set by members of this organization and, thus, the association of the Salt Lake Typographical Union, Local No. 115, with *The Tribune* is as old as the newspaper itself.

Contents

Preface

THIS ACCOUNT OF *The Salt Lake Tribune's* first century is unapologetically pro-*Tribune,* but not uncritically so.

For those readers who desire to know the sources and motivations for what they are reading, these explanatory notes are offered to supplement the specific source citations.

The writer has been associated with *The Tribune* for forty years. It has been a pleasant, satisfying and rewarding association. He can therefore be fairly regarded as a *"Tribune man."* But a cardinal requirement of reporters for the newspaper during, and some years prior to, this association has been objectivity. In this assignment the writer has conscientiously sought to comply with that requirement.

One primary source of information for the newspaper's early history is Edward W. Tullidge, one of *The Tribune's* founders and author of one of the most reliable histories of Salt Lake City up to 1885. Other histories have been examined and used extensively as sources of facts, opinions and interpretations of events. The writer has generally accepted Tullidge's version of events during the early years of the many-faceted and bitter conflict between the leadership of The Church of Jesus Christ of Latter-day Saints and *The Tribune,* as spokesman for the non-Mormons (gentiles), for these reasons:

As one of the founders of *The Tribune,* Tullidge was in a position to know the facts and the motives related to the birth of the newspaper.

1

He was an active participant in the so-called New Movement within the church which led to the establishment of *The Tribune* after he and some of his colleagues had been excommunicated from the church for earlier publishing ventures.

In the opinion of this writer he displayed, in his historical writings, a singular lack of bitterness toward the church which "cut him off" as well as toward *The Tribune* after he had disassociated himself from that newspaper and became an outspoken critic of some of its editorial policies.

His objectivity was so highly regarded by his contemporaries that more than 200 of them, including Mormon leaders and prominent gentiles, signed a petition to obtain a $2,500 appropriation from the city to help finance the preparation and publication of his history of Salt Lake City. The petition signers included such prestigious names as Daniel H. Wells, a mayor of the city; Joseph F. Smith, who later became president of the Mormon Church; the Walker brothers (M. H., Joseph R., Samuel S. and David F.); C. W. Penrose, editor of the *Deseret News;* C. C. Goodwin, editor of *The Tribune;* William Jennings, S. H. Auerbach, William S. Godbe, a founder and chief financial backer of the early *Tribune;* Wilford Woodruff, who later became president of the church; and Heber M. Wells, a governor of the state.

The petition signers, in fact, included most of the names prominently identified with the Mormon-gentile controversy, which makes historical writing acceptable to both sides such a delicate and difficult undertaking. The special committee of the city council which recommended the appropriation was composed of Henry Dinwoodey, Daniel H. Wells and A. H. Raleigh.

Other histories used extensively by the writer as sources of factual information and interpretative material include *A Comprehensive History of The Church of Jesus Christ of Latter-day Saints* by B. H. Roberts; *History of Utah* by Orson F. Whitney; *Utah Since Statehood* by Noble Warrum; and *The Great Basin Kingdom* by Leonard J. Arrington. Whitney and Roberts became general authorities of the Mormon Church. Warrum was a non-Mormon but had close ties with many church leaders. Arrington, a member of the church, published his *Great Basin Kingdom,* an economic history of the Latter-day Saints up to 1900, in 1958.

Naturally, one of the most important sources of information for this history has been the columns of *The Tribune* itself. But the columns of its journalistic adversaries have not been ignored.

The obvious reason for preparation and publication of a history of *The Tribune* at this time is its 100th anniversary on April 15, 1971. But the writer has a personal reason for welcoming the assignment. It provided a means of easing a nagging feeling of unrequited obligation by getting into print something about the role of the most important single individual in the 100-year history of *The Tribune.*

That individual — John F. Fitzpatrick — bore the title of publisher from 1924 until his death in 1960. He actually exercised a strong influence upon all aspects of the newspaper from the time of the death of the late Senator Thomas Kearns, its owner, in 1918. Thus it can be properly and accurately said that he was *The Tribune's* guiding hand, fiscally and editorially, for 42 years, almost half its life span. He, perhaps more than anyone else on the non-Mormon or gentile side, was the architect of an accommodation between the forces which made Utah's early history uniquely contentious. In the journalistic field he was, on *The Tribune* side, the individual wholly responsible for an accommodation which brought the feuding *Tribune* and *Deseret News* into a cooperative agency operation covering non-editorial functions.

Nor did his influence end with his death. John W. Gallivan, the publisher who succeeded him to round out *The Tribune's* first hundred years and launch it upon its second century, is a Fitzpatrick trained newspaperman. That means he is thoroughly grounded in the techniques of all phases of the business and indoctrinated in the Fitzpatrick concepts of the proper role and public responsibilities of a newspaper. The present publisher has, during the past ten years, made some changes and will no doubt continue to do so (newspapers which do not change do not observe centennials). But in basic policies, the Fitzpatrick influence will be reflected in the newspaper for no one knows how many years into the future.

It is doubtful that any newspaper anywhere, or at any period, could be the reflection and the handiwork of one man to a greater degree than was *The Tribune* during the Fitzpatrick regime. Yet his name was known to only a small minority of *Tribune* readers, and to some of these he was a sort of shadowy figure.

The reason for this extraordinary contradiction of dominance and obscurity was Fitzpatrick's abnormal aversion to personal publicity. Whether this trait stemmed from shyness or diffidence (he was anything but shy or lacking in confidence around his associates in *The Tribune* organization) or whether it was a deliberate exercise of a style he had found most effective in influencing and gaining the cooperation of people, is an interesting question regarding his complex character. But the fact is that he succeeded to an almost unbelievable degree in avoiding public attention or acclaim in the exercise of a very considerable public influence.

If those who knew and worked with and for him pass on without putting into print something about him and his career there would be left an intolerable void in the history of *The Tribune* and Utah journalism, as well as in the history of Salt Lake City and the Intermountain area. If, for example, someone one hundred years from now should undertake to write a bicentennial history of *The Tribune* from published information heretofore available his name might well be overlooked or appear simply with the notation that he was publisher from 1924 to 1960.

The keystone of his career was appropriately expressed in the title of a eulogy — "The Good Steward" — delivered by then Bishop Robert J. Dwyer, a personal friend. His loyalty to *The*

Tribune as an institution, to his employer, the late Senator Kearns, and to the family which has held the responsibility of ownership for seventy of the newspaper's first hundred years is exemplified by an incident related by the late Mrs. Jennie J. Kearns, widow of Senator Kearns, to her nephew, John W. Gallivan, the present publisher.

On the night of Senator Kearns' death, Mrs. Kearns walked from the death chamber down a staircase in the family home. At the foot of the stairs she found the senator's young secretary waiting for her with a hand on top of the newel. She placed her hand on his and said:

"You are not going to leave me now?"

"Mrs. Kearns," he answered, "I will never leave you."

"And," she added, "he never did."

1

The Irrepressible Conflict[1]

THE SALT LAKE TRIBUNE was born into a frontier world of inflamed conflict — economic, political, ecclesiastical and social. Unlike most newspapers, it was not established primarily as a business enterprise to record the events of the period. It was, initially, a product of and very much a part of the conflict.

The founders, excommunicated converts to The Church of Jesus Christ of Latter-day Saints, could not have been so unrealistic as to expect it to become a profitable enterprise in the foreseeable future. They had had previous journalistic experiences at considerable out-of-pocket expense. They knew their new daily newspaper would be a spokesman for a very small minority. What they probably did not realize at the time was that this minority carried within itself an irrepressible conflict.

It was, as they quickly discovered, made up of dissident Mormons who were opposed to the church's economic and political policies but who were unwilling to crusade for retroactive destruction of the institution of polygamy; of moderate gentiles who were in partial agreement with them; of embittered apostates and excommunicants; of vindictive anti-Mormons who were determined to wage total war upon the church.

While the avowed goal of *The Tribune* founders was to generate and support a New Movement of accommodation to replace the successive policies of, first, isolation and then insulation, their projected coalition was soon shattered by the diverse elements within it, especially those who were unwilling to settle for anything less than extermination of the Mormon Church as an economic and political power and those seeking abolition and retroactive punishment of polygamy.

That their newspaper survived in the face of the obstacles confronting it was a kind of miracle. Even now it is difficult to sort out reasons why *The Tribune* lived on to ultimately become a spokesman for accommodation (the role envisioned for it by the founders) while scores of other crusading publications that sprang up like desert flowers after a rain shrivelled and died in the searing sun of fiscal reality.

Historian Edward W. Tullidge suggested years after he had disassociated himself from *The Tribune* and some of its editorial policies that it survived because it was a great newspaper. Referring to the group which acquired the newspaper from the founders after they had decided the financial burden was too great for them to carry, Tullidge wrote:

It was Mr. Fred Lockley, however, that gave the marked and pungent anti-Mormon character to *The Salt Lake Tribune,* for which it has become famous in the gentile mind, infamous in the Mormon mind. But the *Tribune* is read at home and abroad — read by Mormon and gentile. To accomplish this object was the primal aim of Mr. Prescott and his compeers, and though they much offended the Mormon community, they won golden opinions from the anti-Mormons. Undoubtedly *The Salt Lake Tribune* represents the irrepressible conflict. In this conflict towards the Mormon Church its potency has resided; but *The Salt Lake Tribune* is also a great newspaper, apart from any anti-Mormon mission; and this is the salient point for notice in a review of Salt Lake journalism.[2]

It appears from Tullidge's appraisal that church efforts to prevent Mormons from subscribing to or reading *The Tribune* were only partially effective. But the ban was not openly flouted. City councilmen, for example, felt constrained when they attacked *The Tribune* to explain that they did not take or read the newspaper but that the offending article had been called to their attention.[3]

To understand and appreciate the conditions into which *The Tribune* was born it is desirable to review certain pertinent events of preceding years.

The violent expulsion of the Mormons from Ohio, Missouri and Illinois; the perils of the great exodus to the valley of the Great Salt Lake; the trials of establishing a viable community in a desert wasteland were matters of history; but it was such recent history that the persecutions and hardships endured during this period had not yet become mere memories in the minds of the participants.

The period of isolation was drawing to a close with the completion of the transcontinental railroad in 1869 and with the stimulus this was giving to a fledgling mining industry.

The Mormons and moderate gentiles were intensifying efforts to attain statehood — the Mormons to get rid of a hated federal judiciary for one thing and the moderate gentiles to advance, they believed, the cause of accommodation.

Part of the grand design of the Mormon prophet Joseph Smith to colonize the Great Basin and Pacific slope and thereby create a galaxy of new states with political power to protect his people had been accomplished by his successor, the great colonizer Brigham Young; and part had been abandoned or placed beyond reach by events.[4]

What amounted by reason of numbers to a one-party political system was in operation in the territory. The church, however, was not fully in control of government because of the imposi-

8

tion of gentile governors and a federal judiciary upon the territory.

Church President Brigham Young was implementing a church-controlled, cooperative economic system which non-Mormons regarded as a plan to force them out of the city and the territory.

There is abundant evidence to show that it was the economic issue more than anything else which led to the establishment of *The Tribune*. And if there were one facet of church economic policy which triggered the launching of the newspaper it was the organization of Zion's Cooperative Mercantile Institution.

Polygamy soon became the most strident battle cry in the controversy, but it was economics and politics which really made the conflict irrepressible.

The revolt of *The Tribune* founders and other like-minded Mormons surfaced some two years before *The Tribune* started publication.

In January, 1868, a new periodical — *The Utah Magazine* — made its debut with E. L. T. Harrison, general editor; Edward W. Tullidge, dramatic editor; Prof. John Tullidge, musical editor; and William S. Godbe and Harrison, publishers. The same group, with the exception of Godbe, had previously been associated in the publication of *Peep O'Day,* a literary magazine that died from lack of financial support.

The Utah Magazine was apparently launched with the good will and moral support of the church, as it was greeted by the *Deseret News,* the church organ, as an "enterprise worthy of commendation and support."[5]

The *News* was unaware of what was stirring in the minds of Godbe, Harrison and Tullidge. Within a few months there began appearing in the magazine articles which collided head-on with the economic policies of Brigham Young.

Typical of the church-offending articles was an editorial entitled "The True Development of the Territory" which argued

9

that the territory's prosperity depended upon development of mineral resources (mining) rather than manufacturing and agriculture. Editor Harrison asserted that Utah's high cost irrigation agriculture could not possibly compete with California, Missouri and Iowa; nor could Utah hope to compete in manufactured products except in a limited market. He continued:

> Common sense would seem to say, develop that first which will bring money from other Territories and States, and then these factories and home industries which supply ourselves will have something to lean upon. . . .
>
> Summed up in a few words we live in a country destitute of the rich advantages of other lands — a country with few natural facilities beyond the great mass of minerals in its bowels. These are its main financial hopes. To this our future factories must look for their life, our farmers, our stock, wool, and cotton raisers for their sale, and our mechanics for suitable wages. Let these resources be developed, and we have a future before us as bright as any country beneath the sun, because we shall be working in harmony with the indications of Nature around us.[6]

The magazine editors quickly found out that they were not speaking in harmony with Brigham Young's economic plan for the territory. And shortly thereafter they found that disagreement with church leaders on economics was apostasy.

The *Deseret News* of October 26, 1869, retracted its endorsement of the magazine by publishing this announcement with the signatures of Brigham Young, George A. Smith, Daniel H. Wells, Orson Pratt, Wilford Woodruff, George Q. Cannon and Joseph F. Smith:

Our attention has been called of late to several articles which have appeared in *The Utah Magazine.* . . . An examination of them has convinced us that they are erroneous, opposed to the spirit of the Gospel, and calculated to do injury. According to the practice of the Church, teachers were sent to labor with the editor and publishers, to point out to them the evil results which would follow a persistence in the course they are pursuing. This did not have the desired effect, and they have since been tried before the High Council, and after a thorough and patient investigation of the case, it was found they had imbibed the spirit of apostasy to a degree that they could not any longer be fellowshiped (sic) and they were cut off from the Church. *The Utah Magazine* is a periodical that in its spirit and teachings is directly opposed to the work of God. Instead of building up Zion and uniting the people, its teachings, if carried out, would destroy Zion, divide the people asunder, and drive the Holy Priesthood from the earth. Therefore, we say to our Brethren and Sisters in every place, *The Utah Magazine* is not a periodical suitable for circulation among or perusal by them and should not be sustained by Latter-day Saints. We hope this will be sufficient, without ever having to refer to it again.[7]

Publication of this ban on their magazine presumably did not come as a surprise to the editors and publishers. For in the October 2, 1869, issue they had published a "Notice to Patrons" asserting their intention of continuing publication despite "certain Church requirements lately made upon us."[8]

However, on second thought, the aroused journalistic triumvirate of Godbe-Harrison-Tullidge decided to abandon the maga-

zine and launch, with the beginning of 1870, a weekly newspaper — *The Mormon Tribune.* So they announced:

> The present volume of this magazine [*The Utah
> Magazine*] was commenced by the publishers with
> the express purpose of presenting before the people
> of Utah some of the broad and grand conceptions of
> God and humanity which they felt themselves
> called upon to present. . . . In the face of special pro-
> hibition by the absolute ecclesiastical authority
> which has prevailed in this territory, it has run its
> course, a silent preacher of advanced thoughts . . .
> and a steady opponent of absolutism in Church and
> State. It is now withdrawn to make way for a more
> prominent advocate of the same great principle.[9]

Thus, the hope expressed by church leaders that they would
not need to refer to *The Utah Magazine* again was achieved; but
in banning the magazine they possibly contributed to the birth of
successor publications to which they would be referring for many
years to come and which would make the offenses of the magazine seem like pinpricks.

The New Movement for which *The Mormon Tribune* and
The Salt Lake Tribune successively served as spokesman had
been incubating for some time. It began taking on tangible form
in the fall of 1868 when Godbe and Harrison made a trip to New
York City. An incident of the trip was later related to Tullidge
by Utah historian T. B. H. Stenhouse:

> Away from Utah, and traveling over the Plains, the
> old rumbling stagecoach afforded the two friends,
> as every traveler in those days experienced, an ex-
> cellent opportunity for reflection. On their way,
> they compared notes respecting their situation of
> things at home, and they spoke frankly together of
> their doubts and difficulties with the faith. They
> discovered, clearly enough that they were — in the

12

words of the orthodox — 'on the road to apostasy,' yet in their feelings they did not want to leave Mormonism or Utah. A struggle began in their minds. One proposition followed another, and scheme after scheme was the subject of discussion, but not one of those schemes or propositions, when examined, seemed desirable; they were in terrible mental anguish. Arrived in New York and comfortable in their hotel, in the evening they concluded to pray for guidance. They wanted light, either to have their doubts removed and their faith in Mormonism confirmed, or yet again to have the light of their own intellects increased that they might be able to follow unwaveringly their convictions. In this state of mind the two elders assert that they had an extraordinary spiritualistic experience.

They returned to Utah, and to a very small circle of friends confided what has here been only briefly related, and their story was listened to. Elder Eli B. Kelsey, a Mormon of 27 years standing, and who was also a president of Seventies, was the intimate friend of Mr. Godbe, and Edward W. Tullidge, another Seventy was a bosom friend of Mr. Harrison. Elder Henry W. Lawrence, a wealthy merchant, a bishop's counsellor, and a gentleman of the highest integrity, was early informed in confidence of this New Movement and gave to his friend, Mr. Godbe, valuable material support. [10]

This was presumably the experience which gave birth to the so-called Godbeite or New Movement. The two elders did not have to make a decision as to their formal relationship with the church. That was taken care of by their excommunication. This, no doubt, spurred them on to accelerate their crusade for reform, both for vindication and because they too believed in their cause.

13

This must, in fairness, be assumed in view of the money and effort they poured into it.

During the incubation period of the New Movement, Brigham Young and his top associates had organized Zion's Cooperative Mercantile Institution. While the cooperative approach to temporal matters was nothing new in the Mormon Church, the establishment of this enterprise served to bring the economic controversy to a head. To the New Movement Mormons it was a pronouncement that the closed economic system to which they objected was going to become completely closed. To the gentile businessmen it was a threat to their very existence. To the non-cooperating Mormons it was an ultimatum to join or get out of the territory.

The message came through loud and clear when Brigham Young, in response to a question as to what would happen to the Mormon merchants who did not choose to join the cooperative, replied: ". . . we shall leave them out in the cold, the same as the gentiles, and their goods shall rot upon their shelves."[11]

Reacting to this, Tullidge wrote:

> This surely was implacable; but, as already observed, Brigham Young and the Mormons as a peculiar community had in 1868 come face to face with implacable necessities. They had, in fact, to cease to be a communistic power in the world and from that moment exist as a mere religious sect, or preserve their temporal cohesiveness. The Mormons from the first have existed as a society, not as a sect. They have combined the two elements of organization — the social and the religious. They are now a new society-power in the world and an entirety in themselves. They are indeed the only religious *community* in Christendom of modern birth. . . . They intend forever to preserve themselves as a community; that was the plain and simple meaning

14

of Brigham Young's answer concerning the merchants in 1868. It was not an exodus which was then needed to preserve them, but a Zion's Cooperative Mercantile Institution.[12]

Brigham Young made it abundantly clear that his cooperative merchandising plan was not a mere church-backed competitive force. It was designed, through the headquarters store in Salt Lake City plus local branches, to become the sole merchandising facility for members of the Mormon Church wherever their number was large enough to justify a branch.

Inventories placed in the cooperative pool to start the enterprise amounted to $450,000. The contributors were William Jennings, $200,000; Eldredge and Clawson, $75,000; N. S. Ransohoff & Co., $75,000; Henry W. Lawrence, $30,000; Bowman and Co., $15,000; David Day and Co., $10,000; Woodmansee Bros., $5,000; others, $40,000.

The 1870 incorporation papers show paid-up stock of $199,000 distributed as follows: Brigham Young, representing the church, with 772 shares (par value $100 each for a total of $77,200); William Jennings with 790 shares ($79,000); other cooperating merchants with 260 shares ($26,000); and 16 other shareholders with a total of 168 shares ($16,800).[13]

Notable absentees from the list of cooperators were Godbe and the Walker brothers who qualified as members of the city's wealthy merchant princes. Godbe's absence has already been explained. The Walker brothers had left the church some time earlier. The incident marking their final break, as related by T. B. H. Stenhouse in his book *The Rocky Mountain Saints,* involved the payment of tithing. In response to a call from a church emissary, the firm sent a check for $500 as a "contribution to the poor." The bishop of the ward later informed them that Brigham Young would not accept the check; that he "would make them pay their 10 per cent tithing or he would cut them off the

Church." Whereupon J. R. Walker tore the check to bits in front of the bishop and said, "cut away." [14]

Z.C.M.I. was an immediate success from a profit standpoint, and sales of the gentile and non-cooperating Mormon firms went into a steep decline. "Walker Brothers, for example, claimed that their sales decreased in a brief space from '$60,000 to $5,000 per month,' and that those of the Auerbach Brothers fell off in like ratio." [15]

Both firms informed H. H. Bancroft, western historian, that they had offered to sell their stocks to Z. C. M. I. for fifty cents on the dollar and leave the territory, but that the offer had been refused.

The claims of the non-Mormon and non-cooperating Mormon firms as to loss of business are not borne out by tax records of the period, according to Leonard J. Arrington in his thoroughly researched and documented economic history of the church, *Great Basin Kingdom:*

> The monthly reports of dealers' sales, for example, give no perceptible decline in Walker Brothers' sales after Z.C.M.I. opened for business, and indeed, their sales for March and April 1869 are almost double those reported for the same months in 1868. Throughout the year 1869, the dealer sales of Z.C.M.I. averaged $106,000 per month, while those of Walker Brothers averaged only $29,000 per month. On a basis of the evidence available in tax memoranda, three things appear to be true: (1) that Z.C.M.I. absorbed the business of the cooperating merchants, while Walker Brothers absorbed the business of the non-Mormon merchants who decided to leave the territory; (2) that Z.C.M.I. effectively prevented Walker Brothers from expanding as rapidly as they would have done upon completion of the

16

transcontinental railroad; and (3) that Walker Brothers' retail sales (as contrasted with their wholesale business) may have suffered temporarily from the church boycott. [16]

Arrington's conclusions as to the impact of Z.C.M.I. upon other merchants are supported in part by observations of Stenhouse. While he asserted that the business of the non-Mormon merchants dropped drastically for a short time, it was soon regained and that within one year from the time the New Movement began the stores of these merchants were so crowded during church conferences that it was difficult for them to serve their patrons. From this it would appear that a significant number of Mormons reacted to the boycott of non-Mormon merchants as they reacted to the ban on reading *The Utah Magazine* and, later, *The Salt Lake Tribune.*

In this economic climate Godbe, Harrison, Kelsey and Tullidge launched their weekly *Mormon Tribune* with the first issue appearing on New Year's Day, 1870.

Editorially, this newspaper followed the policies which had brought them into direct conflict with Brigham Young in *The Utah Magazine.* The news columns were loaded with activities in the mining camps and the editorials emphasized the economic urgency of development of the mining industry; the social need of cooperation between Mormon and gentile; and argued the case for voluntary freeing of politics, and therefore local government, from ecclesiastical directive and control.

It soon became apparent to the New Movement founders of the paper that the name *Mormon Tribune* was inhibiting sorely needed financial and reader support from non-Mormons. A political movement to organize a new liberal party also encouraged a change in name. For these reasons the publishers of the weekly, presumably with promises of wider financial support from the small non-Mormon community, decided to expand their New Movement horizons.

Accordingly, they announced in a prospectus plans to begin the publication of a daily newspaper under the name of *Salt Lake Daily Tribune and Utah Mining Gazette.* (The name was soon changed to *The Salt Lake Tribune.*) The prospectus announced:

> The Daily Tribune will be a purely secular journal devoted entirely to the presentation of news and to the development of the mineral and commercial interest of the Territory.
> It will have no sectarian bias, and will be the organ of no religious body whatever.
> The aim of the publishers will be to make it a newspaper in every sense of the word. . . .
> On political and social questions the policy of the paper will be to sustain the Governmental institutions of the country. It will oppose all ecclesiastical interference in civil or legislative matters, and advocate the exercise of a free ballot by the abolition of 'numbered tickets.' . . .
> As a journal the Tribune will know no such distinctions as Mormon or gentile and where sectional feelings exist it will aim for their abolishment by the encouragement of charitable feelings and the promotion of better acquaintance.
> Correspondence is invited on all public questions of general interest from all those who have anything to say and know how to say it with due regard for the opinion of others. We shall lay our columns open to the public for the freest criticism on public questions, provided disparaging personalities are avoided, and principles are handled rather than men. [17]

It was a high road that the founders laid out for themselves. They soon discovered that it was an incredibly rocky road as well; that the base of support for a journal avoiding disparagement of personalities and ignoring religious distinctions was small indeed. They learned the hard way that the irrepressible pressures of the times were in the direction of a gloves-off fight on ecclesiastical as well as economic, political and social issues; that while there were moderate gentiles and Mormons of the same mind as themselves, they were not numerous enough to make such a newspaper as they had pledged to publish economically viable.

The first issue of the new daily newspaper which was destined to beat the formidable odds against survival, observe a centennial, and move into its second century as a great newspaper, appeared April 15, 1871. The publishers were Godbe and Harrison. The managing editor was a newcomer to the territory — Oscar G. Sawyer. Associate editors were Tullidge and George W. Crouch. Business manager was William H. Shearman.

The journalistic gunboat of the New Movement was afloat and there were menacing shoals just ahead.

2

Schism Within a Schism

ON THE SURFACE, the new daily *Salt Lake Tribune* began publication with somewhat brighter prospects of success than its predecessors.

The talented staff of the weekly *Mormon Tribune* had been ostensibly strengthened by Godbe's appointment of Oscar G. Sawyer as editor-in-chief. But Sawyer, an experienced journalist trained on James Gordon Bennett's *New York Herald,* quickly became the focus of a schism between the schismatic elders who founded the newspaper and the gentiles who had joined with the New Movement group to bring about economic and political reformation in the territory.

Under Sawyer the newspaper became pungently anti-Mormon — a course that was distasteful to Tullidge, Harrison and others associated with the enterprise. Although they had been placed outside the pale so far as the church was concerned, they did not consider themselves anti-Mormon. On the contrary they regarded themselves as missionaries seeking to bring the church into conformity with the laws of the land and thereby save it from destruction and its membership from hardships more severe than those they had already suffered.

Tullidge's reaction to the Sawyer appointment was later expressed in his history of Salt Lake City with the comment: ". . . a Utah journalist ought to have perceived the unfitness of the *New*

York Herald Bohemian to take the editor-in-chiefship of *The Mormon Tribune.*"[1]

Tullidge attributed Harrison's resignation as editor-in-chief to an unwillingness to serve as a subordinate on a paper which he and his compeers had founded, although he conceded that the editor was worn out and suffering from health problems, the reason publicly given for the resignation.

The depth of the incompatibility thus introduced into *The Tribune* organization can be imagined from a recitation of a few incidents involving the schismatic elders and some conjecture about Sawyer and his supporters.

The aim of *The Tribune* and the Liberal Party, as Sawyer would see it, was to break Brigham Young's economic and political grip on his people. This was not likely to be accomplished by the New Movement people (about one of twenty on a basis of election returns) without outside help. The obvious source of outside help was the federal government. So the obvious strategy was to continue and intensify the campaign to arouse the federal government to action.

The Achilles heel of the church, as an outside journalist would likely see it, was polygamy. Trained, as he was, in the school of the era's master in newspaper sensationalism, Sawyer could see that polygamy was a sure-fire reader interest issue. Whatever it might have been to spiritual-minded Mormon elders who entered into the practice, it was sex to the outside world. And, since the beginning of communication media, practitioners of the art of arousing human emotions had found nothing which could be used more effectively than sex.

It was polygamy, for example, which gave currency to the phrase "irrepressible conflict." When Stephen S. Harding, the federally appointed territorial governor, delivered his message to the legislature in 1862, he might have applied the phrase to the economic or the political controversies. But he chose to apply it to polygamy by saying:

21

I lay it down as a sound proposition that no community can happily exist with an institution as important as that of marriage wanting in all those qualities that make it homogeneal with institutions and laws of neighboring civilized communities having the same object. Anomalies in the moral world cannot long exist in a state of mere abeyance; they must from the very nature of things, become aggressive, or they will soon disappear from the force of conflicting ideas. This proposition is supported by the history of our own race, and is so plain that it may be set down as an axiom. If we grant this to be true, we may sum up the conclusion of the argument as follows: either the laws and opinions of the community by which you are surrounded must become subordinate to your customs and opinions, or, on the other hand, you must yield to theirs. The conflict is irrepressible.[2]

Back during the presidential election of 1856, it was John C. Fremont who campaigned on the Republican Party platform which called for the abolition of those "twin relics of barbarism, polygamy and slavery."[3]

It may have been politics which prompted successive threats of military action against the Mormons, but it was polygamy and the charges of insurrection linked to the practice which were used as justification. It was polygamy which could be used to heat up and inflame public opinion back in the states to a point which would compel politicians to resolve the long smouldering and politically annoying "Utah problem."

Moreover, if the job couldn't be accomplished with polygamy, certainly it could not be accomplished with publicity about a co-operative mercantile institution which was hurting the business of some non-Mormon shopkeepers; nor by complaining that Mormons outnumbered their opponents by about twenty to one in elections.

Whether this was the line of reasoning which prompted Sawyer to broaden the scope of the attack on the church is, of course, conjecture. But it is plausible conjecture.

The resentment his editorial policy generated among the schismatic elders who founded, and who were still writing for, the newspaper can be imagined from their known views on polygamy.

Godbe, at his own expense, had traveled to Washington in 1870 to intercede with President Ulysses S. Grant, Vice-President Schuyler Colfax and Rep. Shelby M. Cullom for moderating changes in the latter's pending bill to prohibit polygamy and punish polygamists. He also succeeded in convincing Cullom to refrain from pressing for passage of the bill in the Senate, although the congressman explained that he was bound to vote for it in the House.[4]

When Governor J. Wilson Shaffer was sent to Utah by President Grant in 1870 with the implied instruction to settle the "Utah problem" by military rule, and armed force if that proved necessary, he sought the advice of New Movement leaders, including Godbe and Eli B. Kelsey. Kelsey, in his first interview with the new "war governor," eloquently pleaded the case against an anti-polygamy crusade:

> I will present my own family case. It is that of tens of thousands in their family relations. My wives entered into marriage relations with me with the purest of motives, and from a conscientious religious conviction. They have children by me. Before I will forsake my wives and bastardize my children, I will fight the United States down to my boots! Governor Shaffer, put yourself in my place: What would you do?

The Civil War general paced the room for awhile and then turned to Kelsey with his reply: "By G-d, Mr. Kelsey, were I in your place I would do the same."[5]

Similar sentiments were expressed to General Phil Sheridan, sent to Utah by President Grant as an observer. On the basis of reports subsequently sent to Washington by Governor Shaffer and General Sheridan, the administration modified its initial policy to one designed to avoid, if possible, a rupture with the Mormon leaders.

A Liberal Party convention in 1871 was thrown into chaos and the prospective campaign aborted over the issue of polygamy. The schismatic elders were infuriated by the attacks on polygamy, and symbolically exploded when Judge Dennis J. Toohy of Corinne, who later became a small shareholder and a director of The Tribune Publishing Company, denounced the church on ecclesiastical and moral grounds:

> Here in Utah . . . sensuality and crime have found a congenial home; here immorality has been lifted up where virtue ought to reign. If I had time I could prove the leaders, not the people, were to blame for this. The people of Utah were originally as good as people elsewhere; but have they found freedom and equality in Utah? No; no more than in Turkey; less than in Ireland, and a great deal less than in any kingdom on the globe. . . . The best blood of Europe has been seduced to come here to Utah, and bow down before a false shrine; all except the people of old Ireland, where the Catholic religion holds them true. Not an honest Irishman ever became a Mormon, not one. The Irishman who could become a Mormon and obey their priesthood — what flattery to call him a man.[6]

The widest rift between Sawyer and the founding editors of *The Tribune* was undoubtedly over the question of polygamy. The schismatic elders, as unapologetic polygamists themselves, had neither the background nor the will to attack the doctrine. While some of the New Movement group favored abolition of the practice as a pragmatic concession to public sentiment in the outside world, they resented the use of the ecclesiastical doctrine of plural marriage to inflame opposition to Brigham Young's economic policies.

But to Sawyer, and the next succeeding ownership of *The Tribune*, there could have been no doubt as to the potency of the doctrine as a weapon in the battle for public opinion in the national arena. This had been dramatically demonstrated two years earlier by the Pratt-Newman debate in the Mormon Tabernacle.

Dr. J. P. Newman, a Methodist minister and a chaplain of the United States Senate, construed a suggestion by a Salt Lake City newspaper editor that he debate the issue in the Tabernacle as a challenge from Brigham Young and, with a great fanfare of publicity, accepted the "challenge." But the head of the church was not about to give Washington's most conspicuous anti-polygamy crusader the prestige and national prominence which would arise from a direct encounter with the great religious leader and colonizer, Brigham Young.

Brigham coolly informed Dr. Newman that he was unaware of having issued any challenge. The minister nevertheless came to Salt Lake City and there ensued several days of publicity-generating argument over who was willing and who was unwilling to debate. The upshot was that Brigham Young designated John Taylor or Orson Pratt as his representative. Dr. Newman protested that he wanted to debate the head of the church himself, but finally agreed to meet the substitute. The exchange of correspondence was published in the *New York Herald,* the local press and other major newspapers throughout the country.

The proposition agreed upon was: "Does the Bible sanction polygamy?" Professor Orson Pratt, a leading theologian of the church and one of its most eloquent orators, was the Mormon spokesman. Thousands attended the discussions; major newspapers sent special correspondents to the city to cover the event, and the telegraph company's press business reached an unprecedented level.

The debate was one of the big stories of the period, both locally and nationally, and it received some attention internationally. Some papers covered it in the language of the prize fight ring, giving a blow-by-blow account of the verbal exchanges — a feint to the chin with this Biblical quotation, a solid punch to the midsection with that quotation; a counter-punch with another quotation, and so on.

Judging from press reaction outside Utah, it appeared that neither Dr. Newman nor Professor Pratt scored anything close to a knockout. But it was Tullidge's opinion that Professor Pratt won on points:

> Each day's apostolic fight was glorified with a verbatim report in the *New York Herald,* and every leading newspaper in the country devoted its columns to a daily synopsis of the arguments. Never before, in the whole Christian era, had polygamy been so elaborately and ably discussed between two divines, and certainly never was a religious debate so extensively published and read. Millions of readers followed the arguments . . . and it is safe to estimate that quite two-thirds of them yielded the palm to the Mormon apostle and were convinced, though against their inclination, that upon strict Biblical grounds Mormon polygamy could not be successfully met.[7]

Because of the differing notions regarding polygamy and other ecclesiastical issues, it can easily be deduced that an explosion waṣ building up within *The Tribune* staff. To the discerning reader the conflict was disclosed in an erratic editorial policy which sometimes reflected Sawyer and sometimes the founding elders. The Sawyer critics fumed and waited for an opening to bring the schism to a head. It came when someone charged that Chief Justice James B. McKean, an anathema to both orthodox and schismatic Mormons, had been allowed to write editorials sustaining his own decisions in *The Tribune*. Justice McKean, incidentally, was a somewhat controversial personality within the legal profession nationally, as well as in the Utah Territory. His judicial competence had been questioned by numerous individuals, associations and publications who did not question his personal integrity. One of his most widely publicized actions was to assert in court, when Brigham Young was being tried for bigamy under a territorial statute, that "while the real title of the case at bar is called *The People Versus Brigham Young*, its other and real title is *Federal Authority Versus Polygamic Theocracy*."[8] The principle of trying a system in the form of an individual, and under a statute which was certainly of doubtful application, prompted many commentors to brand the proceedings as a crusade rather than a judicial trial.

At the insistence of Harrison, now a director, Tullidge and George W. Crouch, an ex-Mormon elder associated with the Godbeite movement, a meeting of the directors and staff was called. Participants included J. R. Walker, David F. Walker, Henry W. Lawrence, Benjamin Raybould, John Chislett, Sawyer, Crouch, Harrison and Tullidge. Harrison presented the case on behalf of those protesting the editorial direction taken by Sawyer. The case, as summarized by Tullidge:

> Mr. Harrison stated the case, and in very severe language denounced the course which the manag-

ing editor had been taking. He stated the object for which the paper had been started—namely, to maintain the cause of freedom and the rights of all classes, without distinction of Mormon or gentile; that it had been specially named *Tribune,* as explained in its opening issue, to signify its character—*The Tribune* of the People; that it was not the organ of radicals, nor the enemy of the Mormon people, but rather it was designed to protect and defend them. At first it was called *The Mormon Tribune,* to show its mission in this respect, though since it has changed its name to *The Salt Lake Tribune,* so that it might more fully represent all classes, yet remain true to its original aims. Mr. Sawyer, he said, had been brought out to Salt Lake City, by Mr. Godbe, with the expectation that he would carry out the design of its founders; that he, Harrison, had resigned the editorship, and control of the paper, to give himself a temporary rest, with the said understanding; that Mr. Sawyer, having obtained control, had turned *The Salt Lake Tribune* in a new direction and given it other aims and purposes from those for which it was established; but above all he impeached the managing editor on the specific charge of having permitted Judge McKean to write editorials sustaining his own decisions.[9]

Sawyer told the directors that they were merchants; that they knew nothing about journalism whereas he was a trained journalist. The upshot of the meeting was the resignation of Sawyer, who gave as his reason a "journalistic incompatibility" between himself and the directors.

Fred T. Perris, who had been serving as business manager, was placed in charge of both business and editorial departments but the schismatic elders who founded the paper were in fact at the editorial helm of what looked, at that juncture, to be a fiscally sinking ship doomed to fall into the hands of salvagers.

Despite Sawyer's departure to other journalistic ventures, there was still friction within *The Tribune* organization and its chief backers. Some influential non-Mormons whose support was vital to the fiscal success of the newspaper felt that it was hopeless to simultaneously attack some policies of the church and defend others.

Viewed in retrospect, it appears that the founders were somewhat less than realistic. Leonard J. Arrington, in his *Great Basin Kingdom* describes them as "talented Mormon intellectual 'liberals.' " [10] But they obviously lacked the pragmatic toughness to challenge the great Brigham Young, who was revered by the orthodox Mormons; admired by many non-Mormons in the territory, the states and abroad for his extraordinary accomplishments as a colonizer, and reluctantly respected by many who hated him.

Godbe, a native of London, was bound to a shipping company prior to his conversion to Mormonism. He had traveled extensively in Asia, Europe and Africa and was a self-educated man of the world. On the basis of his achievements, he was far above the average in business ability. He became wealthy as a merchant after arriving in Utah; was a confidant of Brigham Young until he launched the New Movement; and was responsible for some sizeable and profitable mining developments after he abandoned the publishing business. But his journalistic ventures were fiscal disasters. Tullidge estimated that his losses in this field exceeded $200,000, which was a fortune in that era.

Both Tullidge and Harrison were talented writers. But they were apparently too independent-minded for strict orthodoxy and too idealistic and sensitive for effective leadership.

On the plus side a good case could be made for the proposition that their formula for settlement of the Utah problem was

29

substantially the formula which eventually did settle it—elimination of the closed economic and political society and a repudiation of the practice if not the doctrine, of polygamy. Had they been able to foresee the course of future events their sense of defeat would have been softened by the vision of ultimate victory. But while their ends were met, they clearly at that time did not have the stomach for the means.

In any event their crusading journalistic venture never really got off the ground financially and by mid 1873 the publishing company was without funds and in debt. At this point the salvagers—who came to look more like scavengers to the founding elders and orthodox Mormons—appeared in the form of three journalists from Kansas.

3

"The Border Ruffians"

ON THE MORNING OF July 24, 1873, there appeared at the top of the editorial section of *The Salt Lake Tribune* a public announcement. It was the valedictory of Fred T. Perris as general manager of the newspaper and marked the beginning of a new ownership and a new editorial policy, with a different style and content. The retiring manager ended his announcement of resignation with the comment: "As *The Tribune* in the future will be conducted by strangers to the Territory and to myself, I cannot say what its future course will be." [1]

Three days later, on July 27, the new owners — Fred Lockley, George F. Prescott and A. M. Hamilton — addressed themselves to the question left unanswered by Perris:

> We shall make *The Tribune* a live paper, and in conducting it to a position respected by all and respecting all, we shall fearlessly announce our views, independently of all factions, combinations or cliques, whether religious, political or financial. In discussing the questions of the day, we shall, as we have ever done, preserve our self-respect by carefully, patiently and sincerely regarding and weighing the opinions of all others.
>
> In matters of religious faith we shall pursue the course demanded by constitutional sanction, urging

complete immunity for religious liberty among all the people. Bad men and bad women of whatever nationality, creed or profession, will be held responsible through these columns for their misdeeds by fair and honest criticism, alike free from vindictiveness, acrimony and passion.

Salus Populi Suprema Lex est, is the grand principle which, as firm as the rocks of the everlasting hills that look down upon this beautiful valley, forms the substratum of our Republican system. This maxim shall never be lost sight of; and we say woe to him who shall disregard it, be he Jew, Gentile, Christian or Pagan, Romanist or Mormon. The errors of all who may be in power over the people, whether politically or religiously, as officers of the law or as officers of the Church, we shall feel free to combat from the standpoint of journalists, entirely independent of every consideration other than the good of the whole people. We conceive that a public journal actuated by any other motive is unworthy the confidence and patronage of an intelligent public.

The general interest of the Territory, now our home, shall have our undivided zeal and earnest attention; whether those interests pertain to Mining, to Agriculture, to Commerce, or to any other source of wealth and greatness.

Believing that the cause of Republicanism — of freedom — of liberty in its largest sense — is best promoted by general intelligence, we shall at all times advocate the cultivation of the masses, and to that end, free education for the rising generations.

The Tribune shall be a family paper — one that the most sensitive and delicate may not fear to receive into their families. No coarse epithet, no vulgar-

32

isms, no harsh names, shall have place in its columns. We shall strive to make it a newspaper essentially, and worthy a place among the journals of the day.

In short, we conceive it the business of the journalist to publish a newspaper — and we propose to attend strictly to business. [2]

For the next six weeks the tone of *The Tribune* was not markedly different from what it had been under the founding schismatic elders. Sharp criticisms were directed toward certain policies of the Mormon Church — generally the same policies which *The Tribune* had been founded to oppose. But on September 10, 1873, the new owners issued their declaration of a no-holds-barred conflict with the church.

The Mormon city council, infuriated by a *Tribune* account of a previous meeting, ejected the newspaper's reporter and adopted a motion closing the chamber thereafter to representatives of the newspaper.

The response of the new ownership was carried at the top of the editorial page under the heading — "Our Reporter and the City Council":

. . . Our mission is to advance the interest of the city and territory, to promote the cause of education and to ally our efforts with those of our fellow Mormon citizens in furthering any object that would tend to the general good. Several long-time residents have suggested to us that we were pursuing an unwise course. 'You never can disarm the hostility of the Mormons,' they would say; 'your truckling to their abuses will never aid you. The first moment you assume the right of free speech they will come at you with their old time rancor. You must lend your hand to brush them aside, for you never can live peaceably with them.'

This prediction is more than verified. The rancor and the illiberality that rankle in the minds of the Mormon officials are shown in their insane action last night. It was uncalled for. We are unconscious of one word having appeared in our columns since we (the present editor) have had control of it that could possibly hurt the sensibilities of any public man who is endowed with one particle of brains.

The fight has been thrust upon us. It is not of our seeking. The issue is as plain as noonday. On one side are free speech, the solemn guarantee of the Constitution, advancement and Christian charity; on the other side bigotry, fraud, rancor and delusion.

Judge which shall win in the contest. [3]

It would be naive to believe that this declaration of journalistic war and its implementation over the ensuing decade was caused solely by the closing of the council chamber to a reporter. This was not the first time a reporter had been ejected and it wasn't going to be the last.

What is more easily believable is that the new owners from Kansas had surveyed the local situation, consulted with prospective allies and arrived at a conclusion that they could survive only by making a much stronger appeal to the anti-Mormon element than the founders and former owners of the paper were willing to make.

With the *Deseret News* serving as the voice of the Mormon leadership and the *Salt Lake Herald* (founded the year prior to *The Salt Lake Tribune)* serving as the church's lay supporter — or, as *The Tribune* put it — "the minor voice of the church," there simply was no place for another newspaper which could be accused of being "soft" on Mormonism.

The key to the future policy announcement was the reference to the advice of long-time residents. They were clearly telling the newcomer publishers that to recruit and hold a constituency they were, figuratively speaking, going to have to throw a few Christians to the lions.

It would be illogical to suppose that the Kansas men, who were experienced journalists, would enter such a bitterly controversial field; assume the debts of a newspaper that had already failed financially; and start subsidizing it anew, without prior investigation. And the situation that would emerge from such an investigation was substantially this:

To make *The Tribune* a profitable enterprise it would be necessary to break, or at least loosen, the church's grip on the economic life of the community and its political control. This could come about through some substantial changes in church policies, which did not appear to be in the offing; through an infusion of non-Mormon population sufficient to create a viable balance of power, and the prospects of this happening in the foreseeable future were indeed dim; or through federal intervention on a scale which had theretofore been frequently threatened but never carried out.

The non-Mormon element at that time was looking to federal intervention as its best bet for solving what it, and much of the rest of the country, called the "Utah problem." That is why it was so stubbornly opposed to statehood at that time. The battle to bring about the federal intervention it desired clearly had to be fought out in a national as well as a local arena. A vigorous fight had to be waged in the local arena to inflame national sentiment to a point which would compel effective federal intervention.

If the new publishers of *The Tribune* had paid any attention to Utah history since the exodus of the Mormons to the valley of the Great Salt Lake, they were aware that they were challenging a formidable adversary. Brigham Young was one of the outstanding figures of his time; and he was revered by the overwhelming majority of the Mormons and respected by many non-Mormons. He was, on a basis of the historical record, a superb diplomat and charming personality when he wanted to be. Many federal officials sent to Utah by the federal government to get tough with the stiff-necked Mormons, and who arrived in the territory with blood in their eyes, experienced dramatic changes in attitude after conferring with Brigham Young and his associates and viewing their handiwork.

President Grant, for example, visited Utah in 1875 to personally observe the situation that had prompted him to send a tough military man to the territory to clean up the Mormon problem. After conferring with Brigham Young and observing a welcoming demonstration by hundreds of Mormon primary children, he turned to Governor George W. Emery and muttered, "I have been deceived."[4] Mrs. Grant was overwhelmed emotionally at an organ recital in the Mormon Tabernacle and let her good feelings toward the Mormon people be known.

When Senator O. P. Morton of Indiana visited Salt Lake City in 1871 to personally investigate charges of outrageous and unjudicial conduct by federal judges his party included Grace Greenwood (Mrs. Lippincott), a widely read author of the era. She sent back to the *New York Herald,* which was raising an editorial uproar over polygamy, a letter describing Brigham Young in these terms:

> I did not see a common, gross looking person, with rude manners, and a sinister, sensual countenance, but a well dressed, dignified old gentleman, with a pale, mild face, a clear grey eye, a pleasant smile, a courteous address, and withal a patriarchal, paternal air, which of course, he comes rightly by.

The great Chicago fire occurred during this visit and the author, reporting on the local campaign to raise relief funds, wrote:

> There is to me, I must acknowledge, in this prompt and liberal action of the Mormon people, something strange and touching. It is Hagar ministering to Sarah; it is Ishmael giving a brotherly lift to Isaac. [5]

Several years before the founding of *The Tribune* but while other short lived journalistic critics of the Mormon Church were charging it with bringing shiploads of the dregs of Europe to the territory, Charles Dickens, the great English novelist and journalist, published an article describing a Mormon emigrant ship in Liverpool harbor just before its departure for the states. He described the more than 800 Mormon converts aboard as "in their degree, the pick and flower of England;" and concluded the article with these comments:

> What is in store for the poor people on the shores of the Great Salt Lake, what happy delusions they are laboring under now, on what miserable blindness their eyes may be opened then, I do not pretend to say. But I went aboard their ship to bear testimony against them if they deserved it, as I fully believed they would; to my great astonishment they did not deserve it; and my predispositions and tendencies must not affect me as an honest witness. I went over the *Amazon's* side, feeling it impossible to deny that, so far, some remarkable influence had produced a remarkable result, which better known influences have often missed. [6]

Captain Howard Stansbury and Lieutenant John W. Gunnison of the United States Topographical Engineers had earlier written widely quoted testimonials to the industry, sincerity, organizing talents, orderliness, hospitality and colonizing abilities of the Mormon pioneers.[7] Some of the federal judges had, unintentionally of course, improved the image of Mormonism by actions which were indicted not only by residents of the territory but by federal colleagues and bar organizations.

The Mormons had scored a public relations victory over their adversaries with the enactment by the territorial legislature of the first woman's suffrage law.[8] This blunted the attacks designed to equate the polygamous wives with the slaves of the south. It was not customary for masters to give the vote to their slaves.

These incidents and viewpoints, selected at random, are merely illustrative of hundreds of others which were available to the new publishers of *The Tribune* in making their assessment of the policies most likely to prove effective. They could not help but notice the frequency with which tributes to the Mormons and their accomplishments were prefaced with the disclaimer of any sympathy with or support of polygamy. This could only enhance in their minds the usefulness of this doctrine in the public relations battle to bring about a federally enforced solution to the "Utah problem."

The decision of the new publishers to pull off the editorial gloves and start endearing themselves to the anti-Mormons was surely based on something broader than the closing of a city council chamber to one of their reporters. This incident was the occasion, but not the reason, for the declaration of war.

For a few weeks the editorial policy of the paper continued to reflect an ambiguous attitude toward the church. But this was largely due to the fact that Tullidge was still on the staff and contributed lead editorials from time to time under his own name.

In one of these he argued that the cooperative movement had already failed; that the scheme to place in the hands of the church authorities a stupendous church monopoly which would exclude gentiles and individual Mormons "from all independent commerce and industry" had been thwarted. He asserted that the prior four or five years had brought about a great loosening of the "closed society;" that the "polygamy mania" which had earlier swept the church was subsiding; that inflow of gentiles into the mining industry, plus the heretic Mormons, were having a leavening effect on church political power; and concluded:

> And to this may be added that as a social revolution
> almost has been wrought out in Utah in four years
> from ourselves, without much help from Congress,
> the nation can afford to let the same causes consum-
> mate the work, and save itself from the betrayal of
> all our political principles by adoption of a crushing
> out method of despotism. [9]

But the soft, considerate, reasoned approach of Tullidge was tolerated only occasionally and for a short time by the new owners of *The Tribune*. They speedily began implementing a policy which impelled Tullidge to publicly disassociate himself entirely from the newspaper and which earned them the name of "Border Ruffians" among Mormons and their sympathizers.

A more representative sample of the new policy was an editorial carrying the caption — "A Holy Institution — A wife who couldn't see the Beauty of it." There followed an emotion-packed account of the suffering of an unnamed wife when her husband contracted a second marriage, and of the husband's responses to her protestations. It then concluded:

> How any human being who is not degraded below
> the level of a brute, can profane the holiest of
> human affections by putting into a woman's mouth
> any such sentiment as the one given above, passes
> all reasonable comprehension. [10]

Thereafter *The Tribune* attacked the church's tithing doctrine, declaring the one-tenth rate was economically self-defeating; that it was crushing to all useful industry.

> No legitimate business can stand a tax of ten per
> cent, and prove remunerative. Economical law con-
> demns any such exaction. It is a fraud upon the face
> of it, and it is suicidal also. . . . [11]

The divorce suit of Ann Eliza Young against Brigham
Young was covered in great detail, including publication of all
the documents filed by the plaintiff. [12] The Mormon city council
was attacked for its dealings with the church-owned gas company; for neglecting the streets; for tolerating unsanitary conditions in the city; for spending too much money for the wrong
things and too little for the right things. Correspondents from
the mining camps were permitted, and perhaps encouraged, to
express their views of church policies.

As a special feature for the church's conference in October of
1873 *The Tribune* published what it called a picture gallery of
the leaders. The article, with verbal and artist sketches, carried
these sub-heads: "The Ecclesiastical Despots Who Rule Utah and
Eat Tithe;" "A Short and Concise History of Their Rise and
Progress — From Milk to Tithe."

These excerpts from the sketch of Brigham Young are representative of the style and flavor of the series.

> There is such a fund of humor in this Brigham
> Young as a prophet, that we like him in that holy
> calling immensely, and we pray every morning,
> noon and night that he may live long upon the
> earth. Brigham is a jocular fellow, with seventeen
> present wives, and a much larger number in times
> past; but he promises, to all appearances, to be good
> for some years to come. We like Brother Brigham;
> he is so much like the Prince of Denmark, in the
> play of Hamlet. . . .
> For his years, he is a spirited young man, and we
> like his style, Brigham says 'the Lord knows a

thing or two,' but he personally knows more,
and he wants to introduce to the world a system
that will last forever.[13]

To the publishers of *The Tribune* during the 1873-83 decade,
objectivity was a vice not to be tolerated in news columns, editorials or correspondence from readers. The news columns and correspondence were frequently more opinionated than the editorials, possibly because the reporters and correspondents were
more opinionated than the editorial writers.

A few excerpts from reports on the quarterly conference of
the Center Stake in 1880 will illustrate the point:

> Young Brig [Brigham Young, Jr.] then made his ap-
> pearance [on the speakers stand] and after sundry
> coughs, barks, growls and scowls, proceeded to
> stammer forth how glad he was to meet the brothers
> and sisters in their new and commodious building.
> Brig was exceedingly troubled in consequence of a
> belief dominant in his mind that all did not pan out
> as well as they ought to. He said he was 'mighty
> liberal' himself, and his personal friends and ac-
> quaintances he knew, contributed largely also. 'But
> did every person do that?' After repeating this
> query about fifty times, he gave his pantaloons a
> hitch upward, grunted and took his seat.

Another part of the report was captioned "Afternoon Exercises" and then continued:

> The exercises of the afternoon opened with a hymn
> and a prayer by Bishop Woolley, in which he cor-
> rected any false impressions the Lord might have as
> to the building in which his Saints were worship-
> ing, or as to the character of the meeting.

41

Penrose Talks

Everything being satisfactorily adjusted, the box
was opened and Granny's Imp jumped up.[Granny
was *The Tribune's* nickname for the *Deseret News*
and its Imp was Charles W. Penrose, the editor].
Brother Angus [Cannon] pulled the strings, and the
thing commenced to jump and talk. He said he was
unexpectedly called to talk, and as his shirt front
was very dirty, it is to be presumed he told the
truth.

At another point *The Tribune* report stated:

Brother Goddard then took his seat, and Brother
Taylor, the city sexton, read recommendations from
the bishops of the several wards, nominating candidates for Elders. They were voted on singly, and
nearly all unanimously elected, except in the case of
the Sugar House Ward, when *The Tribune* man
thought it to be his duty to vote against the candidate on that occasion.[14]

During this period of uninhibited journalistic expression; of
studied insult; of subtle and coarse humor; of venomous denunciation; and all-around bad manners, *The Tribune* was "taking
it" as well as "passing it out."

The *Deseret News,* as the official voice of the church, let the
Herald [the minor voice of the church to *The Tribune*] do most of
the eye-gouging in-fighting. But on occasion it joined in with a
snarling exuberance not exceeded by either *The Tribune* or the
Herald. As a typical example, *The Tribune* reprinted an article
which had appeared in the *News* of March 31, 1880, for the purpose of answering it. The *News* fumed:

There are certain would-be witty persons who think
they are uttering a good joke at the expense of the

42

Mormons by repeatedly quoting the words of the late Brigham Young — 'We can produce the greatest and smoothest liars, or any other shade of character, you can mention.'

The fun of it is they are quoting against themselves. They and their tribe — the manufacturers of anti-Mormon sensations; the scavengers of the press; the slanderers of the living and defamers of the dead; the garblers of public speeches; the blasphemers of sacred things; the cowardly libellers of women and children; the dirty-minded scandal mongers; the craven dastards who fling their filth at those they know will not retaliate; the pen-stabbers; the character assassins; the authors of false telegraphic dispatches; and their aiders and abetters — are the characters referred to. We have had such things among us from the beginning of Utah's settlement.

They have multiplied upon us as opportunities have increased for the paying exercises of their perverted faculties.

Produce them? Yes we could point them out at any time. But no respectable Mormon recognizes their presence or would be seen in their society, and they are permitted to lie on, and fill the cup of their iniquity, unnoticed. . . . [15]

As a final example of the journalism of the day may be cited *The Tribune's* reaction to the foregoing. It was a retort that showed none of the poise or sense of humor that sometimes added a badly needed grace to *The Tribune.*

It [the *News* article] emanates from the pen of a three-ply polyg, who, if he had his just deserts, would be keeping company with George Reynolds in the Utah Penitentiary, and instead of writing editorials for the lying Church organ, would be engaged in playing checkers with his nose on the prison bars. [16]

4

End of a Dynasty

THE PREEMINENT news event of the decade that Lockley, Prescott and Hamilton published in *The Salt Lake Tribune* was the death of Brigham Young on August 29, 1877. As editors, they fumbled the big story initially but quickly recovered and gave it the attention it deserved.

In the issue of August 28, *The Tribune* reported that the prophet had been stricken with a serious illness. The article speculated that the illness might have been caused by the shock of survey taken by his "minions" and reported to him at a priesthood meeting the previous evening. This survey, the article continued, showed that the prophet's power was slipping; that of some 30,000 residents in the center stake, less than 8,000 could be classed as faithful followers. "Brigham," the article concluded, "could not believe it. He said the report was inaccurate, and he therefore refused to accept it, directing the bishops to have their teachers do their work over and bring the figures up to a respectable showing." [1]

It should be noted here that *Tribune* reports of events within the church, which probably were supplied by disgruntled Mormon participants, were sometimes proved to be wildly inaccurate by subsequent disclosures.

In the issue appearing on the morning of August 29, *The Tribune* reported that the prophet's bowel derangement had taken so serious a turn as to threaten a speedy death and, ghoulishly, devoted the remainder of a full column editorial to speculation on possible successors. From time to time *The Tribune* editors, in a sarcastic vein, would point out that they were not endowed with the gift of prophecy. On this occasion they refrained from making a precise prediction. However they did categorically affirm that for years it had been Young's ambition to found a "prophetic dynasty" and that he had laid careful plans to ensure the succession of his son, Brigham. The editorial expressed doubt that this would happen, because of the unpopularity of the son, and paid the paper's disrespects to several other possible prospects and concluded:

> But whomsoever may be the winning man, there will be widespread dissension in the Mormon ranks and no other leader can hope to possess the influence that Brigham Young has possessed. The death of the Mormon chieftain will not be apt to cause the instant dissolution of the decaying ecclesiastical edifice but it will give it a terrible shock.[2]

In the issue of August 30, 1877, *The Tribune* announced the death of the great colonizer and church leader in a news story of less than a column on an inside page. In the same issue there appeared a much longer editorial article renewing, in summarized form, attacks that *The Tribune* had been pouring out upon the prophet during the prior five years. The bitter spirit of conflict, the editors seemed to be saying, was not going to be softened by death alone. Yet they did, in some paragraphs of the article, concede that the church leader was an extraordinary character and a great, if not a laudable, man. The article continued:

> It is an easy matter to criticize the manner in which he has performed his great work, and to depreciate

his personal qualities. As we have said above, he was illiterate and has made a frequent boast that he never saw the inside of a school house. His habit of mind was singularly illogical and his public addresses are the greatest farrago of nonsense that ever was put in print. He prided himself on being a great financier, and yet all his commercial speculations have been conspicuous failures. He was a blarophant, and pretended to be in daily intercourse with the Almighty, and yet he was groveling in his ideas, and the system of religion he formulated was well nigh Satanic. Yet with this grossness, this illiteracy, this entire ignorance of the art of government, he has succeeded, during an entire generation, in holding absolute sway over a hundred thousand followers, in directing their confidence and affections as to stand to them a very Deity. His death is regarded as the fall of a great man in Israel, and thousands mourn his loss as a personal bereavement.

Yet we believe that the most graceful act of his life has been his death. . . .

. . . If the death of Brigham Young shall be supplemented this fall by an act of Congress giving the people of Utah a free ballot and an amended jury law, the extirpation of priestly tyranny will be complete and Utah will be Americanized and politically and socially redeemed.[3]

The day before the funeral *The Tribune,* assuming the role of fallible prognosticator if not infallible prophet, told its readers that it had been intimated that among the instructions left by Brigham Young to be read on that occasion was one elevating First Counsellor John W. Young (a son) to the "prophetic throne."

46

The article continued:

> Brigham's ambition to found a dynasty has long been known, and during his long rule the Mormon Church has become so completely centered in himself . . . that he would not hesitate or question his right to dispose of it by heritage as if it were his own personal estate. That this will be distasteful to the congregation of Saints, there is no room for doubt. . . .[4]

The forecast proved wrong, as did some others relating to the church leader's will.

On September 4, *The Tribune* editors, apparently more impressed with the importance of the event they were covering than when Young died, devoted fully one-half the front page and columns on inside pages to the funeral service. For a week or more thereafter the newspaper carried a veritable cascade of articles, editorials, and comments of correspondents on the life and death of the prophet and on such related subjects as the succession, the will and the condition of the church's fiscal and business affairs.

Scores of editorial comments from other papers around the country were reprinted by *The Tribune* along with its own appropriate or inappropriate (depending upon the point of view) observations.

The Utica (N.Y.) *Herald* commented that "The career of this man has been in one sense the most remarkable in American history."

The *New York Post* characterized him as a "master of men" and opened its editorial with these paragraphs:

> The phrase which Dickens put into the mouths of all Americans as descriptive of pretty nearly every

American of prominence, fairly belongs to Brigham
Young. The most obvious reflection that his death
suggests is that he was 'one of the most remarkable men in the country.'

In one respect he was a vulgar cheat, of course. In
his character he was essentially coarse and brutal,
without refinement, without culture, without the
finer instincts of men. He gave free rein to the worst
passions of his own nature, and made the worst passions of other men his tools. Yet he was a man of almost unbelievable force of character of a certain
kind.

The *St. Louis Republican* described him as "one of the most
noted men of our times." But the *Omaha Republican* commented
that: "The death of Brigham Young is a mere incident of the day,
having no more national importance than the demise of any
other prominent citizen."

The *Omaha Herald* editorial writer who had met Brigham
Young personally, wrote that he had been struck with the man's
frankness and candor, and impressed with the belief that he was
"a terribly honest as well as a sincere man" and added: "That belief has not been changed by the clamor of his enemies."

The *Indianapolis Sentinel* rated him "a conspicuous figure in
history" and the *San Francisco Call* referred to Brigham Young
and the Mormons as that "extraordinary man and people."[5]

Whether one regarded the departed church leader as a saint
or a sinner, the *Omaha Republican* was certainly wide of the
mark in dismissing his death as a mere incident of the day. In
whatever category he might be placed, he was a giant-size and
an extraordinary character.

What other citizen of Utah, before or since, could generate
the outpouring of editorial comment that Brigham Young did,
both in life and in death? What other citizen of any territory, or

the states, could attract the qualified tributes that Brigham Young did from people who hated him?

He had, without doubt, stirred the imagination of a huge number of people in this country and Europe. His name had been given currency throughout the English reading world by such literary stars as Charles Dickens, Oscar Wilde, Mark Twain and many others. Had television been in existence at the time, and had Brigham Young appeared as a guest, how many individuals of that era could have scored a higher audience rating?

Edward W. Tullidge, one of the schismatic elders who founded *The Tribune,* described Brigham Young in his history of Salt Lake City as "one of the greatest colonizers the world has seen in a thousand years."[6] This, of course, would not have impressed *The Tribune* owners of this period, as they undoubtedly regarded Tullidge as an excommunicant who never, in his heart, left the church and who was its militant apologist whenever it came under severe attack.

This is indicated in a *Tribune* response to an editorial in the *Deseret News:*

> An anonymous writer in our Grandmother, whom we take to be Elder Tullidge, bears testimony to the high moral excellence of his late master, Brigham Young. The devout Elder grows indignant at the 'most outrageous and unwarrantable scandals' which have been heaped upon the memory of the defunct Prophet. He does not produce any of these charges and refute them; that would be too much like the Babylonian method of making an argument. He prefers to reason by induction. 'Can we glance over the fertile valley of Zion,' says the Elder in substance, 'rescued from the naked savage, the wolf, the jackal, the mountain lion and the wildcat, and believe that the man who brought

about this change was the accomplice of assassins? Can we look at the thrifty farms, the smiling homes with the herds and flocks on every range, and believe that Brigham Young was not the father of this people and the friend of education?'

This mode of reasoning resembles that adopted by a western pleader who had a petty larceny charge to defend. 'Gentlemen of the jury,' said he, 'do you believe that my client who lives in the great State of Kentucky, where the land is rich and the soils are fertile, would be guilty of so contemptible an act as stealing eleven small skeins of cotton?'[7]

When the church failed to act in conformance with *Tribune* forecasts as to succession, and the authorities published in the *Deseret News* and *Herald* an epistle by the Twelve Apostles designating that body as the "presiding quorum and authority" of the church, *The Tribune* suspected that internal frictions were too strong to permit selection of a president at that time.

But when at the October conference John Taylor was sustained as president of the twelve but not, as *The Tribune* interpreted it, president of the church, the editors greeted the result as a gain for the liberties of the people. In a lead editorial the newspaper said:

It is not probable that the supreme government of the Mormon Church has been constituted to suit *The Tribune,* but we are free to admit that we are well suited with it. A ruling theocracy is an affliction under any form, but there are degrees of wrong, and we prefer to take it in the mildest form obtainable. The dictatorship of Brigham is not to be reproduced, it was offensive to the whole country and irksome and oppressive to the members of the Church.

Twelve men are now the ruling power, and if one man gets too full of deviltry, his eleven compeers will be apt to tone him down. John Taylor is ostensibly at the head, but he holds divided power.[8]

With the anti-Mormons' ogre, Brigham Young, removed from the scene, the aggressive, red-headed editor of *The Tribune,* Fred Lockley, no doubt felt some pressures from the more moderate elements of the community to ease off in the attacks on "Mormondom." It is reasonable to believe that some *Tribune* supporters who felt that the founding schismatic elders were too "soft" had by this time concluded that the "border ruffians" from Kansas were too abrasive.

In fact, such a reaction was intimated by Lockley in some of his editorials after Brigham Young's death. In the lead editorial of the issue of September 22, 1877, for example, the editor felt impelled to restate the newspaper's position under the heading "Our Position Defined."

Captain Codman [probably John Codman, author of *Mormon Country*] jocosely tells his friends that the only sober face he saw at Brigham Young's funeral was that of the red-headed editor of *The Tribune.* This leads to the inquiry why that individual should put on a solemn look: was he grieving at the Prophet's demise? The old salt's eyes twinkle at this (and here's where the laugh comes in); 'No,' he will reply, 'but he felt his occupation was gone; he was wondering where he would find staple for his future editorials.'

For a joke, this is well enough, and if this editor had been keeping up a senseless tirade against the Mormon chief merely because it made his paper sell, the sally would have some relevancy. But our condemnation of the departed Prophet was based upon his arrogant assumption of irresponsible power, and his obstinate opposition to all progress and improvement. In this perfidious work he was sustained and assisted by all his subordinate priests, and the death of the chief obstructionist has not removed the evil we were combatting. Mormonism, as preached and practiced in Utah, deprives the people of sovereignty and elevates one individual or, on his removal, a privileged class to supreme power. This is anti-republican, and its evil consequences are shown in the enslavement of the minds and faculties of the people and the suppression of an active and healthy public sentiment. Thus our fight is directed not against any individual, however obnoxious may be his character, or however flagitious his conduct, but against the system which subverts the relations of society and places one man, or a certain number of men, at the base. [9]

So *The Tribune's* shafts continued to fly, and a counter-shower came flying back from the *Deseret News* and *Herald. The Tribune's* targets were more widely dispersed, with the towering figure of Brigham Young gone, but this did not dilute the virulence of the journalistic controversy, which was but a reflection (though perhaps an exaggerated one) of the conflict in the whole fabric of the Salt Lake City community.

On one morning *The Tribune* would question the solvency of Zion's Cooperative Mercantile Institution; the next morning it would accuse the church-controlled government of taxing gentile homes twice as high as Mormon homes; of chasing gentiles out of a public park where a Mormon social was being held; of trying to stop mining, and drive gentiles out of the territory, by excessive taxation; of charging gentiles more than Mormons for goods they had to sell. Incoming newspapers and magazines were searched for articles attacking the church or its leaders and the most provocative reprinted in *The Tribune.* Sometimes outside articles favorable to the church would be reprinted, but these were invariably accompanied by *The Tribune's* corrections or an invitation for the writer to come to Salt Lake City and get the facts.

For the next few years Lockley devoted himself with unflagging zeal to demonstrating that the death of Brigham Young had not deprived him of an occupation. But by 1880 there began creeping into the newspaper signs that the "Border Ruffians" were tiring or running short of money. The stage was being set for another change in ownership and perhaps a change in editorial policy.

5

"My Friend, the Enemy"

THROUGHOUT THE TEN years the "Border Ruffians" published *The Salt Lake Tribune* they were obviously harassed by financial difficulties. They took the paper on trial from the founding schismatic elders, who were happy to be relieved "of the heavy burden of their subsidies, which had hitherto sustained it."[1] The Kansas trio also assumed some debts which they were still trying to pay off when they sold the newspaper ten years later.

At the first meeting of the board of directors after the ownership change the capitalization of the enterprise was increased from an undisclosed figure to 300 shares of stock with a par value of $100 per share. Meetings of the board of directors were held at irregular intervals, or minutes were not always written down or were lost before the corporate records were turned over to the next succeeding owners. But such minutes as are still available show clearly that there was more exuberance in the editorial office than in the business office.

At a board meeting on December 24, 1873, the directors engaged in "a general discussion of the possible success of the enterprise" and a resolution was adopted to try the venture one more year, "provided sufficient patronage was given to enable us to pay the current expense of publishing." Present at the meeting were Fred Lockley, who acted as chairman; George F. Prescott, who was president of the corporation; A. M. Hamilton;

George W. Reed, who had been associated with the founding group in the business office and was retained by the new owners; W. H. Taylor and James R. Schupbach, who had joined the Kansans in ownership of the newspaper.

By February 15, 1875, Reed reported to the directors that "conditions were improving" and that the only debts were "the unpaid wages of the executives." Obviously Reed referred to the condition of operating funds and not to debts assumed when the paper was taken over; for three weeks later, at another board meeting, the discussion was devoted to a debt of $11,236.11 in the form of notes given to Walker Brothers, Henry W. Lawrence and William S. Godbe. It was agreed that an attempt would be made to reach an agreement with the creditors, the inference being that funds were not available to pay off the notes and that a compromise settlement at some smaller amount would be sought. Whatever proposal was submitted to the creditors, it was not accepted as the unpaid notes continued to bob up at directors meetings.

At another meeting Prescott reported that "other stockholders" took no interest in the newspaper but "were seemingly willing that it should continue so long as they were not called upon to render financial aid."

On March 5, 1875, Lockley reported to his fellow directors that it was "only a question of time when *The Tribune* might be made a good property, but whether the present management would tire before the difficulties were overcome, time alone would determine."

The unpaid notes, after growing to $16,216.45 by reason of unpaid interest, were finally consigned to Schupbach. Two stock assessments were subsequently levied to make two $3,000 payments on the notes. [2] Whether the remainder was paid is one of the many bits of *Tribune* history lost because corporate records were not kept for periods running into years at a time or were lost.

Lockley's optimistic judgment that *The Tribune,* in time, could become a good property was certainly sound. But his pessimistic inference that he and his associates might tire before that time was reached, and thus not be around to reap the financial rewards, proved to be prophetic.

One of the early signs that Lockley, at least, was tiring occurred in the spring of 1880 when a new editorial writer was employed. Small wonder that the red-headed editor felt the need of some help. Although by-lines were rarely used at this period in Salt Lake City journalism, the Lockley style identified much of the material he contributed to the newspaper — a prodigious outpouring of editorials, articles on major news developments and commentaries on a wide range of subjects. Day after day he wrote thousands of words of copy under what must have been nagging, and at times depressive, pressures. From time to time he intimated in his articles that living and working in a city where one knows he is hated by most of the people he sees and meets is a wearing and exhausting experience.

The new editorial writer was C. C. Goodwin, an experienced and able journalist who later became a partner in the ownership of the newspaper. He was destined also to become the most widely known and quoted editorial voice of *The Tribune* which, except for the Goodwin era, has been far better known as an institution than as a springboard for personal journalistic fame.

The employment of the new editorial writer was announced in the issue of May 23, 1880, under the heading — "A Word Personal":

> Tomorrow Mr. C. C. Goodwin of the *Virginia Enterprise* connects himself with *The Tribune* editorial staff. While congratulating ourselves upon the accession of one whose abilities as a trenchant and accomplished writer are conceded, we also congratulate our readers, who will enjoy in the future the re-

sults of his busy pen. Mr. Goodwin has been on the coast for years, enjoys a popularity second to none in his profession, has helped to build up the great mining interests of the coast, and with his settling down in Zion as a home, not alone the progress of Liberalism and the mining industries, but the welfare of the entire Territory will be advanced. His coming to this field of labor is, we trust, but the signal of an exodus of Nevada miners soon to pour into our mining camps and bring Utah her rightful position as a mineral producing region.[3]

Editor Lockley probably did not realize at the time that he was introducing to *Tribune* readers a journalistic warrior who would overshadow his own image as a hard-nosed, skillful, unrelenting crusader. But such was the case. For the entrance of Goodwin on the Salt Lake City scene set the stage for an editorial battle which was to excite, delight and infuriate territorial readers for more than a decade. And because of the national interest in the "Mormon problem," it was a journalistic confrontation which was watched with interest throughout the country.

Goodwin's major editorial antagonist was Charles W. Penrose, perhaps the most brilliant and provocative editor produced by the *Deseret News.* In a way the two men helped each other professionally. The verbal thrusts of one sharpened the retaliatory instinct of the other. Just as any extraordinary skill is more impressive in confrontation with another extraordinary skill than in isolation, the lustre of one added lustre to the other.

While in the columns of their papers the rival editors devoted themselves singlemindedly to slugging each other and crusading for their respective causes, there are reasons to suspect that they privately respected and admired each other. After the most intense phase of the battle had passed Penrose would refer to Goodwin as "My friend, the enemy;"[4] the sentiment was undoubtedly reciprocated by Goodwin. It was, indeed, a sentiment which was in all probability much more prevalent in the territory during this uproarious period than the published records suggest.

Anyone who has lived in a bitterly divided community is aware that people are often more venomous and stubborn collectively than they are individually. It is only reasonable to assume that personal friendships did reach across the abyss which separated the contending forces in the "irrepressible conflict" which divided Salt Lake City and the Utah Territory; and that these friendships, in due time, helped bridge the abyss.

One of the most noticeable changes which Goodwin brought to *The Tribune* was a broadened interest in politics. He apparently had some personal acquaintance with many political figures of the west and a journalist's background knowledge of leading political figures of the nation. He had decided opinions about most of them and an extraordinary facility for expressing those opinions in print. He was not reluctant to become personally involved in the political processes. And certainly *The Tribune* raised no objections to personal involvement of its editor, so long as he was active in behalf of the right side — the Liberal or anti-Mormon Party.

Whether Goodwin was brought to *The Tribune* by Lockley because of an expected upturn in political activity, or whether the timing was accidental is an interesting point of conjecture. Up to 1880 the Mormons had almost totally dominated the political life of the territory, except for the interventions of federally appointed officials. The Liberal Party had entered candidates in most elections for delegate to Congress but not with any expectation of winning. Their purpose was to designate a candidate to challenge the seating of the successful Mormon candidate.

The strategy proved partially successful in 1880 when George Q. Cannon ran for a fourth term in the office. He was opposed by Allen G. Campbell, the Liberal Party candidate. The

Liberals took their usual drubbing at the polls, the vote tally being 18,568 for Cannon to 1,357 for Campbell.

Viewed in retrospect, with no knowledge of the circumstances, conditions, or influences existing on that election day, the result looks like a miserable showing on the part of the Liberals. For they fell far short at the polls of the then existing ratio of gentiles to Mormons. The 1880 United States census classified Utah's population of 143,963 as follows: Mormons, 120,283; Gentiles, 14,156; Apostate Mormons, 6,988; Josephites, 820; Miscellaneous or Doubtful, 1,716.[5]

But it soon became apparent, following the election, that the revival of interest in Liberal Party ranks stemmed from something other than expectations of a big upturn in voting strength. Orson F. Whitney, in his *History of Utah,* offered one reason for the 1880 political revival among the gentiles:

> History may not hit upon all the reasons for that change of policy, but we think we can name one. It was that the whilom lethargic Liberals now had a Governor [Eli H. Murray] who was a man after their own hearts, who could be relied upon to assist in the furtherance of any scheme having as its object the discomfiture of Mormonism.[6]

At another point, historian Whitney elaborates on this view:

> There is little doubt that the extraordinary activity displayed by the Liberal Party in the fall of 1880 was but part of a preconcerted plan, a general and widespread conspiracy for a tremendous assault all along the line of Mormon defenses, secular and ecclesiastical. This conspiracy was double-rooted, having as its origin religious rancor as well as political animosity. Its field of operation was not only Utah, but various other sections of the Union,

59

whence all efforts converged toward and found a
focus at the national capital.[7]

The Tribune provided most of the journalistic ammunition
fired during the campaign of that year. Without burdening this
record with copious quotations from its editorials during this period, it can be said that Lockley and Goodwin agreed with some
aspects of the Mormon historian's appraisal of the situation.
Their editorials, for example, supported Whitney's contention
that the campaign was intended as an "assault all along the line
of the Mormon defenses, secular and ecclesiastical." But they
maintained, in effect, that any assault had to be secular and ecclesiastical, as the two were inseparable in Mormonism. They too
saw a multi-rooted (rather than double-rooted) conspiracy in the
confrontation and constantly reiterated that this was what *The
Tribune* had been fighting for a decade and would continue to
fight until it was destroyed — a conspiracy to fasten permanently upon the territory an ecclesiastical, economic, political and social dictatorship.

As to what the Liberal Party leaders had in mind in the election, the subsequent developments spoke for themselves.

Before the election returns were opened in the presence of
Governor Murray on December 14 a protest against the issuance
of an election certificate to George Q. Cannon was filed on behalf
of Campbell. The substance of the protest was that Cannon was
an unnaturalized alien and therefore ineligible to hold the office
of delegate to Congress; that his alienage was aggravated by
polygamy, which was incompatible with citizenship and inconsistent with the oath of office; that there was nothing tending
to disprove Campbell's qualifications for the office; that the
certificate should be issued to Campbell and not to Cannon.

Answering the protest from Washington, Delegate Cannon
took the position that only the House of Representatives was em-
powered to judge the qualifications of its members. He also re-

plied to each of twelve allegations and concluded with the assertion that he could not be denied the certificate "without the grossest violation of law and of official duty."[8]

Governor Murray nevertheless awarded the certificate of office to Campbell. But the clerk of the House of Representatives, on a basis of certified statements that Cannon received the greatest number of votes, placed Cannon's name on the roll and he continued to draw the salary.

Thus the battle over who was to be seated was shuttled back to Washington but in a few months was being fought on another front in the federal court of the territory. The controversy created a political-religious din in Washington, Utah, and, through the press and various political and religious organizations, throughout the country.

Chief contributors to the uproar in Utah Territory were Goodwin and Penrose, with the pro-church *Herald* ably assisting the *Deseret News*. Goodwin stole a march on Penrose by getting his own version of "The Mormon Situation" into *Harper's,* a popular and prestigious monthly magazine. Penrose replied in the *Deseret News:*

> We notice it [the Goodwin article] because *Harper's* is a popular and respected monthly, with a large circulation and a deservedly high reputation, not because the author of the article is of any particular importance. He is a comparative stranger to this Territory, having been here but a short time, is densely ignorant of the system which he undertakes to assail, knows nothing of the people he so shamefully reviles, and follows the business of writing against them and their religion for pay. We have read the article through carefully, with the view of discovering some redeeming features in a series of untruths presented without the slightest attempt at

proof, but in vain. . . . That a moderately cultivated mind should stoop so low for the purpose of defaming a creed and people who do not happen to fall in with his notions of right, is indeed lamentable and cause for pity as much as contempt. . . .[9]

In the journalistic atmosphere of the time, this was, to Goodwin, high praise from a rival. He returned the compliment in this fashion: ". . . any charge which the *News* may make against any gentleman is merely the act of a slave, forced by the lash of the master to do his bidding. No one ever blames the bear for dancing when he is placed on the hot iron, and in the same way the contortions of the *News* only excite pity."[10]

Penrose, according to Historian Orson F. Whitney, attempted to answer Goodwin in *Harper's* but the magazine refused space for his article.[11]

During the uproar over the Cannon-Campbell contest for the seat in Congress, President James A. Garfield was assassinated. From July 2, 1881, when he was shot, to September 19 when he died of the wound, this nationally traumatic event dominated the newspapers and, in Salt Lake City, produced a lull in the seating controversy. But even this tragedy was projected into the conflict over Mormondom. The *Boston Watchman,* a church publication, printed a dispatch in which it was stated: "It is an interesting fact that on the day set apart for prayer by the President . . . the *Deseret News,* organ of the Mormons, declared that the 'Praying Circle' of the Mormon Church was engaged in continual supplication for the death of President Garfield." The *News* denounced this as an "atrocious untruth" and challenged the *Watchman* to present proof. No proof was offered, according to Whitney.[12]

The upshot of the year-long court and congressional contest over the Utah seat was that the Committee on Elections adopted and the House approved a resolution denying the seat to both

Cannon and Campbell. On the face of it, this looked like the Liberal (gentile) and Peoples' (Mormon) parties had fought to a draw. But, as subsequent events proved, it was in fact a victory for the Liberal Party. The Liberals had tried before, without success, to prevent the seating of Mormon delegates elected from Utah. So, from their standpoint, keeping the seat vacant was half a loaf. But more important than preventing the seating of Cannon was legislation which followed in the wake of the seating controversy. For the political and religious spleen stirred up during the debates on the Cannon-Campbell contest certainly helped to push through Congress in March of 1882 the Edmunds Act, a revised anti-polygamy law designed to plug up loopholes punched by the United States Supreme Court in earlier laws aimed at polygamy. From this law there flowed five years later a further revision (of the original 1862 anti-polygamy act) known as the Edmunds-Tucker Act. This law was enacted without the signature of President Grover Cleveland. As will be pointed out later, it was a blow which landed in the vital sector of the church.

During the seating controversy and passage of the Edmunds Act the church and the Peoples' Party were not without friends in Congress and the national press. Generally the "outside" newspapers which opposed denial of the House seat to Cannon and enactment of the Edmunds law, and apparently a majority of them did, voiced their disapproval of polygamy but took the position that the proposed remedies would make a shambles of the Constitution. When Colonel Henry Watterson, the famous editor of the *Louisville Courier-Journal*, defended Governor Murray's issuance of the certificate of election to Campbell, the *Louisville Post* retorted that the editors of the *Courier-Journal* must be "either corrupt or crazy."[13]

In the Congress, support for the Mormon position came largely from Democrats and the southern states. It can reasonably be inferred that this support was not wholly motivated by sympathy for the Mormon cause. It stemmed, in part certainly, from a detestation of what the southerners viewed as a program to "reconstruct" Utah Territory with the federal power. Whatever their feelings might have been about polygamy, the cooperative or collectivist economic system espoused by the church, or the effective control of politics with a church-based party, such feelings were but faint stirrings by comparison with their hatred of "carpet-baggers." It is doubtful that Goodwin or Penrose at their denunciatory best, could have improved upon the style of Representative House of Tennessee when he presented his reaction to the Edmunds Act and closed with this paragraph:

> Let the carpet-bagger, expelled finally from every State in the American Union with the brand of disgrace upon his brow, lift up his head once more and turn his face toward the setting sun. Utah beckons him to a new field of pillage and fresh pastures of pilfering. Let him pack his grip-sack and start. The Mormons have no friends and no one will come forward to defend or protect their rights. A returning board, from whose decision there is no appeal, sent out from the American Congress, baptized with the spirit of persecution and intolerance, will enter Utah to trample beneath their feet the rights of the people of that far-off and ill-fated land. Mr. Speaker, I would not place a dog under the dominion of a set of carpet-baggers, reinforced by a returning board, unless I meant to have him robbed of his bone. A more grinding tyranny, a more absolute despotism, was never established over any people. [14]

To the Liberals and their party organ *(The Tribune)* back in Salt Lake City this was, of course, hyperbole. But the rejection of Cannon for the House seat he had held three terms, plus enactment of the sharp-toothed anti-polygamy law, did represent a notable step toward their goal. The policy of waving the inflammatory polygamy flag to mobilize strength for a broader assault on the church position was beginning to pay off. For the accelerating crusade to stamp out polygamy was going to shake to its foundations what economist Leonard J. Arrington refers to in his *Great Basin Kingdom* as "the unique and noncapitalistic economic institutions for which the Mormons had been noted."[15] It was also going to be an important factor in the process of separating church and state, or at least of putting a few layers of insulation between the two.

In short, the anti-polygamy crusade was going to advance on the economic, political and social fronts the cause for which *The Tribune* was founded to serve as mouthpiece. The methods used to achieve the advance were going to be unpalatable to some, if not all, the schismatic elders who established the newspaper, but deliciously palatable to the "Border Ruffians" who succeeded them. But the Kansas trio was not fated to savor the upcoming changes, at least not as publishers and editors of *The Tribune*. For as Lockley suggested in his report to the directors back in March of 1875, the management might "tire before the difficulties were overcome" and *The Tribune* "made a good property." There are good reasons to believe that Lockley and his associates were beginning at this point to tire, either of the rigors of underdog editorial crusading or of the nagging struggle of trying to keep income ahead of expenses, or of both. In any event a new ownership, along with the infusion of new capital into the enterprise, was just around the corner. And a new chapter in Mormon-gentile relations, perhaps more bitter than the previous splenetic chapters, was beginning to unfold.

6

New Owners Take Over

THE YEAR 1882 WAS A busy and exciting one for editors
C. C. Goodwin of *The Tribune* and Charles W. Penrose of the *Deseret News.* The year was notable because of the empty seat in
Congress to which the territory was entitled; the enactment of
an anti-polygamy law which was still to be implemented; and a
sharp upturn in Liberal hopes of a victory at the polls by reason
of a provision in the new anti-polygamy law disenfranchising polygamists.

Goodwin and his chief rival on the *Deseret News,* as well as
the writers for the *Herald,* were at their best in political infight-
ing. So the three newspapers squared off for a lively and what
looked like the territory's most important election campaign up
to that time.

Two Utah historians, who were on-the-scene observers, are
agreed that the campaign represented a new highwater mark in
politics. Orson F. Whitney wrote in his *History of Utah:*

> . . . for the first time in history of Utah, political pa-
> rades, with bands of music, torches, Chinese lan-
> terns, Roman candles, and other pyrotechnics illu-
> minated the streets, whose stones re-echoed to the
> tramp of marching hosts filling the air with hopeful
> shouts and stentorian prophecies of victory. Each
> party put forth its utmost exertions, the orators on

either side vieing with their opponents in eloquence, wit and satire. [1]

Edward W. Tullidge, in his *History of Salt Lake City,* said this about the campaign:

It was the first time in our elections that the two parties had fairly recognized each other frankly and conjointly accepting the idea of the "irrepressible conflict" between them, to be fought out by political leaders and the votes of American citizens. Hitherto our election contests had been rather between the Mormons, as a church, and the anti-Mormons, as a body of crusaders in deadly conflict to overthrow that church. This time, at least in profession, they informally agreed to accept each other as purely political parties, contesting for the rule of the Territory by the sovereign votes of American citizens. [2]

Tullidge was no doubt right as to the professed acceptance by the two parties of each other as political parties. But his implied conclusion that the old Mormon versus anti-Mormon nature of the contest had somehow been changed does not appear to be warranted by the platforms subsequently adopted.

The Liberal Party platform, in fact, affirmed in the preamble that the division was on church lines and that the partisan distinctions known in other portions of the United States "were of minor importance." [3] At least nine of the twelve planks comprising the platform were aimed directly at the church, and the other three were indirectly aimed at the same target. The document said in part:

We arraign the Mormon power in Utah on the following grounds: it exalts the Church above the State in matters of purely administrative and political concern. It perverts the duty of the representative in official and legislative matters by demanding that the interests and wishes of that sect and of the priesthood shall be made paramount considerations. It destroys the freedom of the citizen by assuming the right to dictate his political actions and control his ballot. It teaches that defiance of the law of the land when counseled by its priesthood is a religious duty. It encourages jurors and witnesses, when attempts are made in the ordinary course of law to punish the crime of polygamy, to disregard their duties in order to protect offenders who are of their faith.

Continuing with a long list of indictments that included church control of public lands, its negative influence on commerce and business, its exploitation of women and its treasonable and disloyal conduct toward the United States, the Liberal platform concluded:

For these offenses, to which many more might be added, we arraign the Mormon power in Utah, and invoke against it and its monstrous pretensions and practices the considerable judgment of the citizen voter, the statesman and the Christian, and humbly submit that our attitude toward it is not only justified but demanded by every consideration that ought to control the true American citizen in discharge of political duty. [4]

The platform of the People's Party denied point by point the accusations of the Liberal Party and threw the charge of treasonable practices back at the adversary in these words:

We believe that any party or faction of a political community that seeks to subvert the institutions of local self-government, aims a deadly thrust at the Constitution, and that such party or faction is unworthy of the suffrages of a free people.

We believe that any official who attempts to stifle the popular voice as expressed at the ballot box is guilty of treason against a sovereign people.

With its list of denials complete and its countercharges firmly lodged, the People's Party platform pledged itself to the:

. . . maintenance and defense of constitutional principles and the inalienable rights of mankind, and proclaim ourselves the friends of true liberty — civil, political and religious, to all people in every part of the habitable globe. [5]

The Liberal Party nominated Philip T. Van Zile, a prominent gentile lawyer, for the House seat after Campbell, a wealthy mining man, had declined to run a second race. The People's Party nominated John T. Caine, an eminent citizen, a Mormon, but not a polygamist. The party leaders knew that at this point a victory at the polls with a polygamist candidate would be a hollow one. For the Edmunds Act, passed earlier in the year, had disenfranchised polygamists and established a federal commission which by the election of 1882 was already beginning to purge the voter registration rolls of polygamists and all, male or female, who had lived in a polygamist relationship since enactment of the 1862 anti-polygamy law.

The Salt Lake Tribune, with Goodwin firing the editorial barrages, campaigned vigorously for the Liberal Party candidate. The *Deseret News*, with Penrose wielding his exuberant, penetrating and sarcastic editorial pen, campaigned just as vigorously for the People's Party candidate. Both men could stand squarely on the platforms of their respective parties, inasmuch as they were probably the chief contributors to the documents.

The *Herald,* which *The Tribune* sometimes denounced as caustically as it did the *News* and sometimes dismissed as the "minor voice of the church, not worth answering," ably supported the People's Party and its candidate.

The campaign editorials on both sides were pretty much a symphony, or cacophony, of variations on the platform themes. Nothing basically new was added to the debate but the editorial writers distinguished themselves for eloquent, inflammatory and sarcastic elaboration of the platform planks. They did not strive for, or stoop to, subtlety.

Despite the disenfranchisement of polygamists and the strenuous campaign put on by the Liberals, their candidate went down to crushing defeat on election day. Van Zile polled 4,884 votes to 23,039 for Caine. This was better than the fourteen-to-one disaster inflicted upon them in the prior election, but this time they had no hope of successfully contesting the result. For Caine was issued a certificate of election by the federally appointed commission. The only question that could be raised was whether he, Caine, was entitled to serve out the unexpired term, which had been denied both candidates. The House did accept him for the unexpired term. Judge Van Zile, a lawyer who knew how to accept defeat when it couldn't be avoided, gracefully acquiesced and extended congratulations to his successful opponent.

Caine's initial act in the new Congress was to introduce a bill for admission of Utah to the Union. It was referred to a committee and there died. Although he was unable to make any headway toward statehood, Caine was reelected four times. The tone of Liberal Party and *Tribune* attacks upon him indicated that they were somewhat less allergic to him than to prospective replacements, even though he was president of the company which published the *Herald.*

An ecclesiastical event of 1882, which in later years acquired significance in *The Tribune's* history, was the sustaining of Heber J. Grant as a member of the Mormon Quorum of the

Twelve Apostles. For when a bridge of accommodation was thrown across the abyss dividing Utah's residents, key anchors on their respective sides were Grant, as president of the church, and *The Tribune.*

But at this point in history the climate was far from friendly to accommodation. By October, 1883, *The Tribune* was expressing disgust with enforcement, or lack of enforcement, of the Edmunds law; charging the federal government with selling "indulgences" to the church; and calling upon the press and people of the country to demand enforcement of law in Utah. On October 13, *The Tribune* said editorially:

> East and West the public press is demanding to know why in Utah the crimes which are punished everywhere under the flag, are converted into graces too precious to be interfered with. And this has not come from the insidious teachings of *The Tribune;* it is due solely to the positions taken by the high priests of the Mormon Church, as they in solemn conference stood up to teach their people. The people of the land are slowly awakening to the disagreeable fact that there is really an alien kingdom here, which holds nothing in common with the Republic, which is bound by no rules which bind Americans; which is managed by a code aside from the codes of the country; and which is permeated through and through with treason. These are unpalatable facts, and they are a great humiliation to the wise asses of the East, who have insisted so long that all that is needed in Utah is the spread of intelligence to cure the evil. But it will not last long. The excitement will pass away in a few days; Congress will receive its instructions, as usual, from the railroad corporations and the wholesale merchants of

the great cities, to see to it that the stuffing is kicked out of any law which would, if passed, make the Mormons trouble; the agents of the Church will be on hand when Congress meets to explain to Democratic members that the agitation in Utah is due to a little squad of just such unprincipled carpet-baggers as devastated the South, and another year will go by. In that year 4,000 more supports will be imported from Europe, 3,000 or 4,000 more babies will be born, and very soon the old cry will be in order: 'You would not arraign a whole people for treason, would you?' because in this land, when a mighty number engage in violating the laws, it is not criminal any more, but rather a grace. The Saints need not be alarmed. They are rich enough to buy indulgences from the Government of the United States. [6]

The leaders of the church had a somewhat different view of what the Edmunds Act was going to mean to their people. John Taylor, then president of the church, warned that a "tempest of tribulation" was about to burst upon the Latter-day Saints. At the General Conference on April 7, 1882, President Taylor alluded to the coming storm and commented: "Let us treat it as we did the snowstorm through which we came this morning — put up our coat collars . . . and wait until the storm subsides. After the storm comes sunshine. While it lasts it is useless to reason with the world; when it subsides we can talk to them." [7]

Taylor's forecast of events for the ensuing few years was much more accurate than that of *The Tribune,* which was no doubt delighted at its own misjudgment of the temper of the federal government.

Whitney, in his *History of Utah,* appraised the situation at that period in these words:

The general condition of society and the state of the public mind in Utah . . . has been pretty well indicated. Mormons and gentiles, at times friendly and sociable, were gradually 'drawing the lines' more tightly than ever in places — 'taking sides' and surveying each other with mutual suspicion and dislike. Congress, by its late drastic legislation, supplemented by the acts of the Utah Commission — which the Mormons regarded as partial — had done much to divide the never-too-friendly wings of the commonwealth, and the efforts of the local agitators [meaning principally *The Tribune,* no doubt] had well-nigh effected a complete separation. [8]

In Whitney's view the forces arraigned against the church at this point included: sincere and patriotic men who would have welcomed an end of "war" had the church been willing to surrender polygamy and the political union of church and state; Mormon-haters who would settle for nothing less than the utter extirpation of Mormonism; men who made money out of the agitation and who, as a consequence, did not want a peace which would end the profitable agitation; a majority of the non-Mormon merchants and businessmen, who were not in sympathy with Mormonism but who preferred peace and goodwill because it would bring them Mormon patronage.

The events of this period and the commentaries on them suggest that Whitney's analysis of the anti-church forces was both perceptive and accurate. The position of *The Tribune,* as reflected in numerous editorials, was that the categories specified by Whitney had their opposites on the church side of the abyss and that it was this situation which made the "irrepressible conflict" irrepressible.

Before the approaching storm broke, *The Tribune* was to acquire a new owner. In September, 1883, Lockley and his associates had either grown tired of the grinding fight or were presented with an offer they regarded as too good to turn down. Whatever the reason, they sold out to Patrick H. Lannan and C. C. Goodwin, who, as we saw in an earlier chapter, joined *The Tribune* as editor in 1880. Lannan, whose interests appear to have been centered on the business rather than the editorial side of newspaper publishing, came to Salt Lake City from Nevada. Very little information about him appeared in the local press. He had known Goodwin in Nevada and probably came to Salt Lake City on Goodwin's recommendation. No announcement of the change in ownership was published immediately in *The Tribune*, but some of the weekly papers reported the transaction. The published reports — and there is no reason to doubt their accuracy — were to the effect that Lannan and Goodwin had acquired a fourth-fifths interest; Colonel O. J. Hollister and his family, who had bought into the corporation about one year earlier, had retained a one-fifth interest. The purchase was financed with a $60,000 loan from John W. Mackay who had acquired a fortune of many millions from Nevada and California mining. Obviously the confidence and respect Goodwin had earlier shown when he rose to one of his higher levels of editorial rage in defending Mackay from press attacks were reciprocated by the latter.

With Goodwin already at the editorial helm there was no particular reason for announcing an ownership change from that standpoint. The scanty corporate records of *The Tribune* from that period include a ledger sheet, carrying the notation that it was presented to Lannan and showing an estimated net worth at the time of $39,483.44. This is probably close to the price paid by Lannan and Goodwin for a four-fifths interest, inasmuch as it is consistent with the $10,500 paid by Hollister for his one-fifth interest the year before. Seller of a one-fifth interest was J. R. Schupbach, a founder and first publisher of the *Park Mining Record*.

The ledger sheet given to Lannan indicated that the receipts of *The Tribune* for the previous six months amounted to

74

$35,794.36 and expenses $22,060.31. This indicated an operating profit of slightly more than $2,000 per month. But it is uncertain whether the expense total included salaries of the owner executives. Expenses during this period were sometimes reported at the directors' meetings "exclusive of unpaid executive wages." Thus the $2,000 plus per month may have represented executive salaries and profit or profit after salary payments. One thing is certain; financially, *The Tribune* was no "bonanza" up to this time and successful mining prospectors were doing a lot better money-wise than newspaper editors and publishers.

The change in *The Tribune's* ownership made no change in basic editorial policy but it did alter the style somewhat. With the new infusion of capital, the appearance of the newspaper in a very short time reflected installation of new equipment. News coverage was improved and features added. Editorially, the old fight was pressed with unrelenting vigor but the voice was not quite so shrill as it had been under Lockley and associates. For example, on October 23, 1883, the lead editorial started out in this fashion: "There are many men, sincere in their beliefs in the main principles taught by the Mormon creed, who can not understand why they are opposed by the world at large, and especially by gentiles here who can not but see that they are industrious, peaceable, honest in their relations with their fellowmen, and true to their families." [9]

The remainder of the editorial made it clear that *The Tribune* was not softening its opposition to the church practices. But the new tone must have set extremists on both sides of the conflict wondering what was going to happen.

On New Year's Day, 1884, there appeared a long editorial which was, no doubt, intended as a declaration of policy for the new owners. The general tone is reflected in these excerpts:

> *The Tribune* hails another New Year's day, cheered
> by the support of more friends than have ever gath-
> ered around it before, and exultant with more hope

than it was ever permitted to indulge in. It enjoys steady prosperity, its bitterest enemies sadly acknowledge that it is a tremendous power, and that its supporters are those people who by right of intelligence and character should shape and lead public opinion in this region. It has had many dark days in the past. . . . Its chiefest gratifications are that financially it is on a steadily increasing paying basis, and that it could not be hated as furiously as it is in some quarters, did not a consciousness of its power add fuel to the anger of its enemies. But its greatest hope is that, by and by, to the minds of those who most bitterly inveigh against it now, there will come the consciousness that, after all, it is right, has been right from the first, and that the happiness, self-respect and real prosperity of the majority here have been retarded just in proportion as they have refused to accept its counsels. At present it gives its patrons fuller news than the patrons of any other journal can get. . . . In appreciation of this the public extends to it a generous support. Aside from this it is the only real missionary journal, its mission work being the attempt to convert this region to a full allegiance to American laws, and to draw around home the sanctity which is the foundation for greatness in a people. . . . And so we hail the New Year exultingly, and so warmed by the joy which there is in the present, and by the hope which cheers with promise the future, with malice toward none and with good wishes for all, we extend a 'Happy New Year' to our patrons and to all the homes of Utah. [10]

In other words the new owners believed *The Tribune's* policies in the past were right on fundamentals and that a continuation of those policies would shortly usher in a new day of dissipated hatreds and brighter prospects. But, the "exulting" optimism of *The Tribune* notwithstanding, the brighter day was not to dawn in the new year nor in the thirty that followed.

The issues which provoked the founding of *The Tribune* by dissident members of the church were as inflammatory as ever. New points of difference were constantly agitating the already turbulent surface of community life. *The Tribune*, on the one side, and the *Deseret News* and *Herald* on the other side, continued to take delight in raising an unending stream of issues to enliven the editorial feud. They could get into snarling arguments over the question of whether hooligans in the public parks, or on excursion trains, were gentile or Mormon young people. *The Tribune* would denounce a freight rate increase on outgoing ores as a conspiracy between the railroad barons and the church to close the mines until the Mormons got ready to exploit them. The Mormon "Word of Wisdom" relating to liquor, tobacco, tea and coffee appeared to come into greater prominence after the death of Brigham Young and provided topics for editorial outbursts. For example *The Tribune*, in irritated response to speeches of church leaders on the liquor problem, struck back with this article on August 9, 1893:

> While our Mormon friends are posing as advocates of temperance, and claiming, with their usual disregard of truth, that the gentiles introduced drunkenness into Utah, it may be well to place on the record the condition of things in Utah when none but Mormons lived here. Following is a transcript from official sources, of the persons who owned and worked distilleries, and at what places and for what periods. The record extends only from 1862, when the tax on distilled spirits was first levied. What happened before that we have no way of knowing. It

closes with the coming of the Union Pacific Railroad in 1869, which was also, substantially, the beginning of the gentile era in Utah.

There followed a list of thirty-six distilleries, along with names of the owners and operators. The list included three municipal corporations — Salt Lake City, Provo, and St. George. In true form the article continued:

> Joseph Horne, to whom William Howard's distillery was sold about the time that the Salt Lake distillery was closed and dismantled, was a cover for the First Presidency of the Church. They, or at least Brigham Young and Daniel H. Wells, gave their notes to Howard for the property and set Horne up as a figurehead to run it. The product, some 10,000 or 12,000 gallons, we believe, was sold to the city by Wells, for the most part at $4 per gallon. This continued a year or more or until the Pacific railroad was finished and a branch was well on its way here from Ogden, when they compelled or induced Howard to give up their notes and take back the distillery, probably because they found or feared there was no money in it.

Referring again to the thirty-six distilleries and the Mormon controlled municipal corporations, the article concluded:

> When all these stills were running there were no gentiles in Utah, and the population was less than 70,000. Salt Lake, Provo and St. George cities engaged in the business, running a rectifying and a wholesale and retail liquor house, and taxing all opposition without justice or reason or mercy, until Zion's Co-operative Holiness to the Lord Mercantile

78

Institution was organized and became its heir. That institution, of which the Church owns one-third of the stock, sells more liquor without doubt than any other house in Utah. The First Presidency of the Church and its members never tire in these days of bewailing the evils of tippling and the helplessness of the people, being a Territory, to restrain or abolish it. And this is a fair sample of their consistency in all their teaching and preaching. A more muddle headed, or a more fraudulent set of word-mongers never lived. If the Mormons hang together until they become numerous, wealthy and powerful, it will be made plain that a system which endeavors to adapt the law to the appetite instead of to bring the appetite within the law, is as fatal to moderation in the use of alcohol as it is to moderation in salacial indulgences.[11]

7

Polygamy Crusade

THE RELATIVELY SOFT and conciliatory tone of *The Tribune's* 1884 New Year's editorial proved to be a temporary lapse. Before the year's end the "irrepressible conflict" reached a new high in bitterness, and the journalistic spokesmen for the contending sides were striving for new lows in lacerating editorials.

On November 7, *The Tribune*, under a heading "The Beast of the 'News' " started an editorial with this sentence: "The bastard in charge of the *News* again last evening filled his dreary columns with an attempt to convict a man before trial, to advertise a young girl's shame and everlasting disgrace, and to seek to make out that *The Tribune* was trying to conceal and apologize for a crime. . . ." [1]

The *News* replied that evening in similar tone and phraseology, scoring a point with a less biting but more intriguing heading — "The 'Gentlemen' of the *Tribune*." [2]

The reason for the upturn in venomous editorial exchanges was the beginning of the crusade to enforce the recently enacted anti-polygamy Edmunds Act. It was a crusade which, embarked upon, could scarcely be stopped without surrender by one side or the other. To *The Tribune*, "crusade" was an inappropriate term to describe the implementation of the new law. But that was the name it acquired in the histories of the era. To the editors of *The Tribune* it was a simple proposition of a theretofore spineless, indecisive federal government finally being forced by public opinion to enforce its laws in Utah Territory.

In the eyes of *The Tribune* publishers and editors, the Edmunds Act was the beginning of a governmental assault upon one aspect of an all-encompassing theocracy which was in revolt against the federal government; it was something the newspaper had been fighting for from the time Lockley and his associate "Border Ruffians" took control of the newspaper from the founding schismatic elders who were forced by economics to abandon their fight from within the church to change its economic and political policies; finally, it gave *The Tribune* and its allies a bludgeon which they unrestrainedly used over the ensuing decade to effectively assault all aspects of the system which they claimed had generated the "irrepressible conflict."

The importance of this bludgeon (polygamy and the Edmunds Act prosecutions) as a causative element in the conflict can easily be exaggerated, but its importance as a weapon and the extent of its use as such can hardly be exaggerated. Week after week and year after year *The Tribune* devoted more space to polygamy than to all the other issues of the battle combined. Naturally this concentration by the editors on what they deemed their most effective weapon is reflected in the history of the newspaper from the initiation of the crusade to the termination of church sanction of the practice of plural marriages.

While *The Tribune* could greet the federal government's campaign to enforce the anti-polygamy laws as a long step toward eventual victory, it became over the next several years an ordeal for all but the most insensitive and vindictive of Mormon-haters. It led to the hunting, harassing and imprisonment of women and their babies and of venerable old men whose lives *The Tribune* would concede had been exemplary except for a defiance of law dictated by religious conviction.

Orson F. Whitney, devout Mormon and later an apostle, wrote that those pressing the fight on polygamy were not scoun-

81

drels who found gratification in gloating over human suffering. They were motivated by a conviction that they had a duty, however unpleasant its performance might be, to bring obstinate law-breakers into conformity with law for the ultimate benefit of the territory and all its inhabitants. As Whitney pointed out, some of the Mormon-detested and gentile-admired federal officials were confronted with a problem which impelled them to accept the philosophy of Hamlet with respect to the Queen Mother: "I must be cruel in order to be kind" only to find themselves caught up in the unpleasantries of the second line of the couplet, "Thus bad begins, and worse remains behind." [3]

Obviously *The Tribune,* many of its supporters and most of the federal officials embroiled in the Utah problem underestimated what was going to be required to break the polygamous system. They believed, and frequently expressed such belief, that once the leaders of the church were confronted with conviction and imprisonment they would recognize the hopelessness of their position, agree to abide by the law themselves, and advise their followers to do likewise, without necessarily repudiating polygamy as an ecclesiastical doctrine. This illusion was soon dispelled by the first prosecutions under the Edmunds Act.

The first case instituted under this law which actually came to trial was against Rudger Clawson, a young man then who later became a member of the Quorum of Twelve Apostles. The defense tried first to quash the indictment on grounds that the grand jury was invalid because of the exclusion of Mormons for their response to questions on their religious beliefs and attitudes toward polygamy. The motion to set aside the indictment was denied by Judge Charles S. Zane. Clawson then pleaded guilty to the charges (which were cohabitation and polygamy) and the trial was held beginning October 15, 1884. When the non-Mormon jury split eight for conviction and four for acquittal *The Tribune,* with characteristic bluntness and disregard for legal niceties, responded with this editorial:

THE BEAUTIFUL QUARTETTE

A week's work in the effort to bring a criminal to justice has miscarried through a failure on the part of the jury to agree. The dissenting jurors are Messrs. Woodman, Forbes, Loder and Scribner. In ordinary cases the public and the public press are careful about criticising the motives of men in reaching a conclusion as jurors. The circumstances which attended upon and surrounded this case make impossible a charitable conclusion as to the motives and convictions of the jurors who, by their decision declared that nothing has been established against Rudger Clawson. They did, in effect, what Rudger Clawson in his nastiness and his crime still had too much manliness to do; they declared him innocent. He, in his degradation and shame, had not the audacity to face the court and make the same claim for himself. They did what Lydia Spencer, when there was no alternative left except to conclude that she was either a wife or a kept mistress, had too much truth and womanhood to do; they, in effect, declared that she was a mistress. In their anxiety to shield Rudger Clawson from conviction of a crime which was charged and proved against him, they have convicted him of being an adulterer, and have charged adultery upon an innocent woman. . . . [4]

The remainder of the long editorial was devoted to a review of the testimony and some uncomplimentary conclusions about motives of the dissenting jurors.

Six of the eight jurors who were for conviction came to the defense of their fellow jurors in this letter which was published in *The Tribune*:

In your issue of today is an article . . . in which, in our opinion, the dissenting jurors in the Rudger Clawson case are very unjustly criticised. As jurors in that case we were all of us in a position to know at least as much of the evidence in the case as your reporter or informant could know; and a ten-hour interview with the dissenting jurors in the jury room enables us to judge better than you can of the freedom with which they discussed the matter and of the probable motive actuating their verdict. Now as a matter of fact the dissenting jurors, or at least a majority of them, discussed the matter freely, and in such a manner as to lead us to believe that their verdict, while it differed from ours, was honestly arrived at and free from improper motives. Even were the facts otherwise, we regard the singling out by name of jurors, and the bringing against them of distinct charges of cowardice, stupidity or moral obtumen, in a powerful journal, as not only unjust to the individual jurors themselves, but as tending to defeat the ends of justice by leading men of self-respect to avoid a position where they are likely to be individually attacked in such a manner.[5]

Whitney footnotes in his history a report that two of the jurors — one favoring acquittal and the other conviction — got into a fist fight in the jury room. Whitney also assumes that it was the one favoring conviction from whom *The Tribune* drew its information on what took place in the jury room.[6]

Clawson's defense counsel sought a postponement but the prosecution insisted upon immediate retrial of the case. Defense counsel then sought a change of venue on four grounds, the fourth being: *"The Salt Lake Tribune,* a paper widely circulated and very influential among non-Mormons, by its abuse of witnesses and jurors during and after the late trial, had aroused a

84

bitter prejudice against the defendant, who therefore felt that he could not have a fair trial in this court."[7]

The court overruled the motion, the case was retried and a non-Mormon jury took seventeen minutes to return a verdict of guilty. When Clawson appeared for sentencing and was asked by the judge if he had any "legal cause to show why judgment should not be pronounced upon him," he replied:

> Your honor, since the jury that recently sat on my case have seen proper to find a verdict of guilty, I have only this to say why judgment should not be pronounced: I very much regret that the laws of my country should come in conflict with the laws of God, but whenever they do I shall invariably choose the latter. If I did not so express myself I should feel unworthy of the cause I represent. The Constitution of the United States expressly states that Congress shall make no law respecting an establishment of religion or prohibiting the free exercise thereof. It cannot be denied, I think, that marriage, when attended and sanctioned by religious rites and ceremonies, is an establishment of religion. The law of 1862 and the Edmunds Law were expressly designed to operate against marriage as practiced and believed in by the Latter-day Saints. They are therefore unconstitutional, and of course cannot command the respect that a constitutional law would. That is all I have to say, your honor.[8]

There it was, clearly and briefly stated. There was no room for compromise. The confrontation between church and federal government on this issue could be resolved only by capitulation on the part of one party or the other.

Judge Zane, according to historian Whitney, seemed to be taken by surprise. He remained silent for a minute or two and then said:

> The Constitution of the United States, as construed by the Supreme Court, and by the authors of that instrument, does not protect any person in the practice of polygamy. While all men have a right to worship God according to the dictates of their own conscience, and to entertain any religious belief that their conscience and judgment might reasonably dictate, they have not the right to engage in a practice which the American people, through the laws of their country, declare to be unlawful and injurious to society . . . I confess that I should have been inclined to fix this punishment smaller than I shall, were it not for the fact that you openly declare that you believe it is right to violate the law. [9]

The sentence imposed was a fine of $500 and imprisonment for three years and six months for polygamy; and a fine of $300 and imprisonment for six months for unlawful cohabitation, the second term to begin after termination of the first.

The case was immediately appealed to the Supreme Court of the territory on a writ of *habeas corpus* and the decision of the trial court confirmed. The *habeas corpus* case was in turn appealed to the Supreme Court of the United States.

The Clawson case generated intense interest and received widespread attention primarily because of the timing, the fact that it was a test on both polygamy and cohabitation provisions, and because the defendant was a member of a prominent Mormon family. Incidentally, he served in the penitentiary longer than anyone else convicted during the crusade. This, in the society in which he lived, made him a man of distinction.

Some bigger fish were soon to be caught in the polygamy net. And one of the biggest was Lorenzo Snow, an apostle of the church and subsequently its president. He, like the members of the First Presidency, had gone into exile at the beginning of the crusade but returned secretly to his home in Brigham City for a visit. Someone tipped the officers and seven deputy marshals surrounded the home and arrested him when they discovered a trap door under a rug and found him in an underground apartment.

"The arrest of Elder Snow," Whitney said in his *History of Utah,* "caused a widespread sensation, not only in Utah, but beyond her borders. His prominence and influence made him the most important prisoner that had yet fallen into the hands of the crusaders. The Mormons, as a matter of course, much regretted what had befallen him. The anti-Mormons were correspondingly elated." [10]

Gentiles, *The Tribune* and the federal officials were indeed elated with the arrest of Lorenzo Snow, but not because of vindictiveness toward him. On the contrary they were elated because they saw in his trial a possible opportunity to bring the polygamy hunt to a deeply desired end.

The Tribune expressed the hope in editorials. The prosecuting attorney, Victor Bierbower, expressed it at the beginning of the trial in these words:

> Mr. Snow stands before this jury in a dual capacity, as an individual and a representative. He is acknowledged to be one of the most learned and scholarly of all the Apostles. His collegiate training, his extensive travels . . . his eloquence in the pulpit, and his vast wealth, all combine to make him preeminently the representative of his people. One word from his eloquent tongue, or one line from his caustic pen, would go farther toward settling this

vexed question than any other dozen men in the Mormon Church. I verily believe that the example of his conviction will be more potential for good than would the conviction of three score of Elders, Deacons and Bishops. In this case we are fighting the throne itself. And I will venture to prophesy now, that with his conviction, and those that are to follow, the time is not far distant when there will come a new revelation which will put an end to polygamy. [11]

The Snow case promised to clarify two aspects of the Edmunds Act. First, it would serve as a test of an interpretation given by the trial courts that the law was aimed at polygamy; that it was not necessary, for conviction, to prove sexual intercourse, or occupancy of the same house, but only that the defendant was living or associating with two or more women as his wives. Secondly, it would serve as a test of the prosecution's theory of "segregation" whereby separate offenses could be charged for separate periods of time during which the offense continued. The prosecution was ultimately upheld by the Supreme Court as to the first point but the "segregation" approach was rejected.

After the jury had found Mr. Snow guilty he was given the usual opportunity to address the court. His statement only served to freeze the problem more solidly into the pattern it had already taken. He said in part:

I have ever felt to honor the laws and institutions of my country, and, during the progress of my trials, whatever evidence has been introduced has proved my innocence. But, like ancient Apostles when arraigned in pagan courts, and in the presence of apostate Hebrew judges, though innocent, they were pronounced guilty. So myself, an Apostle who bears witness because of his calling and the revelations of God, that Jesus lives, that He is the Son of God — though guiltless of crime, here in a Christian court I have been convicted through the prejudice and popular sentiment of a so-called Christian nation.

In ancient times the Jewish nation and Roman empire stood vs. the Apostles. Now, under an apostate Christianity, the United States of America stands vs. Apostle Lorenzo Snow.

The trial judge, Orlando W. Powers, then asked the standard question for persons convicted under the Edmunds Act:

"Mr. Snow, the Court desires to ask, for its own information, what course you propose to pursue in the future concerning the laws of your country?"

The reply concluded with these words:

"Having been condemned here and found guilty after having obeyed the law, I am sorry — I regret that your Honor should ask me that question, and, if your Honor please, I should prefer not to answer it."

Judge Powers, in imposing sentence, remarked:

"The Court, Mr. Snow, from its own knowledge of you and your reputation . . . is aware that you are a man of more than ordinary ability. The Court is aware that you are a scholar. The Court is aware that you are naturally a leader of men; that you have a mind well adapted to controlling others, and for guiding others. No matter in what land you might have lived, or in what position you might have been placed, you have those attributes which would naturally have caused people to turn towards you for advice and for counsel. . . .

The Court feels that, in view of your past life, of the teachings that you have given to this people, of the advice and counsel, that you desire to stand as an example of one who advocates, and, the jury has found, also practices in violation of the law, the Court must pass sentence in these cases in a way and manner that will indicate to this people that the laws of the land cannot be violated with impunity, even by one as aged, as learned, and as influential as yourself.

At another point in pronouncing sentence the judge added:

I sincerely believe that Lorenzo Snow could cause this people to obey the laws of the Union, and put an end to the trouble and discord in this Territory . . .[12]

The Snow case almost certainly sounded the death knell of any hope on the part of federal officials and gentiles that the polygamy issue was going to be resolved by leading church members promising to obey, and advising members to obey, the Edmunds Act as interpreted by the Supreme Court. Trial after trial came to the same dead end. To the non-Mormons it all sounded like forked-tongue evasion. To conforming Mormons it obviously sounded like courageous martyrdom for compliance with God's law. But on a few occasions the pattern was broken.

In Ogden Bishop Francis A. Brown didn't quibble. He told the court and jury that he had two wives, that he lived with them and that he had children by them. He concluded his statement prior to sentencing with this declaration:

I expect to stand before the bar of God in the court above, and give an account of the deeds done in the body, and if I cannot obtain my rights in the courts on earth, I have no fear but what I shall receive equity and justice at the hands of God in Heaven, and I can afford to wait. . . . May God have mercy upon

90

this court, and all who are engaged in this unholy crusade against an honest, virtuous, industrious, and God-fearing people! [13]

This was something *The Tribune* editors could admire, and applaud with an editorial which included this comment: "F. A. Brown, the Mormon Saint convicted in Ogden on Tuesday last by his own testimony, had the courage of his convictions. However much one may deplore such wrong-headedness, the admission must be made that here is a man; one who does not quibble and lie, and who scorns to show the white feather." [14]

Another type of deviation which *The Tribune* applauded and the *News* criticized occurred in the case of Orson P. Arnold, a highly respected member of the church. He pleaded guilty to the charge and promised to obey the law thereafter. He was fined $300 and released.

The reaction within the church, as recorded by historian Whitney, was one of astonishment and grief. Said the *Deseret News:* "Notwithstanding the course taken by Brother Arnold which received the encomiums of the court and its officers and the approval of a portion of the spectators, his example is not one that any consistent Latter-day Saint can afford to follow." [15]

Whitney notes that "Mr. Arnold afterwards redeemed himself in the eyes of his people, by going to prison for the sake of his religion." [16]

Despite this clear warning to members of the church, a much more prominent member followed the same course several months later. Bishop John Sharp pleaded guilty, paid a fine of $300 and was discharged.

Whitney said in his history that this created one of the major "sensations" of the crusade. "Bishop Sharp," Whitney wrote, "was not one of the general authorities of the church, but one of a score or more of bishops presiding severally over the ecclesiastical wards of Salt Lake City. Socially and financially, however, he was one of the foremost characters in the community. Nor was

this entirely due to his wealth, to the influence that it commanded, or to the ability by which it had been acquired. He was the
possessor of sterling qualities, for which he was widely honored
and esteemed." [17]

In passing sentence, Judge Zane remarked: "In view of the
statements which you have made, I am disposed to exercise the
discretion which the law gives me, so as not to impose any imprisonment." [18]

The Tribune, in applauding the position taken by the court,
said in an editorial:

> Bishop John Sharp did a manly thing yesterday,
> and confirmed the impression which his daily life
> makes upon those who see him as a thorough, high-
> minded man. He has the sense to see that the posi-
> tion of the Mormons before the country is that of a
> people who are in open defiance of its laws. He
> knows that in his business, if an employe obeys only
> such instructions as he pleases, there is every mo-
> ment danger of collusion, confusion and anarchy. So
> he knows that when a faction of people within a re-
> public assume to judge for themselves what laws of
> that republic they will obey and which they will
> deride, either they must give up that position, or it
> can only be a question of time when the republic it-
> self will topple and fall in ruins. Knowing his full
> responsibility to his church and to his adopted
> country, he yesterday, before the court, promised
> hereafter to live within the laws and never to ad-
> vise anyone to do anything else.
>
> If John Taylor and George Q. Cannon would come
> from their secret hiding places and do the same
> thing, and advise their people who are involved as
> they are, and as Bishop Sharp was, to follow their
> example they would come nearer to proving that

they are fit to be the shepherds of their flock than by anything else they have done for a year. [19]

The Bishop Sharp incident provided one more point of conflict between *The Tribune* and the *News*. *The Tribune* charged that the church directed various forms of retaliation against the bishop for his refusal to perjure himself and for promising to obey the law. The *News* stoutly denied that he suffered any mistreatment at the hands of his church associates. Whitney, in recounting the event some years later, had this to say about it:

> As apparent from Judge Zane's remarks, when pronouncing sentence upon the Bishop, it was the defendant's example that was chiefly valued by the anti-polygamists; an example which, it was hoped, would be followed by all the Mormon leaders. It was the example that the Mormons also took into account, in passing judgment upon their co-religionist, and it was because of the possible effect of that example upon the Mormon cause that many found it difficult to excuse him; to extend the consideration to which his friends deemed him entitled. It is a fact that he was in poor health at this time; in no condition to endure the rigors of penitentiary life. For this reason his course was palliated. . . . John Sharp resigned his office of Bishop of the Twentieth Ward, but it was at the request of the Presidency of the Stake, who thought it advisable under the circumstances, to relieve him of that responsibility. No further action was taken or contemplated in his case, and when he died a few years later, the principal men of the church attended his funeral and otherwise manifested their esteem for their old-time associate. [20]

While Utah was the focal point of the crusade against polygamy, numerous prosecutions took place in Idaho and Arizona and a few cases arose elsewhere.

The Tribune covered the trials in minute detail, frequently straying from objective and factual recital of testimony, with such headlines as: "Judge Bennett's Weak Defense of the Criminal Clawson;" "George Q. Cannon, the Wonderful Knownothing;" "Witnesses for Defense Admit That They Are Perjurers."

Throughout this period *The Tribune,* like its journalistic opponents, utilized the "bludgeon" type editorial. It was always blunt and sometimes brutal. But on occasion it would try a more deft approach. One such example appeared January 21, 1886, in the running editorial dispute with the *News* as to whether polygamous wives really did accept the practice. *The Tribune* flatly rejected public statements of individual women, or resolutions adopted by groups of women as believable evidence; it regarded such declarations as perjured testimony given under ecclesiastical duress.

Under the heading "I Saw It in Her Face," the editorial started out in this fashion:

> There are two men high in the Mormon Church who have recently taken second wives. That is, the general understanding is that they have. It is the quiet talk of both gentiles and Mormons. Two Mormon women met on the street a few mornings since and talked so loud that it was impossible for those near not to hear them. The talk ran as follows: 'Say, is it true that Brother ---- has married a second wife?' 'Yes, it is true.' 'How do you know?' 'I saw it in his first wife's face.' [21]

8

"The Madam"

MIDWAY IN THE anti-polygamy crusade a counter-attack was launched which cooled, temporarily at least, the enthusiasm of some of the "cohab hunters." The opening shot in this counter-attack was the arrest of a deputy United States Marshal named Oscar C. Vandercook on a charge of violating a city ordinance covering lewd and lascivious conduct. The federal official was arrested when he alighted from a train from Brigham City, where he had headed the search resulting in the arrest of Lorenzo Snow.

Vandercook offered no resistance to his arrest by the city police on a warrant issued by Alderman Adam Spiers upon a complaint filed by B. Y. Hampton, city license collector. He declared it was a "trumped-up" maneuver by the Mormon city administration and police to intimidate those engaged in the apprehending and prosecution of suspected Edmunds Act violators. According to historian Whitney, the arrest, and others immediately thereafter, resulted in considerable consternation, if not intimidation. Whitney's account continued:

> At the time set for the trial of Deputy Marshal Vandercook, the Police Court was thronged. The news of the arrests had spread like wild-fire. Not only was general interest awakened; but in some quarters absolute consternation reigned. This was

95

caused by a rumor — which proved to be well founded — that the police were liable at any moment to
be taken into custody, for practices similar to those
charged against the official named. Some of the
prospective defendants were men who had served
warrants, sat upon juries, and played various parts
in the anti-polygamy movement then in progress.
Just where the lightning would next strike was uncertain. Suspense added ten-fold misery to the fears
of those who found themselves occupying positions
the reverse of invulnerable. It was said that those
whose names were 'on the list' had been caught *in
flagrante delicto* by detectives, who, in collusion
with fallen women of the town, had undertaken this
little diversion with a view to balancing the scales
of the Blind Goddess in Utah, and visiting the rigors of the law upon certain crimes against which
the Federal courts were not then proceeding, and at
which, it was held, the Edmunds Law did not aim.
. . . What lent additional terror to the situation
was the significant fact that the charges in these
cases did not consist of glittering generalities. Details were given; names, dates, circumstances were
all set forth. In short, it was just such data as eye
witnesses would naturally be expected to produce;
and eye witnesses the complainants claimed to be.
License Collector Hampton was the leader of the de-
tective force, which included several members of
the regular police. [1]

The Tribune wrathfully charged that it was all a brazen conspiracy aimed at intimidation. The newspaper's version was that
Hampton had recruited the cooperation of a "madam" from San
Francisco, set her up in business in Salt Lake City at a cost of
several hundred dollars, and agreed to pay her a fixed fee for

each client enticed into the house and compromised to a degree which would support a conviction. The "madam" was obligated to supply names, dates and other information pertinent for arrest and prosecution.

The *News, Herald* and the city officials involved took the position that the arrest of Vandercook and others was simply an extension of the crusade to purify the moral atmosphere of the community begun by the Edmunds Act prosecutions and that the net was designed to catch all possible offenders — Mormon, gentile or Jew.

After a few days of legal maneuvering, some of the defendants were tried and convicted in police court and sentences imposed of $299 fines and three months imprisonment. The defendants then appealed to the District Court (which was federal) and all were dismissed on the grounds that the prosecutions were the result of a conspiracy of entrapment. In making the motion for dismissal, Assistant United States Attorney C. S. Varian is reported to have said in reference to the witnesses who had testified against the defendants that he "would not believe such scoundrels on oath, even in the high court of heaven itself. . . . I refuse to prosecute them [the appellant-defendants], or to allow them to be prosecuted; I am sure they could not be convicted, and am certain they ought not to be." [2]

This disposed of the cases initiated by the city police. Hampton was indicted by the grand jury for conspiracy and convicted. His defenders claimed he was convicted on the testimony of witnesses whom Varian had called untrustworthy scoundrels. He was sentenced to one year in prison and served the full term.

The participants in the anti-polygamy crusade could now breathe easier, so far as the city law was concerned. However, it may be presumed that some at least, who found entrapment to be an adequate legal defense, found it less effective when they were confronted by an enraged monogamous spouse at home.

The biggest single sensation in the anti-polygamy crusade was the arrest on February 13, 1886 of George Q. Cannon at Humboldt Wells, Nevada. He was the second man in authority in the Mormon Church and was regarded by some, including *The Tribune*, as the number one man in actual influence. His apprehension, in fact, brought *The Tribune* and the *Herald* to one of their very rare points of agreement. A *Tribune* editorial on February 17, 1886 said:

> The *Herald* yesterday said that George Q. Cannon's arrest had been more desired than that of any other Mormon. This is true. There were ample reasons for it. He was the power behind the throne in this absolute Mormon Kingdom. It was in his power to have caused peace and quiet here. . . . [3]

While the arrest of the church official was an event which plunged Mormons into deep depression and provoked jubilation among anti-Mormons, it was a series of related and subsequent developments which make the case the most sensational of the crusade.

Federal officials had been watching the Cannon farm southwest of the city for some weeks, probably because of tips that the church leader might appear there. It was presumed, and correctly so, that he and President John Taylor were keeping in close touch with each other during their exile so they could make joint decisions regarding church business. (Joseph F. Smith, the other member of the First Presidency, was abroad at the time.) Rumors had been circulated that both Taylor and Cannon were together in hiding in some home in the vicinity of Salt Lake City. The telegraphed report of Cannon's arrest in Nevada was therefore presumed by many to be in error when it was first received. But positive confirmation was shortly received from U.S. Marshal E.A. Ireland, who telegraphed that Cannon had consented to return to Salt Lake City without papers.

It was later disclosed that Cannon had indeed been in the Salt Lake area with President Taylor; that he had agreed to go to Mexico to negotiate for land on which the Mormons might settle without giving up polygamy; that he and his party had traveled to Ogden in a freight car; that they had been taken from there by team to the vicinity of Willard in Box Elder County where they boarded a west-bound Central Pacific train. Someone apparently had recognized him along the way and tipped off Marshal Ireland who had posted a reward of $500 for such information. A Nevada sheriff, in response to a message from Ireland, boarded the train at Winnemucca and made the arrest when the train stopped at Humboldt Wells.

Marshal Ireland and another officer traveled by train to Winnemucca to take custody of the prisoner. During the return trip sensation began piling on sensation. While the train was passing along a bleak waste near the shores of Great Salt Lake Marshal Ireland discovered that his prisoner was not aboard.

Cannon next showed up at Promontory in custody of a deputy marshal. He had a broken nose, a large gash over the left eye and most of the skin scuffed off the left side of his face. He explained that he had accidentally fallen off the train. Naturally, the incident touched off a heated debate between Mormons and anti-Mormons and their journalistic spokesmen as to whether he had fallen off or jumped off in an escape attempt. The argument was not resolved. It appears that, whether he fell or jumped, he did not try to escape after the fall.

The next episode in the drama was the circulation of a rumor that Cannon's friends were planning to rescue him from the federal officers. The military authority at Fort Douglas sent a small body of soldiers to join the party at Promontory. The next rumor was that the rescue attempt would be made at Ogden. The soldiers aboard the train were ordered to load their guns when that city was approached. Nothing happened. At Salt Lake City the soldiers were again prepared to meet any resistance, but none was offered.

The prisoner was immediately taken before Judge Zane. United States Attorney William H. Dickson requested that bail be fixed at $25,000, justifying the abnormally large amount on the grounds that the prisoner had attempted to bribe an officer at Winnemucca; that he had tried to escape; and that he was a high church dignitary wielding immense influence over the Mormon people. F. S. Richards, Cannon's attorney, protested the "exorbitant" bail but Judge Zane granted Dickson's request and John Sharp and Feramorz Little, two of the city's most prominent citizens, were accepted as sureties. Bail was then fixed at $10,000 for each of two additional indictments charging unlawful cohabitation. Mayor Francis Armstrong and General H. S. Eldredge were accepted as sureties for these amounts. Thus the total bail was $45,000 for alleged offenses carrying a maximum penalty of $300 fine and six months imprisonment. It seemed a fantastically excessive amount at the time.

The next episode in the case was a fistic attack on United States Attorney Dickson by Hugh J. Cannon, a son of the church leader, who was infuriated by questions asked of his mother before the grand jury.

The "catechising" of Mrs. Cannon before the grand jury provoked a large mass meeting of women in the Salt Lake Theater and adoption of a memorial of protest which was taken to Washington by Emmeline B. Wells and Dr. Ellen B. Ferguson, two of Utah's most prominent women.

The climax of the drama was not reached until the day set for trial, March 17, 1886. The defendant failed to appear and so did his bondsmen. In the afternoon when the defendant again failed to appear, Sharp and Little promptly paid over the $25,000 bail. But the sureties for the two $10,000 bonds elected to test in the courts the question of excessive bail.

The Tribune, to no one's surprise, denounced the church leader's bail jumping but dealt editorially with the incident with an "I told you so" attitude. The newspaper commented:

> That portion of the public which has been at all swayed by the plea that excessive bail was asked in the case against George Q. Cannon will no doubt be greatly surprised to learn that even such heavy bonds did not hold him. The other, and more intelligent portion of the public which knows that no bail is properly styled excessive which can be easily and freely given, will not be surprised at all. They have recognized from the first that it was simply a question of whether Cannon preferred to stand trial or forfeit any bond given, the amount not being material, since he would not be impoverished and the Church or its agents in the matter were well able to pay. The one thing Cannon did dread was an inside view of the penitentiary. . . . [4]

The remainder of the editorial reiterated a theme frequently expounded by *The Tribune*: denunciation of top leaders who went into exile or "underground" while calling upon others to endure any hardship they might be called upon to make for the church, including imprisonment. Denunciation of the leadership was usually coupled with contemptuous or pitying criticism of those who were going to prison for the cause for meekly accepting the role of "dupes and slaves."

The bail jumping incident provoked a mixed reaction among Mormons according to Whitney, who wrote:

> Many at first regretted the occurrence; for it was supposed that President Cannon's failure to appear for trial would render the situation of his brethren who might be arrested thereafter exceedingly dis-

agreeable. The 'tremendous moral effect' that would have followed his conviction and imprisonment was also a theme much dwelt upon. Now, it was argued, it would be more difficult to convince the world of the sincerity of the Mormon leaders, and those arraigned in the future need expect no mercy. Bail would be refused them, or placed at such a figure that scarcely any would be able to procure it; and if President Taylor should be captured, one hundred thousand dollars would not suffice to secure his liberation pending trial. Such were the arguments and reasonings afloat. [5]

While Mormons generally were not yet apprised of the fact, Cannon had simply followed President Taylor's counsel. This soon became public knowledge, and it was not long until Cannon's disapproving co-religionists were zealously justifying his actions.

As for the forfeited bail, the test over the $10,000 bonds went through the Utah courts and was transferred to Washington. There the cases were ultimately dismissed and, through the intercession of influential friends, congressional action was taken to restore the $25,000 paid over by Cannon's bondsmen.

By this time (early 1886), signs were cropping up here and there that even the wielders of the polygamy stick were growing tired of beating the church over the head with it. *The Tribune,* and many others, had no more illusions that the arrest of a few prominent Mormons would start a stampede of polygamists promising the courts to obey the law in the future. It is possible that, had this happened, the polygamy ruckus could have been resolved without legislation dealing more directly with church economics and political influence. In this sense, a premature solution of the polygamy issue might well have been a defeat for the cause espoused by *The Tribune* and a victory for the church.

Some persons removed from the scene of the crusade still harbored the belief that polygamy could be quelled with a little understanding diplomacy. One who held this view was Caleb W. West, who was appointed governor of the Utah Territory by the Democratic president, Grover Cleveland, when the administration deemed the time to be politically ripe for the removal of the Republican-appointed Governor Murray.

Governor West arrived on a beautiful spring day on May 5, 1886. He was sworn in the next day by Chief Justice Zane and, two or three days later, went to the penitentiary on what he thought was going to be a triumphant mission of reconciliation. He told the polygamous prisoners that he regretted that there existed such an unpleasant state of affairs in Utah but believed there was a remedy at hand. He explained that it would not be necessary for the Mormons to abandon the religious doctrine of polygamy but only the practice, as the conflict with the laws of the land related only to the practice, and not the belief. Most of the discussion was between the new governor and Apostle Snow.

Governor West then left to give the prisoners time to think it over. Before his second visit, the Snow cases were argued before the United States Supreme Court and that body evaded the issue by dismissing the cases for want of jurisdiction. It had earlier accepted jurisdiction in a similar case and, to make the record consistent, reconsidered that case and dismissed it on the same grounds. This left the polygamists and the anti-polygamy crusaders just about where they were before.

On the second visit the governor interviewed Apostle Snow. An official summary of the discussion furnished to the Salt Lake newspapers by the governor indicated that it followed the same general course as scores of discussions between court and defendants in the trial of the polygamy cases.

At one point the summary quoted the governor and Snow as follows:

Governor — Upon consultation with Judge Zane and Mr. Dickson [the prosecuting attorney] and their supporting the view I have suggested, I have come to say to you and your people here that we will unite in a petition to the Executive to issue his pardon in these cases upon a promise, in good faith, that you obey and respect the laws, and that you will continue no longer to live in violation of them. Snow — Well, Governor, so far as I am concerned personally, I am not in conflict with any of the laws of the country. I have obeyed the law as faithfully and conscientiously as I can thus far, and I am not here because of disobedience to any law. I am here wrongfully convicted and wrongfully sentenced. [6]

The interview continued through several more pages, always coming around to the same dead end.

The offer of amnesty was then proferred to the other polygamist prisoners with the suggestion that they take time to reflect before answering. They gave their answer in writing on May 24, 1886. The closing paragraphs indicate the nature of the entire reply:

The proposition you made, though prompted doubtless by a kind feeling, was not entirely new, for we could all have avoided imprisonment by making the same promise to the courts; in fact, the penalties we are now enduring are for declining to so promise rather than for acts committed in the past. Had you offered us unconditional amnesty, it would have been gladly accepted; but, dearly as we prize the great boon of liberty, we cannot afford to obtain it by proving untrue to our conscience, our religion and our God.

As loyal citizens of this great Republic, whose Constitution we revere, we do not ask for, but claim, our rights as freemen; and if from neither local nor national authority we are to receive equity and mercy, we will make our appeal to the Great Arbiter of all human interests, who in due time will grant us the justice hitherto denied.

That you may, as the Governor of our important but afflicted Territory, aid us in securing every right to which loyal citizens are entitled, and find happiness in so doing, we will ever pray. [7]

The reply was signed by a cross-section of the most prominent names in the church including Lorenzo Snow who was soon to become its president.

Governor West was sorely disappointed by the rejection of his plan to conciliate this issue, but it was not because he had been misinformed on this aspect of the "irrepressible conflict" by *The Tribune* and other crusaders in the anti-polygamy movement. While the church, a few years later, did take the position urged upon the prisoners by Governor West, the time was not ripe in 1886. Indeed, some individuals were still taking the same adamant, unyielding stand on the issue in the 1930's and 1950's when they were in revolt against both the laws of the land and the Mormon establishment.

The Tribune extended Governor West a polite welcome when he arrived even though he was a southern Democrat replacing Republican Governor Murray whom *The Tribune* supported and admired both because of his personal qualities and because he was so detested by the church. The new governor's conciliatory visit to the imprisoned polygamists drew this rebuke from the newspaper:

There is, in the East, a large class of people who really believe that the gentiles of Utah are a bad lot. We wonder if the scene at the Penitentiary on Thursday will change their views any. When the Governor of the Territory went there, and, picking out one class of criminals, humiliated himself enough to beg them to receive a pardon from the Government, his offer was not only scornfully refused, but he was made to listen to an arraignment of the faithful officers who have been doing their duty; of the Christian church under which he grew up, and he had flung in his face not only a defiance of the Government under which he is an officer, but had it compared in cruelty to the Pagan governments of antiquity. How will the soothing syrup apostles of the East like that picture? How will the President of the United States look upon it? What will the Congressmen, who have learned to echo Caine's and Gibson's cry of persecution, think of it? Will there not some time a dim consciousness of the real facts begin to dawn upon them. . . .

Of the written reply of the prisoners, *The Tribune* editorial continued:

There is nothing in the reply . . . which either of half a dozen of their number could not have prepared in an hour. The conclusion, then, is irresistible that the document was prepared in some depot of the "underground" and the wretches in the Penitentiary simply signed it. It is not their will, but simply the will of Cannon or Taylor or Smith, or some other skulker who proves by his acts that while he is willing for the men in the Penitentiary to rot there, he does not mean to join them. Hence all the professed devotion to a cause which is in-

cluded in the letter is simply the dictation of some
fraud who, at a distance, explains how willing are
the martyrs to suffer; but who at the same time is
most determined never to join the unfor-
tunates. . . . [8]

Governor West, having received the answer to his hopeful
gesture of conciliation, had to revise his stance. It was an answer
he could not misconstrue. One phrase in the letter put it in a nut-
shell — "Had you offered us unconditional amnesty, it would
have been gladly accepted." To a governor of a territory, a more
precise way of putting it would have been — "Had you offered us
unconditional surrender on this point, it would have gladly been
accepted."

That the polygamy crusade, distasteful as it probably was to
many of the hunters and all the hunted, was inflaming rather
than reducing the Utah problem, was painfully apparent. A few
excerpts from editorials of the period suggest that conclusion.

On May 8, 1886, under the heading "Why Were Gentiles
Asked," *The Tribune* editorialized:

The Mormons gave Governor West a grand reception and ball last night. That was all right and
proper, for Governor West, by virtue of his office
and the reputation he brings with him, is entitled
to every mark of respect. But why were all the
prominent gentiles in the city invited? Why was it
necessary to place the gentiles in the position of
either seeming to slight the governor or of being
on the most friendly terms with the Mormons?
Some gentiles at least, are not adept in the business of seeming to be in love with the people they
do not care for. . . .[9]

This comment was, in part, a reply to one carried a few days earlier by the *Deseret News:*

> The indiscriminate association of Mormons and non-Mormons, innocent and designing, chaste and immoral, can not be otherwise than bad in its results, and they ought to be frowned down and discouraged by Latter-day Saints generally, and every publication that claims to be in the interest of morality. And we would advise our correspondent, and all others who value the purity of their sons and daughters, to keep them from the contaminations of all such badly mixed gatherings. . . .
>
> Would that the barriers between the pure and the impure, between Zion and Babylon, might be rendered stronger and, if possible, impassable. . . . [10]

Going even further on May 1, *The Tribune* drew some parallels between the Confederacy and the Mormon Church:

> Without desiring to be disrespectful either to Jeff Davis or the Mormons, we cannot help but note striking similarity between the arguments of the two. Both, if we believe them, were original noncombatants; neither ever desired anything except their constitutional rights; both have been oppressed by an unjust government and a vicious people; both are certain that history will vindicate them. And still the world keeps on in its course, and the Republic still lives. It is not necessary to criticize the statements of either. A dozen chiefs of the Confederacy have placed on file their solemn statements that Jeff Davis was a sordid, mean, dishonest and untruthful man while he was president of the Confederacy, and we suspect that if

Bishop Sharp's real sentiments could be obtained he would say the same of at least one of the First Presidency of the Mormon Church. Despite all the persecutions Jeff Davis, while parading his noncitizenship, is permitted to hurl his scorn at the Government which spared his forfeited life and has ever since protected him; the men, who with him tried to destroy this Republic and build up a slave empire are now in political control in this country. The temple at Logan is still smoking with plural marriages, and still Jeff Davis is telling of the wrongs in Alabama, and we now and then receive a mournful protest from George and John from the underground. . . . [11]

The Tribune frequently reiterated its reasons for opposing statehood at this period in the territory's history. Some of the reasons it advanced in editorials were that anyone who dared to express an opinion not in accord with the dominant religion in the new state would have to emigrate or fight; that statehood would probably ignite civil war in Utah; that if statehood were then given to Utah George Q. Cannon, whom *The Tribune* regarded as the real power in the church following the death of Brigham Young, would nominate all officers in the state, decide which laws would be repealed or passed and, in short, would govern the state as an absolute dictator.

Nonetheless, some winds of change were beginning to stir, though not discernibly at that moment; and *The Tribune's* campaign was moving more surely toward partial victory than the editors realized.

9

The Raid

DISCOMFORTED, AND AT TIMES sickened, by the brutalities which the polygamy crusade unavoidably imposed upon women, children and the non-polygamous Mormon majority, gentile leaders were nevertheless unwilling to abandon their most effective weapon in the "irrepressible conflict." They were, however, in a mood by 1887 to soften the pressures on polygamy and wage a more direct attack on the church's economic fortress. A weapon suitable for this purpose had been provided by the Edmunds-Tucker Act on which Congress completed action in February, 1887. This new act revised in several respects the anti-polygamy laws of 1862 and 1882 and gave them "teeth." One of the sharpest was a directive to the attorney general of the United States to "institute proceedings to forfeit and escheat all property, both real and personal, of the dissolved church corporation held in violation of the 1862 limitation. . . ."[1] That act had disincorporated the church and restricted its holdings to not more than $50,000 and property used exclusively for the worship of God.

The mood of the gentile community at this point in the struggle was summed up by Whitney, a devout Mormon historian, in these words:

> . . . the Edmunds Act of March 22, 1882, was a disappointment to those who had taken upon them-

selves 'a mission for the social and political regen-
eration of Utah.' That law was not far-reaching
enough to satisfy an element which, not content
that pains and penalties should be visited upon the
polygamous minority among the Mormons, desired
something that would effect the destruction or
emasculation of the entire Mormon system. 'We
care nothing for your polygamy,' the gentiles were
wont to say in private, to individual Mormons. 'It's
a good war-cry and serves our purpose by enlisting
sympathy for our cause; but it is a mere bagatelle
compared with other issues in the irrepressible conflict between our parties. What we most object to is
your unity; your political and commercial solidari-
ty; the obedience you render to your spiritual leaders in temporal affairs. We want you to throw off
the yoke of the Priesthood, to do as we do, and be
Americans in deed as well as in name.'
Such were the frank admissions of those who were
reasonable in their opposition to the Mormons, and
did not hate them with that deep-rooted rancor
that brooked no thought of reconciliation between
the two classes of the commonwealth. Even the
most radical expressed these sentiments at times.
Seldom, however, did such modified utterances —
never, so far as polygamy was concerned — find
place in their public speeches and documents, particularly those sent abroad and used for political effect at the Nation's capital. These were always full
of polygamy, priestcraft, tyranny and treason.[2]

It was a fair appraisal of the position of the gentiles by a
champion of the Mormon cause except on one point. The comment that the gentiles never admitted in public statements

that their primary target were issues other than polygamy was something less than accurate with respect to *The Tribune.* On more than one occasion *The Tribune* stated in articles and editorials that its primary targets were political and economic domination by a closed religious society.

In a comment on a *Herald* editorial, for example, *The Tribune* stated:

> The *Herald* assumes that polygamy is the chief bugbear with gentiles here, and with the nation at large. It is by far the lesser crime. It is merely the nasty cement in the wall of Mormonism; the solid matter in that wall is church rule, the utter vassalage to which the State is subjected, making the abject prostitution of the ballot a natural result; delivering the consciences of the people bound and gagged into the keeping of their chiefs, cementing an organization together, over which some bold ruffians hold the keys of life and death, and causing a whole people to stand ready to execute the commands of those chiefs, no matter what crimes those commands might include. . . . [3]

The local news and editorial content of *The Tribune* during this period indicated that the policy makers did not fully appreciate the potency of the weapon which had been placed in the hands of the gentiles by passage of the Edmunds-Tucker Act — specifically the sections directing the United States Attorney General to dissolve the church corporation and to escheat for the benefit of the district schools of the territory all real and personal property held in violation of the $50,000 limitation fixed in the 1862 law but not enforced up to this time.

The Tribune had vigorously supported the new law and editor Goodwin had spent some time in Washington serving as an adviser to representatives of Utah's gentile community sent to the capitol to lobby for its enactment. The newspaper castigated senators and representatives who opposed the legislation as "Jack Mormons" and, by implication at least, applied the same tag to President Grover Cleveland because he refused to sign the bill, permitting it to become law without his signature.

The term "Jack Mormon" was applied during this period to non-Mormons who collaborated with Mormons. It was a wildly elastic term which the most rabid Mormon haters sometimes hurled at *The Tribune* itself, or at Goodwin, if they suggested Mormon-gentile cooperation on a Fourth of July celebration or on some community enterprise or on some inconsequential political matter.

While federal officials were preparing to wage a direct assault upon the church's temporal power by seizing its property, *The Tribune* centered its editorial fire on two other targets — a test oath provision in the Edmunds-Tucker Act which was designed to prohibit polygamists from voting, holding office. and serving on juries and a church-sponsored renewal of the old campaign for statehood.

The Tribune, and gentile leaders generally, were dissatisfied with the test oath approved by the federally-appointed Utah Commission. *The Tribune* campaigned unsuccessfully for changes which the Mormons insisted, and the commission agreed, went beyond the provisions of the law.

The campaign for statehood was denounced by *The Tribune* as obvious trickery. The fact that the Mormons proposed to put into the state constitution an article prohibiting and punishing polygamy, *The Tribune* argued, was *prima facie* evidence of fraud. Who, *The Tribune* asked, could be so gullible as to believe that the same church leaders who had gone underground and into exile rather than obey a law prohibiting polygamy, really intended to enforce a state constitutional provision prohibiting the practice?

If statehood were granted, *The Tribune* asserted, church-controlled courts, legislature and executive department would ignore the polygamy prohibition or the church-controlled electorate would be directed to repeal it.

In an editorial under the heading "How to Secure Statehood," the newspaper said:

> The movement for Statehood is plainly nothing but an attempt to put off or turn aside the the inevitable. . . . There is a way to proceed which will insure the stopping of any further legislation, the prevention of partition, and the securing of Statehood in three or four years from now. Let John Taylor and George Q. Cannon tomorrow call at the District Court rooms, plead guilty to the indictments there filed against them, promise to obey the laws and resume their places in the community. Let them declare that there must be no more polygamy in Utah until it shall be made legal by the competent authorities of the Republic; that in politics the people must henceforth use their own judgment, that the priesthood has no more political control over them. Then let the Legislature meet and make polygamy unlawful by a special act, and let the people live up to their duty and exercise their political privileges, and the whole trouble that has vexed Utah so long will be ended in a day. Let this be continued for three or four years, and the gentiles will join in asking for Statehood. That is much sooner than it will be secured with any guarantee that trouble will not follow. [4]

In pursuit of statehood, the People's Party went ahead with the mass meeting without gentile participation and elected delegates to a Constitutional Convention which assembled in Salt

Lake City on June 30, 1887. After seven days of deliberation a constitution containing an article prohibiting polygamy was approved and a committee appointed to make arrangements for submitting the document to the electorate at the general election in August. The proposed constitution was approved by the voters in the election by a ratio of about 26 to 1 and it was submitted to Congress in December by Delegate John T. Caine. As *The Tribune* predicted, that was the end of the trail for that statehood bid.

During this eventful year of 1887 two developments occurred which suggested that perhaps both Mormons and gentiles were becoming increasingly weary of the strains and stresses of the "irrepressible conflict." One of these events was the formation in April of the Salt Lake Chamber of Commerce and Board of Trade, as it was called initially. The initiative for the organization was provided by gentiles, one of the leaders in the movement being Governor Caleb West who served as chairman at the first meeting. Stated purposes of the new organization was to revive trade, establish home industries, and attract capital and population. A motto of "No politics or religion in the Chamber" was adopted, probably with the hope that this would permit gentiles to join without being denounced by extremists as "Jack Mormons" and Mormons to join without being denounced by their own extremists as traitors to the church.

With the strong backing of Governor West and many of the territory's most prominent leaders, the chamber moved through the processes of organization and incorporation with relative speed. Signing the articles of incorporation were a number of prominent Mormons, including Heber J. Grant, but its real strength lay in its gentile signatories, one of whom was P. H. Lannan, principal owner and publisher of *The Tribune*.

Early pacification achievements credited to the influence of the Chamber of Commerce were joint Mormon-gentile Fourth of July celebrations in 1887 and 1888. While the two sides of the "irrepressible conflict" had previously observed the nation's Independence Day with joint celebrations, this had not been the pattern during the quarter of a century just past. July 4, in fact, had on several occasions generated volatile situations. One of the most explosive had occurred only two years earlier when, on the morning of the Fourth, flags at City Hall, the County Court House and at many Mormon business houses were hanging at half-mast. When puzzled gentiles learned that the purpose of the half-masting was to signify mourning for the death of the liberties of the large majority of Utah's citizens, menacing incidents began erupting throughout the city. The gentiles quickly formed a committee which demanded an apology by the city and immediate raising of the flags. The Grand Army of the Republic, celebrating at Lindsay's Gardens, adopted a resolution declaring the half-masting to be an insult to the flag. Eli H. Murray, who was governor at the time, telephoned General McCook at Fort Douglas for military aid to compel the raising of the flags. The general, whose head was cooler than most in the city at that juncture, declined to interfere with the military. By mid-afternoon a milling crowd, with patriotism inflamed by liquor, was threatening to break into closed buildings to raise the flag. Shootings were threatened by partisans of both sides at several sites of half-masted flags. But bloodshed was avoided. Repercussions from the incident continued for weeks and it snowballed into a sort of national issue with the gentiles capitalizing on it as proof of the treasonable attitude of the church. A report was spread that the Mormons planned to again fly the flag at half-mast on Pioneer Day, July 24, and this impelled President Cleveland to order the commanding general at Omaha to keep all posts of the Western Platte Department in full strength and prepared for any emergency that might arise in Utah.

One incident of that tumultuous Independence Day involving *The Tribune* was the prompt raising of the flag at the Salt Lake Theater. *The Tribune,* the following day, credited this action to William A. Rossiter, a Mormon who was under bond awaiting trial as a polygamist, and commended him for his loyalty. Rossiter promptly rejected the commendation in a letter to the *Deseret News* — "I take this method of assuring you and my friends that I do not deserve this praise, especially from that source. Respecting the flags being at half-mast, I feel exactly as all my co-religionists do — that it was a proper manifestation of our feelings upon the occasion. If Liberty is not dead, at least she lies bleeding."[5] In the light of such proceedings, the Mormon-gentile cooperation on July 4, 1887, was an encouraging sign indeed.

The second event of 1887 which served to stimulate communication between the warring factions was the election of five liberals to the Territorial Legislature. One liberal had previously been elected to that body but he had been so completely ignored by the Mormon members that he was, in effect, not seated. The liberal breakthrough for five seats was not a result of Mormons switching to the enemy side but of the test oath disenfranchisement of some of the Mormon voters and a redistricting of the territory under the auspices of the Utah Commission. *The Tribune*, exulting in the political victory, said:

> The gentiles won a mighty victory yesterday. They secured a fighting minority in the next Utah Legislature. . . . The spell is broken. There will be such a working force in the Legislature as will put the Church on record at least. But this is not the best feature of all. It will give the gentiles confidence which will cause them to see to it hereafter that they are registered. . . . Who says the dawn has not come?[6]

At the end of the session the gentile members praised the Mormon leadership for the consideration shown them and the leadership commended the gentile members for their contributions. This was probably polite window-dressing. But at this

juncture in Utah's history even a display of good manners between the two groups was a notable step forward.

The major territorial news event of the year was the death
on July 25, 1887, of John Taylor at the home of Thomas F.
Rouche in Kaysville. To the Mormons President Taylor was a
martyr who stood fast for ecclesiastical doctrine through persecution and exile from family, friends and church brothers. His
death was a deep personal bereavement for his faithful following
and a great shock to them collectively, coming as it did at a
time when the church was under tremendous pressures — ecclesiastical, political and economic.

To the gentiles, the departed president was an important
personage but hardly in the same category as Brigham Young. If
The Tribune reflected the attitude of the gentiles at that period,
the real strong man of the church was his first counselor, George
Q. Cannon.

In an editorial on the death of President Taylor, *The Tribune*
said in part:

> It has come down to us from ancient times that we
> should speak no evil of the dead. It is a good maxim,
> too; but when the happiness of thousands is in-
> volved the truth must be told, even down to the
> sepulchre. . . .
>
> The best energies of his life were devoted to the es-
> tablishment of a hostile kingdom in the midst of a
> free Republic, a kingdom in which the tyranny of
> the ancient Asiatic world was to be reproduced, and
> where the many were to be but the unquestioning
> slaves of the few. In the face of the law he married
> many women, and though he saw the effects of po-
> lygamy in the family of the founder of the creed in
> Nauvoo, and the effects in his own family in this
> city, he clung to it, and when there was at last a law

framed that struck a direct blow at the crime, with a kind of fury he drove his people into the commission of that crime, offered rewards to such as would commit it; treated with his displeasure those who refused, and withdrew his confidence and approval from such as having committed it, in good faith tried to make amends before the outraged laws. He not only exerted his influence as a man, but urged his commands upon a confiding people in God's own sovereign name. Hence, above his grave, it is but fair to record what he did, and to add the manifest fact that his lifework was a grievous failure. [7]

President Taylor's death dissolved for the third time the First Presidency of the church. As on prior occasions, the Council of Twelve Apostles became the governing body and Wilford Woodruff, as its senior member, became the virtual head of the church although he was not sustained to the position of prophet, seer and revelator held successively by Joseph Smith, Brigham Young and John Taylor, until April, 1889.

The Tribune's first editorial comment on the new church president was in the nature of a qualified commendation, with the qualification receiving more emphasis than the commendation. Under the heading "Too Sweet," the newspaper said:

Apostle Woodruff is now virtually the head of the Mormon Church. As such, and in behalf of the Twelve, he has caused the publication of an epistle to the Saints 'throughout the world.' It has a more Christian sound than anything that ever emanated from John Taylor or either of his counselors. In the course of it he says:
'Let all Israel remember that the eternal and everlasting Priesthood is bestowed upon us for the pur-

pose alone of administering in the ordinances of life and salvation, both for the living and the dead, and no man on earth can use that Priesthood for any other purpose than the work of the ministry, the perfecting of the Saints, edifying the body of Christ, establishing the Kingdom of Heaven and re-deeming Zion.'

If the foregoing be true, then the Priesthood pertains solely to the relations which man has to his Maker — it is solely a religious affair. There is nothing there which would seem to include the running of a political party; nothing about handling the stock of a co-op store; nothing about nominating men for office and compelling the masses to vote for them whether they would or not; nothing about the temporal affairs of men; nothing to indicate that this Priesthood is a law unto itself, and regards no laws which conflict with its sovereign prerogatives. Did Apostle Woodruff mean it that way? We fear not. He holds a hope to men's lips; we fear he will when he gets ready break it to their hearts. Still, it is a pity. The Church at this crisis might extricate itself from its troubles if it would but give up what civilization demands from it. Power is too sweet and the hope of cajoling and defrauding the nation is too strong. We are afraid the epistle is too sweet. [8]

Had the editor of *The Tribune* been able to peer into the next few years, he might have strengthened the commendation of President Woodruff's epistle and omitted the last sentence of the editorial.

While *The Tribune,* as heretofore noted, was belaboring what it deemed deficiencies in the test oath and warning gentiles not to be taken in by the church-sponsored campaign for statehood, the newly appointed United States District Attorney for Utah, George S. Peters, was priming the economic weapon provided by the Edmunds-Tucker Act for use against the church.

The opening shot in the "raid" upon church property was fired July 30, 1887, the day following the burial of President Taylor. Two suits were filed in the Supreme Court of the territory pursuant to provisions of the Edmunds-Tucker Act directing that the corporation of The Church of Jesus Christ of Latter-day Saints be formally dissolved and that property held by the trustee-in-trust in excess of $50,000 be escheated to the government and used for the benefit of the public schools. The federal government contended that the church held real estate valued at more than $2,000,000 and personal property in excess of $1,000,000 which was subject to escheat.

The government won the preliminary legal skirmishes challenging the competency of the territorial court to hear the suit. This victory induced the church to voluntarily surrender some of its properties with the understanding that an appeal would be taken to the United States Supreme Court. The government then filed a rash of suits in the district courts seeking property which it contended had been transferred to stakes and individuals under secret trusteeships for the purpose of thwarting the law. These suits were later settled, by a compromise cash payment offered by the church, accepted by the receiver and approved by the court.

By mid-1887 the receiver had taken over property of a stipulated value of $807,666 but the actual value was probably substantially in excess of that amount.

Leonard J. Arrington, in his economic history of the church, *The Great Basin Kingdom,* reached this conclusion from his extensive research on this point:

> When one considers the value of the items not stipulated, and the gross undervaluation of some of the

properties, it is probable that the actual value of the properties surrendered was well in excess of $1,000,000. Nevertheless a comparison of the properties confiscated with the list of properties which belonged to the Church shows that the stratagems of the trustee-in-trust paid off in part. The receiver probably did not get a third of the value of the properties belonging to the Church at the time of the passage of the Edmunds-Tucker Act. Of greater importance to the Mormon economy, the receiver did not take possession of the Church's bank stock, nor of its holdings in the key institution, Zion's Cooperative Mercantile Institution. [9]

The property "raid" produced a series of disputes involving legal and receiver fees, conflicts of interest, legal and ethical properties; but the upshot of these challenges was that the "raid" was upheld as to procedures and by the United States Supreme Court as to constitutionality. While much of the church-owned property might have escaped the escheatment net, the blow was a staggering one to the temporal strength of the church. Unlike the polygamy crusade, this was something that hit the leadership as well as the general membership and its direct effects could not be avoided by going underground or into exile. The direct effects of the "raid" were supplemented by a general economic disruption arising from the polygamy crusade. Arrington sums up the economic plight of the church and its members in these words:

> With almost all leaders of Latter-day Saint communities in prison or in hiding, business establishments were abandoned, or were kept in operation by inexperienced wives and children. The ownership of most of the co-operatives drifted into the

hands of a few individuals and were eventually converted into private enterprises. Those United Orders which had survived until this period were discontinued. There were no further meetings of Zion's Central Board of Trade. Almost every business history, in short, shows stagnation; almost every family history records widespread suffering and misery. Above all, the Church, as the prime stimulator, financier and regulator of the Mormon economy, was forced to withdraw from participation in most phases of activity. The 'raid,' in other words, was a period of crippled group activity of every type, of decline in cooperative trade and industry — a period when, above all, Church economic support was essential but not forthcoming — a period when planning would have saved much, but when planners dared not plan. [10]

Gentiles as well as Mormons were bitten by the general economic disruption, although less severely. Surely there must have been a growing longing in the territory for an end to the strife which was depressing the economy and frustrating the desires of those who were looking forward to a more tranquil social and political life. One manifestation of this feeling was the organization of the Chamber of Commerce by both gentiles and Mormons. *The Tribune,* too, on occasion paused in its vitriolic crusade against the power structure of Mormondom to express this mood in a lyrical outburst. One such editorial which appeared April 26, 1887, under the heading "It's All Right" said:

Let us all who have watched and waited and hoped against hope for the coming of the transfiguration of Utah take heart, for the dawn is here. After the sun gets high in the heavens in the spring, there are cold storms and frosts, but we know it is spring

123

nevertheless, and that in a little while longer the roses will bloom, the birds will build their nests and the fruition of the harvest will come. We will have many disappointments still. Men will be weak or perverse; much that we had a right to count upon will be denied us; promises will be broken and more than one will be destroyed in the house of friends, but it will not all matter, because forces are on the march that will, in a little while, make us independent of outside influnces.Utahwas long ago fixed to be the home of a free people, and at that time there was placed in the hills and in the valleys the means through which that freedom might be worked out. The hands of labor are even now closing upon this work, and when they all strike in accord there will be no further need of discussing the Mormon question. It will regulate itself. There is nothing to despair about, rather there is everything to hope for and the hope is going to be realized before the most sanguine dream of it. [11]

This time the writer, presumably Goodwin, seemed to be doing something he would really liked to have done more often.

10

Year of Political Ferment

SIGNS OF A SPRINGTIME of reconciliation, forecast by *The Tribune* in 1887, continued to appear from time to time in 1888 and 1889. One of the most dramatic, which would have been inconceivable a few years earlier, sprouted in the Salt Lake City municipal election in February.

Leaders of the People's (Mormon) Party, who well knew that they would win the election as they had in the past, decided to offer the Liberals four places on their municipal ticket which would then campaign as a fusion ticket. The proposition was presented to a committee of prominent Liberals and accepted by them. It was then proposed to the newly organized Chamber of Commerce and endorsed by about a two-thirds vote of the membership. Next the proposition was laid before the convention of the People's Party, which adopted it by unanimous vote. A ticket was then nominated comprised of the following:

Mayor, Francis Armstrong; aldermen, William W. Riter, Thomas G. Webber, William S. McCornick (Liberal), James Sharp, and George D. Pyper; councilors, LeGrand Young, John Clark, A. W. Carlson, Thomas E. Jeremy, Jr., John Fewson Smith, Samuel P. Teasdel, John M. Dooly (Liberal), M. B. Sowles (Liberal) and Bolivar Roberts (Liberal); recorder, Moses V. Thatcher; marshal, Alfred Solomon.

Although a small committee of prominent gentiles, mostly businessmen, had indorsed the plan, it quickly generated a feud within the Liberal Party. At a meeting in the Chamber of Commerce a larger group of Liberal Party members denounced the fusion movement as a trick to advance Mormon purposes in Washington and it was rejected by majority vote. The group then proceeded to nominate Henry W. Lawrence, a former Mormon who helped financially to launch *The Tribune,* for mayor and appointed a committee to complete an all-Liberal ticket.

Some of the most adamant opponents of the fusion idea were people who had left or been cut off by the church. Among the gentiles who supported fusion were Governor West, who seemed to be motivated by a deep desire for conciliation despite brusque rejection of his overtures in this direction by imprisoned polygamists; U.S. Marshal Frank H. Dyer; J. R. Rawlins, a prominent attorney who had drifted out of the church; W. H. Dickson and C. S. Varian, both former federal officials; *The Tribune* and its editor, C. C. Goodwin.

Goodwin not only defended the fusion approach in editorials but appeared at a meeting of Liberal Party members to urge its acceptance by the membership. Some, he said, regarded it as a trick. And he conceded that efforts would be made by the People's Party to make capital out of it. But even if this did happen, he argued, it would not hurt the Liberal Party as much as to reject the offer. The Liberals, he argued, had nothing to lose and much to gain and, in any event, should give the Mormons credit for sincerity. In the political climate existing at that time it called for considerable courage for gentiles to publicly advocate fusion. Ironically, it exposed to jibes of "Jack Mormon" *The Tribune,* which Mormons regarded as their arch-enemy, and several former and incumbent federal officials who had been roundly denounced as persecutors of the Mormon people. [1]

The fusion, or citizens' ticket, won as expected but very few Liberals voted the straight ticket.

Soon after this election two changes were made in the federal judiciary of the territory. The changes were pleasing to the Mormons and displeasing to the more stiff-necked gentiles. But even this sort of disagreement served to increase and strengthen the tenuous lines of communication across the chasm separating the community. Chief Justice Zane was replaced by Elliot Sandford of New York, and a fourth judge was added in the person of John W. Judd of Tennessee. Both new appointees were, of course, Democrats. Socially, both mixed more freely with Mormons. Judicially, both took a softer stance on polygamy than had Judge Zane.

One of the sensational events of the year was the appearance in court on the morning of September 17, 1888, of Apostle George Q. Cannon to plead guilty to two previous indictments brought against him under the anti-polygamy laws. *The Tribune* had, with almost tiresome frequency, urged Apostle Cannon and other church leaders in exile or in hiding to take such action. But this is not mentioned to suggest that Cannon was reacting to advice from that source. Other reasons which might have prompted his action at that particular time were pending efforts of the church to win statehood; the conciliatory attitude of the new judges; the widespread feeling among gentiles, and some of the less devout of the church membership, that the leadership should show more willingness to take some of the medicine they were advising their followers to take.

Whatever the reasons for his surrender after he had previously jumped a total of $45,000 bail to avoid sentencing, it proved to be an opportune time to clear the record. He was treated softly by Judge Sandford who did not ask for a direct pledge as to future conduct with respect to the anti-polygamy laws but accepted in lieu thereof the defendant's assent to a statement made by the court: ". . . your submission is an acknowledgement — at least, admission — that you submit yourself to the authority of the law and admit the supremacy of the law, which every man must bow to and give obedience to."[2]

The judge imposed sentences for the two counts of 175 days in prison and fines totaling $450. Other convicted violators of the anti-polygamy laws followed the same course that day and on succeeding days, some receiving suspended sentences if they were aged or unable to pay a fine, and all receiving relatively lenient treatment. It was clearly a signal that the newly appointed federal judges were going to ease off on the polygamy crusade. Many gentiles, including *The Tribune* policy-makers, did not like the new policy and said so frequently and vehemently. Idaho's delegate to Congress, Fred T. Dubois, who as a federal attorney in Idaho had vigorously pressed the polygamy crusade in that state, introduced a resolution in Congress designed to put some pressure on President Cleveland for his use of the pardoning power in polygamy cases. The only tangible result of this maneuver was a report from the attorney general showing the disposition of each earlier case. This report showed, in addition to pardons granted, that up to that time there had been 500 convictions in Utah and 89 in Idaho under the provisions of the anti-polygamy acts of 1882 and 1887.

At the election in the fall John T. Caine was routinely re-elected to Congress on the People's Party ticket. His opponents were Robert N. Baskin, Liberal; and Samuel R. Thurman, the nominee of a newly organized Sagebrush Democratic Party. Among the organizers of the new Democratic Party was Anthony W. Ivins, who later became a member of the First Presidency of the church and a potent force in the pacification of the "irrepressible conflict."

Early in 1889, with the Republican Party back in power and with Benjamin Harrison as president, the statehood drive was renewed by the Mormon Church.

The Liberal Party sent Baskin, J. R. McBride and E. P. Ferry to Washington to lobby against the proposal, and Lannan of *The Tribune* spent a good part of the winter there assisting the committee. Governor West likewise appeared in Washington to oppose the statehood bid, but even in opposition he lowered some barriers to dialogue between the warring forces in the territory. Appearing before the committee considering the statehood bid, the governor asserted that progress had been made and was being made in bridging the chasm that had separated the Mormons and non-Mormons since settlement of the territory; that the Mormons had relaxed their old rule of rigorous exclusiveness; that they had exhibited a spirit of liberality and enterprise in appropriating money for charitable and educational institutions; that they had joined with non-Mormons in promoting the economic welfare of the territory; that they had liberalized municipal governments wholly in their control.

"I shall not arraign the Mormon people," he continued, "as wanting in comparison with other people in religious devotion, virtue, sobriety, industry and the graces and qualities that adorn, beautify, and bless life." But none of these things, he concluded, could justify statehood at that time because of the "despotism of the Mormon political system." [3]

The elation of the Mormons over the appointment of federal judges who took a more tolerant attitude toward anti-polygamy law violations was short-lived. Republican President Harrison was less sensitive about playing the party patronage game than had been Democratic President Cleveland, a champion of civil service. Within six months after becoming president, Harrison replaced Governor West with Arthur L. Thomas, who had served as secretary of the territory under Governor Murray; and the two judges who had been so considerate of convicted polygamists — Sandford and Judd — were pushed aside for Republican appointees. Judge Sandford was replaced by his predecessor — Charles S. Zane. This change, or restoration, created an uproar in the local and national press. Criticism of the appointment was not directed so much at Judge Zane as to the nature of the removal of Judge Sandford. In a brief, curt communication, the attorney general notified Judge Sandford that he had been directed by the President "to advise you that in his opinion the public interest will be subserved by a change in the office of Chief Justice of Utah, and this being so, he would be pleased to receive your resignation as such Chief Justice."

Judge Sandford responded with an inquiry as to whether any changes or complaints had been preferred against him and the comment "that if a change is necessary *for political reasons only*, the President can have my resignation as soon as the business of the court and the proper disposition of matters now pending before me will permit."

The attorney general replied that there had been some complaints about the manner in which the judge had discharged his judicial duties and added: "Independently of these particular complaints, however, the President has become satisfied that your administration of the office was not in harmony with the policy he deemed proper to be pursued with reference to Utah affairs, and for this reason he desired to make a change, and out of courtesy gave you an opportunity to resign. As you did not see fit to embrace this opportunity, the President has removed you and appointed your successor."

Judge Sandford retorted: ". . . I have the honor to say that my earnest purpose while on the bench, as Chief Justice of this Territory, has been to administer justice and the laws honestly and impartially to all men, under the obligation of my oath of office. If the President of the United States has any policy which he desires a judge of the Supreme Court to carry out in reference to Utah affairs, other than the one I have pursued, you may say to him that he has done well to remove me."[4]

While every political realist of that period, or any other period, was aware that policy changes are frequently made through the appointive power, it was not something to admit with respect to the judiciary. The administration had asked for it; and Judge Sandford gave it to them, right on the chin. The judge clearly won the encounter in terms of editorial reactions, though not with the help of *The Tribune*. But the gentiles took comfort from the belief that they had won in terms of substance. The incident, however, turned out to be closer to a stand-off than a clear-cut victory for either side. For Judge Zane thereafter was more moderate than either the Mormons or gentiles expected him to be. Historian Whitney's appraisal of the restored judge was summed up in these words:

"His [Zane's] course thereafter was not what many [Mormons] feared it would be. He seemed to be actuated by a kinder or more conservative spirit than formerly, and eventually became popular with many if not most of the Mormon people; and that, too, while retaining his popularity with the gentiles." [5]

Thus it can be inferred that this incident, as abrasive as it seemed at the time, served, on balance, to promote rather than blight the cause of accommodation.

Politically, the "impossible" happened in February, 1889. The Liberals carried Ogden City in a municipal election and elected a non-Mormon city administration headed by Frederick J. Kiesel as mayor. The Mormons charged that the Liberals won by bringing in unregistered railroad workers and getting their ballots in the boxes and counted through connivance of registrars and election judges. *The Tribune* attributed the victory to the "glorious generalship of the Liberal leaders," the excellent work by United States Marshal Dyer and a sprinkling of Mormons who had decided it was time for a change.

In an exulting editorial *The Tribune* said:

The magnitude of the victory achieved by the Ogden Liberals grows in thought the more it is contemplated. Indeed, it was not all accomplished by the Liberals. At least a few of the Saints must have decided it was time for a change, and so voted for the Liberal candidates. It makes an epoch in our sister city; it is an absolute revolution. . . . [6]

131

In response to critical *Deseret News* comment that the new mayor's statement — "I shall not forget that I was elected by a party" — had a genuine American political ring to it, *The Tribune* asked:

> Is it peculiarly American? . . . Can the *News* point to any man elected by that [Mormon] party during thirty-eight years who ever for a moment forgot that he was elected by a certain party? Can it point to one contract or one day's employment given by those officers to any gentile in all those thirty-eight years? . . . And how many Mormon officers in all the world could add what Mr. Kiesel adds: 'I shall endeavor to administer the affairs of my office without partisanship and also without discrimination in the matter of public works.' . . .[7]

But the gentile gloating in February soared to gentile ecstasy in August when they, unbelievably, carried Salt Lake in a legislative and county election by a margin of 41 votes. *The Tribune* hailed this event with these headlines: "Salt Lake City Goes Liberal; The Death Knell of Mormon Rule; The City Is Gentile by Forty-one Votes; People Wild with Enthusiasm; Pierce, Allen, Williams, Ferry, Kimball, Smith, Benner and Hall Elected; Moyle, LeGrand Young, Clark and Others of the Holy Priesthood in Sack Cloth and Ashes."[8]

In an editorial under the heading — "Victory! Victory!! Victory!!!" — the newspaper said:

> Is it not immense? The Central Stake of Zion, on the popular vote, has gone from fifty up to perhaps one hundred Liberals. It is a day that when we predicted its coming, a few years ago, men tapped their foreheads and shook their heads most piteously. We fully believe that the majesty of the Republic would

after awhile assert itself; we believed that even as
the thief on the cross repented at last, a sense of justice would at last pervade Mormonism itself. The
victory yesterday was not won wholly by gentiles.
The quicksand conscience and expanding Ameri-
canism in many a young Mormon's heart helped to
swell the glory of yesterday. . . . [9]

The *Deseret News, Herald* and many leaders of the opposition screamed fraud. But even assuming some election day irregularities, which would not have been unique to that time or
place, it was big political news. For the non-Mormons up to that
time had been too impotent in the political elective apparatus to
even steal an election in Salt Lake.

Whitney's comment on the event in his *History of Utah* was:

That the Liberal majority of forty-one was real, in
the sense of being legal, was much doubted by their
opponents. It was charged that impersonators of
dead or absent voters, as well as soldiers from Fort
Douglas, had been allowed to cast their ballots, and
that this was the basis of Liberal predominance.
Whatever the facts in the case, the leaders of that
party now went to work, laying their plans for the
capture of Salt Lake City in February. [10]

In the light of the population division as between Mormons
and non-Mormons at that time, there are good reasons to suspect
that either there was some ballot box stuffing, as suggested by
Whitney; or that some Mormons crossed over to the Liberal side,
as asserted by *The Tribune;* or that there was some of both.

As forecast by the political events of 1889, the warring
parties did go all out to win the Salt Lake City election of 1890.
Both sides organized clubs throughout the city. Marching bands

were formed; campaign songs were composed and the best orators of the city tried mightily to enhance their reputations for
swaying the populace. The Liberal campaign was directed by
General Patrick E. Connor, the father of the Liberal Party,
as titular and honorary head, and by Judge Orlando W. Powers,
a skilled political tactician and brilliant orator, as the field general. Spearheading the People's Party campaign were F. S.
Richards, able lawyer and political general, and R. W. Young.

Commenting on a grand parade of the Liberals before the
election, editor Goodwin of *The Tribune* launched into one of his
characteristic editorial prose poems:

> When, after days of heat and prostration around
> rocky promontory, the breeze grows fresh and the
> combers from the deep sea come rolling in to break
> in fury against the headland, all things animate
> and inanimate, seem to be roaring around the de-
> voted shore. . . . Utah has long been a rocky prom-
> ontory. It has been a moral storm center. For two
> score years it has been reckoned a coast so danger-
> sous that the prudent mariners have been headed
> away from it; but at last the signals have come of
> something which will clear the air, and though the
> shore may be rocked by the storm, all know that
> when it shall have passed away, the land will be
> better for the visitation. Leaving metaphors aside,
> the display last night was new proof that Salt Lake
> City is being rapidly Americanized. . . .
> The grandest feature of the moving picture last
> night was that there was nothing but joy in the
> hearts of the men in line. If a fair prospect of victory
> seemed to shine from their eyes, the thought that
> warmed and cheered was that it would be a double
> victory if achieved — a victory for the Liberals, and,

though they cannot see it yet, a victory for the men
who are opposing the Liberals. This is true, for
this Territory cannot much longer remain un-
Americanized. . . . [11]

The flavor of the People's Party campaign can be tasted
from some sample stanzas of one of their campaign songs,
inspired by a postponement of a scheduled Liberal parade because of inclement weather to a later date "if weather
permits."

The Liberals one evening postponed their parade,
Because of the weather they felt much afraid.
The fact of the matter their "Gineral" admits,
But they'll have it hereafter, if weather permits.
Hurrah, hurrah, "free water," they cry;
But they're not fond of it, even when dry.
Hurrah, hurrah, free whiskey they'll try,
But as for free water, that's all in your eye.
They call us priestridden, but what shall we say
Of that tyrant, the tripod they trembling obey?
They'll vote as they're told when *The Tribune* ring sits,
And they won't vote at all unless TRIBBY permits.
Hurrah, hurrah for the people! Three groans
For the party whose conscience Pat Lannan still owns.
Perhaps it is treason to talk in such tones;
But they live in glass houses and shouldn't throw stones. [12]

Perhaps more important than the parades, campaign songs
and oratory in the election campaign was the registration drives.
And here the Liberals had a clear advantage. The city registrar
was the secretary of the federally appointed Utah Commission
which supervised elections and he was a gentile. His five depu-
ties were Liberals, four of them were candidates on the Liberal
ticket. Court rulings in polygamy cases were used to disqualify

some of the Mormon voters and charges were made that the Liberals registered and voted workmen on the Denver and Rio Grande Railroad from as far away as Grand Junction, Colorado. The registration process produced a rash of court challenges. But here again the Liberals had the advantage of gentile judges and their position generally prevailed in the test cases. Legal challenges continued throughout the campaign, on election day, and for some time thereafter. But the Liberals elected their entire ticket, headed by George M. Scott as mayor.

At the county election in August a ticket was entered by the Independent Workingmen, which was adopted by the People's Party except as to one candidate, and the Liberal and fusion tickets split the offices.

All in all 1890 had been a year of political setbacks for the People's Party and a year of triumph for the Liberal Party. But the elections were not the most serious blows suffered by the church that year. On February 3 the United States Supreme Court declared the Idaho test oath, which in effect disenfranchised Mormons, to be constitutional. Mormons were astounded and anti-Mormons were jubilant. The decision immediately activated a movement among Utah anti-Mormons to press for a federal act to accomplish the same purpose in the Utah Territory. A bill, more stringent than the Idaho law, was introduced into the Congress — the Cullom-Struble Bill. But some of the Utah gentiles were far from jubilant about this turn of events. One such, and he presumably represented a substantial segment though not a majority of the gentiles, was Fred Simon, vice president of the Salt Lake Chamber of Commerce. In a letter to Governor Thomas and former Utah Governor West who was then in Washington to support the proposed bill, Mr. Simon wrote:

> It was our conservative policy, of which you [West]
> were the leader, which made it possible for the Liberal Party to win; but for this work, the radical Lib-

eral element would be as little advanced as it was five years ago. And now our wheels of progress are to be turned backward, and a policy inaugurated which in ten minutes' time shall settle what ought to take from five to ten years to accomplish. Take a stave and try to bend it into a hoop by a sudden motion and you will break it; only by gradual bending can the work be accomplished.

From the moment the Cullom bill is passed, we must make up our minds that we have in every Mormon a conspirator who will lie awake night after night, and think and plan how to get even. It seems to me that the bill has been conceived in hatred and vindictiveness, and will bear poisoned fruit, which will not only poison the make-up of the average man, but will also inoculate itself upon those who are now advocating this policy.

To attempt to build a commonwealth with two hundred thousand conspirators in our midst, vastly outnumbering the other side, is like erecting a building, the foundation of which rests upon a sand bank. Sparta had in its own midst Helots whom they conquered, and history well proves the result of their work. [13]

This bill was not fated to become law, for something was about to happen which would relieve the tremendous economic and political pressures bearing down on the church. That something was Wilford Woodruff's official declaration that he would submit to laws forbidding plural marriages and use his influence with other members of the church to have them do likewise. It was what has become known in Utah's unique and troubled history as the "Manifesto."

137

11

End of Church
Sanctioned Polygamy

THE "MANIFESTO," issued by President Wilford Woodruff
of the Mormon Church September 24, 1890, was undoubtedly the
most important news event relating to the "irrepressible conflict" between Mormons and non-Mormons in the lifetime of *The
Tribune*. But the big story came to the newspaper totally unexpected and unanticipated through a sort of "back door."

On the morning of September 25, *The Tribune* published on
its front page a 27-line dispatch sent from the Chicago office of
the Associated Press. Over the dispatch were these headlines:
"Why The Devious Way?" "The Mormon President's Artfully
Promulgated 'Manifesto';" "He Does Not Encourage Polygamy: And His 'Advice' to the People, by Way of Chicago, Is
to Obey the Law — Will It Be Read at the Tabernacle?"

The dispatch, carrying a Salt Lake dateline, follows:

> President Woodruff of the Mormon Church today is-
> sued a manifesto in which, referring to the state-
> ment in the report of the Utah Commission that
> plural marriages have been solemnized during the
> past year, and that the leaders of the Church have
> encouraged the continuance of polygamy, he enters
> a sweeping denial that such things have occurred.
> President Woodruff further says that inasmuch as
> the law forbidding polygamy has been pronounced
> constitutional by the court of last resort he hereby
> declares his intention to submit to those laws and

use his influence with the members of the Church to have them do likewise. There is nothing in his teachings to the Church or in the teaching of his associates during the time specified which can reasonably be construed to inculcate or encourage polygamy and when any elder has used language which has appeared to convey such teachings, he has been promptly reproved.

I now publicly declare that my advice to the Latter-day Saints is to refrain from contracting any marriage forbidden by the law of the land. [1]

The *Deseret News* published the announcement in its afternoon edition of September 25, after it had appeared in *The Tribune*.

The Tribune, gentiles generally and probably most of the Mormons were flabbergasted by the development. The quizzical skepticism reflected in *The Tribune* headlines on the dispatch pervaded editorial comment the following day in which it said:

There is something about this dispatch itself which causes people familiar with Mormon ways to be suspicious. It does not come in the authoritative manner in which the orders of the Church are generally clothed. President Woodruff says: 'My advice to the Latter-day Saints is to refrain from contracting any marriage forbidden by the laws of the land.' He speaks merely as an individual. He does not speak as though that advice had come authoritatively by revelation, but as a poor human being in perplexity he gives his flock the advice of a patriarch. The question is, how will they understand it. . . . [2]

In the light of *The Tribune* editorials over the preceding twenty years, its complaint that Woodruff's declaration was not

139

a revelation seems somewhat inconsistent. For *The Tribune* has said over and over again that if John Taylor and George Q. Cannon would go into court, plead guilty to anti-polygamy law violations and promise to observe the law in the future, the polygamy issue would disappear. Now the president of the church was saying that he would not only observe the law but would advise all members of the church to do likewise.

What *The Tribune* reaction really reflected was the deep-seated distrust which divided the community at that juncture. It was not a mere credibility gap but a chasm.

A few days later when the "Manifesto" was submitted to the general conference of the church in the Tabernacle, and sustained without a dissenting vote, *The Tribune* had to reassess its attitude toward the pronouncement. In the issue of October 7 it said:

> *The Tribune* has fought a long battle and received a few vindications in the past. The growing city, the advancing values, the hopes that thrill this people are all vindications of *The Tribune*. But the crowning vindication came yesterday when the President of The Church of Jesus Christ of Latter-day Saints announced to a breathless multitude in the Tabernacle, that the people should listen and henceforth obey. In the most authoritative manner possible, the Mormon Church yesterday repudiated polygamy as a tenet of its faith. That is, instructions were formally given to the members of the creed to cease plural marriages. . . .[3]

In this second reaction *The Tribune* could be, and no doubt was, accused of exaggerating the import of the church action. It was indulging in satirical license with such phrases as "the Lord of Heaven and earth had bent and endorsed *The Tribune*, also." For the declaration sustained by the conference was the same one which *The Tribune* had stressed was not a revelation. All in all, the newspaper's reactions to the "Manifesto" could not be counted among its most brilliant editorial efforts.

Whether viewed as an act of capitulation or of statesmanship, the effect of the abandonment of the practice of polygamy was to greatly relieve the pressures which were threatening the temporal foundations of the church. President Woodruff was not exaggerating when he wrote in his journal: "I have arrived at a point in the history of my life as president of the Church . . . where I am under the necessity of acting for the temporal salvation of the Church." [4]

Politically, the church had just suffered its first defeats in the major population centers of Salt Lake and Ogden; Congress was threatening to pass new legislation which would disenfranchise Mormons; the property escheating "Raid," which had been expanded to cover cash, had created a financial crisis. As Arrington summed it up in his economic history of the church; "Old notes were met by new notes, and the Church's debt continued to increase as interest pyramided." [5]

The immediate effect of the "Manifesto," as concisely summed up by Arrington, was this:

> Northern purity leagues lost interest in trying to reform Utah and 'Christianize' the Mormons. 'Polyg hunts' by deputy marshals became less and less frequent; judges showed more leniency in dealing with 'cohabs' brought before the law. Government attorneys, with the acquiescence of the attorney general in Washington, adopted the policy of being 'light' and 'humane' in their prosecutions. There was a noticeable decline in the vigor with which government attorneys pressed the Church case, the receivership, and the escheat of Church property. Territorial judges reflected the same poli-

cy of leniency by slowing down the judicial processes by which the Church would be finally deprived of its wealth. As the Church demonstrated
its good faith by strengthening its enforcement of
the Manifesto, there was a growing opinion among
political circles that to complete the escheat of
Church property would be both unfair and dangerous — dangerous from a political point of view because of the possible reaction of sympathy toward a
group which was believed to have suffered much
persecution in the past. [6]

The termination of officially sanctioned polygamy can surely be credited with making possible the achievement of statehood
in 1896; of impelling the dissolution of the People's Party and the
organization of the national Republican and Democratic parties;
of prompting the restoration of church property in 1894 and 1896
and the granting of amnesties to polygamists in 1893 and 1894.
Statehood, in turn, freed the Mormons of unwanted appointed
governors, judges, marshals, attorneys and commissioners.

What was generally termed a "surrender" by the church on
the issue of polygamy was, by any pragmatic, practical measur-
ing rod, a defeat for the anti-Mormons who hoped to use it for
the total destruction of the institution; a victory for the more
moderate gentiles who desired and hoped for conciliation of the
"irrepressible conflict."

The reformation of the political system made possible by the
"Manifesto" started immediately after the declaration was issued. Some abortive efforts, in fact, had been made prior to the
"Manifesto" to organize a Democratic Party. But it quickly became apparent to the organizers that with only one national
party functioning the old Mormon versus anti-Mormon pattern
would continue under different terminology.

Although not formally disbanded until later, the Liberal (gentile) and People's (Mormon) parties sang their swan songs in the fall of 1890 in an election to name Utah's delegate to Congress. The People's Party renominated John T. Caine, the sitting delegate and former editor of the *Salt Lake Herald.* The Liberal Party nominated Goodwin, editor of *The Salt Lake Tribune.* With the abandonment by the church of officially sanctioned polygamy, the Liberals had lost their most effective issue and it was no surprise to either Caine or Goodwin or their supporters when Caine was reelected with the usual overwhelming majority.

Soon after President Benjamin Harrison visited Utah in May, 1891, a group of supporters of the Republican Party at the national level organized the Central Republican Club of Utah. A few days later Franklin S. Richards, chairman of the Central Committee of the People's Party, called a meeting of the Salt Lake leaders and proposed that the party be disbanded. All present favored the proposal.

About this time (the exact date was apparently not recorded for posterity), an extraordinary meeting was held in the Gardo House, the official residence of the president of the church which was started by Brigham Young but first occupied by John Taylor. This meeting, the purpose of which was to give official church sanction to a political division of Mormons between the two national political parties or to direct such a division, was for many years thereafter a subject of political discussion. Varying versions of what happened were circulated. The account accepted by the writer of this history is that of James H. Moyle, the last surviving participant and a Democratic Party leader in Utah from early manhood until his death February 19, 1946, at age 87. Moyle wrote:

> I do not remember who were at this meeting other
> than John R. Winder, who was chairman, Franklin
> S. Richards, Richard W. Young and myself. There

> were, of course, many others. . . . My recollection is
> that it was only the city committee and leaders of
> the People's Party. We were there for some time,
> but little, if anything, was done until we were ad-
> vised that George Q. Cannon, then on the under-
> ground, was to be present.
>
> I can now see the view of President Cannon's en-
> trance into the large room on the west side of the
> building. He entered from a door on the east. Al-
> ways well dressed, he wore on this occasion a dark
> suit. He was not a large man, but solidly built, with
> large, prominent blue eyes. I think he would have
> commanded attention anywhere on account of his
> personality. . . . After passing through the door,
> he moved to the front of the room, his person radiat-
> ing greatness. All eyes were upon him. [7]

Cannon, according to Moyle's recollection, told the group
that most Mormons were Democrats, not necessarily because of
party principles, but because they were traditionally oriented
toward the Democratic Party. He said it would be folly to continue the old political division of Mormons versus gentiles and
made it clear that the church leadership deemed it advisable to
abandon the People's Party and divide the members on national
party lines. But it would not do, he explained, for all the Saints
to become Democrats. This would simply push the gentiles into
the Republican Party and perpetuate the division on church
lines. He suggested that the division would, to accomplish the
desired end, have to be genuine and not merely nominal.

"We don't want the old fight to continue,"[8] he added with
emphasis.

No one objected to Cannon's proposal. But Moyle responded
with the comment that his sympathies were with the Democratic
Party; that while attending law school in the East he had sup-

144

ported that party because he believed in its policies; that he was willing to continue working in the People's Party as long as church leaders wished; but if that party was to be abandoned he wanted to be free to follow his own political convictions.

Cannon agreed that Moyle, feeling as he did, should be free to join the Democratic Party; that others with convictions should likewise feel free to join the party of their choice. Those without strong predilections on politics, he continued, could join the Republican Party and thereby create a desirable balance. He then emphasized a second time the position of the church leadership that "the old party fight as between the Mormons and non-Mormons must not be allowed to continue." [9]

Moyle's impression was that Cannon's remarks did not amount to a church fiat that the People's Party was to be dissolved and the membership divided between the national parties. But he had no doubt that Cannon was expressing the wishes of the other two members of the church presidency as well as his own.

Whether Cannon's message was intended as advice or a directive, it did set in motion the dissolution of the two territorial parties and organization of the two major national parties. But some of the Liberals were still unwilling to give up the old fight. They were suspicious of Mormon intentions and feared, rightly as subsequent events proved, that establishment of national political lines in the territory would clear the way for statehood, which they did not want.

In the August, 1890, election the Liberals and the newly organized Democrats and Republicans entered tickets for the legislative body. The Democrats won twice as many seats as the Liberals while the Republicans ran a poor third, electing no members.

In the next election (for delegate to Congress in 1892) John T. Caine, who had held the position through five terms, was persuaded not to run for reelection, presumably on the theory that a change would accelerate the process of burying the old political system and creating functioning national parties. Accordingly, the Democrats nominated Joseph L. Rawlins, an agnostic son of Mormon parents. The Republicans nominated Frank J. Cannon, son of George Q. Cannon. The Liberals, with the support of *The Tribune,* pig-headedly entered a third candidate, C. E. Allen.

Rawlins, the Democrat, won by a plurality of 2,811 votes and the Liberal candidate ran a poor third. The refusal of *The Tribune* to assume leadership in the organization of a Republican Party, which it enthusiastically supported nationally, stemmed from a fear that the church would dominate both Democratic and Republican parties and that the Liberal Party was still a political necessity locally from the standpoint of gentiles. The victory of Rawlins over Cannon served to strengthen this fear. Attributing the election result to a "deal" between the church and the Democratic national administration whereby Utah would be given statehood in exchange for three Democratic members of Congress and three electoral votes in 1896, *The Tribune* said editorially:

> . . . of course they will deny that there is any contract, but we care nothing about that. They denied . . . that there was any contract to have a Democratic delegate elected, but all the same the son of an apostle [Cannon] was defeated by an apostate [Rawlins]. There is not a child 10 years of age in the Territory who does not know that, except for the contract, Mr. Rawlins would have been snowed under so deep that he would not have dug out until late summer. [10]

Not until after the elections of 1893 was *The Tribune* willing to toss in the Liberal sponge and recommend a Republican-Democratic political alignment within the city and territory. In the city campaign of that year Mayor Baskin, an organizer and for years a leader in the Liberal Party, ran for reelection on the

Citizens' ticket, which opposed the Liberal ticket, and won handily. In the legislative election the Republicans won fifteen seats, the Democrats thirteen and the Liberals eight.

Following this election *The Tribune,* in an editorial under the heading: "WHAT NOW? " said:

> . . . some of the best and truest men of the Liberal Party, considering the full situation, declare that the time has come when a full trial of the people of Utah on the American plan should be made. . . . We subscribe to that view. We think all Liberals should remain alert Liberals, that is, they should always keep a jealous watch on events as, from day to day they transpire, but should cease to act as a separate political organization. . . . [11]

The Tribune, which from the inception of the Liberal Party had been its inspiration and spokesman, can hardly be credited with leadership in its dissolution. But it did recognize that the party was in its death throes; that the mood of the people, both Mormon and gentile, was to merge into the national political pattern and try to bury the past. The *Deseret News* made a valid point when it said, in a comment on *The Tribune* editorial: "We believe it would have been better if this decision had been reached sooner." [12]

Viewed in retrospect, it appears that affairs in Utah were working out in accordance with the desires expressed by *The Tribune* for years; that the changes it had been predicting were taking place with remarkable rapidity; that the territory was indeed being "Americanized." It was perhaps the editor's belated, and seemingly reluctant, recognition of the dramatic changes that prompted the remark, attributed by the editor of the *Manti Times-Reporter* to Frank J. Cannon: *"The Tribune* is like an old hag — blind and deaf, mumbling and grumbling, praying for the dawn, when the sun is already shining brightly." [13]

Responding to *The Tribune's* advice, the gifted O. W. Powers resigned the chairmanship of the Liberal Party, thereby completing its burial and paving the way for the organization of an effective Republican Party.

One reason, perhaps the major one, for *The Tribune's* reluctance to liquidate the Liberal Party was a fear, frequently expressed, that Mormon Church influence would be exerted in behalf of the Democratic Party under the national party system. Many church leaders, including President Woodruff, were traditionally Democratic; the Mormon defenders in Congress were mostly Democrats and most of these were southerners; Democratic appointees to federal positions in the territory had been much more conciliatory toward the church than Republican appointees; and the church was looking to a Democratic administration for the long-sought statehood.

But there had already been some indications that what *The Tribune* feared would not necessarily occur. The first such incident erupted in 1892 in Logan, one of the most orthodox Mormon strongholds in the territory. A communication written on the letterhead of the First Presidency of the church and signed by George F. Gibbs, secretary to the First Presidency, was circulated in the city. It contained the sentence: "The men who have at heart the welfare of Utah want Logan to go Republican in this election." [14]

Angry Democratic leaders reacted by appointing a committee to demand an explanation from the First Presidency. The committee was made up of four Mormons and three non-Mormons. They were received by President Woodruff, his counselor, Joseph F. Smith, and John Henry Smith, a general authority and a leader in the organization of the Republican Party. The Mormon members of the Democratic committee were Richard W. Young, grandson, and LeGrand Young, nephew of Brigham Young; Franklin S. Richards and James Henry Moyle. The non-Mormons were Joseph L. Rawlins, Parley L.

Williams and United States Marshal Frank Dyer. Rawlins and Williams were both of Mormon parentage but had left the church.

Rawlins and Williams, both skilled lawyers, subjected Gibbs to "pitiless and unrelenting" cross-examination until President Smith interceded with the comment: "This is a tempest in a teapot." Rawlins, with face scarlet with rage, shouted: "You will find, sir, that this is a whirlwind, and not a tempest in a teapot," and started to march out of the room.

He was induced to return and President Woodruff, the aged, fatherly diplomat who had issued the "Manifesto," calmed the rising tempers with the comment: "Come back, gentlemen. I want to talk to you. I'm a Dimicrat myself [the spelling is Moyle's version of Woodruff's pronunciation of the name]. And all my forefathers were Dimicrats, too." Moyle, the last surviving participant of this meeting as well as the one in the Gardo House, described Woodruff's subsequent unrecorded remarks as a "masterpiece of diplomacy and conciliation."

The committee departed, ostensibly satisfied with Woodruff's remarks. Soon thereafter, the First Presidency issued a statement over the signatures of Woodruff and Smith (Cannon was out of the territory) which said in part:

> If any man claims that it is the wish of the First Presidency that a Democrat shall vote the Republican ticket or a Republican the Democratic ticket, let all the people know that he is endeavoring to deceive the public and has no authority of that kind from us. We have no disposition to direct these matters, but proclaim that, as far as we are concerned, the members of the Church are entirely and perfectly free in all political affairs. [15]

The incident is related here, perhaps with excessive detail, because it was the beginning of a continuing string of similar in-

149

cidents which have erupted in Utah politics over the years.

The Tribune's hesitancy in embracing the national two-party system for Salt Lake City and the territory (it was enthusiastically Republican nationally) was discernible also in its attitude toward statehood. It had, in its editorial advising liquidation of the Liberal Party, endorsed statehood in these words:

> All working together, we can make a great state of Utah. . . . Their [the Liberals] record is as fine as anything in history or romance. For no personal purpose they raised a standard of right and of light in Utah. If Utah is ready for American self-government, they will be glad to see that standard lowered. If they lower it now and events establish that it was too soon, they will raise it again. [16]

The Herald complained that The Tribune's editorials supporting statehood were satirical and insincere. The Tribune retorted:

> If the Herald construes what we have said in the past as being in the nature of jeers and gibes, we will come to an understanding right now and say that we favor the measure with all heartiness; that further we are anxious to see the matter brought speedily to trial. . . . [17]

Regardless of what might have been imbedded in the minds or emotions of Lannan and Goodwin, they were intelligent men. One would have had to have been dull-witted to fail at this point to see that the die had been cast; that statehood was inevitable; that the only remaining question was: how soon?

12

A New State Is Born

ON SEPTEMBER 6, 1893, Delegate Rawlins of the Territory of Utah introduced into the House of Congress an enabling act to authorize the territory to frame a constitution and take other steps necessary for admission to the Union. The act was passed by the House on December 13, 1893, and the Senate on July 10, 1894. On July 16 the bill was approved by President Cleveland and the first high hurdle on the statehood course had been cleared.

The outlook for clearing the remaining hurdles was excellent. Only the timing remained in doubt. Utah had, in all substantial respects, met the conditions demanded by non-Mormons and their spokesman, *The Salt Lake Tribune,* for admission. Virtually all Mormons and most of the influential gentiles, including *The Tribune,* now favored statehood.

The Mormon and anti-Mormon political parties had been abandoned and the two major national political parties were functioning in the territory. To hang back because of a fear that Mormon leaders might exert influence in politics was an absurdity; to demand assurances that this would not be done was to demand the impossible. A cohesive majority in the Territory of Utah, or any other territory or state, was certain to exert influence in politics. With the formation of the Democratic and Re-

151

publican parties, there was a built-in protection against church domination, for there were prominent and influential Mormons in both parties. Under a system which distributes the graces, favors and spoils of politics on a partisan basis, they would serve as watchdogs to see that this did not happen, if only as a matter of self-interest. That this protective device would work had already been demonstrated by the Logan incident.

The practice of polygamy had been officially abandoned. To ask that it be totally eradicated would be asking for the impossible. The test here was not whether some members of the church would continue to practice polygamy, but whether the church would give its sanction to such practice.

The closed economy, which had been so bitterly denounced by gentiles, had never really been established in anything like the degree contemplated and enunciated by Brigham Young when Zion's Cooperative Mercantile Institution was founded. The goal of Mormons trading only with Mormons was achieved to a substantial degree initially, but it had been in process of breaking down for two decades. It was no longer a serious infraction for a Mormon to buy a sack of flour at Walker Brothers store. And there are good reasons to believe that *The Tribune* had some Mormon subscribers. The era when a *Tribune* in the hands of a Mormon was an indication that the possessor was either on the road to apostasy or was willing to run the risk of odium among his compatriots to keep informed on what the devil was up to, had not completely disappeared, but it was fading.

The closed society was likewise breaking down. Many Mormons and gentiles were now collaborating in the Chamber of Commerce, the political parties, the municipal government and the territorial legislature that the term "Jack Mormon" was losing its sting.

If the church had not met the conditions demanded by non-Mormons for statehood at this point, there was no reason to believe that the Mormons would or could meet them in ten, fifty or a hundred more years.

The 1894 election, first held under the national two-party political system, confirmed that the Mormons had actually divided on Republican-Democratic lines and, incidentally, gave the Democrats a rude shock. The Democrats nominated for delegate to Congress the incumbent, Joseph L. Rawlins and the Republicans again nominated Frank J. Cannon. This time Cannon won with a majority of 1,819 votes and the Republicans elected sixty of one hundred and seven delegates to the Constitutional Convention provided for in the Enabling Act, a majority of thirteen.

The widespread assumption, among both Democrats and Republicans, that the traditional ties of the church to the Democratic Party would almost surely make Utah a Democratic state was thereby placed in doubt by the first test. If *The Tribune's* claim in the 1892 election that the church leadership had made a deal to deliver Utah to the Democratic Party in return for statehood was valid, this election indicated that the church leadership was unable to control the election. Soon after the campaign, the charge of political deals by church leaders was shifted to the Republican foot with a long article in *The New York Times* which was reprinted by *The Tribune* and *Salt Lake Herald.* The article charged that George Q. Cannon had entered into agreements and understandings with national Republican leaders to make Utah a Republican state with trust-favoring senators. In return eastern financial interests would finance ventures in which Cannon and other high church officials were interested. [1] Cannon flatly denied the charges. James H. Moyle described the Democratic defeat as an example of "serious ingratitude" on the part of the voters. His explanation of why it happened was more plausible than were the alleged deals between various church leaders and national political party leaders. Moyle attrib-

153

uted the surprising result to two principal factors: An economic depression which the Republicans claimed could be cured by abandonment of Democratic free trade policies and restoration of Republican tariff policies; and a personality issue. The personality problem for the Democrats, in Moyle's opinion, stemmed from the selection for state chairman of the politically talented Orlando W. Powers, who only two years earlier, as the Liberal Party leader, had been vitriolically denouncing Mormons. The dominant figure in the Republican Party was John Henry Smith, a member of the Council of Twelve Apostles. "Many people felt safer with that [Smith] type of leadership, and the non-Mormon members of the party [Republican] did not resent it so long as it brought victory." [2]

Moyle pointed out that the protective tariff issue was particularly effective among mining and agricultural people and commented that he and Anthony W. Ivins were among the very few Democratic livestock men who did not shift into the Republican Party because of that issue.

The uproar created by this first battle between the Democratic and Republican parties and the rash of charges of church interference provided convincing evidence that the American political system was actually in operation in the territory — that the Mormons were no longer a cohesive, obedient political group marching to the polls to do the will of their leaders. Prominent members of the church were at each others' throats politically. Both Mormon Democrats and Mormon Republicans were aligned in the fray with gentiles who a short time before were emissaries of Satan to many of the church members.

B. H. Roberts was not overstating the situation when he wrote: "This [the issue of which national party was entitled to Utah's gratitude] gave rise to a very bitter local controversy in which prominent members of the church participated against each other as partisans with a zeal that carried them beyond the limits of what calm reason would dictate; and the literature of the campaign . . . ran the whole gamut of intense debate."[3]

During the campaign President Woodruff made some remarks about the role of the church leaders in politics at a stake quarterly conference in Provo on September 23, 1894. The following day *The Tribune* quoted from his speech as follows:

> It is generally thought the First Presidency should have nothing to say about politics. I picked up a paper this morning saying that we had no business to meddle in politics. We have a right to lead the people in spiritual and temporal affairs. We have the same rights of leadership that President Young and that the Prophet Joseph Smith had. In temporal affairs? Yes. In political affairs? Yes. We have a right to advise both Democrats and Republicans to lead a pure campaign. We have a right to say to the people that they must be pure in politics as well as in temporal affairs. We have thousands of children growing to manhood in Zion. I am interested in their welfare, and I would like to see them brought up under proper influences and not under the influence of such a campaign as we had two years ago.

The editors of *The Tribune* apparently had some doubts as to the precise meaning of the remarks and immediately sent this letter to Woodruff:

> The purpose of this inquiry is to ascertain with exactness: First, whether your remarks were precisely as reported, and, if not, wherein they depart from precision.

Second, if the remarks were as reported, then in what sense do you wish them to be understood: whether as a claim to control of the political actions of your people absolutely, or only as a citizen to advise the right.

Third, the claim is apparently made in your remarks that the church authorities claim the right to direct the people in their business and politics, and, in general, their temporal affairs, as well as spiritual. It is desirable to know whether this claim is really made and insisted upon at this time, and is to be in the future, while the public has been led to believe that claim is a thing of the past.

In his reply Woodruff said his remarks as published in *The Tribune* were "substantially correct" and then answered the specific questions:

The control of the political actions of our people absolutely is not set up as a claim in my remarks, and I certainly would not wish them to be so understood. I hold that it is the right of the priesthood to advise at any and all times and under any circumstances those who profess to respect its powers, in all matters pertaining to their temporal welfare and their spiritual salvation; in the matter of politics, that the Latter-day Saints should be governed by pure principles, and in political affairs should realize and act upon their responsibilities as saints and citizens. This is not to claim the right to advise them how or for whom they should vote, or which party they should join. We emphatically and sincerely approved the divisions of the "Mormon" people on party lines, and we recognize every man's agency

156

and respect his right to choose in these matters for himself.

The Democratic *Herald,* which was easy to please on this subject, expressed complete satisfaction with Woodruff's statement.

The Republican *Tribune,* which was extremely difficult to convince on the subject of church interference in politics, accepted the answer as satisfactory with this editorial comment:

> The reply is not a retraction of any powers professed by the church, but it does declare that no member of the priesthood would think of advising any Mormon to vote any ticket, only claiming the right, both as a man and a priest, to watch over the morals of the people and as far as possible to shield them from all that may be debasing or immoral in politics. [4]

The Woodruff statement of policy, apparently acceptable to all concerned at that time, did not put the issue to final rest. If Utah were to be held ineligible for statehood until the political parties stopped vying for support of church leaders, and complaining that they didn't get it, or that their opposition did, she would even now be waiting for admission, with dim prospects of success in the foreseeable future.

There were, no doubt, some on both the Mormon and gentile sides still opposed to statehood at the beginning of 1895. Ironically, these groups had something in common. They both viewed the "Manifesto" as an unmitigated disaster but for differing reasons. To the uncompromising anti-Mormons, the Woodruff pronouncement had deprived them of the weapon with which they hoped to totally eradicate the church influence, ecclesiastical as well as political and economic. To the uncompromising Mormons the "Manifesto" was an indefensible surrender or capitulation on the part of church leadership. But the extremist groups on both sides were relatively small in number and neither had an established voice for the recruitment of support.

In Washington the executive branch and the Congress had every reason to welcome statehood for the territory, if for no other reason than to get rid of the "Utah problem" which had been a hairshirt for generations of politicians. In Utah, the press, the established organizations, and the great majority of the people were not only ready for, but eagerly looking forward to the change from territory to state.

It was under these conditions that the newly elected delegates to the Constitutional Convention convened on March 4, 1895, the first Monday in the month, and embarked upon the task of framing a constitution which would meet the conditions laid down in the Enabling Act.

The Republicans, with a majority of thirteen (sixty to forty-seven members for the Democrats) organized the convention and elected John Henry Smith president. While recent developments within the territory theoretically made religion irrelevant in a political body, there was undoubtedly considerable public interest as to church division. The membership was made up of seventy-nine Mormons and twenty-eight gentiles. According to a computation made by Stanley S. Ivins in an article, "A Constitution for Utah," published in the *Utah Historical Quarterly*, the gentiles compensated for their numerical disadvantage by occupying the floor almost half the time. Mr. Ivins calculated that the twenty-eight gentiles accounted for forty-six percent of the speeches recorded in the two large volumes of the convention proceedings.[5]

Three of the delegates were then or were in the future to be associated with *The Tribune*. Editor C. C. Goodwin was a delegate from Salt Lake City. Two of the four delegates from Summit County were David Keith, a co-owner of the newspaper from 1901 to 1918, and Thomas Kearns, co-owner from 1901 until his death in 1918. Kearns, who started as a mine-mucker and became Park City's wealthiest mine owner, was destined to play a major role in the history of *The Tribune* as well as the political and economic affairs of the state for two decades. Moreover, *The Tribune* was destined to remain in the ownership of his family, and thereby to perpetuate the memory of his name, into the second century of the newspaper's history and beyond to a date which only future events can fix.

Although a wealthy mine owner and operator at the time, Kearns was still sympathetically tied to his pick and shovel days and demonstrated a consciousness of his kinship with and responsibilities to his miner constituency in the Park City district. As a member of the majority party, he was assigned to the chairmanship of the Committee on Mines and Mining, member of the Executive Committee and member of the Committee on Salaries of Public Officers. Throughout the sixty-day session, the main focus of his interest and activity was on the labor article. During the April 18, 1895, session he summed up his philosophy and aims with respect to this article during debate on a motion to delete a protective amendment he had proposed.

"I think," he told the body "it is the duty of every man in this Convention to throw around the laborer of this territory all the protection we can." [6]

He did not get all he sought in the article. But for that period it was a progressive article which looked to the future rather than the past. He fought hard for a section providing for an eight-hour day on public works and in mining and manufacturing. He had to compromise with an article specifying eight hours as a day's work on state, county and municipal undertakings and directing the legislature to "pass laws to provide for the health and safety of employes in factories, smelters and mines." [7] The section he proposed carried a mandatory directive to the Legislature to enact an eight-hour day law covering mines, smelters and factories. While this was eliminated, the fight he made for it in the Constitution undoubtedly did prompt the Legislature subsequently to enact such legislation.

Other provisions of the article he guided through the convention prohibited: The employment of women or children under the age of fourteen years in underground mines, the contracting of convict labor, the use of convict labor outside prison grounds except in public works under the direct control of the state, the political and commercial control of employes, and the exchange of "black lists" by railroads, corporations, associations or persons. [8]

The stickiest problem confronting the convention was how to make certain that polygamous or plural marriages would be "forever prohibited" as was required by the Enabling Act. There was no disposition to evade the condition but questions were raised as to possible loopholes of escape at some future time. The convention adopted, on this subject, the language of the Enabling Act:

> First, that perfect toleration of religious sentiment shall be secured, and that no inhabitant of said state shall ever be molested in person or property on account of his or her mode of religious worship; provided, that polygamous or plural marriages are forever prohibited. [9]

This was further buttressed with the provision that the ordinance be irrevocable without the consent of the United States and the people of Utah.[10] But Delegate Charles S. Varian of Salt Lake City was not entirely satisfied even with this double guarantee. He pointed out that the constitutional prohibition was not self-executing; that it might not be made effective by the Legislature; that on a basis of this possibility opponents of statehood might use it as a weapon of obstruction in Congress. He suggested that, as a further expression of good faith, a portion of a territorial legislative enactment against polygamy be incorporated into the Constitution. He explained that he desired the inclusion of only a portion of the territorial law because this would prohibit future polygamous marriages but would not make subject to prosecution the polygamous relationships that had been entered into in the past under the sanction of the church. Delegate Varian was the same Mr. Varian who, as United States District Attorney in Utah, had prosecuted many polygamous cases during the "crusade" and he did not want to see that unpleasant experience renewed. His amendment seemingly accomplished what most of the delegates wanted and it was approved by a large majority vote. But a complication arose later when a code commission appointed to compile the laws of Utah erroneously included the portion of the territorial law which Varian's amendment had excluded.[11]

According to church historian B. H. Roberts, however, the solution intended by the convention was accepted by the state and became policy.

> The melancholy finality contemplated in that settlement was not remote and is practically an accomplished fact now — the elimination by death of that generation of men and women who were involved in the system of plural marriage under sanctions of the Church of the Latter-day Saints. There are but a few of them left now — 1930 — 'and time is on the wing!' Indeed such families are practically extinct.[12]

The Tribune was generally satisfied with the job of the convention, as were the other newspapers. Delegate Goodwin could hardly claim that the Mormons were sticking together to vote only for Mormons after he had been elected from Salt Lake City. The election of some of the gentiles — Kearns and Keith for example — could be anticipated because of the make-up of their constituencies. But the editor of *The Tribune* could not have been elected from Salt Lake City without some Mormon Republican votes.

In the election of 1895, the territory elected a full slate of state officers in anticipation of statehood. Again the obvious assumption that the orientation of Mormons toward the Democratic Party in the past would make Utah a Democratic state proved faulty. For the Republicans elected a full slate of state officials, a congressman and a majority of the Legislature which would elect the state's two United States senators. Heber M. Wells, a Mormon and son of the civic and church leader (Daniel H. Wells), was elected governor; and C. E. Allen, a non-Mormon, was elected congressman. Already the political parties had started dividing the major nominations between Mormons and non-Mormons, a practice which was frequently followed in later years but which was placed beyond the control of the political parties by enactment of the direct primary law prior to the 1940 election.

The old bugaboo of church interference in politics, which in theory had been laid to rest, erupted anew in this first state election. Again it was the Democrats who complained that the influence was being used in behalf of the Republicans. The issue stemmed from the fact that the Democrats had placed on their ticket two general authorities of the church — Moses Thatcher, a member of the Council of Twelve Apostles, and B. H. Roberts, a member of the First Council of Seventy. Midway in the campaign Joseph F. Smith, a member of the First Presidency, reproved these church officials for accepting nominations without consultation with or approval of their ecclesiastical superiors. The haggling over this incident continued for some time in both the political and ecclesiastical arenas. One of its off-shoots was the issuance by the Mormon Church of a political manifesto in which the salient points were made in these excerpts:

We unanimously agree to, and promulgate as a rule, that should always be observed in the Church and by every leading official thereof, that before accepting any position, political or otherwise, which would interfere with the proper and complete discharge of his ecclesiastical duties, and before accepting a nomination or entering into engagements to perform new duties, said official should apply to the proper authorities to learn from them whether he can, consistently with the obligations already entered into with the Church upon assuming his office, take upon himself the added duties and labors and responsibilities of the new position. *To maintain proper discipline and order in the Church,* we deem this absolutely necessary; and in asserting this rule, we do not consider that we are infringing in the least degree upon the individual rights of the citizen.

We declare that in making these requirements of ourselves and our brethren in the ministry, we do not in the least desire to dictate to them concerning their duties as American citizens, or to interfere with the affairs of state; neither do we consider that in the remotest degree we are seeking the union of church and state. [13]

The political squabbling in Utah did not impede the machinery already set in motion to make Utah a state and on Saturday, January 4, 1896, President Grover Cleveland signed the proclamation accomplishing that long-sought and elusive goal. When the news was flashed to Utah it was greeted with the firing of guns, ringing of bells, blowing of whistles and street demonstrations.

The Tribune headlines on its story occupying virtually all of the front page on January 5 said: "UTAH State;" "The Forty-fifth Star Shines Resplendent;" "The Transition From a Territory to a State;" "All Conditions Satisfied."

In the same issue *The Tribune* said editorially:

> It was a joyous day in Utah yesterday. The news reached here early that Statehood had really come to Utah, and gun and bell and steam whistle all joined in an acclaim; and for a time at least, the people seemed to listen as though the mingled voices were echoes of their own heart's voices. Then bunting began to appear; flags went up as the night drew down; the great Temple blazed out in illumination. . . . To other states, statehood came as a matter of course; to Utah it came as a sacred deed of trust put in the hands of the people. The joy was too deep for any outward violent demonstrations; but that did not disguise from any looker-on the truth that the people were immensely, intensely moved. Tomorrow will come the demonstration. With organ and choir and with all ostentation the praise service will be given and we may safely predict that the people will take on anew the resolve that there will never be anything done in Utah to make them or their children regret the coming of statehood to Utah. Our star will be the forty-fifth. Let us all determine that whatever clouds may obscure the other stars in the august galaxy, ours shall always shine on with no mist or cloud or eclipse to dim its perfect splendor. [14]

Inaugural day was as grand as *The Tribune* forecast. The lead paragraph of its report on the event read:

> All nature smiled upon the birth of the State of Utah. and Inaugural day was as perfect midwinter

164

weather as the genial climate of Salt Lake ever afforded. Not a cloud was visible in the blue sky, and the sun's rays were warm enough to cause a slight thaw and make the temperature just right for outdoor exercise. [15]

The Tribune, like the January weather, was in a genial mood. It had started the new year out that way in a January 1 editorial summarizing the history of the newspaper and its progenitors — *The Utah Magazine* and the *Mormon Tribune*. The editorial pointed out that for many years *The Tribune* had had a hard struggle for existence because of its championship of the gentile cause; that it had survived because it had always kept abreast of the times, constantly improving staff and publishing facilities. It reviewed very briefly the conflicts it had fought and closed this portion of the editorial with the comment: "But the days of bitterness having passed, it is useless to refer further to them, now that *The Tribune* has such a hold on the friendship of the masses, including all factions and classes. . . ."

The editorial then expressed pride in *The Tribune's* New Year's edition and the all-around quality of the newspaper in these words:

> In the past twenty years the New Year's *Tribune* has been the source from which facts regarding Utah and its resources have been obtained for use in magazine and newspaper articles sent East; for facts for use in advertising pamphlets, or for business letters bringing capital here; in fact it has been about the only source from which correct information of this class could be obtained without great cost. It has certainly cost *The Tribune* much money to lay before our readers such a mass of information as we have from year to year.

165

Aside from these special efforts, *The Tribune* is always replete with all the news from both home and abroad. To accomplish this has required a constant growth in facilities for getting news; extensive correspondence over the country; growth in the editorial departments; extensive outlays for perfecting presses, for linotype machines, etc., and all these under the most progressive management of the affairs of The Tribune Publishing Company. . . . [16]

The tone of the newspaper at this juncture revealed an expectation on the part of the management and editors that the columns of space previously devoted to the problems arising directly from the "irrepressible conflict" could in the future be devoted to more general issues. From this day forward they hoped to lend their efforts to denouncing the "crime" of demonetization of silver; argument of the case for the free coinage of the metal; defense of the protective tariff system; support of the Republican Party; and castigation of the *Herald,* not as the "minor" voice of the Mormon Church, as in the past, but as the "major" voice of the Democratic Party.

13

Senatorial Fiasco

WITH STATEHOOD ACHIEVED, Utah immediately set about choosing two senators to represent the new state in Washington, D.C. When the Republican - dominated legislature, elected the previous November in anticipation of a formal declaration of statehood, convened in Salt Lake City in January, 1896, one of its first orders of business was the selection by the State Senate of Utah's two United States senators. *The Tribune* behaved sensibly with regard to its old bugbear of church meddling in politics. True, the newspaper was not satisfied with both senators but its objections ran against the gentile elected rather than the Mormon.

The procedure for electing senators at this time may be briefly summarized: First, the parties held conventions and nominated one or more candidates to give the voters some idea of whom they might be supporting for senator, but the conventions were not required to make nominations. It was generally understood, and accepted, that the party winning a majority of the state legislature was entitled to the U.S. Senate seats. Just before the legislature convened, or shortly thereafter, the parties would hold caucuses to seek unanimous agreement on whom the legislative members of the party would support for senator. To refuse to accept a party caucus decision was a serious partisan "sin" excusable only for some overriding objection on the part of the defector. The majority party caucus, in effect, elected the senators. The minority party caucus was largely a matter of form, unless the majority party legislators happened to split on the issue and open the door to a floor contest.

In 1896, the Republicans controlled the legislature, but their convention had not made senatorial nominations. Thus, the door was open for the candidacies of any who wanted to formally declare or work for the honor without a formal declaration. Among the candidates who did not declare, but who had substantial support, was the admittedly outstanding church, civic and political leader, George Q. Cannon. A declared candidate, who had campaigned throughout the state for a Republican victory, was his son, Frank J. Cannon.

The Tribune editors made it very clear before the legislature convened that they would regard the election of the father as a repudiation of the separation of church and state understanding and that they would view the failure to elect the son as an act of perfidy on the part of the Republican legislators. On the eve of the caucus George Q. Cannon announced that he would not, under any circumstances, present himself as a candidate. *The Tribune* promptly commended him for the decision in these words:

> . . . No one better than he understands what some
> of the effects of such [his] candidacy would be. He
> has not since the division movement prominently
> identified himself with either party, and if any man
> has ever heard that he considers himself a Demo-
> crat or a Republican, we have never heard of that
> man. Hence, if elected to the Senate, he would not
> be elected as a Republican or as a Democrat, but
> simply considering his clerical position as he who is
> second in authority in the Mormon Church; the
> country would accept his election as a certain indi-
> cation that the old order of things, so far as church

168

rule was concerned, had been restored. It would cost
Utah millions of dollars by turning back people who
are now contemplating making this their home. It
would disintegrate the Republican Party, if not
both the Democratic and Republican parties. . . . [1]

Three days later *The Tribune* ran a long editorial presenting
the case for Frank J. Cannon's election:

> The Republicans made no nominations for senators
> in their convention, but it was just as well under-
> stood on that day and every succeeding day during
> the campaign, that in case of Republican success,
> Hon. Frank J. Cannon would be one of the senators.
> It was an understanding universally conceded
> throughout the length and breadth of Utah . . . As
> we look upon it, there is not a Republican member
> of the Legislature who was not elected under an
> implied promise at least that he would vote for
> Frank J. Cannon. . . . [2]

Had the writer been able to gaze a few years into the future,
he could have added that the election of George Q. Cannon, the
father, would probably produce a long and controversial investigation as to his eligibility for the seat and that history would record, instead of the "Smoot investigation," the "Cannon investigation" with this difference — Cannon was a practicing polygamist, whereas Smoot was not.

The Republican caucus and legislature did half its duty, as
The Tribune saw it, by electing Frank J. Cannon. But the newspaper was appalled by its selection of Arthur Brown for the other
Senate seat. Brown, a gentile and a lawyer, had represented a
considerable number of defendants under the anti-polygamy
laws. The two senators drew lots to determine which would serve
the short and which the long term. Brown drew the short term.

169

In an editorial congratulating Frank J. Cannon upon his nomination and election, *The Tribune* had this to say about Brown:

> . . . It was unexpected, and will strike the people as something in the nature of a trick and bad faith. Mr. Brown deserves nothing from the Republican Party. He is not of the stuff that the ideal Senator is made; he has none of the qualities that are looked for in the incumbent of that high and illustrious position, but many that one would suppose should forbid any one thinking of him in that connection. The caucus action as to him can only be explained on the theory that a sudden madness overtook the members, and in their frenzy they recked not of consequences. His election will mean nothing good for Republicanism locally; it will signify nothing for Utah before the nation. [3]

B. H. Roberts, in his history of the Mormon Church, took a dim view of both senatorial selections: "Mr. Arthur Brown no more fittingly represented the better class of non-Mormon Republicans in Utah than Mr. Frank J. Cannon met the standards of the Latter-day Saints of Utah." [4]

But his appraisal of the two men might have been colored by hindsight. He was writing after Senator Cannon had, in Roberts words, "turned professional anti-Mormon" and after Brown, again in Roberts words, had been "shot to death in a Washington, D. C., hotel, by a discarded mistress." [5]

In the 1896 general election Utah participated for the first time in the election of a president and vice-president. Party alignments were thrown into chaos by the money issue. William J. Bryan's "cross of gold" campaign shattered the party loyalties of both Republicans and Democrats and *The Tribune* was confronted with a choice of supporting the Democratic national ticket or turning its back upon the cause of bimetallism for which it had vigorously crusaded since "the crime of 1873" — (the demonetization of silver). Apparently the choice was not a difficult one. From the outset of the campaign, *The Tribune* sounded its editorial trumpets for the election of Bryan; the remonetization of silver on a ratio of sixteen to one with gold; the election in Utah and other states of Republican senators and congressmen who were "right" on the money question; and the election of Republican state legislatures.

The election turned out to be a lost cause for *The Tribune* all the way around. Bryan carried Utah by a huge majority but lost the nation. The new state elected a Democrat to the House of Representatives and a Democratic state legislature.

William H. King was the Democratic nominee for Congress. He won by a margin of almost 20,000 votes, and thereby launched a political career which led to the United States Senate where he served continuously from 1917 to 1941. When the Democratic legislature convened the contenders for the U.S. Senate seat held by Brown were Joseph L. Rawlins and Moses Thatcher. Rawlins, although a "drop-out" from the Mormon Church, was the author and chief sponsor of Utah's Enabling Act and author of the act which returned to the church about a half-million dollars in personal property which had been escheated to the federal government during the polygamy crusade. Interestingly, he was described by Roberts, the Mormon historian, as "a lawyer of recognized ability, of statesmanlike quality of mind and temperament and a man of temperate habits."[6]

Thatcher, a prominent Mormon leader, had at this time been deposed from the Council of Twelve Apostles because of his refusal to accept the rule of the church respecting the acceptance of other positions without permission of ecclesiastical superiors.

The contest was close and extended through fifty-three ballots over a period of fourteen days before Rawlins won. In this instance *The Tribune* was not distressed to see a Democrat replace

Republican Brown, who had drawn a short term of barely more than a year when the state elected its first senators.

Utah again went Democratic in the 1898 election and the Democratic legislature, which had the responsibility of selecting a successor to Republican Frank J. Cannon, produced what became known in Utah political history as the "senatorial fiasco of 1899."

The circumstances, briefly outlined, were: Senator Cannon, although elected as a Republican, felt he was entitled to reelection by the Democratic legislature because he, with other western delegates, had bolted the regular Republican Party convention to form the free silver wing of the Republican Party. His chief opponent initially was Alfred W. McCune, a wealthy mining and businessman. There was at the time a sort of unwritten, informal understanding that one senator should be a Mormon and one a non-Mormon. [7] Inasmuch as Rawlins was a non-Mormon, the Mormons had a claim to the new member. McCune soon won the support of the majority of the legislature but was unable to reach the two-thirds majority required for election. [8] The deadlock continued until near the end of the session when the able and overpowering George Q. Cannon emerged as an independent candidate. He too was unable to muster the required majority. With time running out, the Democrats begin turning to James H. Moyle, then the party's state chairman, and on the 169th ballot he was just behind Cannon with twenty votes. A Democratic caucus was called and soon the word was being passed around that Moyle had been agreed upon. But by this time the session had fallen into pandemonium — no doubt with a few pushes from jeering Republicans — and some of the members were leaving. Before the Democrats could reassemble their forces the clock struck midnight and Utah was left with one of its Senate seats vacant. [9]

But this was not the only fumble of the Democrats in this election. They had nominated B. H. Roberts, a general authority

172

of the church and a polygamist, for representative to Congress. He easily won the election but the House voted to exclude him on the ground that he had violated anti-polygamy laws. Thus the Democrats had exposed themselves to the charge that they were responsible for the state's having only one of the three seats in the Senate and House to which it was entitled. Despite this campaign weapon placed in the hands of the Republicans, the Democrats won a special election in April of 1900 to elect William H. King to fill the seat Roberts was denied.

A newspaper development of this period was the purchase by McCune (in furtherance of his candidacy) and some associates of the *Salt Lake Herald, The Tribune's* most consistent journalistic sparring partner over a period of a quarter of a century. A short time later the newspaper was sold to former Senator W. A. Clark of Montana, a major sponsor of a company organized to build a railroad from Salt Lake City to Los Angeles (San Pedro, Los Angeles and Salt Lake Railroad Company). Inasmuch as Clark was a Democrat, the *Herald* remained a spokesman for that party until its subsequent sale to the Republican Party.[10] It continued its friendly policy toward the church but *The Tribune's* claim that it was the "minor voice" of the church had less validity than in earlier days. Although the editorial feuding between *The Tribune* and *Deseret News* established the bench mark in bitterness, it subsided and rose from time to time. But it was a rare day when *The Tribune* and *Herald* were not at each others' throats over some religious, political or civic issue.

Another major news event of this period was the death of president Wilford Woodruff at age 91 on September 2, 1898, in San Francisco, where he had gone seeking relief from a health problem. *The Tribune* devoted more than half its front page and almost a page inside to an account of his life and to the background of Lorenzo Snow, who, it correctly assumed, would be the next Mormon president. In the news story *The Tribune* said:

The news of President Woodruff's death was received in Salt Lake with very general manifestations of sorrow. His simple, kindly nature and his unassuming character endeared him even to those who were not of his faith and they shared the sorrow of the bereaved Mormon population. . . .

In its editorial, which made no mention of the "Manifesto" banning polygamy, the newspaper said:

We suspect that his sterling honesty was his most pronounced trait. His beliefs were strong; he would have died for them at any time and would have smiled as he died, but he was destitute of all arrogance and all pretension; his greatest desire was to perform within his sphere his duty, and to do that without the slightest ostentation or self-glorification. No man was ever more loved by his people. There will be sorrow for him wherever there are Latter-day Saints, for he was more of a father to them than president. . . . [11]

While there were still many bitter words to be exchanged between Mormon and non-Mormon in Utah, between *The Tribune* and the journalistic defenders of the church there was at this time a notable softening of old animosities. This era of good feeling had been conspicuously evident a year earlier, in 1897, during a four-day observance of the fiftieth anniversary of the arrival of the Mormon pioneers in Salt Lake Valley. At the dedication of the Brigham Young monument at the head of the city's Main Street, Goodwin of *The Tribune* delivered a speech on the "Utah Pioneers" which Roberts described as "A bit of western American literature of high class, a western classic in English in fact."

174

The closing paragraphs:

> Whatever the future holds in store for Utah, that story of toil and suffering and final triumph [of the Pioneers] should be held as sacred history to every man who honors devotion to duty in men, and self-sacrifice in women.
>
> It should be taught to the children in schools, and one lesson that should be impressed upon the mind of every child is, that a wrong act on his or her part would be a reproach to the brave men and women who came here in the shadow of despair and by incessant toil and by life-long self abnegation laid solidly here the foundations of a state.
>
> And out of the granite of these mountains should be hewed an imperishable monument, which should be set up in some conspicuous place, and upon it, should be embossed words like these:
>
> *They wore out their lives in toil. They suffered without plaint. From nothing they created a glorified state. Honor and reverence and glory everlastingly be theirs.*[12]

The election of 1900, a presidential year in which a full roster of state officers was elected, produced a minimum of complaints about church interference in politics. Otherwise, the pre-election campaign was typically uninhibited with the two major parties playing the role they are supposed to play in politics and with their journalistic spokesmen slamming each other with unrestrained exuberance. *The Tribune* had concluded that there was no future for bimetallism in the Democratic Party and was now back in the Republican fold without reservations. The *Herald* was as ardently Democratic as *The Tribune* was Republican. Both candidates for governor — Republican incumbent

175

Heber M. Wells and Democrat James H. Moyle — were Mormons. The candidates for delegate to Congress were George Sutherland, a Protestant who was in good odor with the Mormons,[13] on the Republican ticket, and William H. King, a Mormon, on the Democratic ticket.

The Republicans, who were enjoying a brief interlude of unity, skillfully tailored their protective tariff and "full dinner pail" issues to Brigham Young's economic doctrine of building up home industry as opposed to import encouragement, and thereby reversed the Democratic tide which had been building up in the state. They carried the state for McKinley over Bryan; elected a full slate of state officers and won a substantial majority in the state legislature.

One defeated Democrat who left a bit of testimony as to the effectiveness of the role played by *The Tribune* in the campaign was Moyle, a man of unquestioned party loyalty but an intelligent realist who was not blinded by his loyalty. In his papers, and in discussions with this writer, he expressed the view that a major factor in his own, and his party's defeat, were the editorials of Goodwin and cartoons of Charles C. Worthington in *The Tribune.* "This combination of editor and cartoonist was a more effective opponent than all the stump speakers the (opposition) party could rally." [14]

While the issue of church interference in politics had been relatively dormant during the pre-election campaign, it again exploded in an unprecedentedly virulent form when the Republican legislature prepared to convene the following January to, among other duties, elect a United States senator. The impassioned charges of church intervention were directed not at Mormon political cohesiveness in behalf of Mormon candidates; not, as might reasonably be expected, at the Mormon leadership pushing one of its own for political preferment; but at the alleged support of the highest Mormon leader for a wealthy Catholic mining man. The targets of the furious political outburst were the president of the church, Lorenzo Snow, and Thomas Kearns, a man destined to play a major role in the history of *The Tribune,* as its owner and its policymaker for eighteen years, and a significant role in the economic and political history of the state. He had by this time already made a fortune in mining, was an influential member of the Republican Party, and had served as a member of the state's Constitutional Convention in 1895. However, the general public did not yet regard him as a leader nor as a logical prospect for a seat in the United States Senate.

14

Thomas Kearns[1]

THOMAS KEARNS, who arrived in Park City in 1883 when that community was a booming mining center of about 3,000 population, was born April 11, 1862, in Woodstock, Ontario, Canada. His parents, Thomas Kearns and Margaret Maher Kearns, both from Ireland, eventually settled near O'Neill, Holt County, Nebraska, a community founded by Irish immigrants. The father was a farmer and the six children (Bernard, Mary, James, Thomas, John, Margaret) early became acquainted with hard work, but their opportunities for formal education were limited by both location and economics.

Thomas, known as Tom throughout his life, had no more than a grammar school education but his aggressive ambitions impelled him to devote considerable effort to self-education throughout his life. Physically, he was compact, muscular, remarkably strong and agile. He was an excellent wrestler and, from early youth, well able to take care of himself in the rough and tough frontier mining camp environment in which he spent much of his life. Farming did not appeal to him, and by the time he was seventeen he was itching to strike out on his own and try his luck in the mining industry which was being glamorized at that time by stories of rich strikes and quick fortunes throughout much of the west.

He no doubt had been planning a break with family ties for some time but a Saturday night brawl in a poolhall provided him with an occasion or an excuse for the action. On Sunday morning the Catholic parish priest had some pointed and critical remarks to make about the incident in which Tom was involved and he named names in church where all could hear. Indignant at this public affront, Tom announced his intention to leave home, kissed his mother goodbye and set out on his way to seek fame and fortune — which he found probably in more abundant degree than even he anticipated at the time.

From subsequent incidents in his life there is reason to suspect that, however strong the attachment of the mother for the son, on this occasion she might well have agreed with the remarks of the priest. One such incident occurred several years later. Tom attended a traveling variety show in Salt Lake City in which one of the acts was a professional wrestler who offered a prize of $100 to anyone who could stay on the stage with him without being pinned for a specified period of time. Tom accepted the challenge. He not only kept his own feet but threw the wrestler off the stage onto the bass drum in the orchestra pit. He promptly sent the prize money to his mother who responded with a letter of thanks for the gift and chidings for his violent ways.

Tom first went to the scene of a big gold strike in the Black Hills of South Dakota Territory. Unable to find immediate work in the mines he took a job as a freighter between the railroad terminal at Pierre and the Great Homestake Mining Company's mine at Lead. He later got a job at the Homestake mine, his first taste of the industry which was to provide the fame and fortune of his dreams. He subsequently worked for a South Dakota cattle association, returned for a short time to his home in Nebraska and then took off again for Tombstone, Arizona, scene of the glamorized exploits of lawman Wyatt Earp. There he worked in the mines for a time and as a teamster for a transportation company. The next point in his travels was the Tintic mining district in Utah. He found no immediate jobs open there and so continued on to Springville, Utah, where he worked for the Denver and Rio Grande Western Railroad long enough to accumulate another traveling stake. He then set out for Butte, Montana, site of the "richest hill on earth," but when he reached Pocatello, Idaho, he struck up acquaintance with a group of roving miners who told him about Park City. He abandoned the Butte trip and returned to Utah.

The manner of his arrival in Park City in June, 1883, as recounted to James Ivers, a friend and business associate, was substantially as follows: He dropped off a freight train as he neared Park City and went to a farmhouse in the Snyderville area. The farmer was a Cornishman from England named Tommy Williams. He took a fancy to the young Irish traveler, or bindle stiff (a term applied to nonpaying passengers on freight trains) and invited him to stay a few days. Tom spent the remainder of the week doing odd jobs, pitching some hay and possibly having a few drinks and exchanging ideas and experiences with his host. On Saturday night Tommy Williams took his guest to Park City to attend a Catholic Church fund-raising function and to introduce him around. Cornishmen were known as "cousin jacks" and Williams introduced Kearns around the social function as "my cousin, Tom." The manner of the introduction is mentioned here because some seventeen years later, when Kearns was seeking the United States Senate seat, one of the many charges hurled against him by political opponents was that he had arrived in Park City under an assumed name. The intended inference, of course, was that he must have come to Park City as a fugitive of some kind. The "assumed" name he was accused of using was Tommy Williams.

The priest in charge of the fund-raising social — Father Galligan — possessed business as well as priestly talents. His favorite device for bringing in the money was a contest to choose the prettiest girl in town, or the most popular girl, or man, or miner. The choice was made by votes, and supporters of the competing candidates purchased the votes. The priest's business acumen prompted him to see that the contestants were always drawn from rival mining operations, thereby widening and intensifying the competitive inducements for the purchase of votes. On this Saturday night the contest was to select the most popular mine foreman. The contestants were David Keith of the Ontario and John Judge of the Daly mine. Because Williams' "Cousin Tom" was a newcomer, and therefore not so emotionally involved in the contest as the others, he was selected to count the votes. Judge won over Keith and received a gold watch and chain. Kearns, as the vote tabulator, got acquainted with both. All in all, it was quite an eventful night for young Tom. Keith got him a job in the Ontario mine and a friendship developed which made them life-long partners in mining ventures and in ownership of *The Tribune.* Judge likewise was to be a future partner and was the uncle of the girl Tom later married.

In the Kearns-Keith partnership, Keith was usually awarded the more impressive title. But it was Kearns who had the "take over" drive, and it was he who dominated the operations of both mines and newspapers. Keith had more formal education and social polish than his partner, but it was Kearns who was willing to make decisions and push the partnership into the gambles which were essential to success in the mining industry of that era. Although the partnership no doubt benefited from Keith's caution at times, Kearns was frequently annoyed by what he regarded as the indecisiveness of his partner, and he could express that annoyance in blunt, earthy terms. On one such occasion he irritably told another business associate: "If he [Keith] rushed into an outhouse and it turned out to be a three-holer, he would never be able to make up his mind until it was too late."

Kearns apparently found Park City to be more congenial than the mining camps he had previously tried, for he went to work with a will and either lost, or controlled, his wanderlust. He became a lodger in the same boarding house in which Keith lived. After working his shift in the Ontario mine, he devoted additional hours to studying mineralogy and geology. He also pros-pected or took extra work. Years later, as a member of Utah's Constitutional Convention and the sponsor of an eight-hour work day provision, he argued that any miner could get all the work he wanted in eight hours. But eight hours was not enough to satisfy an ambitious young man like himself who was determined to get ahead and become his own boss.

In his search for extra work and opportunity he was offered a contract to drive a tunnel. The job required a modest amount of capital and Kearns had not been working long enough to accumulate any savings. He presented the proposition to Keith, who did have some capital, and the latter agreed to provide the necessary funds. This was the beginning of the long and successful partnership.

Kearns and Keith, sometimes in partnership with others, continued prospecting ventures but were unsuccessful until they acquired a lease on an undeveloped property known as the Mayflower. This venture was prompted by some observations Kearns had made while working on the tunnel job on an adjacent property and the application of his newly acquired knowledge of geology and mineralogy. Partners in the lease, in addition to Kearns and Keith, were John Judge, Albion B. Emery and Windsor V. Rice. The owners of the property were David D. Erwin of Muskegon, Michigan, and two Park City men — Newell and Hirschman.

They started working the property in February, 1889, and some two months later struck ore which was thirty percent lead and contained about 100 ounces of silver per ton. The first ore shipment brought Kearns some $20,000 and he promptly displayed a characteristic which endeared him to those who came to know him well. He used a good part of the money to purchase a fine home in Nebraska for his aged parents.

At this point Kearns and his partners made a disconcerting discovery about the mining industry; that rich strikes frequently, if not usually, generated expensive lawsuits. This one was not among the exceptions. But Kearns and his partners won the suit.

182

In the ensuing years they often found themselves in court on similar suits. They lost some but won more, and so their fortunes continued to grow. While working the Mayflower, the partners discovered that the main ore vein led toward some claims known as the Silver King. They succeeded, in 1892, in purchasing this property from a group of partners — W. H. Dodge, Martin McGrath, John Farrish and Cornelius McLaughlin — for $65,000. This property proved to be their biggest bonanza. They incorporated the Silver King Mining Company for $3,000,000 represented by 150,000 shares which were divided as follows: Kearns, Keith, Emery and Judge 25,000 shares each; W. H. Dodge, 20,833; D. D. Erwin, 12,500; W. V. Rice, 16,667. Keith was president; Kearns, vice president; Rice, treasurer; and Emery, secretary. At the request of Judge, James Ivers was placed on the board to represent his interests.

Some two years before the organization of the Silver King Mining Company, Kearns had achieved another of the goals he had set for himself soon after his arrival in Park City. He married Jennie Judge, the beautiful 21-year-old niece of John Judge and daughter of Mrs. William Wilson. Jennie's father died when she was two years old and the mother was remarried when the family came to Park City in 1879.

For three or four years Kearns' main distraction from excessively long hours of work had been Jennie Judge and he frequently complained to associates that he didn't have time to court her properly. She had won one of Father Galligan's contests as the most popular girl in Park City. While she was undoubtedly entitled to the title on merit alone, under the priest's fund-raising methods, her victory could be attributed also to the fact that Tom Kearns was able and willing to spend more money for votes than were the supporters of any of the other contestants. This incident was reflective of a characteristic of Kearns. Throughout his life, after he had acquired money, he was willing to spend freely for what he wanted, whether the inducement was love, politics or business.

Under Kearns' management the Silver King mine was soon producing handsome profits and by 1900, when he became a candidate for the United States Senate, it was paying dividends of $1,300,000 annually.

The fact that the mine was able to operate on a profitable basis through the money panic of 1893, and through the violent fluctuations in metal prices (silver dropped from 83 cents to 54 cents per ounce during the five-year period 1892-1897) can be attributed in part to the richness of its ore. But an important additional factor was Kearns' managerial ability and his unceasing drive to reduce production costs without cutting wages. On the issue of mine wages his practice as an operator was consistent with his philosophy as a politician, as expressed in the Constitutional Convention. Sometimes his wage policies did not endear him to fellow-operators. But it did win for him the gratitude of the working miners who, when he returned to Park City after the convention, insisted upon replacing the horses to pull his carriage up Main Street.

Just when Kearns started thinking about raising his sights to include a United States Senate seat is uncertain. But his experience in the Constitutional Convention and the reaction of the miners, working men generally, and some of the business community to his accomplishments in that body, no doubt encouraged the idea, or started it incubating. He had already come a long way for an Irish immigrant farm boy. At thirty-eight years of age he was a millionaire mine operator, an important investor in various enterprises which were building up the economy of the city, state, and western part of the country. He had business ties with men nationally prominent in business and politics and had attained considerable prominence in the Republican Party of the state as a delegate to national and local conventions, a substantial contributor to its treasury and a member of the Constitutional Convention. He was not yet, however, regarded by the general public as a Republican leader of such stature as to en-title him to consideration for the Senate seat. When he announced his candidacy late in 1900 the Democratic *Herald* said:

"As yet there has been no stampede of the other candidates to welcome Thomas Kearns into the senatorial arena. His final announcement has had the reception usually accorded to cold ice down the spinal column of an unsuspicious subject, and no wonder."[2]

The Republican *Tribune* did not at first take his candidacy seriously. It was backing O. J. Salisbury, a wealthy businessman and Republican national committeeman who was under bitter attack from the *Herald*. But the day before the Republican caucus, *The Tribune* began taking the Kearns candidacy both seriously and frantically. On the morning of January 20, 1901, *The Tribune* headlined a two-column, front page story: "Deal With the Church;" "Authorities Said to Have Ordered the Election of Thomas Kearns to the United States Senate." *The Tribune's* version of the deal, as summarized in the article:

> It is charged positively, upon authority of men whose knowledge of the facts cannot be questioned, that Mormon Church, or at least the highest authorities therein, have ordered the election of Thomas Kearns.[3]

Continuing its diatribe, *The Tribune* charged that the church had promised its support to Kearns as part of a package deal involving the purchase of certain Saltair properties and the Salt Lake and Los Angeles Railroad running to Saltair by Tom Kearns and Senator Clark of Montana.

On January, 23, 1901, Kearns won majority support of the Republican caucus and was subsequently elected by vote of all the Republicans in the legislature. Just which portions of the "deal" were true and which portions untrue remained a subject for argument as long as the incident was a topic of political controversy. Senator Clark denied that any such deal had ever been made or discussed. The Saltair properties were not sold to

185

the railroad company, although a portion of the railroad later did become a part of the line to Los Angeles. Kearns did have some discussions with Lorenzo Snow regarding the purchase of Saltair and for a time held an option on the property.[4] But this tentative transaction was never completed. So if such a deal as the one charged had been agreed upon, only one portion of it — the election of Kearns to the Senate — was carried out.

Certainly Kearns could not have been elected had he been objectionable to the church leadership or opposed by them as leaders. This was also true of the other candidates. From the reports, charges and rumors published in the press during the short but hectic campaign, a circumstantial case can be made that the other candidates sought the church support which they claimed was responsible for Kearns' election, and some of them thought at various times that they had it.

The entire contest, including the withdrawal of Apostle Smoot in favor of Kearns, suggested that there was an informal understanding that the seat should go to a non-Mormon, for the Mormon candidates failed to attract significant support, or dropped out early. All four candidates who remained in the race to the bitter end were non-Mormons. It was a plausible assumption that President Snow did favor the election of Kearns and helped him to victory. But it does not necessarily follow that Snow used or attempted to use his church position to coerce reluctant votes. Indeed, the nature of the contest suggested that he supported Kearns as Lorenzo Snow, citizen, businessman and personal friend of the candidate. For if the allegations that President Snow, as head of the church instructed Mormon members of the legislature to vote for Kearns were true, the contest provided a dramatic testimony that the political power of the president of the church was not what it had been in Brigham Young's day.

The Mormon legislators either felt free to support the candidate of their choice, or they staged a remarkably convincing sham battle to mislead; for they were split among the four leading candidates through twenty caucus ballots, spread over a period of four days. None of the participants appeared to be under any inhibitions regarding vote switching or expressing uncomplimentary views about the competing candidates. Kearns and his backers simply managed to get nineteen of the thirty-seven Republican votes before anyone else was able to reach that magic number. Once he achieved that majority of one, the caucus was pledged to give him its unanimous vote for election, just as it was pledged to give any other candidate polling a majority their unanimous support.

Assuming that it was the favor of President Snow which enabled Kearns to get a majority, it was not the kind of church control which *The Tribune* had been denouncing for thirty years. It was not a case of Mormons receiving their marching orders, and then marching. *The Tribune,* nevertheless, was furious at the result and it started screaming church influence and control at the top of its editorial voice. In response to a *Deseret News* editorial defending President Snow, *The Tribune* said under a heading "The Core of The Matter":

> To the *Deseret News:* So you affect to doubt the truth of what *The Tribune* has been saying, to the effect that for money the President of The Church of Jesus Christ of Latter-day Saints had dishonored himself, disgraced his Church and the State of Utah. You affect to sneer at that and to treat it with righteous scorn. Suppose it were not true, how would you be talking? You know that gentiles generally believe it. You know that apostles, patriarchs and seventies know that it is true. . . . Practiced in falsehood as you are, adept at lying as you are, graduate as you did years ago from the university of perjury, it is too much for you; even you dare not deny it. . . . [5]

Then two days after this editorial appeared *The Tribune,* possibly in response to reactions of gentile-Republican supporters of Senator Kearns, took a somewhat softer position with respect to the senator-elect but reiterated its condemnation of church influence in politics. The editorial said:

> The life of Senator Thomas Kearns up to date, has in it material for a story of fact that would exceed in its marvels many a fiction. Fifteen years ago he was a day laborer. His labor made him a part owner in a marvelous bonanza of rich ore. Now he has been elected to the next to the most exalted office in the world, and the business prospect before him is a promise of the possession of untold millions and a career that will link his name with the few who control the finances of the greatest of nations. And he is only about forty years of age. . . .
>
> We utterly condemn the methods which gave him the Senatorship. They amounted to a turning back of political progress; they were a blow in the face of the efforts of those who for years have been struggling to make of Utah an American State.[6]

In Washington the election of Senator Kearns prompted Utah's Democratic Senator, J. L. Rawlins, to hand to the Senate clerk charges that the Mormon Church had ordered the election of Kearns. Objections from the floor prevented the reading of the articles by the clerk but Rawlins proposed in a speech that the Senate look into the affair. *The Tribune,* reacting with an attack on Rawlins more vitriolic than it had been directing at Kearns, fumed:

> Mr. Rawlins is guilty of a stupidity that one would, of all men, have expected to come from a State

rights Democrat. He put forth the astounding proposition that the United States Senate should interfere in the election by the Utah Legislature of a Senator to sit in the United States Senate. . . .[7]

The Democratic *Herald,* which had ceased to be the "minor voice" of the church with its purchase first by McCune and then by Senator Clark of Montana, saw in the Rawlins proposal not stupidity but some clever needling. It commented:

> Fancy the grim satire of asking Republican senators to express condemnation of a Republican success in Utah which was engineered in Washington by some of the senators to whom Mr. Rawlins addressed his remarks. Imagine the levity of imploring Mark Hanna to repudiate the election of a senator from Utah by Mormon Church influence when the Legislature which chose Kearns was elected largely through the efforts of the same Mormon officials, encouraged and aided by Mr. Hanna's committee. . . .[8]

When Senator Kearns visited Park City following his election he was given a hero's welcome. Press reaction to his selection, both within the state and nationally, ran the gamut. He was everything from a dunce to a genius.

One of the more realistic appraisals was penned by the editor of the *Bingham Bulletin.* After expressing the view that the election of Kearns was the "greatest surprise that has ever occurred in Utah politics;" and repeating an earlier editorial comment that "Utah politics are a quality that would make a monkey of the slickest Tammany wire puller," the editor continued:

> But come to think of it, fellers, what's the matter with Thomas Kearns anyway? He has the first

189

great qualification for a United States Senator, considered in these latter days — lots of dough. It is honest money that he got out of the ground. He has pluck, energy, brains (in the rough) and his integrity is unquestioned. He is the peer of the most of the other candidates, barring not being strictly at home in a dress suit. Tom Kearns will act conscientiously and do the very best he can . . . . It may come to pass that he will be more of a credit and benefit to his State than would some of the alleged statesmen who wanted the place, and it is no two to one that he will not succeed himself. Senator Thomas Kearns, here's to you. [9]

The *Bulletin* editor might have lengthened his odds on the chances of Kearns succeeding himself could he have foreseen two important events which were to occur before the year was out. The first was the death of the great George Q. Cannon on April 12, 1901, in Monterey, California, where he had gone to spend the winter. For years Cannon had been a towering figure in the church and the state, in business and politics — perhaps the most influential man in the church without benefit of the presidency. Next to Brigham Young, he was the chief object of *The Tribune's* crusade for the simple reason that the editors regarded him as the most formidable opponent within the church.

From the personal standpoint of Cannon, death came none too soon. For despite his conspicuous qualities of leadership, his willingness to assume responsibilities, the reverence he generated among Mormons and the respect he commanded from non-Mormon friends and foes, he had no wish to become president of the church. He confided the hope that death would come to him before it came to President Snow, to Georgius Y. Cannon, his youngest son and a grandson of Brigham Young. Georgius accompanied him on a trip to Hawaii a year before his death and on the trip to Monterey, California, about a month before his death.

190

On both occasions he told his son that one of the worries of his later years had been that he would out-live President Snow and thereby be placed next in line for the presidency by reason of seniority.

Six months after Cannon's death Lorenzo Snow died on October 10, 1901, at his official residence, the Beehive House in Salt Lake City. The urbane, able and deceptively tough-minded church president had, as B. H. Roberts put it, the qualities that "go to the making of the practical mystic."[10] He had made some notable strides toward extricating the church from the fiscal morass into which it had fallen during the polygamy crusade and "raid." And he was the kind of person who might see in a non-Mormon millionaire mining and businessman the qualities the state would find useful in the United States Senate. But his death, coupled with that of Cannon, brought new leadership to power within the church and undoubtedly diminished the acceptability, within the church hierarchy, of a man of Kearns' type as a representative of the state in Washington, D. C. The point was immediately grasped by Arthur Brown, the clever non-Mormon lawyer who had already clawed his way to one short term in the Senate, and who was a strong competitor for the seat Kearns had won and who was therefore well schooled in the intricacies of Utah politics. The morning after President Snow's death, Brown walked into Hogle's Bar on Main Street, the gathering place for mining, business and professional men of the city; tossed down a stiff drink of whiskey; and, turning to the other morning imbibers, solemnly announced to all who might be interested: "Tom Kearns died last night."[11]

It was, as later events proved, a prophetic pronouncement of a political death. And, carrying prescience one step farther, he might have added that the effect of the physical death of Snow and the political death of Kearns would be another ebb in what appeared at the time to be a tide, rising slowly but surely toward the goal of accommodation between the opposing forces in the "irrepressible conflict." For the spurning of the political aspirations of *The Tribune's* dominant owner was the match which reignited the controversy.

15

Goodwin Out – Kearns In

THE FIRST HINT of a change in the ownership of *The Salt Lake Tribune,* which had had three owners in its first thirty years, appeared in print while Senator-elect Thomas Kearns was celebrating his victory with supporters and friends and preparing to go to Washington to take his seat.

On January 29, 1901, The *Salt Lake Herald* published a rumor story under the heading: "Senator Kearns Does Not Want *The Tribune."* The news item said:

> A rumor has been in existence for the last few days to the effect that Senator Thomas Kearns was about to break into the newspaper business through the purchase of *The Salt Lake Tribune.* It has been said that the Senator had a desire to shine in journalistic circles and that, when notice was given him that *The Tribune* was on the market, he jumped at the opportunity.
>
> Last night Senator Kearns laughed at the idea. 'It is absurd,' said he. 'People say I would shine more as a miner than as the editor of a newspaper and I don't know but what they're right. I certainly have no intention of breaking into the newspaper business at this time. . . .'[1]

Whether the qualification "at this time" was intended to convey the impression that Kearns had not given the idea any thought or that he was not yet ready for such a venture can only be surmised. Sometime during the next nine months he did decide to buy the paper and acted upon the decision.

The night before the senator left for Washington he and Mrs. Kearns hosted a reception in the Knutsford Hotel, then the finest in the city. *The Tribune,* which by this time had recovered some of its poise, covered the event with a four-column artist's sketch of dancing dignitaries under a four-column headline: "Kearns Reception a Brilliant Event." The news story began:

> The Knutsford never saw such a large gathering. Upstairs and downstairs, in corridors, halls, dining rooms and library they crowded and everybody seemed to have a good time. . . . There was music in the air, everywhere. . . . Downstairs in the public corridor Olsen's orchestra, enlarged to fifteen pieces, rendered a choice programme as the hundreds filed through the doorways. . . . When the upper floor was reached alluring strains of another kind were heard coming from the dining-room, such music as only the Christensen orchestra of twelve pieces can produce. [2]

Decorations and ladies gowns were described as was the elaborate array of food, coffee, punch and champagne. Guests included Governor Wells, Mayor and Mrs. Ezra Thompson, members of the State Supreme Court, federal officials, Bishop Lawrence Scanlon of the Catholic Church and such Mormon leaders as Apostles Reed Smoot and John Henry Smith.

On the day of his departure for Washington, Senator Kearns had a pleasant announcement to make. The Silver King stockholders had voted to increase the monthly dividend from $75,000 to $100,000. M. J. Dailey had been promoted from mine foreman to assistant manager with full power to act in the absence of Senator Kearns. James Ivers, a director, supplemented these announcements with the information that ore taken from a lower level than those then being worked showed an average value of $150 per ton compared to about $50 per ton for the levels already developed.

The senator, according to a *Tribune* report, was accompanied to Washington by Joseph Lippman, his campaign manager. But *The Tribune* had apparently jumped to an unwarranted conclusion. They left together but Lippman turned up in San Francisco, where he told a visiting Utahn that he was no longer associated with Senator Kearns.[3] This provided the local political writers with additional material for speculative articles on patronage pressures which were already starting to bear down on the new senator.

Mrs. Kearns remained at home, probably because the representative of a St. Louis decorating firm was in the city to start planning a $50,000 decorating job in the new mansion Kearns was then building on Brigham (East South Temple) Street. (The mansion was later given to the state by Mrs. Kearns for a governor's mansion and it is now the home of the Utah State Historical Society.)

With the national press re-echoing *Tribune* charges that the Senate seat had been sold to Kearns by the head of the Mormon Church and *The Tribune* still condemning the "deal" in its editorial columns, Senator Kearns was sworn in on February 4. He was escorted to his seat, which was temporarily located on the Democratic side, by a Democratic colleague, Senator Rawlins, and on his desk was a massive array of American Beauty roses bearing the card of Mr. and Mrs. Frank J. Cannon. After the flowers had been admired, Representative William H. King of Utah, also a Democrat, escorted the new senator and a small party to the Senate dining room for an informal luncheon.

Among the guests was Perry S. Heath, a man who was to play a rather important role in the history of *The Tribune*. Heath, a former Indiana newspaperman, was then secretary of the Republican National Committee.

Much of the national publicity about the new Utah senator during his first few months in office was devoted to his rise from pick-and-shovel miner to millionaire silver mine owner. Various publications estimated his wealth at figures ranging from $1,000,000 to $10,000,000. Incidents in his background which received frequent mention of the outpouring of magazine and newspaper articles about him included a reference to Alaska as an island in one of his speeches, a mispronunciation of the Philippines (Filliponies) and a reference to indigents as "indignant" poor. Most of the writers, who found him an intriguing subject, placed more emphasis on such things as a gift (at the behest of Mrs. Kearns) of $50,000 to a Catholic orphanage (Kearns St. Ann's Orphanage); his championship of protective provisions for labor in the Utah Constitutional Convention; his refusal to cut miners' wages when metal prices dropped sharply; the esteem in which he was held by his employes; his willingness to invest the fruits of his Park City bonanza in other mining ventures and in development of Salt Lake City properties (in association with Keith, James Hogle and others); and his down-to-earth appraisals of himself.

Newsmen were occasionally delighted with some of Kearns' pithy comments or responses to questions. Sample: a sensational New York newspaper sent a group of reporters through the Senate asking each member what they would do if they had $25,000,000. Senator Mason of Illinois replied, "I would erect an insane asylum to accommodate New York editors who get up these foolish questions." Senator Kearns replied, "My son, that is too much money to be disposed of in a few minutes conversation."[4]

In Utah the new senator was "worked over" by the press in a manner that forty or fifty years later would have set any Utah politician to tearing his hair and screaming "libel and crucifixion" to the top of his voice. The Democratic *Herald* kept up a steady drumfire of cartoons, news articles and editorials designed to ridicule the senator's manners, speech and dress. Much of the satirizing job was delegated by the *Herald* editors to a columnist, Joel L. Priest, who wrote under the heading: "Old Sport." Priest was one of the few Utah newspaper writers of the period who enjoyed the distinction of a by-line. He later became a prominent figure throughout the Intermountain West as a public relations man for the Union Pacific Railroad and his son, Joel L. Priest, Jr., served as reporter, city editor, financial editor and managing editor of *The Tribune* during the nineteen-twenties and thirties before he followed in his father's footsteps to join the Union Pacific's public relations department.

The *Herald* worked overtime to sharpen frictions within the Republican Party over patronage and to pit one faction against another in organizational disputes. Although *The Tribune* claimed that the *Herald* was actually a Kearns organ because of the senator's friendship and business associations with the then owner, Senator Clark of Montana, it is unlikely that anyone else could have reconciled that claim with what the *Herald* printed about Kearns. *The Tribune* wavered between hostility toward the new senator one day and what appeared to be an attempt at reconciliation the next.

On some occasions the *Herald* would support the position of Senator Kearns but only when the senator's stance was so popular with the voters that to have opposed him would have been a disservice to the Democratic Party; or when the issue was between Kearns on the one hand and *The Tribune* and Patrick H. Lannan on the other. In these situations the *Herald* was consistently on the side of Kearns.

The *Deseret News* was the most objective of the newspapers toward Senator Kearns and this, of course, was attributed by rival politicians to his friendship with Lorenzo Snow. Some politically oriented weeklies with short life-spans joined in the fray during this period and for the most part they too were critical of Kearns. One of these was *Truth*, a publication which did not always live up to its name but which did print much provocative and some perceptive political speculation and information.

Several months after Kearns was elected, *Truth* published a behind-the-scenes account of events before the election which had an intriguing ring of plausibility about it.

> The true story of what influences induced Senator Kearns to reach for the senatorial toga is known only to a few. It has never before appeared in print, and hence ought to be read with as much interest as though the incident happened but last week or yesterday.

The article then related that a year earlier Secretary Heath of the Republican National Committee had come to Salt Lake with a group of businessmen high in national Republican circles. The main purpose of the visit was to discuss the formation of a company to build the proposed San Pedro, Los Angeles and Salt Lake Railroad. An incidental development was a meeting with leading Utah Republicans to explore the possibilities of turning Utah, which had been voting Democratic, into a Republican state. The visiting Republican leaders, according to *Truth*, invited local party leaders to a conference. A few appeared but others, for various reasons, by-passed the closed meeting.

The *Truth* article continued:

> Can the Republican Party carry Utah? . . . Nearly every one of the Salt Lakers expressed his doubts, and added that he did not know where the money would come from . . . but there was one man in the crowd — Tom Kearns — who had not yet spoken. . . .

197

'Gentlemen,' he said, 'we can carry Utah and we will. . . . We will elect a Republican Legislature that will have the naming of the next Senator. It is true, it will cost a lot of money for the campaign, but I will bear my share of the burden, and if Utah is not in the Republican column when the returns are in, I will pay the whole cost of the campaign out of my own pocket. As to getting help from the outside, I don't think we need it. Utah ought to, and will, make a handsome contribution to the national campaign fund, which I am sure the gentlemen visiting us will appreciate.'

This kind of talk so electrified the visitors at the meeting that they at once took courage. Immediately after adjournment, Perry Heath and his colleagues, made a pledge, each to the other, that they would do all in their power to have Kearns elected Senator from Utah. . . . [5]

Such a meeting did take place. That such a discussion also took place is certainly plausible. The reaction attributed to Kearns was characteristically Tom Kearns. Following the election of Kearns, the *Herald* and other Democratic publications teemed with charges that the election of the "Silver Senator" from Utah was planned and carried out from Washington by such Republican powers as Mark Hanna and National Committeeman Kerens of Missouri.

All this, of course, does not explain Smoot's withdrawal from the contest and President Snow's undoubted interest in Kearns' candidacy. But by indulging in further speculation seventy years after the event, these loose ends can logically be connected. Smoot was interested in a political career and was therefore likely to be cooperative with national Republican leaders. The leaders of the Mormon Church, far from being political babesin-the-woods, had maintained contacts with important political figures in Washington beginning with Joseph Smith. To seek to exert influence through these contacts in the interest of the Mormon people and Utah would have been nothing less than a duty of leadership. It would be naive to assume that President Snow lacked such contacts. And it is possible that his church and the state might benefit from some political cooperation at this point with Republican leaders who had pledged to do all in their power to elect Kearns.

So the final point of the retrospective speculation is that President Snow might well have had a variety of logical, persuasive and wholly defensible reasons for supporting Kearns. It is probable that Kearns was suggested, either directly or indirectly, to the church president by national leaders of the Republican Party. Most of the Mormons prominent enough to have a valid claim for the seat were polygamists and President Snow had every reason to believe that none of these could be seated if elected. At this time political realism, or expediency, favored a non-Mormon over a prominent Mormon. As a Catholic, Kearns was a member of a church which had stood aloof from the bitter crusade against the Mormons as a people. Up to this point Kearns was certainly not conspicuous as an anti-Mormon. Thus the question of whether Snow supported Kearns can be counterbalanced, if not answered, by another question: Why not?[6]

In late February, 1901, Mrs. Kearns and three Kearns children (Edmond J., Thomas F., and Helen M.) joined the senator in Washington for the inauguration of President McKinley and on March 24 they sailed for the Mediterranean aboard the steamship *Aller*. They almost missed the ship, arriving on the pier in a carriage at a gallop after the gangway had been hoisted to the rail. It was lowered again for the Kearns family and a maid to come aboard. The plan was to join Perry Heath and a party of friends in Naples and then tour the major cities of Europe including the British Isles. However, Mrs. Kearns and the children remained in Lausanne, Switzerland, for several months, a change in plans which might have been prompted by an unpleasant and frightening incident at home. Two letters mailed from a Union Pacific train between Omaha and Ogden and delivered to Frank J. Westcott, private secretary to Senator Kearns, in Salt Lake City demanded $5,000 in $20 bills from Senator Kearns. The letters stated that unless the money was immediately sent to a specified post office box in Schuyler, Nebraska, the writer would kidnap and torture the Kearns children and dynamite the Kearns mansion on Brigham Street. Westcott, without confiding in Mrs. Kearns, mailed copies of the letters to Senator Kearns and turned the originals over to the local postal inspector. A few days later a man named Ernest J. Wolter, a merchant in Schuyler and a former resident of Park City, was arrested as the writer of the kidnap threats. Wolter was indicted but an Omaha judge sustained a demurrer to the indictment on the grounds that there was no such crime under United States law as that alleged in the indictment. The threat naturally created considerable apprehension over the children and prompted some wealthy Salt Lakers to employ guards for awhile.

Kearns returned from Europe early in May, leaving his family in Switzerland for the summer. One reason for his shortened European tour was a projected visit of President McKinley to the West Coast and hopefully to Salt Lake City. Kearns had been working before his departure to induce the President to include Utah in his itinerary.

When the senator arrived in Salt Lake City on May 16 he was interviewed by the local press on his European trip; political patronage, the hottest political subject at that moment; and the projected railroad to Los Angeles. The *Herald*, in its characteristic style when dealing with the Republican senator, started its story with the light and irreverent touch. It described Senator Kearns as "wearing a sawed-off derby hat with the cutest kind of French curl to the brim. But with all his travels and his political elevations," the article continued, "Senator Kearns returned without affectations. He didn't say 'bong sewer' when he met his friends or 'oh rivure' when he left them. It was 'Hello Ed,' and 'How are you, Reed' and 'Good Boy, Hebe,' just as in the days of long ago." The *Herald* quoted him in denial that he was "given a key to the side door of the Vatican" while in Rome and the reporter then apparently posed a question as to the construction of the "hot air railroad" — San Pedro, Los Angeles and Salt Lake. Kearns good humoredly replied, "What's that? Hot air road? Why what's the use of my saying it's going to be built? I've said that all along, and I still say so." [7]

The Tribune played the interview straight, pressing the senator for answers on patronage issues. "That business" (federal appointments), the senator replied, "is not ready for consideration yet." [8]

The original plan for the presidential visit to Utah was for the President and Mrs. McKinley to spend a day of rest at the Kearns home in Salt Lake City. But Mrs. McKinley became ill in San Francisco and a number of planned stops were cancelled. The special train carrying the President and his party stopped for twenty-five minutes in Ogden on a Sunday morning (May 26) and President McKinley was introduced to the delegation on hand to greet the train by Senator Kearns.

The senator spent most of the summer in the controversial and divisive job of distributing federal jobs and attending to his personal business. In September the nation passed through the traumatic experience of a presidential assassination and a succession to the presidency.

The Tribune rushed onto the streets an extra announcing the shooting of President McKinley in Buffalo, N.Y., about 6 p.m., Friday, September 6, 1901. On September 7 the newspaper carried numerous stories on the tragedy, including an interview with Senator Thomas C. Platt of New York in which he was quoted as saying: "This is one instance where I think lynch law justified."[9]

The Tribune headlines on succeeding days were: "President Will Recover, Vice President Roosevelt So Informed;" on September 9, "Holding His Own;" on September 10, "Confident He Will Live;" on September 12, "President Is Better;" on September 13, "President Near Death's Door;" on September 14, "The President Is Dead;" and on September 15, "Roosevelt Takes Oath."

An incidental effect of this national tragedy was to place in the White House a man who had taken a special liking to Utah's Silver Senator and the soon-to-be co-owner of The Tribune. Kearns and his partner, Keith, went to Washington together to attend the presidential funeral. A month later, in Salt Lake City, Lannan and Goodwin announced the sale of The Tribune to an unidentified buyer.

In the issue of October 19 there appeared on the editorial page under the heading "An Announcement," which said in part:

> With this issue of The Salt Lake Tribune, its stock, goodwill, franchises, machinery, plant and all its appurtenances, passes from the control of its former owners into the hands of a new management.
>
> It will take some time to develop to the public the improvements contemplated for making The Tribune even greater and better in the future than it has been in the past. . . . Idle boasts, however, count for nothing. Watch and wait.
>
> The Tribune will be essentially a news-gatherer. If money and effort will avail, both will be enlisted in making its field broader, its limitations without bounds in covering the news field of the entire world. Its watchword will be progress and its step forward.

To Mr. P. H. Lannan, who retired after a service covering a period of many years, it bids God-speed in any new field of endeavor his splendid energies may enlist.

To Judge C. C. Goodwin, who retires as editor, whose trenchant pen has given to *The Tribune* a reputation second to no newspaper in the West, nothing we can say can add luster to a fame so firmly established in the State and community he has served so well.

This portion of the announcement was obviously prepared by the new management. The remainder, written in the style of Goodwin, reflected a mixture of confident self-assertiveness, a note of regret at the bitterness of the conflict in which he had been embroiled, and a defense of *The Tribune's* position. The writer emphasized that no "self-reproaches are mingled with the farewell." But, with subdued eloquence, he made it clear that the job of carrying the fight against certain practices and policies of the Mormon Church had been at times a painful one. His portion of the statement continued:

The foregoing explains itself. The change has come. It is immediate and radical.

The men who have been in control of *The Tribune* for the past nineteen years, in giving up their places are glad to feel that the trust they have held goes into entirely competent hands, which supply full promise that the much-loved journal will advance and fill its place in the front of the progress of this great State.

In the same issue which carried the announcement of the change in *The Tribune* ownership, there appeared a brief editorial comment on the newly sustained President of the Mormon Church, Joseph F. Smith, which also sounded like Goodwin. It said:

> The new head of the Mormon Church has held the trust and affection of the very best men and women among the Latter-day Saints. He was hot-headed and passion-tossed in the old days, but experience has much changed him. Since the pronunciamento of President Woodruff, he has seemed to be the most conservative and sincere of all the high Church officials who have, during the past fifteen years, been oftenest mentioned. Under his sway there promises to be little friction within the Church, and no one ought to know better than he what causes friction between it and the outside world. *The Tribune* has no wish for him or his people except increasing prosperity, progress and tranquility. [10]

The issue of polygamy, which had so long dominated the pages of *The Tribune* and Utah news, wherever published, was quiescent at this time. But it did occasionally erupt in the news.

On November 7, 1901, *The Tribune,* for example headlined a front-page story: "Believes in Polygamy; Apostle Heber J. Grant Declares in Interview That Men Should Be Allowed to Take Additional Wives." The article, carrying a Tacoma, Washington, dateline, said that Grant and two other Mormons had gone to Japan two months earlier to open a church mission there; that they had been holding meetings in Yokohama and Tokyo; and that Grant had: "raised a storm of indignation in the cities named by stating in an interview that we [Mormons] still believe that under certain restrictions honorable men should be allowed to take additional wives with the consent of the first wife." The same article explained that Grant, in response to the indignation expressed in the Japanese press, had printed numerous letters clarifying his interview and emphasizing that "they [Mormons] do not teach polygamy, but will fully respect the laws of Japan." [11]

In the light of the commitment made in the Woodruff "Manifesto," this was hardly a basis for a revival of the anti-polygamy crusade by *The Tribune*. For the newspaper had, all during the bitter controversy, taken the position that the right of anyone to believe in the principle of polygamy was not at issue but that all the church was being asked to do was to abolish the practice as long as it was contrary to the laws of the United States. *The Tribune* did not pursue the Grant interview beyond the news story, at least not at that time. But this period was a lull before a renewed storm over the issue which was raised some two years later by the election of Reed Smoot to the Senate and a challenge raised against his seating.

16

The Silver Queen

THE ONLY public disclosure made as to the new ownership of *The Tribune,* at the time of the announced sale was the appearance of the name of Perry S. Heath in the masthead as publisher and general manager. Just how long the general public was unaware that the owners were Senator Kearns and his partner, David Keith, is difficult to ascertain. The law requiring publication of a sworn statement of ownership and circulation did not become operative until October, 1913. But the Kearns-Keith ownership was disclosed publicly long before that.

Some individuals knew at the time of the transaction that the purchasers were Kearns and Keith and many more suspected it. Within ten days after the announcement of the sale the editor of the Challis, Idaho, *Messenger* published an item identifying Kearns as the purchaser and adding that the new editor, Heath, was "not to be compared" with Mr. Goodwin, "one of the ablest editorial writers in the world." [1]

But a few days later the weekly *Truth,* which prided itself on being an authority on both revealed and unrevealed political information in Salt Lake and Utah, published a special dispatch under an Indianapolis, Indiana, dateline and credited to *The Chicago Tribune* which said in part: "Indiana Republicans say they are convinced Perry Heath bought *The Salt Lake Tribune* in order to pave a way to the United States Senate. . . ." [2]

Obviously the editor of *Truth* believed at that time that Heath was the purchaser, for the stock-in-trade of the publication was disclosure of just such behind-the-scenes happenings. Two weeks after the transaction, the *Deseret News* made a reference to *The Tribune* as "popularly believed to be owned by Senator Kearns." [3]

A version of the transaction handed down in *The Tribune* through the years, is that Kearns had Heath buy the paper on behalf of himself and Keith because Lannan would not under any circumstances sell to him. There are ample indications that Lannan had acquired a strong aversion to Kearns, whose election to the Senate over *The Tribune's* candidate, Salisbury, had rudely compromised the position of *The Tribune* and Lannan as the accepted spokesman for the national Republican Party.

The skimpy corporate records of The Tribune Publishing Company for this period show only that all the stock was sold to William C. MacBride (apparently serving as broker) and that he in turn transferred all the stock to Heath. At a meeting on December 31, 1901, the 300 shares were allocated as follows: Heath, 296; David Keith, 1; C. F. Keith, 1; Frank J. Wescott, who was associated with Kearns and Keith, 1; and Joseph Lippman, 1. Heath was elected president, David Keith, vice president, and Wescott, secretary-treasurer. On January 28, 1902, Heath was officially given the titles of publisher and general manager, positions he retained until 1904 when Lippman was named publisher and general manager. The indicated price paid for the newspaper by Kearns and Keith was about $200,000. This was approximately five times the amount Lannan and Goodwin had paid for it nineteen years earlier.

While Heath was negotiating for and buying *The Tribune* for the Kearns-Keith partnership, Senator Kearns sailed to Europe again to bring his family back home. The highlight of this trip, so far as hometown publicity was concerned, was a dinner given in London in honor of the senator by Sir Thomas Lipton, world-famous king of the tea business and builder and racer of sailing yachts. The dinner was attended by many distinguished members of the British Parliament. The social function was widely reported in the United States press. The *Salt Lake Herald* featured the event with a sketch of the two Toms toasting each other from a bottle labeled "hot air" and a verse by William G. Jackson, one of its talented writers, titled "The Meeting of The Toms."

Sound the tom-tom.
Our Tom
And England's Tom
Are seated beside a buried
Tomahawk
Drinking Tom and Jerry
With the Jerry
Left out.

Says England's Tom
To our Tom
"You're a Tom
After my own heart, Tom."
Says our Tom
To England's Tom:
"And you too, Tom."
And then they both say:
"Here's to you, Tom."

And a lot of English
Reporters
Rush to their offices
And grind out
A lot of tommyrot
About the way
The Anglo-American alliance
Is being cemented
By their Tom
And our Tom. [4]

The *Herald's* cartoon and verse moved the *Intermountain Catholic* to publish a long editorial under the caption: "Tale of Two Dinners." The first dinner was one in New York City attended by business and political leaders. The main point of the editorial was an expression of hope that Roosevelt's foreign policies would be more like McKinley's than Cleveland's. Referring to the London dinner, the editorial said in part:

> Nobody will apprehend the comical side of English austerity with better relish than Senator Kearns, and we may include Sir Thomas Lipton as well. And no persons would laugh heartier than these two Toms, could they have seen the cartoon in Wednesday's *Herald* along with what is written by William G. Jackson to give it effect. . . . [5]

When Senator Kearns returned from Europe he was accompanied by Senator Clark of Montana but not by his family. He told a *Tribune* correspondent in New York that Mrs. Kearns would remain in Geneva, Switzerland, until spring as the children were attending school there.[6] The return of Kearns and Clark together revived press interest in the San Pedro, Los Angeles and Salt Lake railroad. Two months later on January 14, 1902, *The Tribune* carried a Washington dispatch which anticipated the first step toward the eventual absorption of the line by the Union Pacific.

The dispatch said that Senator Clark and E. H. Harriman (who had obtained control of Union Pacific) would adjust their differences in the railroad matter and that the San Pedro company would either purchase or lease for a long period that portion of the Oregon Short Line from Salt Lake City, Utah, to Caliente, Nevada.

Upon his return from Europe, Senator Kearns made a quick trip home to Salt Lake City to take care of personal business and discuss patronage problems besetting him at the time, and then he returned to Washington to plunge into the social and legislative whirl of his first full-fledged session of Congress. His first notable legislative coup was the blocking of a mineral lease covering the Uintah Indian Reservation to a private mining company. Unable to dissuade the Secretary of Interior from approving the lease, Senator Kearns introduced a resolution into the Senate to require the Interior Department to furnish to the Senate all documents relating to the lease before its ratification. With the help of the chairman of the Committee on Indian Affairs, Kearns was able to get the resolution adopted. This stopped the lease and Kearns then disclosed that he planned to introduce legislation to open the reservation to settlement. Such legislation was introduced and passed.

The Tribune, as might be expected, applauded the senator for his maneuver to stop the proposed leasing. But so did the Democratic *Herald.* The *Deseret News* conferred its commendation on all three members of the Utah congressional delegation — Kearns, Senator Rawlins and Representative Sutherland. The weekly press of the state generally credited Kearns with thwarting the leasing scheme.

"Senators Kearns" said the *Lehi Banner,* "is all right. He got in his resolution just in time. . . . Tom always gets his licks in at the proper time. Utah made no mistake in sending him to the U.S. Senate." [7]

Another typical comment on the incident appeared in the *Castle Dale Progress.* It lauded the senator's action and added: "And, by the way, the manner in which Senator Kearns is conducting the affairs of Utah at the national capital is agreeably surprising. . . ." [8]

Clearly, this was a case in which public sentiment was so nearly unanimous that political foes felt impelled to give Senator Kearns a pat on the back.

Both in Europe and in Washington, the new Utah senator quickly erased the image given him by political foes during the campaign — that he was a graceless, hard-rock miner who did not know how to wear a dress suit. At the annual charity ball in the Willard Hotel in Washington, the *Washington Star* singled out as a notable group Senator Kearns' party, which included Mrs. Kerens of St. Louis, Mrs. Perry Heath and Mrs. S. B. E. Holmes of Salt Lake City.

The society reporter identified Mrs. Holmes as a "handsome brunette, the wife of a multi-millionaire of Utah."[9] She was that. She was also a millionaire in her own right when she married Colonel Edwin F. Holmes, a Michigan lumberman who had acquired some mining interests in Utah. Susie, as she was always known to close friends; Utah's "Silver Queen," as she was known to society writers covering the equivalent of the present-day international jet set; or Mrs. Susanna Bransford Emery Holmes Delitch Engalitcheff, her full name when she died in 1942, epitomized an era of quick fortunes and expansive living covering the "gay nineties" and the early nineteen hundreds. A member of a Missouri family impoverished by the Civil War, she made the long trip from the Midwest to the California gold country in a 250-wagon train commanded by her father. While spending a summer visiting with relatives in Park City, she met and married A. B. Emery, who at the time was a railroad baggageman and secretary of several mining companies earning a very impressive income of $250 per month. He mentioned one evening to his young bride that if only he had a little money they could become wealthy. Susie thought she knew how to get the needed money. She went to R. C. Chambers, the wealthy manager of the Ontario mine, reminded him that her father had once grubstaked him and negotiated a loan. Emery used the capital to become a partner with the Kearns-Keith group in the Silver King discovery and was soon thereafter the owner of stock valued at more than a million dollars. He died in San Francisco in 1894 while en route from a trip to Honolulu, leaving a young, attractive and, for that period, a very wealthy widow. Susie did not have long to wait until she found herself in court fighting to retain her inheritance. Chambers sued for half her interest on the grounds that the money he had provided was a grubstake. Susie was able to prove to the court's satisfaction, with checks showing interest payments, that the money advanced was a loan and not a grubstake. She won in the trial court and the decision was upheld on appeal.

One day Susie accepted an invitation from Tom Kearns to drive to Park City and meet a widower "worth about seven million dollars." The widower, Colonel Holmes, began courting her and proposed several times. Unable to get a definite answer, the colonel gave a dinner at Delmonico's in New York City for a group of Utah friends, including Susie and Governor Wells. During the dinner Colonel Holmes suddenly plucked an American Beauty rose from a huge bouquet, tossed it on the table, arose and announced their engagement. Susie had not been forewarned, but after thinking it over she decided she needed a husband and protector and decided to let the engagement stand. They were married in the Astor Parlors of the Waldorf-Astoria Hotel. The wedding dinner was supervised by Oscar of the Waldorf. After a few weeks residence at the Plaza Hotel, the couple went on a two-year tour of Europe.

The "Silver Queen" recalled a short time before her death that it was "wonderful" trip but that she was bored by her husband's passion for art galleries. Once, when her husband asked a guide in a Moscow art gallery how long it would take to complete the tour, Susie tartly remarked "about three years at this pace."

Upon their return to Salt Lake City Colonel Holmes heard that the Amelia Palace, the home built by Brigham Young for entertaining guests, was for sale. He promptly purchased it for Susie, and brought a crew of twenty decorators from Marshall-Field's in Chicago to decorate it. The decorators did such a magnificent job on the gold-leaf dining room walls that even the colonel decided it would be inappropriate to cover them with paintings and so built an art gallery in a building adjacent to the house. After a sumptuous reception and housewarming, Susie went to Washington where she attended the charity ball as a member of Senator Kearns' party and was an honor guest at numerous receptions, the hostess at one being Mrs. Mark Hanna. She was introduced by Senator Kearns to President Roosevelt who thanked her for a generous campaign contribution, particularly since she was a southern Democrat by inheritance. She returned home in response to a letter from Colonel Holmes informing her that he was going to close the home unless she did return immediately. Thereater, for almost twenty years, Amelia Palace was Salt Lake City's social center except for periods when the hosts were in Europe or Washington or New York or the Orient.

Friday was at-home day for the "Silver Queen" and as many as 300 to 400 people would call during the afternoon and evening. The guest list for the largest single party given in the home was approximately 800.

Amelia Palace was subsequently sold back to the Mormon Church and torn down to make way for a new Federal Reserve Branch Bank building. Colonel Holmes then bought Susie a mansion, El Roble, in Pasadena, California.

The colonel died in 1927 while Mrs. Holmes was on another European tour. She did not return for the funeral.

"It was better that way," she said years later. "His first family could bury him without interference, and that's the way he wanted it. He left his money to three daughters and a son. And that's the way I wanted it too."

Mrs. Holmes married a Serbian physician, Dr. Radovan Nedelkov Delitch, in 1930 and divorced him two years later. Soon after the divorce he hanged himself aboard an ocean liner and was buried at sea. In 1933 she married Prince Nicholas Engalitcheff, known to his associates as the "melancholy Slav," and he died in 1935.

213

The "Silver Queen's" reign ended in death on August 3, 1942. That she enjoyed her title, and role as a romantic symbol of the West's early mining boom days, was obvious. In her later years she lamented, with sorrow but not bitterness, the passing of an era, "when rich people could live like they wanted to live, and could afford to live, without fear of offending the proletariat." But that she could also view it all with an impish sense of humor was signified by one of the grand parties she liked to recall — a party in Honolulu for "three crowned heads, the tin king from South America, the lobster king from San Francisco and the silver queen from Utah." [10]

While Utah did not have many millionaires at the turn of the century, it had perhaps twice as many in relation to total population as the nation as a whole, principally because of the mining industry. The *New York World* undertook in the 1902 edition of its almanac and encyclopedia to list all the persons in the United States owning wealth in excess of a million dollars. Of the list of 3,600, nineteen were credited to Utah. In addition to the "Silver Queen," Senator Kearns and David Keith, the Utahns listed were S. H. Auerbach, A. G. Campbell, R. C. Chambers estate, Albert F. Holden, W. S. McCornick, A. W. McCune, Henry Newell, Samuel Newhouse, John Q. Packard, Joseph R. Walker estate, Matthew H. Walker, Thomas Weir and Brigham Young estate, all of Salt Lake City; Fred J. Kiesel, David Eccles and the D. H. Peery estate, Ogden. The *Herald* noted that probably a dozen more could be added to the list but did not identify them. [11]

Early in 1902 while Senator Kearns was busy in Washington looking after the state's legislative interests and working to get his choices appointed to federal positions, the *Deseret News* "scooped" *The Tribune* with the announcement of plans to launch a new newspaper in the city. The *News* reported:

> Within the next ten days or two weeks this city is
> going to have another newspaper. It will in reality

214

be an evening edition of *The Tribune* and will be called the *Telegram* to distinguish it from the morning issue.

When Senator Kearns and associates bought *The Tribune* a few weeks ago, they also came into the possession of the one unused Associated Press franchise which P. H. Lannan held under option and ever since that time there has been more or less talk of starting the evening paper. The venture is now undertaken to save the franchise which either has to be taken up or forfeited. . . . William M. Butler of Cincinnati is to be president and general manager and D. Elliott Kelley of Philadelphia, managing editor. [12]

The first edition of the new newspaper appeared January 30, 1902. In reply to the *News* reference to it as the evening edition of *The Tribune,* the *Telegram* retorted that it was "the evening edition of *The Tribune* in the same sense the *Herald* was the morning edition of the *News* — no more and no less." [13]

In choosing this device to declare its independence of *The Tribune,* the *Telegram* pointed up that any inference that the *Herald* was a weak sister to the *News* was far from true. The chief, if not the sole, owner at the time was Senator Clark of Montana. During its life (from June 5, 1870, to its merger with the *Inter-Mountain Republican* to form the *Herald-Republican* in August, 1909) the *Herald* passed through numerous ownerships. Generally, it defended the Mormon Church and its leaders, but it sometimes expressed disagreement with particular actions or policies. The *Park Record,* to cite one example, reported on May 16, 1896, that "B. H. Roberts has resigned as editor of the *Salt Lake Herald,* giving as his reason that the position that the paper had taken on the recent 'Manifesto,' was apt to place him in a false light." [14] While at times it sounded, as *The Tribune* put

.c, like "the minor voice of the church" it certainly did not always adopt *Deseret News* positions. It was a well-written and competently edited newspaper which was at its journalistic best when defending the Democratic Party or attacking *The Tribune*. It was, in short, a tough competitor, and the fact that it was *The Tribune* and not the *Herald* that survived was a testimonial to the strength and staying powers of *The Tribune* and its owners.

17

Polygamy Issue Revived

UTAH'S FIRST election with Senator Thomas Kearns in the Senate and in control of two newspapers — *The Tribune* and the new evening *Salt Lake Telegram* — involved only two public officials and the membership of the Legislature. It was politically important chiefly because the new Legislature would select a United States senator to serve with Kearns.

Before plunging into his first campaign as titular leader of his party, Senator Kearns embarked on his third trip to Europe to bring his family home. In London he and Mrs. Kearns were entertained a second time by Sir Thomas Lipton, this time at a dinner aboard his yacht, *Erin*. This social event prompted the *Baltimore Herald* to editorialize:

> After the wining and dining [aboard the Erin] the Senator and his wife went ashore and the former unbosomed himself to a representative of the Associated Press. Sir Thomas will contest for the Challenge Cup this year and President Roosevelt will be nominated and elected in 1904. Fifteen years ago Sir Oracle Kearns was manipulating a pick in the mines. He struck it rich and now he is a millionaire — the idol of the Republicans, the Mormons and the Roman Catholics of Utah. 'Queer combination,' someone remarked. Yes, but it was a

winning combination two years ago and landed the ex-pickist in the United States Senate. However, Kearns is said to be a splendid fellow and out in Utah they swear by him. He is a free liver and a free giver, with just enough religion to stand in with the churches and just enough sinner to stand well with the politicians. Sir Thomas Lipton is of the same order of humanity, only he is more of a sport than Kearns of Utah who came to America from Ireland via Canada [true of his parents but not of Tom Kearns]. Lipton was born in a poverty-stricken district on the coast of Ireland and had a tough struggle in early boyhood himself. He landed in South Carolina, worked for $10 a month for a time and then had sense enough to break away. He is a many-times millionaire now, a baronet by the grace of God and King Edward and yachting is his fad. There is plenty of romance in the lives of those two men — the one an American Senator and the other a chum of the King of England.[1]

When Senator Kearns and his family returned home in the early fall the political pot was boiling furiously and the fumes were swirling around the name of Kearns for supporting Reed Smoot for the Senate seat and, on the other hand, for not supporting him. Those who said he was supporting Smoot offered the charge as proof of the existence of a Mormon-Kearns machine which had set out to control the state. Those who said he was not supporting Smoot offered it as proof that he was a double-crosser and ingrate, inasmuch as Smoot had withdrawn from the Senate contest two years earlier in Kearns' favor.

Former Congressman William H. King, and other Democratic campaign orators, were warning the voters to beware of the "thirst for power of that syndicate known as the Silver King

E. L. T. Harrison, co-founder of *The Tribune*.

Edward W. Tullidge, historian and one of the founders of *The Tribune*.

Henry W. Lawrence, wealthy merchant and financial backer of *The Tribune*.

William S. Godbe's home in the 1880's.

William S. Godbe, schismatic elder, first publisher and financial backer of *The Tribune*.

Brigham Young, President of Mormon Church and chief target of *The Tribune* until his death in 1877.

George Q. Cannon, regarded by *The Tribune* as the strongest personality in the Mormon Church after Brigham Young's death.

Wilford Woodruff, fourth president of the Mormon Church (1889-1898) who issued "Manifesto" on polygamy.

C. C. Goodwin, *The Tribune*'s most famous and widely quoted editor.

Charles W. Penrose, editor of *Deseret News* and Goodwin's editorial adversary.

Frank J. Cannon, dissident Mormon who became *The Tribune's* editorial writer in the early 1900's.

Frederic Lockley, editor of *The Tribune* during 1870's.

Colonel William Nelson, editor of *The Trib-une* from early 1900's until his death in 1913.

Ambrose N. McKay, general manager of *The Trib-une* from 1911 until his death in 1924.

Senator Thomas Kearns, onetime prospector and mining mogul, became co-owner of *The Tribune* in 1901 and directed its policy until his death in 1918.

David Keith, co-owner of *The Tribune* and business partner of Senator Kearns.

Senator W. A. Clark of Montana, business associate of Senator Kearns.

Utah's Silver Queen, Mrs. Susanna Bransford Emery Holmes Delitch Engalitcheff.

Joseph F. Smith, sixth president of the Mormon Church (1901-1918), withdrew badly needed Mormon support from Senator Kearns in the 1904 election.

Lorenzo Snow, fifth president of Mormon Church who supported Kearns for senate seat.

Senator Reed Smoot, who wrested control of Republican Party from Senator Kearns.

Heber J. Grant, Mormon president who advanced the Mormon-Gentile accommodation.

Anthony W. Ivins, Mormon Church leader and a *Tribune* favorite.

J. F. Fitzpatrick, *The Tribune* publisher 1924-1960.

Gus P. Backman, friend and confidante of President McKay and J. F. Fitzpatrick.

David O. McKay, Mormon Church president when Newspaper Agency Corporation was formed.

J. F. Fitzpatrick, viewing two of his loves — *The Tribune* and Salt Lake City, from his office in Kearns Building.

John W. Gallivan, who became *The Tribune* publisher in 1960.

G. B. (Bert) Heal, a *Tribune* editor from 1927 to 1951.

Arthur C. Deck, executive editor, and Publisher J. F. Fitzpatrick in 1956.

A cartoonist's impression of two political adversaries by Alan L. Lovey of *The Salt Lake Herald*.

WITH MIGHT AND MAIN HE TUGS IN VAIN.

One of a dozen of **Charles V. Worthington's** *Tribune* cartoons which James H. Moyle, the **shoe** clerk here, blamed for his defeat by Heber M. Wells, seated, in the 1900 campaign for governor.

THE BIG MIT OF UTAH G. O. P.—No. 2

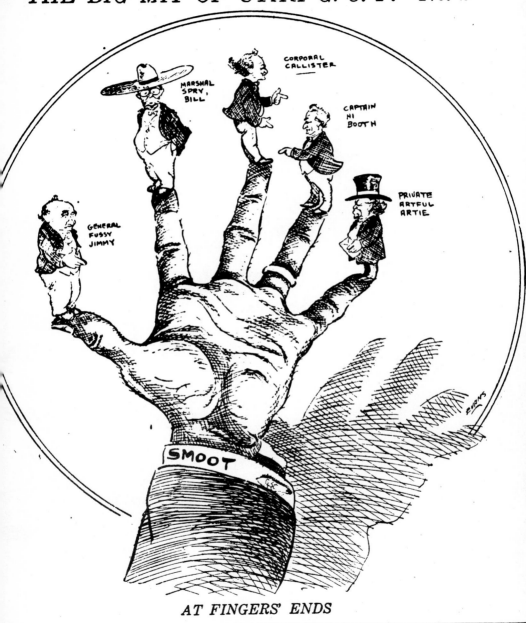

AT FINGERS' ENDS

Key figures in Senator Smoot's "Federal Bunch", reading from thumb to little finger; James H. Anderson, Republican state chairman; William Spry, who later became governor; Edward H. Callister, collector of internal revenue; Hiram E. Booth, United States district attorney; Arthur L. Thomas, Salt Lake City postmaster.

SALT LAKE DAILY TRIBUNE

AND

UTAH MINING GAZETTE.

VOL. I.   SALT LAKE CITY, U. T., SATURDAY MORNING, APRIL 15, 1871.   **NO**

Front page of the *Daily Tribune's* first issue.

" Praise God From Whom All Blessings Flow "

The Salt Lake Tribune.

SALT LAKE CITY, UTAH, WEDNESDAY MORNING, NOVEMBER 8, 1905.

WEATHER TODAY—Fair

TWELVE PAGES—FIVE CENTS

LXXII., NO. 25.

ALT LAKE IS AN AMERICAN CITY!

The orning rs Sang gether d the Sons God out for Joy."

I GO TO SPREAD GLAD TIDINGS

"This is the Victory that Over cometh the World. Even Our Faith."

REAT LANDSLIDE OCCURS

Salt Lake–American Party Owns the Earth

the city election yesterday the American party took all in sight. Ezra Thompson and the entire American ticket has elected by a plurality of seven hundred. It is a glorious victory. It is a triumph of right. It is a victory for the rican home. It sounds the death knell of church domination in Salt Lake and in Utah. It means a greater Salt Lake, a er Utah. It says to the people of the United States that the people of Salt Lake do not indorse, nor condone the acts e hierarch and his band of 26 in their open and defiant defiance of the laws of both God and man. It means the ment of the Apostolic Senator, Reed Smoot, from the Senate of the United States. It is magnificent, and The Tribune ds congratulations to the grand army of men and women in Salt Lake who so nobly stood by the American party in attle of Tuesday. The new Council will stand—eight Gentiles, seven churchmen.

he Councilmen elected yesterday are: First ward, Martin and Crabtree, Americans; Second ward, O'Donnell and Carter, ricans, Fifth ward, Black and Mulvey, Americans; six in all. Third ward, Holley and Fernstrom, Church; Fourth , Hartenstein and Tuddenham, Church. The holdovers are Davis and Hobday, Gentile Republicans; Preece, Mormon blican; Wells and Barnes, Mormon Democrats.

The Tribune's most exuberant front page hailing an American Party victory in 1905.

The Salt Lake Tribune

Salt Lake City, Utah — Monday Morning, July 2, 1956 — Copyright 1956, Kearns-Tribune Corporation

Price Five Cents

28 Perish in Crashes

United Air Lines Wreckage

Tail Section

TWA Wreckage

Wreckage Dots Wall of Canyon

By Robert F. Alkire
Tribune Staff Writer

CEDAR CITY, July 1 — I have just come from the scene of the world's worst commercial air disaster.

There isn't much left.

Bits of torn metal and blackened fire burned areas mark only trace of two giant airliners — A DC7 owned by United lines and a TWA Super Constellation — that Saturday sent 128 persons to death.

The Most Rugged in the World

The site of the crashes is about 22 miles northeast of Grand Canyon, Ariz.

Men who live and work in this country call it "the most rugged in the world."

Near the confluence of the Little Colorado and Colorado Rivers in the canyon, there is a 3,000-foot bluff...

Brothers Report

Fading Rays Of Sun Light Crash Debris

By Robert F. Alkire
Tribune Staff Writer

CEDAR CITY, July 1 — "Everything is wreckage" and "there are certainly no survivors."

That is the way two brothers who discovered the wreckages described the scene.

Palen Haldgin, 25, and Henry Haldgin, 23, operators of Grand Canyon Airlines airport, about 23 miles southwest of the scene came upon the wreckages last Sunday about 3:00 p.m., just as the last rays of the sun were resting the canyon.

Just One Pass

They last time flew just one pass through they saw what seemed to be wreckage as they were able to identify only one — the DC7 — plastered against a 2,000-foot knoll where the Colorado River at the confluence with the Little Colorado.

First reports Saturday were that one was the Constellation. After the one sight, they climbed out to blaze a trail a few miles south of the canyon rim and reported their find.

Darkness Closes

By then darkness had closed in and further identification was impossible.

The brothers at first suspected something Saturday evening. On a scenic flight they noted smoke rising from the canyon floor but attributed it to a lightning strike from Friday's thunderstorms over the region. While eating dinner, they heard news of the disaster.

See Page 4, Column 3

Elm Flattens Car, Kills 7 in Canada

By Associated Press

KESWICK, ONT., July 1 — A giant elm tree, uprooted by storm winds, flattened a car filled with homeward bound holidayers Sunday night and crushed the seven persons inside to death.

The freak accident wiped out the family of Stanley Joseph Gloster, 29, Toronto, and three in laws. They were on their way home from a Dominion Day outing at a friend's cottage on Lake Simcoe, 50 miles north of Toronto.

The dead include Gloster; his wife, Alice, 26; their two sons, Allen, 4, and Donald, 18...

Smashing Winds Flay Eastern U.S.

By Associated Press

Violent winds Sunday flayed the upper part of the nation from the midwest to upstate New York.

Farm buildings were smashed. Power and communications lines torn down. In the midwest, scores of flat roofers and a new-tooled monument were suddenly torn apart.

In the midwest at least the trouble was from...

Thunderstorms rolled in the cooler air.

Chicago had its hottest day of the year and the temperature soared to a sports event...

Incredible Sight

'Copter Crew Finds Crash Bodies Piled

Special to The Tribune

CEDAR CITY, July 1 — A helicopter crew Sunday became the first to reach the TWA Super Constellation, one of two giant airliners that collided in the rugged area.

Page 3, J. Pleas, Lees Air Force Base said by telephone all reaching the scene.

White TWA Found

The first thing I saw was a bit of white metal, he said. "Then we came to the burned area . . . then the big red marker 8 feet wide . . . The biggest part of the plane I saw was a portion of the fuselage which remained windows. He continued. "The bits and pieces were all in the vicinity of the burn."

"Then we saw the bodies. We all worked by them. They are burned and mangled so bad it was hard to recognize them. They seemed to be piled on each other as if the plane had hit in a nose dive."

Rest Underneath

"We reported only 13, but we are sure the rest are underneath."

"I saw safety belts, shoes, children's clothing, lots of black, in steel metal. It was the worst sight I have ever seen."

Capt. Pleas said if weather and landing conditions permit, it is planned to send doctors, the Coconino, Ariz., County coroner, airline officials, the CAA and CAB investigators to the scene on the first trips Monday.

A supply of tarpaulins, blankets and other equipment has been assembled and is ready for use in shuttling the dead from canyon depths to the Grand Canyon Airport by helicopter, Capt. Ryan added.

Steel Strike Sparks Plea For Mediator

Seeks Way To End Dispute

By A.R. Raskin
New York Times Writer

NEW YORK, July 1 — Federal mediators moved swiftly Sunday in an attempt to settle the steel strike.

Purge is Starting'

Reds Tighten Poznan Trap On Bread, Freedom Rebels

By Associated Press

BERLIN, July 1 — Two Polish armored divisions and thousands of police waged a grim house-to-house hunt for hidden leaders in the battered city of Poznan Sunday after crushing a two-day revolt for bread and freedom.

The smouldering city Sunday morning said troops and police had sealed off the big industrial center of 361,000 and started the dragnet operation after finally crushing armed resistance.

Some witnesses estimated the savage street fighting that ended Saturday took at least 200 persons...

Featuring a striking photograph of the crash scene, Tribune ... worst commercial airline disaster. Reporters and photograph-

Grand Canyon crash coverage won *The Tribune* its Pulitzer Prize.

Park City during the 1880s: a mining center, source of silver fortunes and rugged individualists like Thomas Kearns and David Keith.

Main Street, Salt Lake City, as it was at the end of *The Tribune's* first decade.

A section of the city showing *The Tribune* home in 1880s. It was at 22-26 W. 2nd South.

The fifth *Tribune* home at 80 W. 2nd South.

Mrs. Jennie Judge Kearns, widow of Senator Thomas Kearns and principal owner of *The Tribune* after his death.

The mansion of Senator Kearns soon after it was completed in 1903. It was governors' mansion from 1937 to 1956 and is now home for the Utah State Historical Society.

Tribune Building, Main Street, home of *The Tribune* since 1937.

In 1906, the city room of the *Salt Lake Telegram* was headquarters for W. B. Griffin, city editor, at far left; W. E. Traughber, managing editor, next, then W. E. Farr, Percy Cropper, Gordon Place, Elliott Kelly, B. G. Hite, Robert Cochrane, and two unidentified copy boys.

E. A. Vandeventer, second from left, was managing editor of the *Salt Lake Telegram* in this 1930s look in the editorial room when *The Tribune's* sister paper was located at 145 S. Main.

Early *Tribune* community service included mapping roads in Intermountain Area using the Pathfinder automobile shown here in 1910.

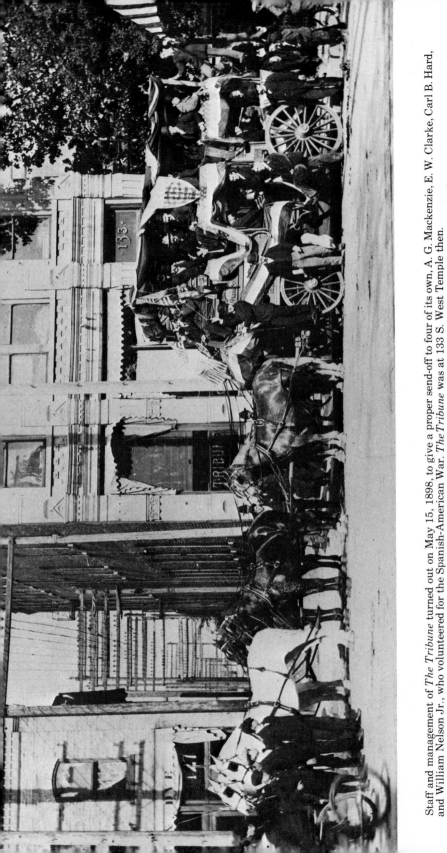

Staff and management of *The Tribune* turned out on May 15, 1898, to give a proper send-off to four of its own, A. G. Mackenzie, E. W. Clarke, Carl B. Hard, and William Nelson Jr., who volunteered for the Spanish-American War. *The Tribune* was at 133 S. West Temple then.

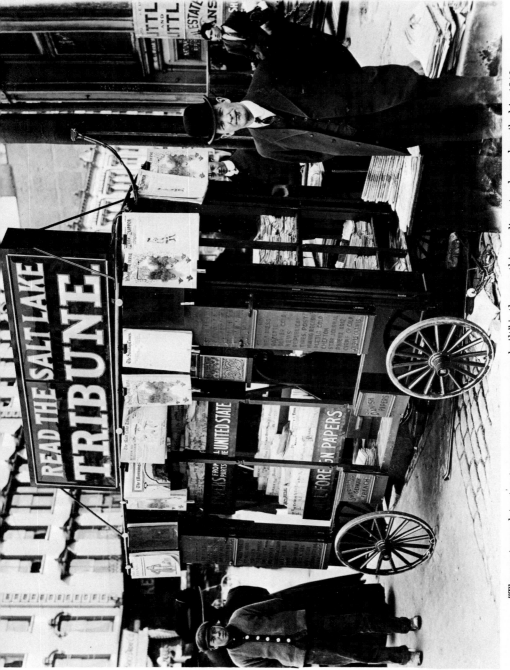

"The most complete street newspaper wagon ever built" is the way this vending stand was described in 1910.

The Tribune in 1906 was the 100th newspaper in America, and the first in the West to install Linotype machines.

Two of these Goss perfecting presses printed *The Tribune* in 1903.

Original Salt Palace interior featured delicate statuary in balcony area. Notice names of states in ceiling panels.

This is lower level of first Salt Palace which opened at 9th South and Main Street on August 21, 1899, at a cost of $60,000. Two-story frame building was destroyed by fire Aug. 29, 1910.

Salt Palace was gathering place for athletes, actors and musicians just as new Salt Palace.

Tribune actively campaigned in favor of bond issue to help finance new Salt Palace for downtown Salt Lake City.

The 14,000-seat arena of new Palace is site of rodeos, concerts, hockey matches, conventions, exhibitions, shows and basketball games.

Major community service program annually for *Tribune* is its Old Fashioned Fourth of July celebration at Lagoon. Thousands relive "good old days" at patriotic observance.

Centerpiece of Salt Lake City's downtown Christmas decorations annually since 1945 has been *The Tribune* Christmas Tree located on Main Street in front of The Tribune Building.

Long an advocate of preserving the environment, *The Tribune* started its Christmas Tree Grove in 1960. Youngsters plant 200 spruce seedlings annually on Arbor Day at the grove.

crowd which was seeking to steal the Mormon church for the benefit of the Republican machine." [2]

Out of the welter of charges and counter-charges, the speculations and exaggerations spewed out by the campaign orators and press there emerged a very blurred picture of the political alignments then existent. It would have been difficult to have separated fact from fiction at the time, and it is even more difficult retrospectively with all the participants dead. A few conclusions regarding Kearns which appeared to be supportable are: that he did, as he said he would, refrain from active support of particular Republican candidates; that he did seek to keep the Republican state convention in the control of his supporters; that if he actively opposed a particular candidate for the Senate it was Congressman Sutherland; that he did have misgivings about the election to the Senate of Smoot because of his position as an apostle of the Mormon Church; that he had genuine doubts that Smoot would be seated if elected.

His doubts that Smoot would be seated if elected originated from a high source within the Republican Party — President Theodore Roosevelt. Kearns had reportedly told Apostle John Henry Smith that Smoot would be turned down by the administration, inasmuch as it was feared that the election of an apostle would have an adverse effect on Roosevelt's re-election. This was publicly verified when Kearns issued this announcement: "This afternoon President Roosevelt requested me to state in the manner I am now stating it, that he very much hoped that no apostle would be elected, and that he desired to be placed on record as kindly but firmly advising against the election of any apostle to the United States Senatorship. . . ." [3]

The Smoot supporters, naturally, interpreted this as a Kearns' attack on Smoot. But Kearns insisted that he had nothing to do with the announcement except to make it public at the request of President Roosevelt. Inasmuch as no denial came from

219

the White House, it is to be assumed that Kearns was speaking at the request of and for Roosevelt.

That the President's position was dictated by a desire to avoid "Utah problem" political repercussions, such as had dogged presidents for half a century, rather than any personal aversion to Smoot was indicated by the fact that Roosevelt did support the seating of Smoot after he was elected.

Despite the political brawl then building up in the state, Senator Kearns, on the surface, appeared to be in the driver's seat. He was, as incumbent senator, the generally recognized head of the Republican Party in Utah; he had close ties with President Roosevelt, as well as with other national party leaders; he was probably the most liberal contributor to the party in Utah; he controlled the journalistic mouthpiece of the party, *The Tribune*, and a new afternoon newspaper; he had been commended by Democratic organs for legislative accomplishments, particularly with respect to mining laws and Indian reservation lands; and he had succeeded in placing supporters in several politically important federal positions (although they later showed up as cogs in the "Smoot Machine").

But things were not so rosy for the senator as they seemed. With the death of President Snow, he had lost his most useful contact with the Mormon Church. And he might well have suspected by this time, as subsequent events disclosed, that he was *persona non grata* with the new president of the church, Joseph F. Smith. He had had some disagreements with Representative Sutherland over appointments and the normal and inevitable intra-party feuding over patronage was becoming abnormally bitter. Although credited by his opponents with "controlling" the entire daily press of Salt Lake City, he had a "bad press," in almost all the weeklies and several national publications. He was under constant attack from the *Herald*, which was ably performing its function as a Democratic organ. The *Deseret News*, which was concentrating more on fighting sin at the local level than in the state and national-level political brawling, was more often critical than complimentary. And two weekly publications were battering the senator with crusading zeal.

One of the weeklies — *Goodwin's Weekly* — was edited by the prestigious former editor of *The Tribune*, C. C. Goodwin. He later became reconciled with Kearns and wrote voluminously in the *Salt Lake Telegram*. But he never again quite reached the journalistic heights he had reached on *The Tribune*.

During the campaign Goodwin insisted that Kearns controlled not only *The Tribune* and *Telegram* but the *Herald* as well. As proof of Kearns' control, if not outright ownership of the *Herald*, Goodwin frequently pointed to the fact that the *Herald* did not rally to Sutherland's defense when he clashed with Kearns. It did not seem to occur to Goodwin that the most obvious assumption a reader could reach was that the *Herald*, as a Democratic spokesman, was more interested at that time in cutting down Republican Sutherland, a candidate for the Senate, than Republican Kearns, whose term would not expire for two more years.

The other weekly, *Truth*, published by John W. Hughes, went a few steps farther in attributing a journalistic monopoly to Kearns:

> Soon after Kearns was elected Senator, he obtained control of the entire daily press of Salt Lake City and Ogden and later, with probably one or two exceptions, had the entire country press manufacturing public opinion in his favor. . . . [4]

Scrapbooks of newspaper clippings compiled in Senator Kearns' office show that *Truth* strayed far from its name in stating that the country press, with one or two exceptions, were manufacturing public opinion in favor of Kearns. Many of the weekly papers bitterly attacked him and many reprinted *Truth's* own attacks on him. And a perusal of the columns of the *Herald* and the *Deseret News* during Kearns' incumbency in the Senate suggests that if he did control them, he had some unbelievably strange ideas about the exercise of such control.

If one assumes that the public read political news and editorials with discrimination, it can also be assumed that the effectiveness of the journalistic attacks on the senator was diminished by the excesses and inconsistencies of the attackers. For in many instances they sought to portray him simultaneously as an unlettered ignoramus and a Machiavellian genius. And the incongruous images were not reflected in different publications, but frequently by the same publication on the same day in the same editorial.

Following a tack suggested previously, various newspapers outside Utah concluded that the election of a Catholic senator by a state which was overwhelmingly Mormon meant a political alliance between the two churches. Among the publications which made this assumption was the *Portland Oregonian* and it promptly drew this rebuke from the *Intermountain Catholic:*

> They may have some conscientious reporters upon the *Portland Oregonian* but the one they assigned to write up Utah and its political conditions is not one of them. For a newspaper with so much pretensions as the *Oregonian,* aiming to achieve a national reputation, one would naturally suppose that its information might be regarded as reliable. It may be in some features, but whenever it treats upon Catholic matters its comments have always exhibited the bile of a bigot.

Writing from Salt Lake, this correspondent of the *Oregonian* starts off by saying that Utah politics are a queer jumble. No intelligent observer of events in Utah will dispute that assertion. Endeavoring to analyze this 'queer jumble' he discovers a political alliance between the Catholic church in Utah and the Mormon church. He reasons out such an alliance because in a state where 70 per cent of the people are Mormons, Thomas Kearns, a practicing Catholic, was elected United States senator. Thomas Kearns, also, according to the correspondent, carries a large Catholic vote with him, and has things pretty much his way throughout the state. . . .

A more ingenuous way to pervert fact could scarcely be conceived by other than an evangelical preacher, and it is probably from this source the *Oregonian's* correspondent derived his information . . . we cannot allow such a falsehood about Catholics in Utah to go abroad without rebuke. [5]

Senator Kearns could, of course, dictate content and policies of *The Tribune* and *Telegram* to whatever degree he desired, as the dominant member of the owning partnership. But he soon learned, if he did not know beforehand, that ownership of a newspaper is not an unmixed blessing for a politician. Every *Tribune* or *Telegram* news story relating to the senator's activities in Washington; every editorial pointing out his aims or his accomplishments, provided a fresh target for the opposition press.

The Tribune, which was evaluated by such an unsympathetic critic as the historian B. H. Roberts as "the most commanding and powerful newspaper of the Intermountain West, capable of influencing and molding public opinion as to things anti

'Mormon,' " could do much for those political figures it chose to support.[6] But its praise, when directed toward an owner, was a dagger pointed inward which opponents could thrust with cries of self-adulation and sycophancy. Surely, there must have been times when Senator Kearns wondered if he were not better off with a *Tribune* owned by Lannan and Goodwin attacking, than with a *Tribune* owned by himself defending.

The campaign produced some wildly inaccurate political judgments on the part of the press. But the first prize in this category must be awarded to the Democratic *Herald.* Commenting editorially on Smoot's candidacy for the Senate, the newspaper said:

> He [Smoot] is mistaken if he supposes that the people of Utah are ready to see the power of an Apostle and a United States Senator united in one man's control. . . .
>
> The idea of uniting two such dissimilar positions is as incongruous as would be the thought of sending a Cardinal of the Church of Rome to the Senate or nominating a Methodist Bishop for the vice-presidency. . . .
>
> Concede the impossible, and suppose Smoot were elected and sent to the Senate, what would be the attitude of the other members toward him?
>
> Right or wrong, would not the outside world believe the Apostle's Church had verified the oft-repeated charge of its enemies and consolidated church and state in Utah?
>
> Could any amount of denial convince Utah's friends in the Senate and House that she had kept faith with those who gave her statehood?
>
> The questions answer themselves. . . .[7]

Whatever the philosophical merits of the *Herald's* position and its presentation of the same — and it was a position which *The Tribune* had espoused for many years and which Senator Kearns held at the time — the "impossible" which the *Herald* did not really mean to concede, did come to pass. The Republicans elected Joseph Howell to the House of Representatives to succeed Sutherland, who was looking forward to the next Senate vacancy and did not run for reelection; and elected Smoot to the Senate on the first ballot. He was seated, after a long fight, and remained there for thirty years, an annoyance no doubt to many Democrats but hardly a "humiliation" to the state.

In the ensuing four years, however, the election of Smoot did generate repercussions nationally and locally. It revived the polygamy issue, which had been slumbering for more than ten years; it contributed to a revival, at the local level, of the old Liberal Party under the name of the American Party; it, in short, fired up the old "irrepressible conflict" all over again. And *The Tribune* soon became the focus of one side of the conflict, as it had always been in the past.

Within a week after Smoot's election a protest against his seating was formally initiated by eighteen Salt Lake City residents. Among the signers of the protest were William Paden, pastor of the First Presbyterian Church; E. B. Critchlow, member of a prominent law firm; P. L. Williams, a lawyer and apostate Mormon who had become bitterly anti-Mormon; and C. C. Goodwin, former editor of *The Tribune* who at this time was publisher and editor of *Goodwin's Weekly*. Briefly summarized, the allegations offered in support of the protest were that the president and apostles of the church were, under the doctrine of the church, supreme in all things temporal and spiritual; that they were supreme in the exercise and transmission of the mandates of this authority; that they had not abandoned the principles and practice of political dictation nor the belief in polygamy; that this body of officials, of which Senator Smoot was one, had con-

225

nived at violations of the laws against polygamy and had protected the violators; that this was contrary to express pledges given in procuring amnesty for polygamists; that it was contrary to express conditions upon which the escheated church property was returned; that it was contrary to pledges made to obtain statehood; that it was contrary to the Enabling Act and the state Constitution.

One of the signers of the protest, Reverend J. L. Leilich, filed a separate protest charging that Smoot was a polygamist. This was disproved early in the hearings and thrown out.[8]

The Tribune displayed an uncharacteristic reluctance to become directly involved editorially in the Smoot case. Senator Kearns, it is true, had served as the bearer of advice from President Roosevelt that it would be unwise from the standpoint of the national Republican Party or the state of Utah to elect an apostle of the Mormon Church to the Senate. *The Tribune* gave prominent display on its front page to a news article in the *Washington Post* stating that two years earlier President McKinley in an interview with Smoot had advised him "not to permit the use of his name for the senatorship and not to suffer himself to be elected" because it "would injure the interest of Utah and her people and the Mormon Church. . . ."[9] The *Post* article also attributed the earlier failure of Moses Thatcher to win a Senate seat to the intervention of President Grover Cleveland.

Smoot, it will be recalled, did withdraw his name in 1900.

The Tribune, presumably reflecting the views of Senator Kearns, also made clear its agreement with Presidents Roosevelt, McKinley and Cleveland that it would be unwise from the standpoint of the state and the church to elect an apostle.[10] But in supporting the presidential interventions in Utah's senatorial election, *The Tribune* conspicuously avoided its usual free-swinging, no-punches-barred style of editorializing on political issues. When the Legislature, ignoring the warnings from Washington, did elect Smoot, *The Tribune* took special pains to emphasize that it had no animosity toward the new senator as a person; that it did not question his competence or character.

In an editorial following the Republican caucus which gave Smoot a majority vote *The Tribune* said:

> *The Tribune* has made its position clear in the matter of this candidacy and election. It considers the election of an apostle to be unwise and adverse to the true interests of the State. The President's advice was, we can be sure, not lightly given, and means much more than appears on its face. It is too late now, however, for argument and we have no desire to prolong it. At the same time, we must be allowed to say that we desire to withdraw nothing we have said, holding that it was all justified in the interest of good politics and for the permanent good of the State and its people. And further, that it would have been the part of wisdom for the Legislature to have been guided by it. [11]

After the Legislature confirmed the caucus decision *The Tribune* said:

> We do not know how Apostle Smoot will be received in the national capital as a Senator, but imagine that under the circumstances the atmosphere may be a trifle chilly. However, we have no disposition to bewail the inevitable, to throw any stones nor to put snares in the new Senator's path. We can and do await the result of his election with equanimity, and would be glad to see all the forebodings of evil come to naught. [12]

What the "forebodings of evil" came to can be summarized thus: the heretofore mentioned protest from Salt Lake City against the seating of Smoot; a counter-statement urging his seating, signed by Governor Wells and a score or more of prominent governmental officials and businessmen both Mormon and gentile; a two-year investigation by the Senate Committee on Privileges and Elections which fanned Mormonism and polygamy into a sensational national issue all over again; a report by the Senate investigative committee recommending against the seating of Smoot; and the over-riding of the committee recommendation by the entire Senate and the seating of the Mormon senator from Utah.

Volumes of testimony as to conditions in Utah were accumulated during the hearing and, as Roberts commented in his Mormon Church history, it was "sensationally published . . . as fast as it was given." [13]

Senator Smoot was undoubtedly helped in his fight for the seat by President Roosevelt, who had strongly and publicly advised against his election. In a letter published some six years later in *Colliers Weekly,* a national magazine, the then ex-President Roosevelt said:

> As for the case of Senator Smoot himself, he came to me of his own accord, and not only assured me that he had never had any relations with any woman excepting his own wife; and I may also add that it was the universal testimony of all who knew anything of his domestic life that it was exemplary in every way. He also assured me that he had always done everything he could to have the law about polygamy absolutely obeyed, and most strongly upheld the position that the church had taken in its public renunciation of polygamy and that he would act as quickly against any Mormon who nowadays made

a plural marriage as against a gentile who committed bigamy. I looked into the facts very thoroughly, became convinced that Senator Smoot had told me the truth, and treated him exactly as I did all other senators — that is, strictly on his merits as a public servant. I did not interfere in any way as to his retention in the Senate, save that when senators came up to speak to me on the subject, I spoke to them freely along the lines I have here outlined. . . .[14]

Thus it can be surmised that with the majority of the senators, as with Roosevelt, it was Smoot's personal life which enabled him to win the fight for his seat; that the legalistic and philosophical issues involved were brushed aside by the senators in favor of a moralistic consideration which was epitomized in a comment attributed to Senator Boies Penrose of Pennsylvania: "I think the Senate should prefer a polygamist who doesn't 'polyg' to a monogamist who doesn't 'monog'."[15]

A subsidiary effect of the Smoot investigation was an investigation within the Mormon Church as to compliance with the Woodruff "Manifesto" of 1890. This resulted in some excommunications, the resignation of two apostles (John W. Taylor and M. F. Cowley) and the issuance by President Joseph F. Smith and acceptance by the church general conference of 1904 of a statement reiterating the pledge given in the original "Manifesto." The statement concluded with this sentence:

. . . I hereby announce that all such [polygamous] marriages are prohibited, and if any officer or member of the Church shall assume to solemnize or enter into any such marriage he will be deemed in transgression against the Church, and will be liable to be dealt with according to the rules and

229

regulations thereof and excommunicated there-
from. [16]

Once again the "irrepressible conflict" had erupted; and once
again it appeared to have been repressed by the seating of Senator Smoot and the reiteration of the "Manifesto." Once again it
was a lull before a longer-lived eruption which was to be touched
off by Senator Kearns and *The Tribune.*

18

A Redeclaration of War

BY THE SPRING OF 1904 it was time for Senator Thomas
Kearns to make an important decision — whether to seek reelec-
tion or to retire from the Senate at the end of his four-year term.
On the basis of his record his position appeared to be favorable.
He had played the leading role in blocking an unpopular lease of
Uintah Indian Reservation mineral rights to private interests
and opening the lands to settlement. He had succeeded in raising
Fort Douglas to the status of a regimental post. He had won several political prestige fights over federal appointments, the most
notable being the transfer of a tri-state internal revenue office
from Helena, Mont., to Salt Lake City and the appointment of his
candidate, E. H. Callister, to the position of collector. He had
been prominently identified with conservation and irrigation
programs of the Roosevelt administration. He had won recognition as one of the Senate's best informed members on mining law
and mineral legislation. He had been publicly praised by President Theodore Roosevelt as a trustworthy and able representative of his political party and the people of Utah.[1] He had
survived a campaign of ridicule stemming from his lack of formal
education and was now being attacked on more substantial
grounds.

Under an unwritten political understanding then accepted
by both national political parties in Utah, the seat he was occupying was to be filled by a non-Mormon, particularly if the
Senate seated Reed Smoot.

A major negative factor was a festering split in the Republican Party at home which was clearly undermining his influence. Another was the disposition of Congress to do nothing about Utah-sponsored legislation pending a decision on the seating of Smoot.

But these, and many other factors, were inconsequential by comparison with the overriding question on which the decision was almost certain to turn — what was the attitude of the leadership of the Mormon Church toward a Kearns candidacy for re-election?

With the election of United States senators a function of the State Legislature, it was impossible in Utah for anyone objectionable to the church to be elected to that position. Everyone in the state, except political illiterates, knew that to be true, although many pretended not to know it. The best available evidence indicates that Senator Kearns received an answer on his status with the new church leadership in March, 1904, when President Joseph F. Smith came to Washington to testify in the Smoot hearings.

President Smith himself was the source of the information that Senator Kearns did seek and was given an answer to the question, but he made that information public through the voice of B. H. Roberts, the eminent Mormon historian. At a public meeting in Provo on March 14, 1905, Roberts stated categorically that Senator Kearns did pose the question to the church president and added he was making the charge "with the full knowledge" of President Smith and "with his approval." He was, in short, speaking for Smith. Relating the incident, Roberts wrote: "Senator Kearns was told when making the solicitation, both when making it directly by himself and indirectly through another, that the president, Joseph F. Smith, 'was not in politics.'" [2]

It can fairly be assumed that Senator Kearns did not accept the phrase "not in politics" as the total message conveyed by the answer. He, in all probability, interpreted it as notification that he was not an acceptable candidate to the head of the church and then and there reached a tentative decision at least not to embark upon a contest which offered no hope of victory. He did not publicly announce this decision until September 11.[3] And during the intervening six months the Democratic *Herald, Goodwin's Weekly, Truth,* the *Deseret News* and the state and regional press published many columns of speculation on why he would or would not run for reelection. His tactical setbacks and defeats were proclaimed and analyzed in detail; his record was scrutinized, mostly in a critical way; and his political ambitions for the future were anticipated with an unrestrained freedom of opinion which characterized political news and editorial writing of that period. It made interesting reading at the time, but for historical purposes it can be dismissed as irrelevant.

One of the greatest subjects of speculation about Senator Kearns was his relationship with Smoot. The picture created by the collective outpourings of the political writers was that Smoot withdrew in 1900 at the direction of President Lorenzo Snow to insure the election of Kearns; that Kearns and Smoot then formed an alliance to control the Republican Party and elect Smoot to the next Senate vacancy; that there was a falling out between the two; that Kearns opposed Smoot in 1902 and that the latter gained control of the party when he won the seat; that Kearns instigated the contest over the seating of Smoot; that Kearns had the power to prolong the contest or terminate it at any time.

All of this, which has over the years gained a considerable degree of historical acceptance, could have been true. But this version contains enough contradictions to suggest that at least a good part of it was fancy rather than fact. If it were true that Kearns was working to keep Smoot out of the Senate, and that he had the power to turn the investigation on and off at will, surely he would have had the power to prevent Smoot's seating. If the obviously politically self-serving newspaper articles are dismissed as such, there remains considerable evidence to support a version substantially as follows:

233

The opposition to the election of a high official of the Mormon Church to the Senate emanated not just from anti-Mormons in Utah but from leaders, including United States presidents, of both political parties. They did not want to revive a conflict in Utah which had annoyed presidents and political administrations for almost half a century. Thus, in 1895, President Grover Cleveland intervened in opposition to the election of Apostle Moses Thatcher to the Senate. The church, which had some very good reasons for courting the goodwill of the administration (one being the recovery of its confiscated property), responded by censuring the Thatcher candidacy and adopting a political rule requiring church officials to obtain permission from their superiors to run for political office.

In 1900, President McKinley advised Smoot to withdraw his candidacy for the Senate. Church President Snow might well have had some good reasons for courting the goodwill of that national administration. The known facts are that Smoot did withdraw and that President Snow did assist Kearns in his campaign for the seat. There is also convincing evidence that Kearns had, by his willingness to lead and finance a campaign to shift the state to the Republican column, ingratiated himself with national Republican leaders. As previously suggested, it is quite possible that Snow accepted Kearns as a suitable candidate at the behest of national Republican leaders rather than because Kearns had entered into some negotiations for the purchase of Saltair from the church — a deal that was not consummated.

In 1903, Theodore Roosevelt, motivated by the same considerations as Cleveland and McKinley, advised the Republican Legislature not to elect Apostle Smoot to the Senate. In this instance, Joseph F. Smith had presumably given Smoot permission to seek the office under the rule adopted after the Thatcher incident, and Smoot chose not to accept the advice of Roosevelt. When confronted by an accomplished fact rather than the prospect of something which might be damaging to the Republican

Party, Roosevelt changed his stance and assisted Smoot, at least with respect to those senators who inquired as to the presidential position.

The most intriguing unanswered question about Senator Kearns' senatorial career was why he decided to deliver the extraordinary speech he did deliver from the Senate floor four days before the expiration of his term, March 4, 1905. Events leading up to and possibly influencing his decision to deliver the speech, which amounted to a call for reactivation of the "irrepressible conflict" after a lull of almost fifteen years, undoubtedly included the Smoot hearing and its disclosures and his contacts with President Joseph F. Smith. That a definite decision to deliver such a speech, and to break with the Republican Party at the state level, had not been reached by July 1, 1904, is indicated in an announcement of a change in the management of *The Tribune* on that date. The substance of the announcement was that Perry S. Heath, who had held the position of publisher and general manager since the Kearns-Keith purchase of the newspaper, had resigned because of commitments in the East and would be immediately replaced by Joseph Lippman. The announcement closed with this paragraph:

> The new management will issue *The Tribune* as a straightforward, uncompromising Republican newspaper, endeavoring to win all Republicans to the harmonious and united action which will insure to the party in this most important campaign . . . the decisive triumph which the policies and record of the Republican Party have so richly earned. [4]

Certainly, there was no hint here as to what was to come.

In August the Republican state convention met and nominated a state ticket which included John C. Cutler, a businessman, for governor and Joseph Howell of Cache County for representative in Congress. The press seemed to be in rare agreement that the convention was dominated by the Smoot forces. The Democrats met in September and nominated a ticket headed by James H. Moyle for governor and Orlando W. Powers for representative in Congress. The Socialists also nominated a ticket which carried one surprising candidate — C. C. Goodwin for justice of the Supreme Court.

The first tangible signal of the disruptive political storm which was brewing was sent up on September 7. At a meeting in Auerbach Hall the "American Party of Utah" was organized. The featured speaker was Senator Fred T. Dubois, the old Mormon fighter from Idaho, and the keynote of his speech was that a new party in Utah was necessary to protect the political rights of the citizens from destruction at the hands of leaders of the Mormon Church.

News reports of this and subsequent meetings provided no indication that Kearns was involved, directly at least, in the formation of the new party. Among the state committee members were P. L. Williams, Willard F. Snyder and P. J. Daly. Others playing a prominent role in the organization of the party included Frank J. Cannon and Edward B. Critchlow. The party's nominee for governor was William M. Ferry, a business associate of the Silver King group, and for representative in Congress, Ogden Hiles.

Before the American Party nominated its ticket, the Republican State Committee met and passed a resolution renouncing *The Tribune* as its organ. *The Tribune* declined to be "read out" of the party and on September 16 announced that it was still a Republican newspaper which supported the national ticket but would not support a "State ticket nominated by the Mormon Church of Utah masquerading under the guise of Republicanism." [5]

From this point on *The Tribune* waded into the campaign with its old-time zeal and disregard for diplomatic niceties.

Frank J. Cannon was writing the editorials, and the style of some of the articles offered under news headlines, suggested that he was composing some of these. On November 2, for example, a "strictly confidential" letter was directed to Editor Penrose of the *Deseret News* under the headlines: "Church Cinch for Smootler." "Mormon Democrats in Front Line." "Bishop Winkler Counsels Them According to Brother Spry's Boast." The letter:

> Mormonton, Utah, Oct. 31 — Dear Brother Penrose [Apostle and Editor of the *Deseret News*] — This brings us back to the days when the Lord redeemed the children of Israel from bondage and sent them to the promised land in Utah. Everything is coming our way and the gentile enemies of the kingdom are on the run like the devil beating tanbark. I feel to rejoice with exceeding great joy.
> The Mormons are taking to political counsel like a hen takes to grasshoppers. All they want to know is what Brother Smith and Brother Smoot wish them to do and they will do it, if it knocks all the harmony out of the quorum. . . .[6]

The Tribune did support the national Republican ticket, but it devoted much more space to attacking the Republican state and county tickets and to supporting the American Party tickets. In its editorials and political forecasts, *The Tribune* indicated it did not expect an American Party victory at the state level but it did reflect high hopes of a victory in Salt Lake County. Those hopes collapsed on election day. The first venture of the new political party was a fiasco all down the line. The vote for governor reflects the pattern — Cutler, the Republican, 62,446; Moyle, the Democrat, who was once again a victim of wrong timing, 38,047; Ferry, the American, 7,959; and Kaufman, the Socialist, 4,892.

The judgment of American Party backers as to the Salt Lake political climate was not so bad as the 1904 election returns made it appear. For the new party, or revived Liberal Party, later won three successive Salt Lake City municipal elections and controlled the city government from 1905 to 1911.

When the Republican Legislature, elected in 1904, met in early 1905 it selected George Sutherland to succeed Kearns for a full six-year Senate term. It was a Smoot victory, politically speaking. To *The Tribune* it could more accurately be termed a victory for President Joseph F. Smith. As a Protestant, Sutherland qualified (even though his background was Mormon) under the informal understanding that a Mormon and a non-Mormon should occupy the Senate seats.

Thus the stage was set at home for Kearns' farewell address in the Senate. The speech was a masterful distillation of what *The Tribune* had been saying from the time of its founding until after the "Manifesto" and the abandonment of the ecclesiastical political system. It was also a recapitulation of disclosures arising from the Smoot investigation. But its impact was heightened by the fact that it was delivered not during the heat of a campaign, when speeches were rightly discounted by the public but after the political rewards had been distributed. For this reason it was a far more ominous threat to the normalization of Utah politics than were the bitter words of the campaign.

Gaining the Senate floor to speak on a joint resolution introduced by Senator Dubois of Idaho to propose constitutional amendments for the prohibition and punishment of polygamous marriages and plural cohabitation, Senator Kearns began:

> Mr. President, I will not permit this occasion to pass without saying what it seems to me should be said by a Senator, under these circumstances, before leaving public life. Something is due to the State which had honored me; something is due to the record which I have endeavored to maintain honorably before the world; and something, by way of information, is due to the Senate and the country. . . .

He then launched into a recapitulation of Utah's history leading up to statehood and a description of conditions, as he saw them, then existing in the state. He frankly conceded that the power he was denouncing had helped him to the Senate seat:

> I say to you, my fellow senators, that this place of power is infinitely more magnificent than I dreamed when I first thought of occupying a seat here. But were it thrice as great as I now know it to be, and were I back in that old time of struggle in Utah, when I was seeking for this honor, I would not permit the volunteered friendship of President Snow to bestow upon me, even as an innocent recipient, one atom of the church monarch's favor. . . .

Near the close of the long speech which, it can be presumed, nobody found dull, Senator Kearns provided the following propositions in summary:

> Outside of religion the Mormons as a community are ruled by a special privileged class, constituting what I call the church monarchy.
> This monarchy pledged the country that there would be no more violations of law and no more defiance of the sentiment of the United States regarding polygamy and the plural marriage relation.
> This monarchy pledged the United States that it would refrain from controlling its subjects in secular affairs.
> Every member of this monarchy is responsible for the system of government and for the acts of the monarchy, since (as shown in the cases of deposed apostles, Moses Thatcher, and others) the man who is not in accord with the system is dropped from the ruling class.

239

This monarchy sets up a regal social order within this Republic.

This monarchy monopolizes the business of one commonwealth and is rapidly reaching into others.

This monarchy takes practically all the surplus product of the toil of its subjects for its own purpose, and makes no account to anyone on earth of its immense secret fund.

This monarchy rules all politics in Utah, and is rapidly extending its dominion into other states and territories.

This monarchy permits its favorites to enter into polygamy and to maintain polygamous relations, and it protects them from prosecution by its political power.

Lately no effort has been made to punish any of these people by the local law. On the contrary, the ruling monarch [President Joseph F. Smith] has continued to grow in power, wealth and importance. . . .

The senator concluded:

It is the duty of this great body — the Senate of the United States — to serve notice on this church and his apostles that they must live within the law; that the nation is supreme; that the institutions of this country must prevail throughout this land; and that the compact upon which statehood was granted must be preserved inviolate. . . .[7]

Senator Kearns, by his own testimony, regarded the speech as fulfillment of a public obligation. Historian Roberts viewed it as "a revengeful effort to destroy what he could not use to his own advantage."[8] The *Deseret News* described the speech as "his [Kearns] dying wail."[9] The Democratic *Herald*, always alert to capitalize on Republican squabbles, concluded that the real target of the speech was Senator Smoot.[10] *Goodwin's Weekly* coupled an attack on Kearns personally with the judgment that the speech expressed a "clear idea of existing methods in Utah."[11] *The Tribune* editorialized: ". . . until Senator Thomas Kearns stood in the Senate . . . and told all, there had never been made an instant and complete picture of the awful situation in this state. . . . It was a scene to thrill all humanity who witnessed it and to mark a chapter in history which will awaken profound emotions in all who read it. . . ."[12]

The *Ogden Standard*, published by William Glasmann, said editorially:

> The most ardent admirers . . . of the distinguished Utahn never suspected, until yesterday, that he [Kearns] was a great orator entitled to rank with Patrick Henry, Daniel Webster, Rufus Choate, Henry Clay and other silver-tongued orators of the 'Golden Age' of the Republic, or that he was able to fully eclipse all modern senators by the elegance of his diction, the never-ending succession of his periods and the fiery pathos of his invective.[13]

Kearns was not a polished writer or speaker and there was a widespread public suspicion that this speech was written by someone else and much speculation as to who the author might be. B. H. Roberts attributed it to Frank J. Cannon, who was *The Tribune's* chief editorial writer at the time and who remained in that post through the ensuing several years. Commenting on the speech Roberts wrote:

> Here it should be said that the speech of Senator Kearns was not his in fact, either in its conception

or its polished composition. For bad as its reveal-
ments are, and in the main false, it is constructed
by a devilish cunning, and made up of polished sentences and moving tropes—a literary style of which
Senator Kearns, being ignorant and untrained in
such matters, was utterly incapable. The speech
was only his because he adopted it, accepted it from
the brain and hand of another, and read it in the
Senate house. The speech was generally believed to
be in conception and composition the work of ex-
Senator Frank J. Cannon. [14]

Because of Roberts' unconcealed aversion to Cannon, whom
he described as brilliant and cunning but lacking in character, it
might be suspected that he attributed the speech to Cannon because he wanted it that way. But the evidence does support Roberts' conclusion that Cannon was the writer. It sounded like Cannon's style. Cannon was writing editorials of similar content for
The Tribune and he was the person Kearns would likely turn to
for help in preparing such an address. Goodwin or Fred Lockley
might have written it; but Goodwin was an antagonist of
Kearns at the time and Lockley had disappeared from the Utah
scene.

Thus, Roberts' attribution of the speech to Cannon appears
to have been valid. His seeming assumption that Kearns was incapable of authorship is open to question. While Kearns obviously was not a polished speaker or writer, he had a native and un-
polished ability to get to the point and communicate it. On the
basis of his overall record of achievement, there is reason to believe that he knew what he wanted to say; that he had his own
reasons for saying it; and that he called upon an expert to help
him say it effectively, a practice that was not then, and is not
now, uncommon among persons of prominence in politics and
other fields.

In calling upon Cannon to compose his senatorial "swan song," Kearns could deliver it with assurance that it would reflect professional skill. For Cannon had few if any peers in Utah in the art of persuasive and polished speaking or writing. While Cannon's *Tribune* editorials during the next few years strongly suggested that he was personally in accord with the contents of the speech he had written for Kearns, this was not necessarily so, for Cannon could attack or defend a cause with impressive skill. This ability was exemplified by an incident which occurred during this period. His brother, Hugh J. Cannon, was serving a mission in England and had the responsibility of editing the *Millennial Star,* official publication of the Mormon Church in Europe. He wanted to publish some articles dealing with certain aspects of Mormon theology and decided that the person best qualified to write them was his brother, Frank J. Cannon. Although aware of the fact that Frank was no longer in the church fold, he wrote a letter suggesting that his brother write the projected articles. Frank promptly complied with the request. The articles so impressed Hugh that, in a letter of thanks, he asked: "How can you, having lost the faith, write such convincing and moving articles in defense of the faith?"

Frank J.'s reply was brief and to the point: "I wrote them for you, not me." [15]

19

Give 'Em Hell Politics Again

WHEN EX-SENATOR Thomas Kearns returned from his four-year term in the Senate his political allies were licking wounds inflicted the previous November and preparing for revenge in the Salt Lake City election to be held the next year. The Smoot investigation was still in progress in Washington supplying ammunition for the American Party to use in the forthcoming campaign. The Mormon Church, apparently in response to the disclosures being made in the Smoot investigation and in Kearns' farewell speech in the Senate, was cracking down on members who still refused to comply with commitments of the Woodruff "Manifesto" and the reiteration of that document by President Joseph F. Smith at the April, 1904, annual conference.

The Salt Lake Tribune was being operated under the management of Joseph Lippman, a lawyer who was associated with Kearns and *The Tribune* intermittently over a long period, and was apparently making a modest profit. But in October, 1905, Lippman was replaced by Frank I. Sefrit, who served in the role of publisher and general manager for the following six years. Frank J. Cannon was the chief editorial writer, but the executive in charge of the news and editorial departments was Colonel William Nelson, a Civil War veteran of imposing appearance whose career with *The Tribune* spanned thirty-two years.

The Colonel, like some *Tribune* editors and publishers who followed him, had an aversion to personal publicity in the organ

244

under his control or influence; as a result, his name seldom appeared in the newspaper. Other publications frequently identified him as *The Tribune* editor or mentioned him in connection with controversies or libel suits involving the newspaper. Information about him handed down verbally within *The Tribune* organization pictured him as a competent, dedicated, early-west style newspaperman who expected conflicts and threats and who was prepared to meet either verbal or physical attacks. His first act upon arriving at *The Tribune* editorial offices in the morning, according to unrecorded office history, was to remove a revolver from a pocket and place it on his desk within easy reach. He was then ready to go to work.

A native of Scotland, Colonel Nelson came to the United States as a youth and worked for newspapers in Wisconsin and Illinois before joining the Union Army. He distinguished himself in several battles and spent the last few months of the Civil War in the infamous Andersonville Prison. After the war, he resumed newspaper work, served in the Wisconsin Legislature, and, in 1876, received a federal appointment as United States marshal for the Utah Territory. A change in the national administration removed him from this post three years later. In May, 1881, he joined *The Tribune* staff as a reporter. He served successively as city editor, telegraph editor, managing editor and editor-in-chief, the position he held at the time of his death on October 26, 1913.

Historian Whitney characterized him as one of the "pronounced anti-Mormon federal officials," and during his incumbency as marshal he was sued for $25,000 damages for alleged false imprisonment and maltreatment of a prisoner. The suit was brought by Dr. Jeter Clinton, a police justice in Salt Lake City for many years. Dr. Clinton had been arrested on a grand jury indictment charging him with complicity in a murder committed some fifteen years earlier during the so-called "Morrisite War." The murder charge was subsequently dismissed on motion of the

United States district attorney, and the damage action against Nelson was disposed of when the court granted a motion for a non-suit. [1]

The esteem in which the Colonel was held by *The Tribune* owners and by his co-workers was reflected in the newspaper the morning following his death by a three-column picture on page one, an obituary occupying a full column on page one, and several inside columns devoted to feature stories about his exploits as a Union Army officer and as a federal law enforcement official plus tributes from state and city officials and Senator Kearns. The obituary noted that during his thirty-two years of service on *The Tribune* he had been absent from his office for only five weeks — two weeks for a vacation and three weeks for an illness. [2] A *Tribune* editorial stated that his character and career could be summed up with three words — courage, law and order. [3]

The Tribune Publishing Company had been changed from a Utah to a West Virginia corporation in March, 1904 and on October 28, 1905, Kearns was elected a director. It was apparently his first official position with the newspaper, although he had long been identified as the owner in partnership with Keith. He was elected director to succeed Heath, who had resigned four months earlier as publisher and general manager.

Sketchy corporate records indicate that Kearns and Keith spent more on the newspaper than its revenues for the first few years of their ownership. Physical facilities were improved, new equipment purchased, news coverage expanded and various features added. The first dividend of $10,000 was declared on March 1, 1905, and a smaller one followed on June 14. But these were probably the last dividends for several years, as the newspaper was heading into a revival of the "irrepressible conflict" and a succession of operating deficits. Profits were not vital to the survival of *The Tribune* at this particular period. The Silver King Mining Company was still maintaining a flow of dividends to Kearns and Keith ample to subsidize the newspaper without disrupting the living standards of its owners. However, the mine had reached its peak and was soon to start a decline which was going to eventually change the fiscal status of *The Tribune* to that of a business which had to make a profit to survive.

The 1905 municipal campaign was a wild one, even by Utah standards. The Democratic ticket was headed by the incumbent mayor, Richard P. Morris. The Republicans nominated a ticket with William J. Lynch as the candidate for mayor. The American Party mayor candidate was Ezra Thompson, a business and mining man. The Socialists also entered a ticket.

Never in the most bitter days of the conflict between the People's Party and the Liberal Party had *The Tribune* fought harder than it did in support of the American Party in this city election. It attacked the incumbent Democratic administration on a wide range of issues, particularly water, taxation and employment. It tried to convince Republicans that they had no chance of victory and could therefore turn the Democrats out only by joining the Americans. It told the Democrats that the Mormon Church was supporting the Republican Party and that their only chance of not being liquidated by an ecclesiastical party was to vote American. It also appealed to Mormons, particularly the younger generation, to cast off their ecclesiastical political yoke by voting American.

The newspaper showed particular concern about gentile Republicans and Democrats and disclosed that some of them had been very bitter because of *The Tribune's* refusal to wage a war against church influence in the 1903 city campaign.

In one editorial aimed at this group *The Tribune* said with a rare note of conciliation in its voice:

> Let us take a reposeful moment for gentle consideration or argumentation with those ardent gentile Republicans and Democrats who were very angry at

The Tribune about 1903 because this paper did not raise the flag of revolt against existing conditions here and call upon the gentiles to forsake affiliations in politics, in business and in social life with the hierarchy and their institutions.

It is not at all an exaggeration to say that such gentiles were warm to the point of boiling during the period named — and some of them even at an earlier time. They even threatened to launch an anti-Mormon movement without *The Tribune.* . . .

All this time *The Tribune* was devoting itself to making plain the situation as it stood, without any especial attack upon the hierarchy, without any recession from the high ground which it had always occupied on this question, but awaiting only the ripened hour when one call would bring all gentiles in Utah together. . . . [4]

This editorial indicated quite clearly that *The Tribune* had been bitterly criticized by anti-Mormons for softness toward the church while Kearns was in the Senate and that the policy was defended on the grounds that the time was not ripe for finishing the long fight which had been temporarily quelled by the "Manifesto" and the division of Mormons between the two national parties.

The campaign waged by *The Tribune* was appallingly intemperate by standards of political coverage which later became the vogue. But viewed within the frame of then prevailing journalistic practices it was not so shocking. The *Herald,* the *Deseret News* and the weekly publications could hardly be described as objective in their approaches to the campaign issues.

The Tribune editorials, slanted news articles and vindictive cartoons were, of course, offensive to orthodox Mormons. Historian Roberts characterized the American Party campaign as "sensational and unscrupulus."[5] Roberts, careful and objective as he was in the area of historical facts, could be much harsher in his judgments of *Tribune* excesses (and particularly with Cannon as editor) than he was with the excesses of the Democratic *Herald* or the *Deseret News*.

The basic affirmative campaign waged by *The Tribune* in support of the American Party was summed up in this editorial:

> The friends of the American Party . . . believe that a gentile victory next Tuesday will be followed by such an awakening in business that the city will leap into business prominence in a few months.
> They believe that if either of the church-ridden parties is successful there will be no change from present conditions. In fact, it is the conviction of hundreds of the most conservative men in Salt Lake City that a defeat of the gentiles will be heralded by American newspapers as a certainty that the American spirit here has been hopelessly overridden. The effect of this announcement will be to divert homemakers from Utah in even greater numbers than at present. . . .
> We believe that Americans and untrammeled Mormons will deal a decisive blow next Tuesday. If they do, peace will come with increased population, and come quickly.[6]

One of the issues generated by the campaign involved the question of who was boycotting whom in employment. *The Tribune* charged commercial leaders of the church were spreading the word that a gentile victory would result in a systematic discharge and boycotting of many Mormon employes. *The Tribune* replied that boycotting with respect to employment was, and always had been, the other way around. It republished a table of nineteen non-Mormon and nineteen Mormon firms with the number of non-Mormons and Mormons employed by each. It noted that the table had been published a month earlier and that "its correctness has never been disputed even by the shameless liar on the *Deseret News*."

The table showed Keith-O'Brien, a gentile department store, with 122 Mormon and sixty non-Mormon employes. One of the founders was Kearns' partner in the ownership of *The Tribune*. For Zion's Cooperative Mercantile Institution, the major Mormon mercantile business, the division shown was 316 Mormons and nine non-Mormons. Auerbach's, a non-Mormon department store, showed an even division — seventy-five Mormons and seventy-five non-Mormons. Sweet Candy Company, non-Mormon firm, was credited with eighty-one Mormons and forty-nine non-Mormons. McDonald Candy Company, Mormon, was credited with 184 Mormons and eleven non-Mormons.

The table indicated that Mormon banks preferred Mormon employes and that gentile banks preferred non-Mormon employes. The table showed all nineteen non-Mormon firms with some Mormon employes and twelve of the nineteen Mormon firms with no non-Mormon employes.

The breakdown for the *Deseret News* was 282 Mormons and eight non-Mormons. *The Salt Lake Tribune* was not listed. Whether this omission was prompted by modesty or consideration for Mormon employes, if there were any, cannot be determined at this late date as no explanation was offered in the article. In a note at the bottom of the table *The Tribune* conceded that there might be some "slight errors" growing out of the fact "that some Mormons will claim to be gentiles and some gentiles will claim to be Mormons."[7]

On the Monday before the election *The Tribune* charged that the church had "sent out the word" to vote for Lynch, the Republican candidate for mayor. It gave prominent display on the editorial to an article which began:

The whisper has been whispered.

Joseph F. Smith, the prophet of God, has put his lips to the speaking tube and now every subordinate ecclesiast of the Mormon church in Salt Lake City, and every Democrat who is amenable to church influence, has been notified to work incessantly and to vote for William J. Lynch, the 'Republican' candidate for the mayoralty. [8]

Much of the remainder of the article was designed to convince Democrats that they were being betrayed. On the front page of the same issue was a two-column box carrying the heading: "It's a Stampede" and an article with this lead paragraph: "Gentile Republicans and sincere Mormon Democrats, learning of the course of the whisper in Sunday's fast meetings and Sunday-schools were so angered last night that the rush to the American Party is a stampede. . . ." [9]

The city election, it should be noted, was not a battle between a gentile David and a Mormon Goliath, as were state elections, but to some degree the reverse. By *The Tribune's* own calculations there were at this time about 22,000 registered voters in the incorporated city, and of these about 12,000 were gentiles and something over 9,000 Mormons. Prior to the election, *The Tribune* conceded that as many as 2,500 gentiles might vote against the American Party but predicted that this would be offset by Mormons voting for the gentile candidate for mayor.

The election, which brought out a remarkably high percentage of the total registered vote if *The Tribune* calculations were reasonably accurate, produced these mayor totals: Thompson, American, 8,456; Morris, Democrat, 7,797; Lynch, Republican, 4,985.

The Tribune's pre-election forecast of the vote was nothing to cheer about as to accuracy, but the result was and *The Tribune* cheered with its largest type. Across the top of the newspaper's front page on the morning after the election was a line "Praise God From Whom All Blessings Flow." Underneath was *The Tribune* masthead and an eight-column banner line: "Salt Lake Is an American City." Under the banner line was a six-column reproduction of the party's spread-eagle insignia and in the eagle's beak was a scroll carrying this line: "I Go To Spread Glad Tidings." At each side of the eagle were scriptural quotations and beneath it were two more eight-column lines: "Great Landslide Occurs;" and "Salt Lake-American Party Owns the Earth." The remainder of the page was filled with gloating editorial comment and the names of the winning candidates set in large type. [10]

Historian Roberts' comment on the page was: "The announcement of the municipal election victory was . . . most extravagantly, not to say hysterically jubilant." [11]

Despite its jubilance over the result, *The Tribune*, in its hour of glory, humbled itself enough to admit that its forecast was somewhat wide of the results. It had predicted a somewhat larger vote for the American Party with the Republican candidate second and the Democratic candidate third. The fact that the Democratic candidate ran only 659 votes behind the American Party candidate hardly supported *The Tribune* charge that the church was giving all-out support to the Republican candidate. Its explanation for this miscalculation was that midway in the voting Senator Reed Smoot, and other church leaders, learned that the Republican candidate was doing poorly and that the only hope of beating the American candidate rested with the incumbent Democrat, Morris. They then sent word out to the faithful to switch to Morris. *The Tribune* modestly conceded that had this development occurred a little earlier, the result might have been different. [12]

The American Party victory in 1905 was no fluke, as it won two successive Salt Lake City elections with John S. Bransford as its candidate for mayor. The party continued to nominate state and congressional candidates but was never able to make a strong showing in the entire state, which was heavily Mormon. The 1907 and 1909 municipal elections were similar in tone to the one in 1905 except that *The Tribune* and the American Party were defending the administration rather than attacking the administration of the opposition. But in 1911 the American Party and *The Tribune* as its spokesman, suffered a decisive defeat in the municipal election. The party did not recover. This local election was important in the history of the state, the city and *The Tribune* for at least two reasons. It introduced non-partisan elections in the city. It firmly established in the state the political alignment on national party lines which began with the division of Mormons between the national parties back in the 1890's.

One of the new elements in the 1911 municipal campaign was a new newspaper, the *Herald-Republican*. It was born from the merger of the *Inter-Mountain Republican*, established in February of 1906, and the *Salt Lake Herald*, which had been one of *The Tribune's* journalistic antagonists from its birth. The merger, which became effective August 14, 1909, marked the end of a consistent, effective and high-quality Democratic spokesman *(The Herald)* as both papers had been acquired by Republicans prior to the merger. The ownership, which underwent frequent alterations, included Senator Smoot, Governor William H. Spry, D. C. Jackling, the rising star in the Utah mining industry, and several other Utahns prominent in the Smoot political organization.

For eleven years prior to its demise by merger, the *Herald* had been edited by Ambrose Noble McKay, a man whose exceptional talents had been transferred to *The Tribune* earlier in 1911.

In the 1911 municipal campaign the American Party managers were outmaneuvered from the beginning. The heavily Mormon Legislature had enacted a law changing Salt Lake City government from a mayor-council to a commission form. Three political parties or groups entered candidates in the qualifying primary — American, Republican and a non-partisan Citizens fusion group. *The Tribune* immediately smelled a church plot to defeat the American Party. The Republican ticket, according to *The Tribune*, was entered by Smoot to drain gentile Republicans away from the American candidates. The church would support the Citizens ticket, and the Smoot Republicans, if defeated in the primary, would join in that support on a non-partisan basis. Whether or not it was planned that way (or plotted as *The Tribune* preferred) that is the way it worked out. The Citizens and the American candidates qualified, the Smoot organization backed the Citizens candidates and the Citizens ticket won by a three to two margin. *The Tribune* charged that the church was brazenly campaigning for the Citizens ticket, citing as proof a speech in the Mormon Tabernacle by C. W. Penrose, speeches by other church leaders in stake and ward meetings; the appearance of the Citizens non-Mormon candidate for mayor, Samuel C. Park, as speaker at a Mormon church meeting in a ward house; and editorials in the *Deseret News* and the *Herald-Republican* (always referred to as the Smoot organ by *The Tribune*).

The *Deseret News* firmly denied that the church was participating in the campaign [13] and the "Smoot organ" shouted that the "Silver King Crowd" was trying to fasten its control on the city. [14] Both sides accused the other of turning the campaign into a church fight and both sides charged the other with responsibility for the fanning of religious acrimony. Because a majority of the Citizens candidates were non-Mormons, *The Tribune* had to concede that the church was more conspicuous in the campaigning than in the candidacies. In an editorial comment on Penrose's speech in the Tabernacle, *The Tribune* paid the former *Deseret News* editor some qualified compliments. But the purpose may have been to strengthen the charge of church interference in the campaign and to downgrade Penrose's successor rather than to elevate Penrose in the esteem of *Tribune* readers.

The editorial said in part:

> There is this to say about Penrose. He is less of a
> hypocrite than some of those who would cover up
> what they mean by forms of words and in disguised,
> secret action. He has always been rather inclined to
> boldness, although an adept in deceit and falsehood
> whenever he considers these to be most serviceable.
> For a long series of years he was editor of the *Deser-*
> *et News*, and he made it a paper very much superior
> in intelligence and usefulness to what it has been
> since he left it. The deterioration in that paper has
> been very marked of late years. It has lacked the ex-
> perienced intelligence that Penrose had at his com-
> mand, and, while being quite as unscrupulous as
> he made it, there has been an element of uncandor
> and stupidity, as well as proneness to blundering,
> that was but little manifest during his occupancy
> of the editorship of that paper. [15]

Almost a year before the defeat of the American Party in the
1911 municipal election an event took place which signaled a
change in the policy of *The Tribune*, particularly with respect to
the Mormon Church as an ecclesiastical institution. The event
was only partially announced at the time. And as far as this
writer can determine, some of the important aspects of the
event have never since been publicly disclosed until publication
of this history. [16]

The event was a meeting of Senator Kearns and Ambrose N.
McKay, a gentile who for some eleven years had served as editor
of the *Salt Lake Herald*. Senator Kearns had offered the position
of publisher and general manager of *The Tribune* to McKay and
the purpose of the meeting was to arrive at an understanding as
to future policy.

On the morning of January 1, 1911, a Sunday, the appointment of McKay was announced in a brief article at the top of the editorial page:

> On this day Mr. Frank I. Sefrit retires as general manager of *The Tribune* and *The Evening Telegram* [the Sunday issue carried the mastheads of both *The Tribune* and *Telegram*] and is to be succeeded by Mr. A. N. McKay.
>
> The new general manager is well known to the public, and is thoroughly familiar with the local newspaper field.
>
> Both *The Tribune* and *The Evening Telegram* will continue to be vigorous and aggressive in support of those principles and public policies for which they have so long contended. [17]

The announcement was signed on behalf of the two newspapers by Frank J. Westcott, secretary of the publishing company.

In a New Year's editorial in the same issue *The Tribune* had this to say about itself and its policies:

> As is usual in our annual numbers, we have a few words to say this morning on *The Salt Lake Tribune.* And we are glad to let our friends know that its business and prospects were never so sound and solid as now. In subscriptions our list is larger than ever, our advertising more extensive and profitable. The year has dealt very kindly with *The Tribune.* In return, *The Tribune* has been faithful to its trust as the outspoken voice for freedom and personal independence. [18]

A document with a more important bearing on future policies of the newspaper than the editorial was not published. It was an agreement between Kearns and McKay on general policies which were to serve as guidelines for the new publisher. There was nothing startlingly new or sensational in the agreement. To the general public it probably would not have signified any particular change had it been published in *The Tribune*. Its significance stemmed from a combination of two elements — what was said about policy and the man who was to implement the policy.

The first item in the ten-point agreement was: *"The Salt Lake Tribune* is now and will continue to be an American newspaper, devoted to the promotion and protection of American ideals, interests and institutions." *The Tribune,* and virtually all other American newspapers, had said this about themselves.

The second item could mean much or little, depending upon its interpretation and implementation: "Regardless of political preferences it will hold patriotism above partisanism and open its columns to honest opinions, fairly expressed, by reputable members of all parties and denominations." As it was sure to be interpreted and implemented by McKay, this meant that *The Tribune* was going to be far more objective in its news coverage of political and ecclesiastical affairs than it had been in the past.

The third item, when related to the newspaper ideas known to be held by McKay, meant that while *The Tribune* might support various organizations and their objectives, it was no longer to let itself be placed in the role of a dog being wagged by a tail: *"The Tribune* as an independent organ serving the general public, uninfluenced by personal ambition or animosities, but having an undivided interest in the community with entire freedom from extraneous domination of any kind."

The fourth item committed *The Tribune:* "To be a crusader for strict observance of the federal and state constitutions, for law enforcement thereunder, and for equal opportunity for all deserving citizens not motivated by hatreds or intolerance."

257

The remaining items were not especially pertinent to the controversies which had agitated Utah in the past. [19]

McKay, as has heretofore been indicated, was not an eloquent, zealous crusader. He was not a Lockley, a Goodwin or a Frank J. Cannon. He was an unimpassioned, objective newspaperman (an uncommon breed in the journalistic world of the previous century) and he had close personal friendships with and the respect of influential Mormons, gentiles, Democrats and Republicans. He was not the sort of person Kearns would have selected for publisher and general manager of *The Tribune* unless he had decided that the time had come to mute the old fight and strive for an accommodation of the contending forces which had generated the "irrepressible conflict."

The agreement as to *The Tribune's* future policy would have been even more significant at the time it was signed had it been known that in a few years Kearns would acquire full ownership of *The Tribune*; that death would place in his shoes a man (John Francis Fitzpatrick) who was dedicated to repression of the "irrepressible conflict;" that death would place at the head of the Mormon Church a man (Heber J. Grant) who would see eye to eye with Fitzpatrick on the desirability of resolving the "Utah problem" in Utah.

20

A Step
Toward Accommodation

WHY, AFTER RE-IGNITING the "irrepressible conflict"
four days before the end of his Senate term, did Thomas Kearns
decide in late 1910 to change the tone of *The Tribune* in its coverage of political-ecclesiastical affairs?

On the basis of his past record, it was not because he lacked
the stomach for a fight. He had waded into too many conflicts
when the odds did not appear to be favorable to suggest such a
conclusion. One supposition which gained considerable credence
— that the change was more or less forced by the defeat of the
American Party in the 1911 municipal election — is weakened
by the time factor. The decision was reached almost a year before
the election and at a time when there is no reason to believe that
Kearns and American Party leaders were anticipating defeat.

The answer to the question is probably complex, involving
many considerations rather than a single overriding one. On the
testimony of Kearns himself one factor was the economics of
newspaper publishing. A young business associate and confidant, James Ivers, critically posed the question to Kearns some
time after he had detected the gradual shift in policy. Kearns,
striking a characteristic pose with chin on massive chest, grunted a few times and then called through an open door for an aide
to bring in *The Tribune* account books "and show them to my
young friend here." The books showed substantial losses for several prior years. Ivers nodded his understanding and the ex-

senator then offered a few explanatory comments. He told Ivers, in substance, that he had been up and down Main Street contacting virtually every prominent gentile businessman; that they had all encouraged him to keep up the fight; but that none of them was willing to put up a single dime to finance it! [1]

While the losses shown on the books were sizable, they were not unsupportable for the owners. But Kearns had been through enough battles to know that persons who urge another to fight, but are unwilling to make a commitment themselves, are unreliable allies and may turn out to be opponents when the going gets rough. He was perhaps more concerned about the attitude of those he would have to look to for support than the deficits of the newspaper.

Other considerations entering into the decision can be inferred or surmised from editorials published in *The Tribune* both before and after the decision to alter the policy. *The Tribune* had concluded from election returns that the American Party had, in its victories, been losing more non-Mormon votes to the opposition candidates than it had been gaining from the Mormons. The newspaper had noted also that gentiles were showing an increasing willingness to run on church-supported tickets. In brief, the intermingling of gentiles and Mormons in political contests indicated a growing desire on both sides to forget ecclesiastical orientation of politics. This, really, was what *The Tribune* had been fighting for. It may well be that Kearns had concluded, to use a phrase which Noble Warrum had probably picked up from McKay when discussing his agreement with Kearns on future editorial policy, that a new policy was needed "to conform to changing conditions and future prospects of the State." [2]

That a change was taking place under the McKay management was conspicuously apparent in *The Tribune's* news coverage of the 1912 and 1914 election campaigns and editorial comments thereon.

In the 1912 presidential election year three major tickets were entered — Democratic, Republican and Roosevelt's Bull

Moose. *The Tribune* supported the Republican ticket, primarily on the tariff issue. It cautioned that a Democratic victory would mean that Utah's wool and lead would become the first victims of the Democratic anti-protective policies. Allies of all three parties were covered with an impartiality which must have been a shock to partisan readers. Editorial comment on individual candidates opposed by *The Tribune* was, with only occasional exceptions, temperate, reasoned and directed at positions on issues rather than personal deficiencies. A candidate out of favor with *The Tribune* might be misinformed or lacking in comprehension but he was no longer a malicious liar. The harshest *Tribune* criticism was aimed at a Republican ally and journalistic competitor, the *Herald-Republican.* It was always referred to as the organ of Reed Smoot and his "federal bunch." Occasional jibes were taken at Mormon Church meddling in politics but these were wrapped in humor or gentle sarcasm rather than denunciatory spleen. In an editorial comment on a Democratic meeting *The Tribune* quoted, with evident pleasure, some remarks of Simon Bamberger, then a candidate for the State Senate and later governor of the state, about an editorial in the church's *Improvement Era* urging the reelection of William Howard Taft and signed by Joseph F. Smith, president of the church. "This editorial," said Bamberger, "shows that Taft has at least one friend in Utah who is working for him without having any intention to influence a single vote." *The Tribune* article noted that this remark produced an outburst of Democratic laughter. [3]

In an election morning editorial, *The Tribune* refrained from predicting the reelection of Taft by a landslide but said:

> . . . If faithful official service, well performed in the real interests of the people, is going to count for anything then certainly President Taft ought to be absolutely sure of re-election.

261

The next paragraph said:

> Whatever the outcome is, however, we can all say
> with Cardinal Gibbons, whose sermon on Sunday
> was reported in full in yesterday morning's *Trib-
> une,* that the country is safe; that the fathers so
> justly and evenly organized the three departments
> of government so that no one of them would bring
> ruin to the Republic; that whatever the result of the
> election, the Union will be preserved; the Nation
> will progress, and all will be well. [4]

To readers of *The Tribune,* accustomed as they were to a
"raw meat" type of political diet, this surely must have seemed a
switch from the meat-ax to the feather duster.

The Tribune's candidate for president did not win. But Utah
was one of the two states he did carry, aided no doubt by *The
Tribune's* warnings as to what a Democratic victory would do to
lead and wool and by Joseph F. Smith's editorial in the *Improvement Era.* In its post-election editorial, *The Tribune* philosoph-
ically accepted the result, noted that the returns verified the
most extravagant pre-election claims made for Governor (Woodrow) Wilson, and attributed the Republican rout to the division created by Theodore Roosevelt.[5] The Republicans carried
Utah for all state and congressional offices, re-electing William Spry as governor, retaining Joseph Howell for a fifth term
as representative in Congress and electing Jacob Johnson to the
state's newly acquired seat in the House of Representatives.

In the 1914 election campaign, *The Tribune* took a stance
between its placatory attitude of 1912 and its inflammatory
aggressiveness of the pre-1912 days. But it remained much closer to the 1912 pattern than the earlier one. The reason for the
shift in the direction of militancy was the candidacy of Reed
Smoot for his third term in the Senate. This was the first election

under the constitutional amendment requiring the selection of senators directly by the voters instead of by state legislatures, so the Senate seat was a direct rather than an indirect issue in the campaign.

Forsaking its Republican commitment with respect to this office, *The Tribune* opposed Smoot, but not with the strident voice it had customarily used in past campaigns. It focused its opposition on one central issue — that neither Smoot nor anyone else should simultaneously hold the offices of United States senator and apostle of the Mormon Church. In the light of Kearns' speech in the Senate just before his term ended, his newspaper could hardly have done less than this without appearing craven. So even a policy aimed at accommodation, upon which *The Tribune* had now embarked, could not justify silence on this issue.

In this particular instance *The Tribune* could oppose Smoot without in fact being anti-Mormon. Smoot's opponent was James H. Moyle, whose credentials as a solid, dedicated, loyal Latter-day Saint could not be questioned. In this respect Smoot outranked Moyle only in ecclesiastical position. And it was this position which *The Tribune* contended should make Smoot ineligible for the political position. Then too, *The Tribune* could oppose Smoot without indirectly supporting a candidate objectionable to Kearns. There are good reasons to believe that Kearns held Moyle in high personal esteem and refrained from directly and affirmatively supporting him only because of his commitment to Democratic policies which Kearns opposed. Moreover there were some similarities between the Moyle and Kearns positions on the church-state issue. From the time the Mormons were divided between the two national parties, Moyle had consistently reflected, and at times asserted, the position that while high Mormon officials had a citizen's right to seek political office and express political positions, they should be regarded and treated as citizens in their political roles and not as ecclesiastical authorities. The Kearns position was that the two roles should not be mixed in

263

the same individual. Certainly, Moyle bitterly resented *Tribune* attacks on high officials of the church. His view was that when Kearns lost his seat in the Senate, "he used the full power of his paper to revile the Church and fan the fire of hatred already raging over the Reed Smoot situation."[6] But his resentment over this issue apparently did not generate the personal animosity which characterized the period.

Kearns' attitude toward Moyle as a person was expressed at a dinner honoring the latter upon his appointment in 1917 to the position of assistant secretary of the treasury in the Wilson administration. Said Kearns, in concluding his brief speech: "Everybody knows where you stand on any question, and you never hit below the belt." To Moyle the dinner was ". . . an unforgettable occasion . . . not alone for such tributes spontaneously accorded him, but more so for the reconciliation here represented."[7]

In its lead editorial the Sunday before the election, *The Tribune* took what before 1912 would have been a very "soft" position on the candidate it opposed.

> What will Tuesday's verdict be? it asked. Will Senator Smoot be elected his own successor or will James H. Moyle be given the coveted honor?
> Were Senator Smoot not an apostle of the dominant church of the state there could be little doubt of the result. And, even recognizing the tremendous advantage Mr. Smoot's church position gives him, it is difficult to imagine how he can carry Utah, wedded though it is to high protection, in this year of grace, 1914.[8]

The editorial then cited reasons why it opposed Smoot and argued that his defeat or his reelection by a close vote would be a victory for *The Tribune's* position.

When the first returns came in the Democrats were jubilant. Moyle carried Salt Lake County by 1,076 votes. But outlying counties changed the pattern and Smoot won by a margin of 3,152 votes. Democrats raised an uproar over suspected fraud in Weber and Washington counties. But Moyle declined to seek an investigation and a recount.

The Tribune's post-election editorial bore the caption: "Mr. Smoot's Rebuke."

> Tuesday election is full of promise to the people of Utah. Its results were in effect a pledge by the people to themselves of independence in political affairs. If the outcome does not indicate a complete divorce of church and state, it assuredly must satisfy the most radical critic that a tremendous forward movement has been made in this direction.
>
> On Sunday last *The Tribune* commented editorially on the outlook in this state and it indicated, in hope rather than expectation, the possibility of the thing happening that has happened. It pointed out the almost insuperable difficulty of dislodging a man like Senator Smoot, intrenched by his apostleship, and by it elevated in the minds of his co-religionists, above the ranks of his fellow citizens. *The Tribune* also indicated that, in the dozen years Mr. Smoot has occupied the senatorship, a strong sentiment has grown up against the elevation of a high church official to a lofty political position. The impropriety of one man's holding simultaneously two offices — one next to the loftiest in the American government — has been much commented on, and by none in stricter terms of reprobation than by Mormon Republicans, who nevertheless, were more than will-

ing to accept Mr. Smoot in either capacity, but in
one only. . . .[9]

The Tribune, of course, could be accused of self-serving rationalization in interpreting a narrow-margin defeat as a victory. But it could reasonably argue that the close race in a state
which two years before was one of the two in the entire union to
stand firm for the Republican Party; in which the head of the
dominant church had urged support of the Republican presidential candidate; and in which the major economic interests were
strongly protectionist, did reflect a movement toward The
Tribune's position.

As for The Tribune. its coverage of the 1914 campaign
showed that 1912 was not a passing aberration but was intended
as a continuing policy. It had covered the news events of the campaign objectively and impartially; it had opposed a candidate because of his ecclesiastical position without rancor, and without
assailing his religion; it had sought to persuade with reason
rather than inflame with invective; it had pursued a course designed to invite reconciliation rather than to provoke retaliation;
it had begun implementing a policy conforming to changing
conditions and looking to the future prospects of the state.

"Mr. Tribune" Appears[1]

THE ROUTINE employment of a secretary in the spring of 1913 turned out to be the most important action Thomas Kearns ever took with respect to the future of *The Salt Lake Tribune* and the perpetuation of the controlling ownership of the newspaper within his own family.

The new secretary was a 26-year-old railroad employe then stationed in Grand Rapids, Michigan. He had lived for a short time in Salt Lake City three years earlier, liked what he saw and had developed a desire to return. A special attraction of the city was a young girl, Eleanor F. Crawford, who became his wife in 1914. He apparently met and talked with former Senator Kearns when he was stationed in Salt Lake City with the Denver & Rio Grande Western Railroad and he had been recommended by Senator Clark of Montana. On May 26 he received a letter from Kearns inquiring about his availability and promptly responded with a formal application for employment, written on the letterhead of the Pere Marquette Railroad Company, which then employed him.

The letter, dated May 26:

Dear Senator:

Thank you for your kind favor of May twenty-third, which came in hand today.

Not only am I a first-class stenographer, thoroughly

versed in spelling, punctuation, diction, grammatical construction and composition but have the initiative and ability of execution to take up and diplomatically handle correspondence and other matters without dictation, and, in line with your desires.

As previously stated, have been associated with Mr. J. W. Mulhern for the past four years in capacity of secretary and assistant chief clerk, being with him while at Salt Lake City, and the fact that he has taken me with him from Illinois to California, thence to Salt Lake City, and now in Michigan, speaks for itself as to my loyalty and ability, and the confidence he has in me.

In my present position am receiving $120.00 per month, and would be willing to make a change to the West for that salary.

My address here is #260 State Street—am single—my folks residing at #801 South Sixth Street, Burlington, Iowa.

Would be glad of an opportunity of a personal interview with you, and would go to Chicago to call on you at any time that you might be passing through that point.

My only reason for entertaining a desire to change from my present position is a longing to again return to the Western country and locate permanently there.

Assuring you of my appreciation of your consideration and well wishes, which are thoroughly appreciated, I remain,

Yours respectfully

J. F. Fitzpatrick [2]

Shortly thereafter Fitzpatrick was notified that Senator Kearns would be at the Blackstone Hotel in Chicago on a specified date and would like to meet him there. As later recalled by Fitzpatrick, Kearns' first question was when could he report for work and a date was agreed upon. Thus the young secretary embarked upon a career in the service of *The Tribune* and the Kearns family which continued until his death on September 11, 1960. His background provides clues to some of his characteristics; but in many ways he was an inscrutable man, a complex mixture of antithetical traits which, to employes, could be baffling, exasperating and endearing all at the same time. Different persons, or the same person at different times and under varying circumstances, could get an impression that he was predominantly tough or soft; aggressive or shy; adamant or flexible; frank or secretive; aloof or gregarious; autocratic or democratic. A demanding perfectionist at heart, he was not easy to work for, but he was exhilarating.

Born January 18, 1887, in Pottsville, Pennsylvania, he was the eldest of the six children of James Henry and Mary (Goulden) Fitzpatrick. His father was a railroad engineer operating out of Pottsville. A bitter strike which occurred in the year of John's birth left the father both out of work and blacklisted from railroad employment. The railroad managements stood firm against rehiring their own known strikers but, needing skilled workmen, were not too careful about hiring blacklisted men from other areas. So James Henry Fitzpatrick, with other engineers, solved their dilemma by going to Burlington, Iowa, to fill the jobs of engineers blacklisted there while the Burlington engineers moved to Pennsylvania to fill the vacancies at Pottsville.

This, and similar experiences of his father in trade unionism, undoubtedly contributed to Fitzpatrick's sympathy for and genuine acceptance of unions and collective bargaining at a time when most executives with his responsibilities stubbornly resisted or reluctantly bowed to unionism. But his philosophical and practical sympathy for collective bargaining did not extend to all areas of employment. In the newspaper business, for example, he firmly believed that production workers in the backshop should be organized. But he could not understand why editorial employes would want to be represented by a bargaining committee rather than by themselves, individually. Neither could some of his editorial employes who sensed that they would fare better in individual than in collective bargaining.[3]

After graduating from Burlington High School and attending a business college for a short time, Fitzpatrick went to work in the railroad industry and remained there until he was employed by Senator Kearns. He retained throughout his life a sentimental attachment for and a strong interest in railroads, and his railroad training and experience served him well as a newspaper publisher. One particular area in which his early experience proved useful was that of diplomacy. As secretary to a railroad man who was recognized as a genius in operations but a catastrophe in public relations, Fitzpatrick worked to keep his boss out of trouble and to repair public relations damage if he failed. It might well have been this phase of his early experience which led him to follow throughout his life a practice which he frequently recommended to *Tribune* associates: to hold the tongue when anger gained ascendancy over judgment; to commit the angry response to writing; to place it in a desk overnight; to read it next morning and then destroy it. The practice no doubt served him well. On the debit side it left a void in the history of *The Tribune* so far as written documentation is concerned during the forty-odd years of his stewardship.

Fitzpatrick, or "J. F." as he was more often addressed, or "Mr. Smith" as he was sometimes identified within *The Tribune* newsrooms, did not always follow the "write it and destroy it" practice he so highly recommended. In dealing with editorial employes, for example, or with others, including advertisers, he could be awesomely uninhibited when he felt the occasion warranted plain speaking. He could, and often did, denounce stupidities with an Irish eloquence which one would never suspect he possessed until one experienced his verbal lash. The physical signal of an approaching storm was a slight flush rising from the lower neck upwards and an outward slant of both eyes. When the storm was over, it was over, and the victim might soon thereafter become the recipient of a warming commendation for something well done. Rank, incidentally, did not protect one from his "chew-outs." He could be harsher with a top associate than with a subordinate far down the organizational line. Commendations too were distributed without regard to rank.

Don Howard, a veteran employe of the *Telegram* and *The Tribune* who was assembling material for a history of *The Tribune* when he died April 15, 1967, left his impressions of Fitzpatrick in a paragraph referring to a drawing of *The Tribune* publisher in the Mint Cafe. The cafe, located near The Tribune Building, was patronized by a cross-section of downtown Salt Lake, and Fitzpatrick frequently lunched there to broaden his contacts and thereby guard against the error of assuming that what he heard at the Alta Club, the city's most prestigious men's club, represented prevailing public opinion. Howard, after noting the presence of the Fitzpatrick sketch among those of sports world characters, entertainers and men-about-town, wrote:

> So you drop into the Mint for breakfast, or for an afternoon beer, and if you had known John Fitzpatrick during the years he was boss man, you were always aware of his presence; sort of looking over your shoulder to see if you were on the job; and also ready to pick you up if you stubbed your toe. So in retrospect you feel the interest he had in your welfare; his concern if you became ill; his offer of a loan to tide you over in a time of stress or tragedy; and, above all, his fairness in dealing with the people he employed. You never knew what a real 'chew-out'

was until you had it from him; or what a glow of pride could flow from his bare mention of a job well done.

Another long-time *Tribune* employe, who shall remain anonymous because his experience was illustrative rather than unusual, interrupted the recital of a complaint against his employer with an apologetic recollection of his first meeting with Fitzpatrick. He recalled that a few months after he started working full-time for *The Tribune* a recurring health problem required hospitalization for an unknown period of time. To him it looked like a disaster. Having been an employe for so short a time, he assumed that his job was gone. There was no medical or hospital insurance at that time to soften the blow of unexpected bills and, in a state of depression, he was lying in bed wondering how he could possibly meet his financial obligations when Fitzpatrick and Arthur C. Deck, executive editor of *The Tribune,* walked in. Fitzpatrick, who was far less eloquent on occasions of this kind than when he was reacting to a blunder embarrassing to *The Tribune,* expressed sympathy and said: "Now, the only thing you have to worry about is getting well. And don't come back until you are well. You are still on the payroll, your job will be waiting for you when you are able to return, and arrangements will be made so you can pay your bills."

If there was one thing above all others that Fitzpatrick expected and demanded of his employes it was loyalty to *The Tribune,* but not the degree of loyalty he gave it, for that would be demanding the unreasonable and the unattainable. An employe could disagree with the policy of the newspaper and so express himself without offense to the publisher. He could criticize particular aspects of the newspaper and sometimes find the publisher in agreement. But any employe who questioned the integrity of *The Tribune,* inside or outside the organization, simply placed himself beyond the pale of the publisher's tolerance. The offend-er probably would not be discharged but would be welcome to leave at any time, and, having left, he would not be re-employed. It was not an attitude of "the king can do no wrong" but rather a belief that those who questioned the king's integrity, honesty and intentions, should not be in the service of the king.

Examples of *Tribune* employes protecting the interests of the newspaper delighted him, wherever found. On one occasion while walking through the newsrooms he stopped an office boy delivering papers to desks of editors and writers and asked for a copy. The boy politely but firmly told him the papers were for members of the staff and could not be given away to anyone else. Fitzpatrick indicated his understanding of the situation and instructed the editor to increase the boy's salary and watch him in the future.

Fitzpatrick's aversion to personal publicity or public acclaim bordered on the obsessive, and it sometimes created problems and embarrassments for his associates. He would not permit the use of his name in *The Tribune* when, as a matter of news coverage, it should have been used. Had he been arrested for drunken driving his name would undoubtedly have been used at his direction. Any news item carrying the names of the publisher or the owner of *The Tribune* was known in the news department as a "mandatory refer;" that is, it was to be referred to the editor in charge and, by him, to Fitzpatrick or someone delegated by him to act if he were away and could not be reached. The name of the owning family might survive the "refer" but the name of the publisher was almost certain to be deleted, particularly if it was used in a commendatory connotation.

When the University of Utah in 1949 conferred an honorary degree of doctor of laws upon him he at first declined to permit the use of his picture in *The Tribune*. He agreed to waive his role of censor in that particular instance only after associates convinced him that the absence of his picture might embarrass other recipients of honorary degrees.

When he was awarded an honorary degree of doctor of public service by Brigham Young University in 1956 this characteristic was thus noted in the presentation:

> ... Yet so successfully has he avoided the limelight, so carefully has he pursued anonymity, so effectively has he merged himself into the groups with which he has served, that his great achievements have gone largely unheralded and unpublicized. In his varied activities and in his unnumbered contributions to his community, John Fitzpatrick has proved the truthfulness of the statement, 'You can get almost anything done if you don't care who gets the credit.' He would rather see the job done than receive the acclaim for doing it. This characteristic can be attributed both to his fine sense of modesty and his conviction that much can be accomplished if work is uninterrupted by applause. [4]

On another occasion, when a dinner was given to honor a group of men who had played important roles in bringing about something of great economic importance to Utah and the Intermountain area, Fitzpatrick instructed *The Tribune* editor that his name was not to appear in the news coverage of the event by *The Tribune*. The editor and a *Tribune* reporter assigned to the dinner were reluctant to comply with the instruction because they knew, as did the honored guests, that Fitzpatrick had played perhaps the most important role of all. The editor and reporter knew their publisher too well to ignore the instruction without first testing what his reaction would be. So the reporter, within Fitzpatrick's hearing, suggested to the editor that in this case the publisher should waive his authority and permit the editor to make the decision as a matter of news judgment. Fitzpatrick's eyes took the slightly outward turn and the warning flush crept across his neck. "If my name appears in this story," he said in a low voice, "*The Tribune* will tomorrow be looking for a new editor and reporter, and I mean it." Whether or not he really meant it, the editor and reporter believed that he did and his name did not appear in the next morning's *Tribune*.

Among Fitzpatrick's many notable characteristics was a disciplined determination to learn. To learn the newspaper business, or any other, by starting at the bottom and working up to the top requires intelligence and ambition. But to come in at the top, as Fitzpatrick did, and then burrow down to the bottom to learn all the facets of the business, calls for a higher order of intelligence, ambition and disciplined concentration. That is what Fitzpatrick did. He delved into the mechanical production, circulation, distribution, advertising, business management, newsgathering and editorial departments of the newspaper to acquire a detailed knowledge of each. No matter in which department one worked, one was mistaken to assume that Fitzpatrick did not know what was going on or did not have ideas about what should be going on just because he had started newspaper work as the publisher. [5] It was a constant source of amazement to associates as to how, as one editorial writer put it, "he can keep on top of everything, as he does." The most pressing challenge to the political editor, for one, was trying to keep ahead of the publisher in political news. He frequently found himself in the humbling position of receiving his first leads on important upcoming developments from his publisher who had never even been a reporter. Employes in other fields had similar experiences.

While Fitzpatrick's interest and knowledge encompassed the entire newspaper operation, editorial employes always felt that he was, at heart, an editorial man. That is, he viewed a newspaper as something more than a profit-making business. To him a newspaper had public responsibilities and obligations which could not be satisfied by commercial success alone. He recognized that commercial success was, in the long run, essential

275

to the discharge of the public responsibilities; and he worked as hard to keep *The Tribune* economically strong as he did to improve it as a newspaper. But the end product to be striven for was a newspaper which met its public responsibilities, and not merely a profitable business.

Both with respect to *The Tribune* and the area which it serves he took the long-range view. That is why in periods of depression he deemed it more essential to maintain the quality of the newspaper than to maintain its level of profits. To him this was not an impractical, idealistic policy but a thoroughly pragmatic one.

This philosophy can be illustrated by his position on a water development program when the Salt Lake area was threatened with a severe and continuing shortage. One proposed solution involved a transmountain diversion of Colorado River Basin water into the Great Basin. Another involved various water-savings projects within the Great Basin and the diversion into the Salt Lake system of water flowing from the Silver King Coalition Mines property in Park City. Use of the Silver King water would have necessitated a purchase of very substantial size from the mining company whose principal owner was the same Kearns Corporation which owned *The Tribune*.

Fitzpatrick carefully weighed the merits and demerits of the proposed programs, and presumably his responsibilities to the Kearns family corporation. His conclusion was that the projects to conserve and develop water already within the Great Basin, including the Silver King source, could be undertaken twenty-five, fifty or 100 years in the future when it was needed; but failure to start getting Colorado River water allotted under compact could, and probably would, mean its loss forever. Thus, the long-range interest of the area served by *The Tribune* would best be served by the transmountain diversion project. And whatever best served the interests of its territory best served the interests of *The Tribune*. So, he instructed the editor to give unqualified and aggressive support to the program which would bring in Colorado River water.

Intense and serious-minded as he was, Fitzpatrick nevertheless had a relaxing sense of humor and loved a good practical joke. One he often recalled long after the event, and with growing relish, involved a Kearns Corporation employe and the 1936 election. J. E. McGinty, manager of the Kearns Building for many years, was a dedicated Democrat long before Franklin D. Roosevelt came along. With Roosevelt as head of the party, McGinty became both a dedicated and impassioned Democrat who could not comprehend how any intelligent person with any interest at all in humanity could favor Governor Alfred M. Landon over the great F.D.R.

Shortly before the election, Fitzpatrick had *The Tribune* staff make up a front page carrying a multi-column, smiling picture of McGinty, proudly displaying on his chest a huge sunflower campaign badge used in the Landon campaign. Two copies of the newspaper with the McGinty front page were run off the press. One was delivered to his home and the other placed on his desk in the Kearns Building. When he arrived at his office he looked at *The Tribune* on his desk to make sure that what he had seen at home was not, as he surely hoped it was, an aberration or a horrible nightmare. He charged into Fitzpatrick's office, slammed *The Tribune* down on the desk, announced that he was through working for any outfit that would slander a man as he had been slandered and vowed he would sue *The Tribune* for all it, and its owners, and its publisher were worth. Fitzpatrick soothingly sympathized with his distress, explained that he, the publisher, did not know in advance what was going to appear in the news pages and suggested that the matter would have to be taken up with the editor. He picked up his telephone, called Bert Heal, the editor, and conversed with him briefly and then, hanging up the phone, gravely informed McGinty: "Heal says that you can't sue for libel on a picture."

McGinty exploded with a string of unprintable expletives telling Heal where he could go. Even after he had been convinced that only two copies of the offending page had been printed and that he was in possession of both, McGinty remained unconvinced for a few days that the joke was funny. The day after election he could view it with tolerance, and even enjoyment, inasmuch as the candidate supported editorially by Fitzpatrick (Landon) carried only two states and lost Utah by almost three to one.

Not all *Tribune* employes saw Fitzpatrick in the same light. Some were exposed too much to his autocratic side and too little to his democratic side to comprehend the whole man. But as a generalization, it can be said that those who had the opportunity to experience his displeasure and his pleasure most were the ones who held him in highest esteem. That, it seems to the writer, is the meaningful measure of his character.

22

Journalistic Brawl Revived

WHEN JOHN F. Fitzpatrick assumed his new duties as secretary for Thomas Kearns in the spring of 1913 he was embarking upon a far bigger job than he could possibly have anticipated, but the large problems he was to deal with lay in the future. His immediate task was to demonstrate his competence in routine secretarial functions for which he had been employed. One of the first things noted was that the boss's desk was piled high with documents and correspondence. This seeming disorder appalled his orderly mind and clashed harshly with the habits he had formed in the railroad business. So one of his first acts, when Kearns was going to be out of the office for a few days, was to order some cabinets and file the contents of his desk. When an older and more experienced fellow-employe walked into the office and saw a bare desk he reacted with consternation and demanded to know what happened to all the papers. Fitzpatrick explained that he had filed them so he would know where they were. The older employe advised the new secretary to get the papers back on the desk before the ex-senator returned and warned: "If he gets back and discovers that something he wants is filed away where he can't find it, he will file you away." Fitzpatrick did not follow the well-intentioned advice. When Kearns returned he looked at the clean desk, grunted a few times, sat down and called for a particular paper. Fitzpatrick walked to one of the filing cabinets, pulled out the document and placed it on the desk. Then, one by one, Kearns asked for several more documents or correspondence files. Each time Fitzpatrick repeated his first performance. Nothing more was said about the filing system but thereafter the boss worked from an orderly desk. Day by day Kearns became more and more aware that his new secretary had not overstated his qualifications when he wrote, in his application, that he had "the initiative and ability of execution to take up and diplomatically handle correspondence and other matters without dictation, and, in line with your desires." The new secretary was already moving along a course which was to make him indispensable.

The newspaper situation in Salt Lake City at this point was far from stable. The competitive brawl was not quite so wild as it had been four years earlier when five dailies were fighting it out for survival—*The Tribune,* the *Evening Telegram,* the *Herald,* the *Inter-Mountain Republican* and *Deseret News.* All were undoubtedly losing money. The merger of the venerable *Herald* and upstart *Inter-Mountain Republican* to form the *Herald-Republican* had reduced the combatants from five to four, but the available business was insufficient to provide economic viability for four newspapers and it is doubtful that any were showing a profit in 1913. Had a qualified expert in newspaper publishing been making book at the time on the Salt Lake competition he would undoubtedly have picked the *Deseret News* as favored for survival, even though it was not at the top in either circulation or advertising volume. Its church ownership and support guaranteed its continuity, regardless of profits or losses. He would almost certainly have rated *The Tribune* the second best bet for survival, for it was still solidly entrenched in the morning and Sunday fields because of the prestige it had acquired over the years. Its owners had financial resources and were willing to absorb its losses. Additionally, *The Tribune* appeared to be moving in the direction of financial stability. During the two years since the muting of the "irrepressible conflict" it had increased its daily circulation from 16,000 to almost 19,000 and its Sunday circulation from 23,000 to 32,000. More important, from a revenue standpoint, it was beginning to get advertising from firms which, prior to 1911, shunned it for religious reasons.

Thus, the bookmaker would have encountered his most difficult task in rating the *Herald-Republican* and the *Evening Telegram.* The *Herald-Republican,* although fighting for first place in circulation and advertising volume, appeared vulnerable for several reasons. The prestige built up over a period of forty years by the *Herald* as a Democratic organ had been dissipated by its merger with the *Inter-Mountain Republican* and the firm identification of the merged newspaper as the mouthpiece of the Smoot organization of the Republican Party, which was not the entire Republican Party as the editorial feuding of the period clearly revealed. The *Inter-Mountain Republican* editor at this time was Arthur J. Brown, the former United States senator who had energetic detractors both among Mormons and gentiles. Moreover, it had suffered from ownership changes and diffused ownership. Individuals owning more than one percent of the stock at this particular time were Senator Smoot; D. C. Jackling, the guiding genius of Utah Copper Company; H. E. Booth; E. H. Callister; E. E. Jenkins; James H. Anderson; Senator Sutherland; E. M. Allison, Jr., and R. T. Badger.

The status of the *Telegram* changed during the year. Until late 1913 it was owned by the Kearns-Keith partnership and edited by C. C. Goodwin. While Kearns had been in the Senate, Goodwin, who left *The Tribune* when Kearns acquired control, had aimed a steady drumfire of criticism at Kearns. Presumably a personal reconciliation had taken place, or both had decided that an association as owner and editor would be mutually beneficial. But Goodwin was never able to transfer his *Tribune* prestige and reader appeal to the *Telegram,* possibly because he had passed his peak, or because the changing Utah climate had outmoded his talents, or because of over-exposure. He contributed a full page of editorials to the *Telegram* daily.

Late in the year Kearns and Keith sold the money-losing *Telegram.* The purchasers were George E. Hale, who became publisher and business manager, and a group of businessmen which included prominent Mormons and gentiles. Among those owning one percent or more of the stock were such well-known Utah names as J. Reuben Clark, Jr., who later served as United States ambassador to Mexico and in the First Presidency of The Church of Jesus Christ of Latter-day Saints; M. S. Browning and D. C. Eccles of Ogden; Paul F. Keyser, B. F. Bauer, George S. Auerbach, Jay T. Harris, N. W. Clayton and H. A. Schweikhart of Salt Lake City.

Breaking the pattern of the long *Tribune-Deseret News* feud, the journalistic brawling for a few years during this period was most conspicuous between *The Tribune* and the *Herald-Republican,* the morning competitors. Each challenged the other on circulation and advertising figures, even though sworn statements of circulation and ownership were now published semi-annually under an act of Congress which had been enabled in 1912. The splenetic outbursts were not confined to charges of fraud in circulation and advertising reports. The newspapers frequently accused each other of publishing direct or implied falsehoods for the purpose of injuring a competitor. A few examples will suffice to reflect the mood of the period.

The Tribune, always on the alert for opportunities to annoy Senator Smoot, reprinted this comment from *Harper's Weekly*:

> Senator Smoot stands at the head of a bi-partisan machine in Utah whose first rule is that any man who has not the machine's O.K. cannot thrive. The machine has quietly at its service the columns of the *Deseret Evening News,* the official organ of the Mormon church, and openly has the support of the

Herald-Republican, a paper founded by Senator Smoot and his close political subordinates. That there was a combination between the two papers was suspected by many, but this could never be proved until a short time ago when the name of Presiding Bishop [C. W.] Nibley of the Mormon church appeared on the executive committee named to dominate the editorial policy of the *Herald-Republican. . . .* [1]

The *Herald-Republican* screamed "foul," and denounced *Harper's Weekly* for originating and *The Tribune* for perpetuating a falsehood linking Bishop Nibley to the *Herald-Republican* for the purpose of creating an impression that it was a Mormon newspaper and thereby depriving it of liquor advertising. [2]

In an article published in the *Fourth Estate,* a newspaper trade publication, Brown, the editor, and E. H. Callister, the general manager of the *Herald-Republican,* denied emphatically that Bishop Nibley owned any stock in the newspaper or was in a position to influence its editorial policies. The national advertising representative of the newspaper went directly to the heart of the matter in stating:

It has been claimed that the *Herald-Republican* is a Mormon newspaper . . . and that Mormons do not buy whisky, cigars, beer, automobiles or in fact anything that the foreign advertiser would advertise in Salt Lake City. The Mormon question in Utah is a dead issue. The *Herald-Republican* does carry all the beer advertising . . . all the big whisky advertising . . . a majority of the different foreign tobacco advertising . . . a majority of the automobile accounts; in fact, all classes of foreign advertising. . . . [3]

283

None of the articles generated by this controversy provided any hints as to origin of the claim that Mormons did not buy automobiles!

On another occasion *The Tribune* aroused the ire of the *Herald-Republican* by reprinting at the top of a news column a notice of assessment levied against its stockholders and followed by this interpretative comment:

> Since the organization of the *Inter-Mountain Republican* several years ago the men engaged in that newspaper venture have had an illuminating experience in the perils of publication. It is said on good authority that considerably more than $200,000 was spent in the effort to make the old *Republican* go, but without success. . . .

Then, aiming its dart directly at Smoot and other founders of the *Inter-Mountain Republican, The Tribune* recalled the merger of the *Herald* and the *Inter-Mountain Republican* and continued:

> The *Herald* was a sound business with a splendid patronage. It was in excellent financial condition and the new owners, who had failed so disastrously with the *Inter-Mountain Republican,* got along swimmingly for a time. They forthwith claimed all the circulation in town and boasted of great profits being made, though none of the $100,000 in bonds issued on the merged newspapers ever were taken up and no dividends were ever paid to the stockholders. These clamorous claims have long since been silenced and now, in spite of the new venture have been compelled to admit failure and to assess its stockholders in order to meet the expenses of operation . . . [4]

284

Editor Brown of the *Herald-Republican* reacted next day with a half-page editorial under an eight-column red banner line. It started with a sweeping denial that the newspaper was being forced to join *The Tribune* in "its financial misery." But the details hardly supported the generalization that the *Herald-Republican* was in satisfactory financial condition. Brown conceded that the merged papers' hopes of paying the purchase price of the *Herald* out of profits had not been realized. He attributed the disappointment to "the unsatisfactory financial condition of the *Herald*" and to a financial depression which had had "devastating effects" on all Utah business. Then, shifting back to the stance that all was well with the *Herald-Republican* financially, he took the offensive:

> The *Tribune's* invitation to join it in the ranks of the newspaper prostitutes must therefore be declined. . . . The *Herald-Republican* has not sunk $850,000 as has *The Salt Lake Tribune* and the *Evening Telegram* under the ownership of Mr. Thomas Kearns. The *Herald-Republican* has never lost $50,000 in one year as did *The Tribune* and *Evening Telegram* according to the sworn statement of Mr. Kearns himself in the United States Court. The owners of the *Herald-Republican* have never gone into court and blackened the reputation of their own newspaper to rob an employee of a few hundred dollars that were honestly due him as Mr. Kearns did in the case of Frank I. Sefrit.

Making another quick shift in emphasis to justify rather than deny financial woes, Brown informed the public that, after all, the *Herald-Republican* was not launched as a commercial enterprise; that its primary purpose was to protect the people of Utah "from the unscrupulous attacks made upon them by the

Kearns newspapers." Continuing, he elaborated on this point:

> Whatever the silencing of the Kearns batteries of defamation have cost us has been well worth the money, for this newspaper has accomplished the primary purpose of its existence. Within two years after it had entered the field there was an abrupt change in *Tribune* policy. Its campaign of vituperation, so far as it included the columns of that newspaper, was terminated.

Again returning to the financial status of the *Herald-Republican,* Brown admitted that its "revenue is smaller than in prosperous times" but added: ". . . we have suffered less in proportion than most ventures that are now struggling with Democratic prosperity in Utah."

At the point in the editorial the ambivalent Brown apparently decided that he had been overly harsh with Kearns. But instead of softening the fatal product, he concluded: "Mr. Kearns, however, is a vast improvement upon many of those who are supporting him and his newspaper."[5]

Despite all the claims of growing circulation and advertising volume, of bright future prospects, and of "satisfactory financial status," the obvious fact was that the Salt Lake City newspaper structure was and had for some time been in an economic wringer which had forced the merger of the *Herald* and *Inter-Mountain Republican* and which was still threatening to squeeze the life out of one or more of the four survivors. Because of factors heretofore mentioned, the struggle for survival had shaken down to the *Evening Telegram* and the *Herald-Republican.* But the newspaper battle continued for about four more years with four combatants before a break came. A few days after the *Herald-Republican* announced plans for greatly expanding the contents of its Sunday paper, there appeared on the editorial page an announcement that the issue was the last which would appear "under present management."[6] The deal was rather complicated and all the details were not initially disclosed. But the effect was the transfer on a lease of the *Herald-Republican* to the Telegram Publishing Company which started publishing a morning *Herald-Republican-Telegram,* an *Evening Telegram-Herald-Republican* and a *Sunday Herald-Republican-Telegram.* This arrangement continued for only four months. On July 8, 1918, the *Herald-Republican* canceled the lease and the following day started publishing what it described as the "new *Salt Lake Herald,*" a seven-day a week newspaper.[7] The brief amalgamation by lease generated a rash of lawsuits filed by the *Herald-Republican,* which charged breach of contract and asked for a judgment of $157,930.

The new *Herald* offered no explanation of why the *Republican* portion of its name had been dropped. Perhaps the purpose was to dim its image as a partisan political organ; or maybe it hoped to recapture some of the prestige and flavor of that tough and pungent Democratic competitor of *The Tribune,* the old *Salt Lake Herald.* That hope was not to be realized. Economic pressures on the *Herald* increased and on January 1, 1920, a new publisher took over. He was A. L. Fish, a former representative of the *Los Angeles Times* in San Francisco and business manager of the *Oregon Journal* in Portland, a job he had left to enter the Army during World War I. Fish installed G. B. (Bert) Heal as managing editor. Both Fish and Heal were destined to later serve *The Tribune* for many years. During the next few months Fish also negotiated a lease or contract which soon led to the *Herald's* demise. With this lease he assumed operative control of the *Telegram* from George E. Hale who was in failing health. The arrangement included a monthly payment to Hale for life. Thus, in the Sunday issue of the *Herald* on July 18, 1920, this notice appeared:

The *Herald* Passes — With today's issue, the *Salt Lake Herald* suspends publication. Established June 6, 1870, this paper has seen more than 50 years of active service. . . . But now a new era in journalism has come; mounting costs of operation, and the trend of advertising toward the evening field, have made it impossible for the *Herald* to profitably continue publication. . . . The Salt Lake Telegram Publishing Company has made arrangements to take over the circulation and serve the subscribers of the *Salt Lake Herald* with the evening and Sunday *Telegrams*.[8]

Thus, while the *Telegram* took over the expiring *Herald*, it was the publisher and managing editor of the *Herald* who remained to operate the surviving newspaper, the evening and Sunday *Telegram*.

During the lusty and inelegant squabbling among the competing newspapers prior to the demise of the *Herald*, the old *Tribune-Deseret News* feud was notably quiescent. Neither of these veterans of Utah's journalistic wars showed a disposition to reopen the "irrepressible conflict." Occasionally the old mood surfaced briefly. One such incident occurred when the *Deseret News* published an article quoting unidentified sources to the effect that *The Tribune* was an unseen influence in the leasing of the *Herald-Republican* to the *Telegram* and the subsequent cancellation of the lease.[9]

Reacting with old time vigor, *The Tribune* replied over the name of Thomas Kearns that the *Deseret News* had never in its long career of half-truth and defamation printed anything as "distasteful as this innuendo which tries to connect" *The Salt Lake Tribune* "with the unfortunate history of that foul sheet known as the *Herald-Republican*. . . ."[10]

Noting that the vitriol in *The Tribune* statement was aimed at the *Herald-Republican,* the *Deseret News* sought to turn away wrath with a soft answer. Accepting Kearns' statement, the *News,* tongue now in cheek, congratulated him "that he had nothing to do with a campaign which has brought about the present conditions with the *Herald-Republican,* conditions which for some months practically removed that paper from the field of competition with *The Tribune.*" [11]

While *The Tribune* was still disposed to bare its teeth on occasion in the give-and-take of the competitive newspaper war, A. N. McKay, the publisher, presumably with the assent of Kearns, had drastically toned it down in the political arena. In the 1916 election, for example, the old brawler which had lived most of its life in the eye of a political hurricane, stood placidly on the sidelines. It expressed a polite preference for Charles Evans Hughes, the Republican presidential candidate, over President Woodrow Wilson and his "he kept us out of war" reelection campaign; but it took no editorial position on candidates within the state and was impeccably objective in its news coverage. It was accused by the *Herald-Republican* of supporting Simon Bamberger, the Democratic candidate for governor; but this charge would have been difficult to support by anything which appeared in its columns prior to election day. The *Herald-Republican* would have been right had it said that the owners of *The Tribune* favored Bamberger over Nephi L. Morris, the Republican candidate for governor, and William H. King, Democrat, over Republican incumbent George Sutherland, in the United States Senate contest.

The Tribune's preference stemmed not so much from any aversion to the Republican candidates as from their association with and obligation to Senator Reed Smoot and the *Herald-Republican.* Both gubernatorial candidates campaigned as advocates of state-wide prohibition. *The Tribune,* forsaking its old position that "dry" laws would aggravate rather than eliminate the liquor problem, was now lending its support to the prohibition movement. While *The Tribune* adequately covered the campaign as a non-combatant observer, its rival *Herald-Republican* became directly embroiled. Democratic Party officials ran large advertisements in *The Tribune* asserting that local breweries were influential stockholders in the *Herald-Republican* and charged that the "Smoot organ" had made a deal with the "liquor interests."[12] Whatever the facts, it must have been an intriguing situation for those veterans of the "irrepressible conflict" who had campaigned so long to force the political processes out of an ecclesiastical mold. Their efforts, or events which they did not control, or some of both, had really mixed things up in Utah. The devil's disciple of the campaign was no longer *The Tribune* but the journalistic organ of a political organization led by an apostle of the Mormon Church. The *Deseret News* and *The Tribune* were for once backing the same cause — prohibition. The gubernatorial candidate who proclaimed that he had no ties or obligations to the "liquor interests" was Simon Bamberger, a Jew and the first non-Mormon ever elected governor of the state. His opponent, Morris, who was accused by the Democrats of having obligatory ties with the "liquor interests" was a respected member of the Mormon Church.

Whatever the reaction of the voters might have been to the campaign charges and counter-charges, they gave the Democrats a decisive victory on election day. Wilson carried the state by more than 15,000 votes, King beat Sutherland by some 12,000; Bamberger won over Morris by a slightly lesser margin and carried with him the entire state Democratic ticket and a majority of both houses of the State Legislature. With the predictable help of Republican legislators, Bamberger promptly made good on his promise of a "bone dry" state prohibition law. The law was signed by the governor on February 8 and became effective on August 1, 1917.

Two days after the election *The Tribune,* relapsing into the editorial style of an earlier period, disclosed its views on the election under the heading: "Smoot Rebuked."

> The result in Utah is a statewide rebuke to Senator Smoot. . . . The returns show that within his own church there exists an overwhelming sentiment against the senator's brazen assumption of a three-fold leadership — in religion, in politics and in finance. His amazing arrogance and egotism have finally met with the disaster they invited. . . .

The editorial charged that "Smoot and his fellow ringsters" had prevented the renomination of Republican Governor William Spry and thereby made the greatest of a long series of blunders. It echoed the Democratic charge of a "deal" with the "liquor interests" and added:

> What the terms of the deal might be the public did not know, but when they saw the saloon vote swing suddenly to Mr. Morris they did not need to know the details of the agreement. They made up their minds then and there that the Smoot crowd, which had been tied up with the liquor interests for years, were merely at the old game. . . .
> But this deal was simply one of the many Smootian blunders. The people of Utah had determined to repudiate him and they carried out their purpose in the most convincing fashion. They were done with Smoot and his pretensions forever. [13]

It looked like a sweet political victory for *The Tribune* at the time, but it would have turned sour had those relishing Smoot's discomfort been able to peer into the future and see him occupying a Senate seat and enlarging his influence in that body for sixteen more years.

291

23

Deaths Temper Conflict

IF ONE YEAR were to be singled out as the most eventful and significant in the 100-year history of *The Salt Lake Tribune,* 1918 would be a formidable contender. It was a year of momentous historical events, such as decisive Allied victories which culminated in the ending of World War I; the embarkment by the United States upon what was to become a continuing policy of international aid, rehabilitation and military involvement; and the ravaging Spanish influenza epidemic. It was also a year of death-related internal changes for *The Tribune.*

To the readers of *The Tribune,* and to people all over the world, it was both a depressing and an exhilarating year. The depressive factors, as reflected in the columns of the newspaper, included long lists of Utahns and Intermountain residents killed in the war. Every issue carried two, three or more pictures of young men "killed in action." On the home front the flu epidemic was loading the columns of *The Tribune* with obituaries of prominent and obscure people of all ages, with an abnormally large percentage being men and women in the prime of life. During the latter part of the year, when the epidemic was rising toward its crest, schools, churches, theaters, dance halls and other places of public amusement were closed. Social functions, public or private, were forbidden; shopping hours were curtailed and controlled to minimize contact of people with one another; limitations were placed on the number of passengers allowed on street cars; and Joseph F. Smith, president of The Church of Jesus Christ of Latter-day Saints, was laid to rest without a public funeral service. The medical profession got into a public hassle over the wearing of gauze masks as means of controlling the epidemic. A *Tribune* staff member recalls a vivid memory of the period when in late November he was checked out of the Fort Douglas hospital and registered at the Hotel Utah. About 10 p.m. he walked from the Hotel Utah to the Newhouse Hotel and back, a distance of eight blocks on Main Street, and saw one human being and two cats. The human being, wearing a ghostly white mask, was a night watchman checking shop doors. The cats were, appropriately, black.

Soaring prices and shortages harassed a large majority of the people. *The Tribune,* in a report on Thanksgiving dinner food prices, listed eggs at 72 cents per dozen, oranges at 10 to 15 cents each, turkey at 40-42 cents per pound and spring chicken at 45 cents per pound. [1]

On the cheerful side of the otherwise dismal picture which emerged from the columns of *The Tribune* were large black headlines on Allied victories, capped on the morning of November 11 by a huge eight-column banner line — "The War Is Ended" [2] — and on the morning of November 12 by a slightly smaller line — "125,000 Salt Lakers Go Wild." [3] The Salt Lakers went wild at a spontaneous street celebration. Ironically, the Armistice festivities were blamed by health authorities for aggravating the flu epidemic.

At *The Tribune,* in keeping with the somber atmosphere of the year, death struck swiftly and it struck at the top. David Keith, the long-time partner of Thomas Kearns, died in April, thereby placing a half interest in *The Tribune* in an estate which demanded cash for tax purposes. On October 18 Thomas Kearns died eight days after he was struck down by a Ford automobile near the base of the monument of Brigham Young at Main and South Temple Streets. Death was attributed to a stroke brought on by injuries suffered in the accident. This placed the other half of *The Tribune* in an estate and shifted to the competent shoulders of Kearns' secretary, John F. Fitzpatrick, responsibility for the varied and extensive business interests left by Kearns to his family. The deaths of the two owners of *The Tribune,* instead of jeopardizing continuity of ownership of the newspaper, established it in the Kearns family. For a year later, after Mrs. David Keith had also passed away, David Keith, Jr., administrator of the estate, and his attorney appeared in the office of John Fitzpatrick to offer the one-half share in *The Tribune* for sale. As recalled by Fitzpatrick years later, the executors of the Keith estate said the sale was necessary to raise cash, that they had decided to give the Kearns estate the first opportunity to buy, that if the Kearns family did not choose to buy they would seek to sell elsewhere. Fitzpatrick inquired as to the asking price and was informed that it was $300,000. He thereupon agreed to buy and entered into a contract to pay $30,000 down and the remainder upon confirmation of the sale by the court. The transaction was completed on October 19, 1919. Valued on *The Tribune's* past earning record, $300,000 looked to be a liberal price for a one-half interest. Valued on the newspaper's outlook for future earnings, it was a bargain price. At the time of the sale it appeared to be a reasonable price, as two different sets of appraisers had valued the Kearns half-interest at $175,000. Fitzpatrick looked to the future instead of the past and, as the future demonstrated, made a very profitable investment for the Kearns family.

A third death in 1918 which had an indirect but significant bearing on the history of *The Tribune* was that of President Joseph F. Smith of The Church of Jesus Christ of Latter-day Saints on November 19. The deaths of Kearns and President Smith a month apart had consigned to the past some old animosities which had impeded prior efforts to repress the "irrepressible conflict." The frictions had been reflected in such incidents as Smith's opposition to a second Senate term for Kearns, the sena-

294

tor's indictment of the church from the Senate floor just before his term ended, the organization of the American Party and its support by *The Tribune*, and President Smith's suspected collaboration with Kearns' old political enemy, Senator Reed Smoot. More important to the cause of accommodation were the leadership changes wrought by death. President Smith was succeeded as head of the church by Heber J. Grant, a man who over the next 27 years was to demonstrate a dedication to healing old sores and pushing the "irrepressible conflict" into past history. In this enterprise he had the equally dedicated collaboration of those in control of *The Tribune* — John Fitzpatrick, who after Kearns' death exercized the authority of ownership, A. N. McKay, the publisher, and Homer F. Robinson, a *Tribune* man for more than a half-century, who was business manager.

President Grant's role in the establishment of an accommodation was not a passive one, for he was not a passive man. He was an activist in the movement both at home and abroad. He certainly stands out in the history of the Mormon Church and in the history of Utah as a mighty contributor to an evolutionary process of displacing conflict with cooperation at home and erasing a widely entrenched (primarily because of polygamy) image of his church as an ecclesiastical pariah. The attitude of President Grant toward the gentile journalistic spokesman in the "irrepressible conflict" can be fairly expressed in his own words. Following Joseph F. Smith's death, Grant carried in his pocket a copy of the editorial tribute paid to President Smith by *The Tribune* and frequently read it at meetings to prove that the epoch of distrust and recrimination had really ended. At a Thanksgiving dinner sponsored by the Salt Lake Chamber of Commerce a few days after the death of A. N. McKay on November 18, 1924, President Grant, the principal speaker, began:

> I made up my mind last night . . . that I would devote most of my time in paying tribute to Ambrose

Noble McKay. To his fairness and understanding I attribute the changed attitude of the greatest newspaper in our city.

He then read *The Tribune's* editorial tribute to President Smith and added these comments:

I believe I know who wrote that editorial. Although I asked Mr. McKay if the man I mentioned had written the article he merely said: 'We never give away editorial secrets.' I am satisfied if the party I named had not written it he would have told me I was mistaken, but he did not. [4]

The person who wrote the editorial was Noble Warrum, Sr., then postmaster of Salt Lake City but who later served *The Tribune* for years as an editorial writer. He was a close personal friend of McKay, Grant and Smith.

A few years before President Grant died on May 14, 1945, a *Tribune* reporter called at his home seeking an interview on a European tour the church president had just completed. He found President Grant alone and in a reminiscent mood. After the immediate business had been disposed of, President Grant began recalling past experiences and for about two hours kept a reporter who had to meet a deadline entranced. When the reporter reluctantly informed President Grant that he would have to leave if he was going to "make the Idaho edition" President Grant terminated the interview with substantially this comment:

There is one more thing I would like to tell you. I am a man with a long memory. I am not always so forgiving as I should be. And *The Tribune* has said things about me and many of my friends and associates which I shall never forget or forgive. But I want you and your associates on the paper to know that if suddenly remembering some of these things, I begin expressing my bitterness, I am talking about the past and not the present or anyone now associated with *The Tribune.* For one of my best friends, inside or outside the church, is your publisher, John Fitzpatrick. [5]

A month before *The Tribune* paid its tribute to President Smith, the *Deseret News* published an editorial on the death of Thomas Kearns which indicated that the church newspaper, like *The Tribune,* was willing to let bygones be bygones.

The death of the Honorable Thomas Kearns yesterday . . . removes from this sphere of action with painful suddenness a man who was in all respects a notable figure in the community. He rose by his own energy, industry and foresight — aided perhaps to some extent by what men call luck — from poverty to affluence; he climbed from the station of humble delver underground to the loftiest political position any American state can confer upon one of its citizens — the United States senatorship. To his credit be it said that in the height of his prosperity he never forgot the 'pit whence he was digged,' and he was not too proud to recognize with cheery sociableness and material aid those with whom he toiled in less comfortable days. . . . Hence, with large numbers of men in his employ, his enterprises were singularly free from labor disturbance. His private benefactions were far more numerous than were known to the public, while some of his larger charities will long be memorable. Having gained his wealth in this state, he was loyal enough to use it locally in building up and beautifying the city where he made his home. Of course he had his limitations, as has every man; but he had also many of those fine traits which endear a man to those who know him best. . . . [6]

The Tribune, which had said some harsh things about Joseph F. Smith both before and after he became president of the Mormon church, said this about him in death:

In his earlier days he was fiery, fearless, impetuous and uncompromising, and was therefore looked upon as a fanatic intolerant of moderation and irreconcilable to opposition. But with the coming of age, the assumption of authority, the increase of responsibility and the consequent contact with his fellow men, came a broadening of vision and a softening of his nature which gained for him a recognition of those sterling qualities for which he will be remembered longest and best. . . . [7]

In the benign political and ecclesiastical atmosphere then existing in Utah, The Tribune pursued a policy in the 1918 campaign and election which could offend no one, except perhaps some of its older readers who were used to stronger political fare. It covered the campaign quite fully and objectively and took no editorial position on candidates within the state. It was an off-year and the office of president, United States senator and governor were not at stake. The newspaper did aggressively oppose a proposed constitutional amendment designed to remove constitutional property tax protections from the mining industry. It did indulge in a little political meddling in the affairs of neighboring states by supporting Francis E. Warren, a Republican, for reelection to the Senate in Wyoming and Charles B. Henderson, a Democrat, for reelection to the Senate in Nevada. The newspaper also urged Nevada and Wyoming voters to support "bone dry" propositions which were being submitted to the voters. The strength of the prohibition sentiment then rolling up in the country can be appreciated from the fact that both Nevada and Wyoming did vote "dry," along with Florida and Minnesota. This brought to thirty-three the number of states adopting state-wide prohibition laws before the Eighteenth Amendment was approved the following January (1919) to become effective in January of 1920.

In an editorial comment on the prohibition vote *The Tribune* stated that California failed to go "dry" only because of the San Francisco vote, and with the following statement predicted that national prohibition would surely come by 1920:

> Prohibition sentiment has been growing for a number of years and has at last gathered sufficient momentum to make itself felt. Politicians have long since ceased to call the prohibitionists 'long-haired cranks' just as they ceased calling suffragists 'short-haired females.' Success makes all the difference in the world.[8]

A newsworthy event in the fall of 1918 which served to emphasize the change in the policy of *The Tribune* was the reviving of the old bugaboo, polygamy. The issue was raised not by *The Tribune* this time, but by leaders of the Mormon Church at the semi-annual conference in October. Charles W. Penrose, whose slashing attacks on *The Tribune* while he was editor of the *Deseret News* had brought him more than local fame as a journalist, turned his considerable talents of denunciation upon those members of the church who were persisting in the teaching and the practice of plural marriages. Penrose at that time was a member of the First Presidency and so was speaking with the authority of that body. If anyone doubted that he was expressing the position of the church it was dispelled when President Joseph F. Smith who was making his last appearance at a general conference, and Heber J. Grant, senior member of the Council of Twelve Apostles, concurred in and expanded upon Penrose's remarks. *The Tribune* quoted President Smith as follows:

> I find it imperative upon myself to endorse and affirm without reservation the statement that has been made by President Penrose in relation to the subject upon which he last treated. I want to say to this congregation and to the world that never at any time since my presidency in the Church of Jesus Christ of Latter-day Saints, have I authorized any man to perform a plural marriage and never, since my presidency of the Church, has any plural marriage been performed with my sanction or knowledge or with the consent of the Church. Therefore, such marriages as have been performed unlawfully and contrary to the order of the Church are null and void in the sight of God and man and are not marriages at all. I want you to put this down in your notebooks and remember it as long as you live, because it is true. 9

The Tribune covered the conference sessions in considerable detail and with detached objectivity, a far cry from the earlier conference reports loaded with sarcasm and snide interjections. Unlike *The Tribune* of an earlier period, it kept its editorial mouth shut on polygamy, which was now a problem for the *Deseret News*.

In summary it can be said that 1918 was undoubtedly a more eventful year in the history of *The Tribune* when viewed retrospectively than it appeared at the time. For the significance of some of the developments of that year depended upon their permanence. There had been "springtimes" of accommodation on prior occasions, followed by relapses into the old "irrepressible conflict." Viewed from the vantage point of more than a half-century, 1918 emerges as the year in which policies of conciliation cautiously inaugurated by both sides of the old conflict in 1911 were confirmed and permanently established. It was the year of certain events which assured a continuity of ownership of *The Tribune*. It was the year which solidly entrenched advocates of accommodation in control of the destinies of the newspaper for the next half century and more. It was the year in which economic realities began forcing Salt Lake City's newspaper business into a viable structure. It was the year which sounded the death-knell of the venerable and respected *Salt Lake Herald,* although it lingered on until July 18, 1920, before it actually suspended publication. It was, in short, a year roughly dividing the history of *The Tribune* into two periods. During the first period it distinguished itself both at home and throughout the country as an aggressive, persistent, effective, and sometimes intemperate, voice on one side of a bitter conflict encompassing economic, political, religious and social differences. During the second period it distinguished itself both at home and throughout the country as a consistent, objective, effective and temperate advocate of sensible cooperation among diverse economic, political, religious and social groupings. Throughout both periods it has been an energetic collector and disseminator of news, background information and viewpoints from which its readers of all varieties could draw their own conclusions, objective or otherwise.

301

24

From Brimstone to Soothing Syrup

WHEN THOMAS Kearns died so unexpectedly it was inevitable that his secretary, John F. Fitzpatrick, would take over management of the estate the one-time hard rock miner had accumulated during a comparatively short life. This was so for at least three reasons. In the five years Fitzpatrick had served as the former senator's confidential and chief assistant he had won the complete confidence of his employer. Death transmitted this confidence to Mrs. Jennie Judge Kearns, the widow. No one but he possessed both business experience and a familiarity with the various interests left by Kearns to his family. Thus the selection of Fitzpatrick to take over the responsibilities theretofore carried by Kearns was both a matter of choice and necessity. Still another factor which probably had some bearing on the succession was the willingness of the secretary to assume responsibilities. As he had said in his letter of application for the job, he had "the initiative and ability of execution to take up and diplomatically handle correspondence and other matters without dictation, and, in line with your desires." He was the "take-over" type of man who did not shrink from the exercise of authority, the making of decisions and the acceptance of responsibility for those decisions. And Mrs. Kearns never had reason to wonder whether she had acted wisely in placing so much trust in the ability and fidelity of her late husband's young secretary.

The assets of the estate left by Kearns were appraised for inheritance tax purposes at $2,078,670.59. The major items were real estate, principally the Kearns Building, valued at $1,084,650; railroad bonds valued at $376,630; railroad capital stock valued at $135,117; Silver King Coalition Mines Company stock valued at $170,063; a one-half interest in *The Tribune*, valued at $175,000; Liberty Bonds in the amount of $25,000; and $26,887 cash in bank. Miscellaneous items included a 1908 Pierce Arrow automobile valued at $750 and three old vehicles valued at $1. Actual value of the estate was no doubt somewhat more than the appraised value. Looking a few years into the future, the appraisal was substantially short of the actual values. With respect to *The Tribune*, Fitzpatrick purchased for the estate the Keith half-interest in the newspaper for $300,000 and thereby struck an excellent bargain for his employers. In the following year (1920) the capitalization of *The Tribune* was increased from $200,000 to $1,000,000 and during the next four years it paid $350,000 in dividends. The flow of dividends, however, dwindled markedly as Fitzpatrick took over control. The motions at directors' meetings to authorize dividends were gradually supplanted by recommendations from Fitzpatrick as treasurer that $350,000 be accumulated for a new double octuple printing press; that $50,000 be accumulated for expansion of this or that department, and so on. Fitzpatrick had an inner urge approaching the intensity of a passion for capital investment and accumulation of cash reserves. And he generally got his way. He was not a man to take economic risks unless he had to, and he recognized that the days when the flow of mine dividends could support the newspaper belonged to the past. For mine dividends had already dwindled and publishing costs were swelling.

The heirs to the estate of Kearns, who left no will, were Mrs. Kearns and three children, Thomas F., Edmond J. and Helen. The corporate organization of The Tribune Publishing Company after the Keith one-half interest had been acquired was Thomas F., president and director, Mrs. Kearns, vice president and director, and Edmond J., director, and Fitzpatrick, treasurer. A perusal of the minutes of the board meetings indicates that the influence of the treasurer far exceeded that which normally attaches to that office in corporate organizations.

The day-to-day operations of *The Tribune* were at this time in the capable hands of A. N. McKay, who exercized the functions of publisher and general manager but whose title in the statements of ownership and circulation was general manager; Homer F. Robinson, business manager; and E. H. Holden, managing editor who had recently succeeded F. P. Gallagher in that position. There is nothing in available records to suggest that Fitzpatrick interfered in the operation of the editorial department of *The Tribune* during this period — the late teens and early nineteen twenties. There was no reason why he should; he was just learning the newspaper business and, intelligent and perceptive as he was, he undoubtedly recognized that his proper role, temporarily, was that of a student under the tutelage of the veteran, McKay. Moreover, as the future disclosed, he was in full accord with the general policies being pursued by McKay in accordance with the understanding he had reached with Kearns when he accepted the position in 1911. However, the Fitzpatrick influence was immediately reflected in the over-all business operations of the newspaper in such areas as budgeting and capital improvements.

Robinson, the business manager, had been a dedicated employe of *The Tribune* since 1882 when he started work as a messenger at age 18. He was a product of both periods of *The Tribune's* history and had imperturbably gone about his business of trying to make the newspaper profitable both in the days of bitter conflict and the latter days of conciliation. He was, by nature, better suited to the role of conciliator than crusader but he could play either one with dignity and without personal animosity or obeisance. In outward appearance he was an austere, forbidding individual encased in the armor of gruff sternness. Inwardly he was gracious, sympathetic and tolerant, and he possessed a subtle sense of humor which was not immediately discernible. In his capacity as business manager he was an ally of the editorial department, particularly in the sensitive and frequently disputatious problem of drawing the line between news and unpaid advertising. He never pressured editors to give away in the news department what he was selling in the advertising department. On the contrary, he was more inflexible on this point than some editors and on occasion raised objections to publication of material which an editor was willing to accept on a basis of its news value. He regarded the sale of newspapers or space as a mutually beneficial business transaction which did not call for the giving or the acceptance of favors. The inward nature of Homer Robinson was accurately reflected in a *Tribune* project which he initiated and enthusiastically nurtured until his death in 1939 — the Sub-for-Santa program. The program survived him and at Christmas time still serves as a memorial to a man who probably worked for *The Tribune* longer than any other person — fifty-seven years.

The story of *The Tribune* during the 1920's was one of solid progress in circulation and advertising volume. This reflected comparable growth in its public acceptance as a readable, reliable and objective source of news and opinions. The editorial policy, unobtrusively initiated in 1911 and fortified by the events of 1918, was working as the initiators expected it to work. Its area of acceptability as a source of information was rapidly expanding and its value as an advertising medium was keeping pace. *The Tribune* was on its way to becoming in the new era of accommodation what it had been in the old era of the "irrepressible conflict," the most widely read and quoted newspaper between Denver and the Pacific Coast. In this new era its appeal was aimed at the entire public of its circulation area rather than the combatants on one side of a bitter conflict. Its new role was that of a unifying communications medium for its territory rather than a divisive champion of a cause which by this time had been won in all substantial respects.

305

The change in the fortunes of *The Tribune* was dramatically reflected in the circulation figures. During the first forty years of its life, up to 1911, the daily circulation had crept from approximately 1,000 to 16,000. The Sunday edition, which was launched in 1900 with a circulation of 13,362, had reached 22,783 in 1910.[1] In 1915 the daily circulation was 18,847 and the Sunday 35,526 and by the end of 1919 the daily circulation had passed the 40,000 mark and the Sunday was a few hundred short of 65,000.[2] The growth trend continued throughout the 1920's but slowed drastically for a few years when the depression of the 1930's descended upon the country.

In the political campaign of 1920 *The Tribune's* editorials were even more bland than they had been in 1916 and 1918. It covered the speeches and developments of the campaign adequately, but any satisfaction Republicans or Democrats derived from its editorials had to be strictly negative. The most positive statement in its election morning campaign editorial was that the presidential candidate receiving a majority of the electoral vote would take the presidential chair and "the country would settle down to business." The concluding sentences were:

> Today marks the culminating point of the 1920 campaign. From now on business will improve because the matter of policy for the next four years will have been definitely settled and the businessmen of the nation can make their plans along the lines laid down without fear of interference. There is much reason for optimism at this time.[3]

For *Tribune* readers brought up on the editorials of Lockley, Goodwin and Frank J. Cannon, the editorial page must have been depressingly dull reading.

The election turned out as *The Tribune* forecast — a Republican sweep in the nation and in the state. Warren G. Harding was elected president, Reed Smoot was returned to the Senate for his fourth term, Charles R. Mabey was elected governor and E. O. Leatherwood and Don B. Colton were elected to their first terms in the United States House of Representatives.

In the 1924 campaign *The Tribune* shed some of its neutrality but not its recently acquired soft political manners. It supported, with something less than crusading zeal, the election of Calvin Coolidge who had succeeded to the presidency upon Harding's death. Somewhat more positively, it urged the election of a Republican Congress to support the president. In a pre-election editorial, it said:

> It being practically certain that President Coolidge will remain chief executive of the nation for the next four years, the Republican Party will not achieve a full measure of victory at the polls next Tuesday unless it gains control of both branches of Congress. Otherwise the president's influence for good will be nullified. . . .[4]

The Tribune's assumption that Coolidge would be elected by a large majority proved correct, but its confident prediction that Utah would go Republican proved wrong in one important respect. The Republicans retained their two congressional seats, elected majorities in both houses of the state legislature and elected a state ticket except for the politically most important office of all, that of governor. George H. Dern, a Democratic state legislator, defeated Governor Mabey and thereby pulled off an upset that was stunning to *The Tribune* and the Republicans and surprising to the Democrats. In a post-election editorial *The Tribune* extended the customary congratulations to the winners but it did not radiate enthusiasm for the new governor:

> The Democrats made their drive against Governor Mabey and succeeded in defeating him. He will be succeeded by George H. Dern, a Salt Lake business-

man who has had business experience and who will
no doubt be able to fill the exalted position to which
he has been elected. *The Tribune* wishes him well
and extends the customary congratulations upon
his victory.

Governor Mabey retires to private life with a clean
record as a public official and with the proud consciousness of having performed his duty as he
saw it.[5]

The Tribune editor was surprised by the election of a Democratic governor in Utah but he was astounded by an event in
England which he commented on in the same issue.

Premier Baldwin has not invited David Lloyd
George into his new cabinet but he has done almost
as astonishing a thing — he has made Winston
Churchill chancellor of the exchequer, thus honoring the man who deserted the Tory Party twenty
years ago and who has now come back to eat of the
fatted calf which has been roasted for him by Mr.
Baldwin. . . .[6]

The Tribune, incidentally, devoted a liberal amount of its
space to foreign news and frequently commented editorially on
foreign affairs and events. This was partially but not wholly a response to the increased public interest in world affairs arising
from World War I. For the newspaper, from the time of its
founding, had given more attention to foreign news than most of
its inland contemporaries. The editors were perhaps conscious of
the considerable number of residents in its territory who had
come from Europe as converts to the Mormon Church or to work
in the mines or smelters and who still had strong ties with the
"old country."

Soon after the election, on November 18, 1924, death ended
the long and noteworthy newspaper career of A. N. McKay. One

of his major contributions to Utah journalism during the eleven years he served as managing editor of the *Herald* and thirteen years as general manager of *The Tribune* was the moderation of partisan excesses which characterized newspapers of his era. Politically he was a Democrat and, as editor of the *Herald,* he presided over the general policy of a Democratic newspaper. During his regime it was not Democratic in the same sense that the *Inter-Mountain Republican,* for example, was Republican. The *Herald* was primarily a newspaper and secondarily a party organ. As general manager of *The Tribune,* McKay directed the change in policy of that newspaper which made possible and promoted an accommodation between Mormons and non-Mormons. In the terminology of the day, he was one of the state's outstanding and most influential "Jack Mormons" and he was not apologetic about that role. He was, along with John F. Fitzpatrick in a later period and such Mormon leaders as Heber J. Grant, a key girder of the bridge which first spanned the chasm which the "irrepressible conflict" had created in Utah. He was, on the non-Mormon side, a counterpart to such Mormon leaders as Grant and Anthony W. Ivins.

There was, incidentally, something special about "Tony" Ivins so far as *The Tribune* was concerned. Anyone who started working in *The Tribune* news or editorial departments after the turn of the century soon learned by word-of-mouth or through some experience that the holiest of "holy cows" around *The Tribune* was not a big advertiser or a banker who might be holding a mortgage, but Ivins, who was neither advertiser nor banker. Why or how this relationship started may be explained in some unpublished diary but no clues could be found by the writer in recorded histories. *Tribune* editorials, however, indicate that it started some time prior to 1907. For when Ivins returned from Mexico where he had been a mission president to be sustained as a new member of the Council of Twelve Apostles, *The Tribune* had this to say about his selection:

The reward to Mr. Ivins has been well earned, from the church standpoint. And we believe that it will inject into the quorum better character in the way of independent manhood than the twelve have received for many years. The chief difficulty about it is that he will be away so much that he will not be able to shake loose the barnacles as he could and probably would do were he here all the time. But as there had to be a filling of the vacancy, we certainly approve of A. W. Ivins. We could not have made a better choice ourselves, and this is about the first occasion (unless we except McKay) that we could have said the same. [7]

The Tribune obviously had the same high regard for David O. McKay, who had been sustained a member of the Council of Twelve Apostles in 1906, that it had for Ivins.

This tribute to the two Mormon leaders had come at a time when animosity between *The Tribune* and the church and *Deseret News* was at a peak. *The Tribune* was publishing in every issue from one to a half-dozen editorials denouncing the *Deseret News*, President Joseph F. Smith and other church leaders. The *Deseret News* was reciprocating in kind. A sample of the dozens of *Tribune* editorials published during the same week that the Ivins-McKay editorial appeared started out in this fashion, under the heading — "Its Sniveling Wail":

The *Deseret News* last night put out a long-winded wail about *The Tribune* abusing it and 'fighting the Mormon church.' Of course, *The Tribune* has not been fighting the Mormon church at all. It has been abusing nobody. But it has resented the lies told by the church organ, and has condemned the lawlessness, vice, lechery, tyranny, usurpation and robberies of the Mormon church leaders. . . . [8]

The Tribune's high regard for Ivins personally did not deter it from publishing six days later a purported expose of the new apostle as a post-Manifesto polygamist. Under front-page headings — "Apostle Ivins a Polygamist, Known to be a Two-Ply One, and Reported to Have Other Wives, Takes Plural Wife After Manifesto" — the article began: "The Mormon hierarchy in elevating Anthony (Tony) W. Ivins of Mexico to the apostleship appears to have overlooked a disqualification over his predecessor, the late George Teasdale. Apostle Teasdale was a five-ply polygamist whilst Apostle Ivins can boast of only two better halves. . . ." [9]

Two days after publication of this expose, which was one of a long series, *The Tribune* published on its front page a retraction which said in part that Apostle Ivins "had declared most positively that he is not a polygamist, and never has been, and that he has kept faith with the pledges made to the United States when Utah was made a State. . . ." [10]

In the same issue on the editorial page *The Tribune* apologized to Apostle Ivins for the error but expressed no abashment over the fact that no one had checked the article with Ivins before its publication. The editor excused this omission on the grounds that *The Tribune* had learned from experience that it could not expect to be told the truth by church sources on this subject. The editorial then continued:

> In acknowledging the fact that this [the statement
> that Ivins was a polygamist] was a misstatement,
> *The Tribune* feels so far from being humiliated that
> it would be glad of the privilege of making similar
> confession every day in the week concerning others,
> if only such action could be in truth — as we believe
> to be the case here — and if this whole situation
> could thus be cleared up. . . . [11]

This did not end the really inexcusable (for *The Tribune*) and embarrassing (for Apostle Ivins) incident. Two days later

The Tribune published another editorial, which said in substance that the newspaper had gotten Ivins into trouble with "the old polygamists . . . who are wondering why this 'fresh young apostle' as they call him, should put any black mark upon their countenances." The editorial continued:

> Why does he, they inquire, even before he has become accustomed to his apostle frock, cast aspersions upon their righteous lives? If a thing is to be denied, they reasonably assert, that thing is to be denied only because it is bad. Are they, then, who made of commonplace Honorable Anthony W. Ivins the distinguished Apostle Anthony W. Ivins such a bad lot? We also would like to know.
>
> But let them fight it out with Apostle Ivins, and not let them blame *The Tribune* further. Our columns are open to both proposed controversialists in this particular matter; and while we hold our space in high value, let not either the polygamists or Mr. Ivins stint themselves on that account. Have it out, gentlemen. We were never more ready for such a fray, and our willingness can be exceeded by no other thing than our interest in the outcome. [12]

A measure of Apostle Ivins' tolerance can be inferred from the fact that this affair did not poison his relations with *Tribune* executives, and over the years he grew even larger in their esteem and respect. As a footnote to this relationship, which played no small part in the repression of the "irrepressible conflict," an incident in which *The Tribune* again had some apologies to make to Apostle Ivins is worth mentioning. A year or so before his death in September of 1934, and when he was nearing his eightieth birthday, he took to the hills on one of his favorite horses and bagged a magnificent deer. A *Tribune* sportswriter, who thought the word "senile" signified only age, started his

312

story of "Tony" Ivins deer hunt with the phrase: "Despite his senility. . . ." [13] The consternation in *The Tribune* editorial offices the morning the article appeared was something to remember. The editor waited in dread for a call from Fitzpatrick's office in the Kearns Building across the street from the Tribune Building and glanced across the street from time to time to see if the Kearns Building roof was still in place. When the call came it was, in the light of the circumstances, surprisingly mild. The publisher made it clear that he did not like the choice of words in the Ivins story and suggested that the writer go to the Ivins home to apologize. The sportswriter, who shall remain nameless, willingly but apprehensively complied with the directive and was greeted not by an infuriated President Ivins but a chuckling "Tony." Ivins suggested that perhaps the writer had hit closer to the truth than he (Ivins) liked to admit and assured him that if the article had any adverse repercussions on his job status that he (Ivins) would be happy to intercede in his behalf.

In a tribute to President Ivins upon his death *The Tribune* said in part:

> As a general he would have been gallant and re-
> sourceful; as a judge, impartial, sympathetic and al-
> ways just; as a leader in any cause, courageous and
> consistent. As a successful colonizer he was vigi-
> lant, progressive and enterprising, ably fulfilling
> every essential requirement of guide, commander,
> counselor, advocate and arbitrator. As a churchman
> he was devout but not bigoted; chivalrous in contro-
> versy, reasonable in attitude and argument, toler-
> ant of the honest opinions of others. . . . [14]

Sometimes things are said in death which would seem an exaggeration in life, but no one around *The Tribune* doubted what was said about "Tony" Ivins was really meant by the publisher in death or in life.

25

"J.F."Takes Over [1]

WHEN JOHN F. Fitzpatrick became publisher of *The Salt Lake Tribune* upon the death of A. N. McKay in 1924 he was ready to assume the responsibilities attached to that position. He had been observing and studying the newspaper operation for almost twelve years, and, beginning in 1918 when Thomas Kearns died, he had for all practical purposes, been functioning as the newspaper's owner. Had he been a man of ordinary ambition and dedication he could have continued in that role, delegating the job of editing, publishing and distributing the newspaper to subordinates who had been brought up in the business and who in varying degrees were knowledgeable in the details of the operation. Being a man of extraordinary ambition and dedication, he could be nothing less than a publisher in fact as well as in title. It is doubtful that any man ever applied himself more diligently or learned more about newspaper operation in a dozen years than Fitzpatrick did between the time he became Kearns' secretary and publisher of *The Tribune*. *The Tribune* organization was quickly made aware of the fact that the top man across the street knew what he wanted and was determined to get it. (Fitzpatrick's office was always in the Kearns Building across the street from the Tribune Building.)

The rather relaxed attitude which had developed in all departments of the newspaper as circulation, advertising and profitability had grown under the McKay regime, began evaporating and tensions started building up. In the news-editorial department, for example, an embarrassing error was no longer an occasion for a chuckle and a routine warning not to let it happen again but a painful crisis. Fitzpatrick, of course, did not expect to eliminate errors from *The Tribune*, but he was determined that those responsible were not going to be complacent about them.

Those left in day-to-day charge of the newspaper operation by McKay's death were experienced and competent newspapermen, as they had demonstrated. But they were not businessmen. Wasteful, hit-and-miss practices had been permitted to creep into the operation. To cite an example, editors did not dummy (lay out) inside pages and type was set without regard to the space which was going to be available when the issue was made up. Much of the editing was done after the stories had been set in type and galleys of overset (excess type) littered the composing room after each edition went to press. Fitzpatrick, who always retained an emotional fondness for railroading and its vocabulary, concluded that this was "a hell of a way to run a railroad," and, in 1927, he hired two members of the *Telegram's* staff to reorganize internal operations of *The Tribune*.

For superintendent of the backshop he selected H. Eugene (Mike) Glenn, who had been performing that same function for the *Telegram* on a lean budget and whose newspaper experience dated back to 1908 when he started work as a $3 per week apprentice in *The Tribune's* backshop. Glenn was given centralized control of the mechanical operation and, under Fitzpatrick's guidance, instituted reforms to reduce waste, improve the typographical appearance of the newspaper and, in general, to replace chaos with order.

To fill the void left by McKay's death, the new publisher chose G. B. (Bert) Heal to direct the news and editorial departments with the title of editor. He continued in this position until 1950 when he relinquished newsroom responsibilities and served as editor of *The Tribune* until his death in 1951. Heal was a kind-hearted, self-effacing individual who bore no resemblance to the fictionalized image of the hard-driving managing editor brought in to revolutionize a lackadaisical news department. With the backing and the prodding of Fitzpatrick he proceeded to do the job assigned to him in his own way. Except for an aversion to personal publicity or public attention, he was strikingly unlike Fitzpatrick. In a way they complemented each other. Because of his innate kindness, Heal might have become overly tolerant of shortcomings without some pressure from the publisher. On the other hand, without the insulation he provided between publisher and newsroom, tensions might have reached levels unconducive to efficiency. In any event, the combination did markedly improve the newsroom operation and the quality of the newspaper.

If there was one professional quality which Heal emphasized above all others, it was objectivity and fairness in news coverage. He had a passion for getting both sides of a controversy before airing it in *The Tribune*. To publish a news story which might be injurious to an individual or a group and then give the individual or group the opportunity for rebuttal the following day was not good enough for Heal. He insisted upon giving the party who might be injured an opportunity for rebuttal or explanation in the original story. If, for some reason, this was impossible before an approaching deadline, he preferred to get "scooped" on the story and publish it the following day. If *The Tribune* started covering a trial or adversary hearing, Heal insisted that the job be finished with comparable display. A misjudgment of reader interest in such a news event did not justify, in Heal's journalistic code, abandonment of the story after one side of the case had been publicized. The other side was entitled to "its day in *The Tribune*" as a matter of fairness, even if it was apparent that readers had lost interest in the affair.

Throughout his forty years in the newspaper business, as reporter for the *Ogden Standard-Examiner,* editor of the *Herald-*

Republican, editor of the *Telegram* and editor of *The Tribune,*
Heal immersed himself almost totally in his work. He was in his
office at *The Tribune* during most of the twenty-four hours of
each day; was frequently there on Sunday and took vacations
only when Fitzpatrick insisted that he get away for a week or
two. He had one consuming interest aside from work — children,
everybody's children, not just his own. He was never without a
stock of candy and gum in his pockets and desk to pass out to
children he met on the street or who came to his office. It can be
confidently asserted that the story which gave him the greatest
inward satisfaction of his entire newspaper career involved children.

Shortly before school closed in the spring of 1948 he received
a letter from Miss Elayne Christensen, a teacher in Antimony,
Garfield County. Antimony is an isolated, rural Mormon community of about 250 population 220 miles south of Salt Lake
City. The teacher explained that many of her students had never
been in a city and that she was undertaking a project to somehow
get them to Salt Lake City for a sightseeing trip when school
closed. Could *The Tribune,* she asked, suggest places of special
interest they could visit and assist in making arrangements?
This was something that could really excite the unexcitable
Heal. He immediately sent a reporter to Antimony to inform the
teacher that *The Tribune* could do more than assist her in the
project; it would be happy to make all the arrangements and pay
all the expenses of the trip she was planning. As soon as *The
Tribune* published a feature story about the projected trip, along
with pictures of the children and interviews with them about
what they had never seen and what they wanted to see, the prof-
fers of assistance started pouring into Heal's office. Hotels, restaurants, theaters, amusement parks and industrial plants by
the dozens wanted to serve as hosts for a day or a few hours. The
job of selecting those to be favored became somewhat of a problem.

A large bus was dispatched to Antimony on the appointed day and fifty children, along with several parents as chaperones, were ready and waiting for the adventure. Much to the surprise of the reporter assigned to the story, the public reacted as Heal did. Newspaper readers were in a mood for something like this to provide relief from the heavy newspaper diet of postwar problems. Press services carried detailed accounts of the trip. Magazines sent reporters and photographers to participate in the coverage. The *New York News,* largest circulation newspaper in the United States, devoted the entire front page of one edition to a picture of the Antimony children disembarking from the bus and gazing at the top of the ten-story Hotel Utah which, to them, was a real skyscraper.

It is doubtful that *The Tribune* ever published a news or feature story which generated more letters of appreciation and requests for more of this kind of news than this one. It turned out to be more than a human interest feature story. The articles about the children and their school had described in a rather vivid way the dilapidated condition of the school building and physical facilities. The effect, which was neither anticipated nor intended at the time, was to focus public attention on the need for state aid to upgrade some of the state's rural schools. So the human interest story about children did more to bring about replacement of primitive school houses in rural areas of the state than pages of editorial argument and pleading could have done. Thus, Heal's heartwarming human interest story can be credited with much more than an exciting week for fifty Antimony children.

The assumption by Fitzpatrick of responsibility for the entire *Tribune* produced no startling changes in the general editorial policy of the newspapers, as some ownership or editorship changes in the past had done. The broad guidelines agreed upon by Kearns and McKay some thirteen years earlier were in accord with the ideas of Fitzpatrick, and so there was no occasion for basic policy changes. The new publisher and the executives he brought into the organization concentrated on the achievement of objectives already set but not always effectively pursued.

Viewed superficially, *The Tribune* published under the guidance of McKay and Fitzpatrick might have seemed to some of its readers a repudiation of *The Tribune* of the eighteen hundreds and the early nineteen hundreds. Certainly its journalistic style had changed dramatically. It was no longer the slashing crusader against policies of the majority ecclesiastical group within its circulation area. It was no longer the mouthpiece of a political party or faction of a party, although it asserted political preferences when the publisher felt it had a public responsibility to do so. It shunned assaults on personalities such as it had once reveled in. It deliberately sought to make itself essential as a source of information to the entire public rather than the zealous champion of a segment of that public.

The seeming break with the past, however, was more a matter of tone than of basic substance. From the time it was founded the publishers and editors of *The Tribune* had asserted and reasserted with almost monotonous frequency that their purpose was not to destroy an ecclesiastical persuasion; that if certain policies which they deemed inimical to the community and its future were abandoned the "irrepressible conflict" would disappear. Specifically, the newspaper declared that if attempts to establish a closed economic system, a dominant ecclesiastical political party and a religiously segregated society were stopped there would be no reason for the conflict; that if a genuine effort to suppress the practice of polygamy in violation of law were made *The Tribune* and those for whom it spoke would have no legitimate complaint on that issue; that a belief in plural marriage as an ecclesiastical conviction without practice in violation of law was no concern of those who believed otherwise.

In the light of changes which had taken place when McKay became general manager, and the further changes which had taken place when Fitzpatrick assumed the title and functions of publisher, it would have been repudiation of *The Tribune's* own commitments not to have changed the newspaper's policies. To have continued the old conflict after its causes had disappeared would have been to consign *The Tribune* to the Salt Lake newspaper cemetery which had claimed so many of its predecessors and contemporaries.

Fitzpatrick no doubt made his fair share of mistakes during the early years of his regime as publisher. Experienced staff members sometimes felt he relied too much on the opinions of friends outside the business and too little on in house advice. After all, his own experience was restricted in time and scope and he would have had to possess both genius and luck not to have made some blunders. However, he learned with incredible speed and thoroughness, and before many years passed associates accepted his judgments as well as his directives without question. The attitude of staff members who dealt directly with him is exemplified by one editorial writer who, after lamenting what he believed to be a wrong decision, shrugged his shoulders and began carrying out his assignment with the remark: "He can see around corners and I can't, so maybe it isn't a mistake."

Staff members who communicated directly with him only occasionally, or who never asserted a conflicting opinion in his presence, sometimes felt that he was intolerant of any questioning of his judgment. On many occasions, however, he sought and gave careful consideration to opinions differing from his own, and no doubt sometimes altered his own views and decisions as a result of the differences. But having reached a decision after considering the alternatives, the arguments were over. He expected and demanded that his decisions be carried out.

He rarely wrote editorials himself although he frequently specified in precise detail the position he wanted *The Tribune* to take on those issues he deemed important. Trained as he was in business communication, his own prose rarely satisfied him. He had an extraordinary ability to spot a fuzzy phrase and a talent for clarifying the thought. His most skillful editorial writers were not reluctant to concede that he could often improve their handiwork. He had a special aversion to subtleties carrying overtones of sarcasm, and ruthlessly excised such gems from any copy he edited.

As for news coverage, Fitzpatrick demanded clarity, objectiveness and fairness. Politics has always been an area especially subject to public suspicion of publisher dictation or interference. The writer of this history, during thirty-seven years of political writing for *The Tribune*, received suggestions from Fitzpatrick to give some special attention to political figures on only two occasions. In both instances the suggestions, and they were only suggestions and not directives, were to make a special effort to give complete and comprehensive coverage to events in which the political figures were featured speakers. One incident involved Senator Reed Smoot, a Republican and for a considerable number of years *The Tribune's* No. 1 political enemy. The other involved former President Lyndon B. Johnson, a Democrat.

His attitude toward the use of news coverage to advance political preferences can be illustrated by an incident in which the political writer was accused by an interested party of "slanting" a news story dealing with a controversial issue. The reporter firmly denied the charge of news "slanting" either intentionally or unintentionally, and as an additional defense, added: "But even if it were slanted, the bias was in the direction of *The Tribune's* editorial policy."

Fitzpatrick did not explode, as he was capable of doing in the grand manner. He calmly and coldly remarked:

"If you are going to be influenced in your news writing by *The Tribune's* editorial policy, I suggest that you stop reading the editorial page until this election is over."

If there was bias in *The Tribune's* coverage of the news during the Fitzpatrick era, the fault was in those writing and editing the news; it was not a result of publisher dictation.

Fitzpatrick's basic policy in publishing *The Tribune* was to set unreachably high goals, find key men who would strive to reach them and then drive himself and his key men in their pursuit. He was never the absentee publisher and he did not belong to the school of top executives who believe in delegating authority and then leaving the recipient of the authority to sink or swim without interference. He was, rather, a constant prod to keep his subordinates moving toward the objectives he had set.

26

A Declaration of
Voter Independence

THE GREAT DEPRESSION dominated the 1930's for *The Tribune* and all other businesses. One of its first casualties which directly affected *The Tribune* was the *Salt Lake Telegram*. *The Tribune's* afternoon offspring was then owned by A. L. Fish, Thomas G. Mullin and Edward E. Jenkins, the latter a Salt Lake City businessman. Mullin, a native of San Francisco and a newspaper associate of Fish in Portland, Oregon, had come to Salt Lake City shortly after Fish took over the management of the *Herald* to serve as that newspaper's business manager and together they soon acquired control of the *Telegram* with Jenkins as a partner.

From the time it was launched in 1902 by the owners of *The Tribune,* the *Telegram* was beset by economic difficulties. Its deficits were absorbed by Thomas Kearns and David Keith until 1914 when they tired of the financial drain and sold it. Thereafter, under different ownerships, it continued to sink further into debt and by late 1929 the owners found themselves unable to meet demands for payment of overdue notes held, among others, by The Nibley Company of Salt Lake City. Publication was temporarily continued by issuing new bonds, but by September, 1930, with all resources exhausted and the depression tightening its grip on the economy, Fish, Mullin and Jenkins were forced to toss in the towel. In a letter dated September 26, the partners informed attorneys for The Nibley Company, which held the assets of Charles W. Nibley, that they were "unable to meet payment" and therefore surrendered "all claims to the stock of The Telegram Publishing Company to The Nibley Company."[1]

This posed a problem for the owners of both *The Tribune* and the *Deseret News*. Obviously, neither wanted a third publisher to enter the field. They had been through that before with everyone losing money. Moreover, it was doubtful that any third party would be foolhardy enough to want to acquire a losing newspaper in a period of deepening depression in a market which had never been sufficient to support three separate daily newspapers. For that would mean renewal of the fight for survival against the competition of an afternoon newspaper backed by the resources of The Church of Jesus Christ of Latter-day Saints and an adequately financed, deeply entrenched morning and Sunday newspaper.

The alternatives were for the *Deseret News* or *Tribune* to buy the *Telegram* or let it sink. Fitzpatrick had no desire to re-acquire the *Telegram* for *The Tribune* and was convinced that the best solution was for the *Deseret News* to purchase it, merge it with the *News* and establish then and there what he believed would have to be the ultimate solution — one morning and one afternoon newspaper. Heber J. Grant, then president of the Mormon Church, and his advisers were reluctant to acquire another business enterprise. Their position, Fitzpatrick was advised, was that while the church intended to keep the *News* under any circumstances, they wanted to diminish rather than enlarge the church's competitive business enterprises. The details of just what took place to resolve the impasse are probably unknown to anyone now (1971) alive. The end result of negotiations was the purchase of the *Telegram* by *The Tribune*, abandonment of the *Sunday Telegram* and the merging of operations in *The Tribune* plant. This at least promised some substantial reductions in production costs.

The financial collapse of the *Telegram* as a separate enterprise can be attributed to the inexorable pressures of the changing economics of newspaper publishing. These pressures, stemming both from climbing production costs and changing needs of advertisers, had been rising since the turn of the century and were destined to continue to rise in the future. It was not something unique to the Salt Lake market area but a force which was changing the pattern of newspaper publishing throughout the land and which was just beginning rather than finishing its course. The *Telegram* had competent management, an able staff and a loyal reader following. As a newspaper it deserved to survive, like the defunct morning *Herald*. But economics had decreed its two-step death unless it could outlast better financed and more solidly entrenched competition. As for management and staff, the re-acquisition of the *Telegram* gave *The Tribune* a helpful infusion of experience and newspaper skills. A. L. Fish came to *The Tribune* with the *Telegram* and served as general manager of the combined operation until his retirement in 1947. Thomas G. Mullin came to *The Tribune* in the same manner and served as business manager of the combined papers until his retirement in 1949. Bert Heal, the editor for many years, and Mike Glenn, the backshop superintendent who had reorganized the mechanical operation, were recruited from the *Telegram* prior to its purchase by *The Tribune*. So was Harvey Hancock, the managing editor during the early nineteen thirties. Arthur C. Deck, who served successively as managing editor and executive editor (a position he still holds as the paper rounds out its first century), also came to *The Tribune* with the *Telegram*, as did Theodore Long, editor of the editorial page. Among the reporters who came into *The Tribune* organization with the *Telegram* were A. W. (Al) Ferguson, who started working for the *Telegram* in 1917 and retired from *The Tribune* in 1964; and Clarence D. (Scoop) Williams, whose service with both papers dates back to 1922.

With the *Telegram* back in protective association with *The Tribune* which had given it birth in 1902, Fitzpatrick's overriding responsibility was to batten down the economic hatches and head into the storm of the century's deepest depression with two newspapers and various other interests to keep afloat. Costs were cut wherever possible. Salaries were reduced but not so drastically as on most major newspapers of the country. One *Tribune* staff member who started working just before the severity of the depression at the top reporter's salary of $65 per week found himself three years later in the position of city editor with a salary of $49 per week. His experience was not unusual. No one expected during this period to advance in pay. The height of ambition was to advance fast enough in position to avoid a reduction in pay. The psychology of retrenchment was so strong that a week before the 1932 election seven Utah state officials, whose pay could not be legally reduced, announced they were voluntarily imposing a ten percent salary reduction upon themselves by returning to the state that portion of their pay. It was an experience that undoubtedly contributed, in the area of fiscal attitudes, to what became known some thirty years later as a "generation gap."

Through it all, Fitzpatrick struggled determinedly to avert a deterioration in the quality of the newspapers for which he was custodian. They shrank in size, of course, but the large part of the shrinkage was in advertising volume rather than news content. He maintained, and indeed increased, pressures for improving the quality of the product and, viewed retrospectively, it is doubtful that *The Tribune* was ever more successful in sinking its roots deeper into the territory it served than during the depression years. At the beginning of this period (1930) the newspaper's circulation was 51,280 daily and 69,730 Sunday. By 1935 daily circulation had declined slightly to 50,311. Sunday circulation, aided by the merging of the *Sunday Telegram* with *The Tribune,* had risen to 74,008. In 1936 daily circulation rose to

54,582 and Sunday circulation to 81,029.[2] Thereafter the newspaper continued to grow in circulation and gradually began returning to the normal growth pattern in advertising volume and revenues. Through it all Fitzpatrick succeeded in keeping his newspaper operation out of the red except for one year and by the time the pre-war boom started he was in a position to cope with the problems generated by a quick shift from deflation to inflation. Those same inexorable economic pressures which had doomed the *Herald* and the *Telegram* as separate publishing enterprises forced yet another change in the Salt Lake newspaper structure twenty years later.

While passing through the economic crisis of the depression years Fitzpatrick kept *The Tribune's* policy rudder in substantially the same position he had set it when he took over corporate management late in 1918. In the 1932 campaign *The Tribune* aggressively supported a constitutional amendment to permit first class cities to change their form of government through a home rule procedure. It refrained from endorsing or attacking candidates, thereby continuing a practice it had adopted in 1911. The newspaper's front page columnist, Walter Lippmann, supported the candidacy of Franklin D. Roosevelt, more by criticizing Herbert Hoover than by praising Roosevelt. Will Rogers, who was also carried on the front page, apportioned his delightful political jibes to both sides. *The Tribune,* which had long since stopped complaining that the president of the Mormon Church could dictate election results in Utah, raised no objection when President Heber J. Grant announced in an interview with *The Tribune* that he was supporting Hoover and that he would again vote for Senator Reed Smoot, as he had always done since Smoot's first candidacy. President Grant made one concession to *The Tribune's* pre-1911 position, and to the changed political climate in the state, by emphasizing in the interview that he was expressing his own preferences and was not asking anyone else to vote other than personal convictions dictated.[3] The closest

The Tribune came to taking a position was in an editorial published on November 6, 1932, the Sunday before the election, in which it pointed out that:

> President Hoover has defended the Republican tariff policy with convincing sincerity. Governor Roosevelt has been forced to reassure the farmer that he does not contemplate reduction of duties on their products. But the west is also vitally interested in protection for products of its mines. Prosperity for this industry means employment for its people and revenues for maintaining its institutions. It has waited in vain for an explicit and detailed analysis of Mr. Roosevelt's tariff ideas on this score. Western states must also look to the House and Senate for tariff security. It is evident that tariff reductions spell disaster for the west, dooming its people to idleness and closing its mines and impoverishing the farmer and livestock man.[4]

Democrats could, with defensible logic, interpret the editorial as an expression of preference for Hoover and Smoot. Republicans no doubt regarded it "a far cry" from the ringing endorsements that *The Tribune* once gave to the candidates of its choice. These were probably the precise reactions Fitzpatrick had intended to evoke.

Utah voters were given more attention in the campaign by the presidential candidates than they had been accustomed to receiving. Roosevelt spent a weekend in Salt Lake City and delivered one of his major speeches in the Salt Lake Tabernacle. Hoover spoke in the same place the Monday night prior to the election, stopping in Utah en route to his home in California. *The Tribune* gave both visits elaborate coverage. Then on election day the electorate of Utah demonstrated, if proof were still need-

328

ed at this point in the state's history, that the political preferences of the president of the Mormon Church, of *The Tribune,* or
of both no longer dictated election results in Utah. The Democrats carried the state by more than 30,000 votes, virtually wip-
ing out Republican office holders at the state level and in all the
larger counties. Smoot, whose defeat had been loudly and erroneously predicted on three previous occasions by *The Tribune,*
was overwhelmed by Elbert D. Thomas, a University of Utah political science professor. It was a result which *The Tribune* would
have cheered at the top of its editorial voice prior to 1918, but
those who would have led the cheering were no longer around to
enjoy the downfall of the apostle-senator which the newspaper
had opposed so relentlessly through eighteen of his thirty years
in the Senate.

The 1932 election ushered into Utah a Democratic-New Deal
political era which gave the Democratic Party a monopoly of
Utah state and congressional offices for fourteen years. Henry H.
Blood was elected governor and remained in that office for eight
years; Thomas remained in the Senate for eighteen years; Abe
Murdock was elected to the House and remained in that body or
the Senate for fourteen years, and J. W. Robinson was elected to
the House where he remained for fourteen years. Undoubtedly
the greatest surprise was the defeat of Smoot by Senator Thomas. The veteran senator, no longer involved in feuding with *The
Tribune,* spent the evening in the newspaper's office where he
was provided with all the returns from the state as they were reported. When the early returns showed him to be running far behind he suspected that someone was playing a ghastly joke on
him. The pattern of the vote on president and other offices soon
convinced him that the returns were valid and that his thirty-
year career in the Senate was drawing to an end.

If any of the battle-scarred veterans of the ecclesiastical-
political wars of an earlier day suspected that a president of the
Mormon Church could dictate the outcome of a Utah election by

expressing a party or candidate preference, their suspicions should have been laid to rest by 1932. If any lingering doubts did survive 1932, the 1936 election provided the clincher. In this election *The Tribune* abandoned the soft-spoken near-neutrality which had characterized its editorial page after 1911 and endorsed without qualification a presidential candidate. In an editorial bearing the heading "We Vote for Landon," the newspaper said:

> *The Salt Lake Tribune* favors the election of Governor [Alfred M.] Landon. It believes that this is the quickest and surest way back to constitutional government and the American tradition. It is fearful of a continuation of the class prejudice of the Roosevelt administration, feeling that class conflict is the ultimate result of factional hate. . . .
> The new deal, so called, is a barnacle on the government of the people, unmanageable and uncontrollable by the people, in whom our government is vested. This extraordinary government has cost and is costing a tremendous sum. The people must pay. It has added nearly a quarter of a million employes to the federal payroll, most of whom are beyond the jurisdiction of normal government. It has added bureau after bureau, exhausting the alphabet to find designations for these waifs of governmental experiment.

The concluding sentence declared that *The Tribune* supported Landon because "we do not trust Roosevelt."[5]

It can be presumed that Fitzpatrick took this editorial position as a matter of conviction. Certainly he had no thought of clambering aboard a bandwagon to back a winner, for *The Tribune's* own poll indicated that the Roosevelt tide was running much stronger than in 1932 and that he would carry Utah by the widest margin the state had ever given a presidential candidate since statehood.

The Tribune's endorsement of Landon was mild by comparison with the position taken by the *Deseret News* on behalf of the Mormon Church leadership. In a pre-election editorial occupying four columns at the top of the front page and under the heading "The Constitution," the *Deseret News* said in part:

> One candidate has characterized the Constitution as of 'horse and buggy' days. He has advised members of Congress to join in enacting laws irrespective of the belief of the congressmen as to the constitutionality of such laws. . . .
>
> The other candidate has declared he stands for the Constitution and for the American system of government. He makes it clear that he will keep inviolate the oath which he must take as president of the United States. He has shown himself to be an honest, truthful man, a patriotic efficient public servant. . . .
>
> Church members who believe the revelations and the words of the Prophet must stand for the Constitution. Every patriot, loving his country and its institutions, should feel duty bound to vote to protect it.[6]

No names were used because none were needed. The phrase, "horse and buggy days" identified President Roosevelt as unmistakably as would have the initials F.D.R. It is doubtful that the church leadership had ever taken a stronger stand against one candidate and for another, either publicly or within organizational ranks, than in the 1936 election. *The Tribune's* editorial opposition to Roosevelt, incidentally, was based primarily on the same constitutional issue which evoked the editorial in the

331

church organ. On election day, however, the Utah electorate re-soundingly rejected *The Tribune's* advice and the *Deseret News'* counsel by giving Roosevelt the largest percentage of the total vote (70 percent) ever given to a presidential candidate in the state's history.

Soon after this election a young and recent graduate of Notre Dame University started working full-time for *The Trib-une.* His unobtrusive entrance into the newspaper's organization was little noted by staff members and only a few recognized his appearance as a noteworthy event in the history of the institu-tion. But from the outset he was clearly marked by family connection, personality and ability as the eventual successor to Fitzpatrick as publisher.

The new employe, John W. (Jack) Gallivan, was the only son of a half-sister of Mrs. Jennie J. Kearns, Mrs. Francis Wilson Gallivan. The mother died when Jack was five years old and thereafter Mrs. Kearns assumed responsibility for Jack and his two sisters. Under the watchful eye of Mrs. Kearns, Jack re-ceived his early education at a grammar school in Oakland, Cali-fornia, a junior high school in Berkeley and at Bellarmine, a pre-paratory school operated in connection with Santa Clara Univer-sity. He was then sent to Notre Dame University where he start-ed preparing himself for newspaper work both at the academic and practical experience levels. He served as campus correspon-dent for the *Chicago Tribune* and worked part time in the classi-fied advertising department of the South Bend, Indiana, *News-Times.* While attending Notre Dame he became acquainted with a daughter of a *Chicago Tribune* executive who, impressed by the young man from the west, offered him a job upon graduation.

Primarily interested at the time in a writing career, Galli-van decided that the offer would provide him with the opportuni-ty he wanted so he called Mrs. Kearns on the telephone to tell her about the job offer and his intention of accepting it. Mrs. Kearns kindly but firmly informed him that she had educated him to work for *The Salt Lake Tribune,* not the *Chicago Tribune,* and that she expected him to return to Salt Lake City. He complied with her request and on August 1, 1937, became a full-time employe of *The Tribune,* where he had worked part-time in the circulation department and the editorial library during summer vacations.

If there were any members of the staff who resented his presence because of the element of nepotism in his employment the feeling quickly evaporated. He immediately became a popular, probably the most popular, member of the staff. If there was ever a family member employed by a family corporation who received none of the favors normally suspected in these relationships it was Jack Gallivan on *The Tribune.* He worked longer hours, and, in addition to regular assignments, did more odd jobs which no one else wanted to do, than anyone else on the staff. His first regular job was that of a bookkeeper, surely an affront to an inspiring writer. After a few weeks in this unwanted post he worked in advertising, circulation, and editorial departments, starting on the copy desk in the latter department. In his spare time he was both manager and staff of the promotion department, wrote a sports column twice a week (a concession to his writing aspirations) and produced merchandising bulletins for advertisers. For years he fed *The Tribune-Telegram's* carrier pigeons housed on the roof of the Tribune Building. He did not escape from this chore until years after the sometimes useful and sometimes frustrating pigeons had been outmoded by two-way radio and mobile telephone communications. One of his numerous successful promotion ideas was an invitation during World War II for mothers of servicemen to send in their favorite prayer. One was published each day for several weeks before Thanksgiving Day and war savings stamps given for the one selected for publication on Thanksgiving morning. Gallivan not only fathered the idea but carried it out and he naturally acquired the title of "prayer editor."

333

On a dismal (for Gallivan) Saturday afternoon when his beloved Notre Dame football team was trailing Army's famous Mr. Inside and Outside (Blanchard and Davis) team by about forty points, Gallivan was called from the copy desk, where he was working, to the city desk to take a telephone call. A deep voice inquired: "Is this the prayer editor?" Gallivan, seeking to attune his voice to his title and hide his exasperation over the football game, replied that it was and solemnly asked if there was anything he could do for the caller.

"Why," the muffled voice intoned, "don't you say a prayer for Notre Dame?"

Immediately sensing that his leg was being pulled, Gallivan replied in unctuous tone: "Thou art a sonofabitch." The disguised voice was that of William (Bill) Coltrin, a *Tribune* sports writer.

During his period of training for the top job, Gallivan was "one of the boys" around *The Tribune* and he continued in that role without sacrifice of respect even after he moved into Fitzpatrick's office as assistant to the publisher. He had convinced his colleagues around the newspaper that he was marked for success whether he chose to work for the *Chicago Tribune* or *The Salt Lake Tribune* and that he was clearly the right choice to succeed Fitzpatrick. It was one of those instances when the staff, had they been given the privilege of electing their publisher, would have made the same choice as the owners.

334

27

Prohibition: Sale by Drink

ON APRIL 29, 1886, the *Salt Lake Evening Democrat,* a daily and weekly publication which crusaded against *The Tribune* and the Mormon Church for about two years before expiring from lack of financial support, had hailed as a notable news event: "The *News* and *Tribune* agree—That worthless dogs should be killed."[1]

The point of the *Democrat's* jibe was exaggerated but not grossly so. For it must have seemed to some newspaper readers of that era that *The Tribune* and the *Deseret News* energetically sought out issues to disagree upon, more from a lust for controversy than from dedication to convictions. Any such tendency had completely disappeared by 1911. Thereafter *The Tribune* and *Deseret News* frequently took the same position on public issues and both newspapers quite obviously avoided confrontations over trivialities which in the old days would have put them at each other's throat. Newspaper manners had undergone a marked change not only in Salt Lake City but across the country generally.

Some differences did remain and on occasion the two newspapers found themselves on opposite sides of a controversial issue seeking to persuade the reading public to their respective points of view. Nevertheless, editorial differences were argued on the issue without assaults on the motives, veracity, intelligence and sincerity of the opposition.

One such confrontation occurred in 1933 when repeal of national prohibition came to a head, as a result of Franklin D. Roosevelt's election on a platform pledging repeal of the Eighteenth Amendment and a revision of the Volstead Act.

Almost from *The Tribune's* birth liquor had been a bone of contention between it and the *Deseret News*. Frequently in agreement upon social and moral aspects of liquor consumption and the desirability of temperance, the two papers differed sharply on how best to deal with the problem. Each tended to lay responsibility for the fact that liquor was a problem in Utah at the feet of the other and its constituency. During the first two decades of its life, *The Tribune* often expressed irritation with temperance speeches at church conferences and *News* editorials which in *The Tribune's* opinion implied that it was the gentiles who brought the liquor traffic to the territory and perpetuated it. *The Tribune* devoted columns of news and editorial space to the charge that the liquor problem reached Utah ahead of the gentiles; that the business was monopolized by chosen church members and the church-controlled Salt Lake City government; that the largest distributors were church-controlled drug stores, principally Z.C.M.I.; that the early city ordinances regulating the business were inexcusably lax. Probably the most detailed attack on the church's position on liquor was delivered by Judge O. W. Powers at a Liberal Party rally on July 20, 1890, in the old Salt Lake Theater. It was a distillation of what *The Tribune* had been saying in the two decades past. During the 1908 campaign of the American Party the newspaper revived and republished the speech which would have filled two or three pages of present-day newspapers. Additionally, *The Tribune* published a long editorial lauding the speech.

The following excerpts from the editorial reflect the nature and tone of the speech as well as the editorial comment:

> The peculiar ambition of the Mormon priests all
> through this business has been to enjoy the liquor
> traffic and disclaim responsibility for it. . . .

As we have shown not long since, the early liquor ordinances of this city had no prohibition of Sunday selling; in fact, Sunday was not mentioned at all in the ordinances. There was no provision against women frequenting saloons, nor against minors doing the same, provided the minors were over fourteen years of age. It was probably the most lax, reckless legislation so far as temperance was concerned, and the most abjectly servile to the liquor interests, of any ordinance ever passed in any civilized city in modern times. . . . There was no rectification of conditions until the gentiles came, and showed the community the strictness with which the traffic was regulated elsewhere.

It is probable, judging from present appearances, that a sentiment will be worked up for the passage by the Legislature next winter of a local option law. We presume that there will be no particular opposition to it, nor do we see any reason why anyone should oppose it. [2]

The answer of the *Deseret News* to the charges of *The Tribune,* Judge Powers and other gentile campaign orators, was to hang the early liquor problem around the necks of trappers, soldiers stationed in the area and gentile fortune hunters passing through the city on their way to the California gold fields. There can be no doubt that these groups did indeed contribute substantially to the territory's liquor consumption.

While *The Tribune* opposed national prohibition legislation until the early nineteen hundreds, its objections were based upon the belief that it would not work and that it was not a proper power to vest in the federal government. Its attitude toward the aims of the Prohibition National Party was expressed during the campaign of 1904 in an editorial denying that drinking habits could be governed by statutes and that consequently the Prohibition Party would fail in its appeal.

Soon after A. N. McKay became general manager of *The Tribune* at the beginning of 1911, the newspaper changed its position on the practicality of prohibition legislation. It praised editorially the action of both major political parties in the 1916 campaign pledging state-wide prohibition and commended Governor Simon Bamberger who, having won the election, followed through on the pledge to get a bone-dry law through the Legislature which became effective on August 1, 1917. *The Tribune* also abandoned its earlier objection to national prohibition, commenting in an editorial praising Nevada, Colorado, Montana and Wyoming for joining the prohibition states: ". . . but whatever the west might have been in the long ago, it is far in advance of Massachusetts, New York and Pennsylvania on the great moral question of the day. The people out this way do not cater to vice and do not invoke the doctrine of states' rights to protect the saloon. . . ."[3]

Several years' experience with national prohibition convinced Fitzpatrick that the experiment, however noble it might have been in purpose, was an abysmal failure and should be discarded for some other approach to the liquor problem. *Tribune* editorials began reflecting this viewpoint by the late 1920s and by 1933 it was waging a temperate but persistent campaign for Utah to join the states backing repeal of the Eighteenth Amendment. By this time thirty-three states had voted for repeal and six more were to vote on the issue in that year. *The Tribune* stated editorially:

> There is no national prohibition, in Utah or in any
> other state of the union. This thing they call prohi-
> bition is a mockery and a pretense, a vicious circle
> of hypocrisy and corruption. Decency and respecta-
> bility rebel against it, not because they want li-

cense and liquor, but because they want honesty and temperance.[4]

The tide of public sentiment was running heavily against prohibition in the nation but Utah was a large question mark in the minds of the "wets." The reason was that the leadership of the Mormon Church and some of the Protestant churches were aggressively opposing repeal. The church groups argued, with considerable theoretical logic at least, that the repealists, in calling for an end to hypocrisy and corruption, were really making a case for enforcement of the noble experiment rather than its abandonment.

At the October conference of the Mormon Church, President Heber J. Grant said, in an address opposing repeal: "I have hoped and prayed that we as a people would not vote for abolition of the Eighteenth Amendment." *The Tribune* reported that Melvin J. Ballard and David O. McKay of the Council of Twelve Apostles "followed President Grant with pleas to uphold prohibition, asserting that the people of the church will make history when they vote on the momentous question a month hence."[5] The voters did "make history" in the sense that they placed Utah in the national limelight by voting approximately three to two in favor of repeal of the Eighteenth Amendment and of the state's bone-dry constitutional provision.

The Tribune supported the cause of repeal as unequivocally and as firmly as it had supported its positions while the "irrepressible conflict" was raging. But the tone, the style and spirit of its advocacy bore no resemblance to the slashing editorials of the earlier days. It no longer prefaced its affirmative arguments with a rude assault on the character of the opposition. A typical example of its editorial approach in the repeal campaign appeared under the heading: "The Search for Temperance":

. . . Our people, whether for repeal or against it, are motivated by the same ideal, the protection of

339

society against the moral encroachments of liquor
excesses. We instinctively are a temperate people
with decent motives and righteous ideals. On either
side of the question of repeal we find that the ultimate objective is one and the same, temperance.
. . . There is an honest difference of opinion among
our people as to how we may best reach this
goal. . . .[6]

To the plea of prohibitionists that Utah should stand out
against the national trend and remain dry, *The Tribune* replied:

Utah has nothing to gain by voting dry and remaining wet. It may expect more difficulty in enforcement if it pursues this course. The state will suffer
revenue losses without contributing anything to
the morals of its people. It will be pursued by boot-
leggers and racketeers who will be driven from
their present fields by the reassumption of public
control and assertive government. . . .[7]

The repeal issue cut across political and ecclesiastical lines,
a fact which made victory possible for the repeal forces. Democrats, whatever their religion, were under strong political pressures to publicly support repeal and many did. The state's Democratic congressional delegation endorsed repeal as did many candidates for municipal offices which were to be filled in the election. Even in Cache County, a stronghold of Mormon orthodoxy,
George D. Preston, county attorney and a former Logan city
judge, came out for repeal with the observation: "If everyone who
has violated the prohibition laws will vote for repeal, Utah will
repeal by more than a hundred to one."[8]

Richard W. Young, Jr., then president of the Federal Land
Bank in Berkeley, California, and a former Utah legislator and
author of the state's bone-dry law, endorsed repeal and com-

340

mented that "prohibition in Utah and the nation has been an absolute farce."[9] John F. Bowman, a former mayor of Salt Lake City, was chairman of the Defenders, the state-wide organization formed to oppose repeal. Franklin Riter, a Salt Lake City attorney, served in a similar capacity for organizations set up to campaign for repeal. Ray L. Olson, a member of the Utah Legislature, served as campaign director for the repeal forces. One of the most active organizations backing repeal — The Crusaders — was headed by Clarence Bamberger, prominent businessman and a nephew of Governor Simon Bamberger whose administration had sixteen years earlier fulfilled a campaign pledge to give the state a bone-dry law.

Delegates elected to the constitutional convention set up to act on the repeal issue met in December to formally carry out the mandate of the voters. On the day the final action was to take place it appeared that Utah would be the thirty-sixth, and therefore the deciding state, to approve the repeal amendment. A *Tribune* reporter and a radio broadcaster convinced the delegates that the vote should be delayed until evening. This would give the morning *Tribune* the first break on the story and the delegates an opportunity to participate in a nation-wide radio hook-up. But this plan was thwarted by staff members of the *Telegram,* which by this time was being published from *The Tribune* plant and which *Tribune* staffers were inclined to view as "little sister" but a more pesky competitor in the news field than the rival *Deseret News.* Don Howard, *Telegram* news editor, contrived a fake news bulletin stating that Maine, scheduled to vote for repeal the following day, had decided to convene its convention and act immediately and thereby take the role of the deciding state. The bulletin was shown to some of the Utah delegates who, in a panic, took the decisive action four hours earlier than planned. Utah did become the thirty-sixth state to repeal thus receiving what some regarded as desirable publicity and some as unwelcome notoriety.

Prohibition repeal, incidentally, was a noteworthy event in the history of *The Tribune* for reasons other than the termination of a noble experiment. It demonstrated in more mundane ways that the Utah electorate could react in an unpredictable way; that an ecclesiastical position did not necessarily determine election results; that political dictation, as differentiated from influence, had disappeared from Utah. It demonstrated that the old and disruptive "irrepressible conflict" had been suppressed by an accommodation which permitted differences of opinion on highly controversial issues without the poisonous side effects which were so common in an earlier period. Reduced to a personal basis, it demonstrated that President Heber J. Grant of the Mormon Church and the publisher of *The Tribune* could disagree, and disagree vehemently, on methods of dealing with the liquor problem without disrupting their cooperative relationships within areas of agreement and without engendering personal animosity.

Immediately following repeal the so-called "wets" and "drys," both of whom were classified by *The Tribune* as temperance advocates, collaborated in the preparation of a liquor control law to fill the void. The new act, a product of compromise which did not totally satisfy either side, was duly enacted by the State Legislature. During the ensuing years particular provisions came under attack and minor changes were made from time to time. *The Tribune* was among the early critics who sought changes, particularly with respect to making liquor available by the drink. On two occasions in the 1950s the newspaper supported legislative proposals to accomplish this goal. But the bills died before reaching the voting calendars. This situation finally led to a sequel to prohibition repeal in the form of a sale-by-drink initiative proposal. Convinced that the subject was so controversial that legislators could not sponsor substantial changes without inviting political reprisals, *The Tribune* concluded that the electorate of the state should be given an opportunity to express its view. Accordingly there was launched under the leadership of *The Tribune* a campaign to place a proposed sale-by-drink act on the 1968 ballot. The first phase of the campaign, the collection of some 40,000 signatures of qualified voters on a petition required to place the proposal on the ballot, was accomplished with thousands of signatures to spare and in the face of determined and well-organized opposition to the signing of the petition.

In the second phase of the campaign — that of seeking support for the legislative proposal — *The Tribune's* position was strikingly similar to what it had been as a supporter of prohibition in the early nineteen hundreds and, as a supporter of prohibition repeal in 1933. The newspaper supported prohibition with a conviction that it would promote temperance. It supported repeal with a conviction based upon experience that prohibition had failed to promote temperance, but rather it had promoted disrespect for law and lawlessness.[10]

In 1968, the newspaper urged approval of the sale-by-drink proposal on the grounds that it would substitute a controllable system of dispensing liquor for the uncontrollable system which prevailed under the bottle-only, "brown bag" system.

The 1933 editorial comment that: "Utah has nothing to gain by voting dry and remaining wet" and that "the state will suffer revenue losses without contributing anything to the morals of the people" was, in *The Tribune's* view, as applicable in support of the sale-by-drink proposal as it had been in support of prohibition repeal.

The Utah electorate, however, did not react to Utah's 1968 liquor law as it had to prohibition repeal. The proposal was rejected by substantially the same ratio by which repeal was approved.

The Tribune's unsuccessful campaign, however, did have one effect. It resulted in the adoption by the Legislature which convened two months after the election of a non-profit mini-

343

bottle system for private clubs and restaurants — a solution which had theretofore been an anathema in the state's legislative body.

An intriguing question is why Utah's electorate voted three to two for repeal of prohibition in 1933 and against a rather small liberalization of the liquor laws in 1968. No one, of course, can speak the collective mind of the voters. But some theories which seem plausible to the writer are these:

Prohibition repeal was presented as a simple yes or no proposition: do you want to get rid of what you have and try to work out something better? Under Utah's initiative procedure the only way to get the sale-by-drink issue presented to the voters was by submitting a proposed implementing law. Each provision was to some degree vote-eroding. Had it been necessary, for example, to submit the question of prohibition repeal in the form of the liquor law subsequently enacted, the repeal supporters would have had a more difficult campaign to wage. Some who favored repeal would have voted against the proposed law because it did not permit sale by the drink, or because it provided for a state monopoly, or because it placed too much power in the hands of the Liquor Control Commission, and so on. That is what happened to the sale-by-the-drink law. Opponents of the proposition were in a position to exploit the differences of opinion on details to diminish support for the central position — legalization of controlled sale by the drink. One point of attack was the obvious fact that a drink would cost more under the system proposed than under the prevailing "brown bag" system. The opposition skillfully exploited this fact to win voters who favored sale by the drink but not so strongly as they opposed paying more for the drink.

More important in voter influence than all the divertive "red herrings" which burdened the sale-by-drink proposition, but not prohibition repeal, was the fact that prohibition repeal was proposed by the New Deal Roosevelt administration at the time it

344

was rising to its peak of public acceptance. Repeal posed an issue of political loyalty which brought many people to its support who would not have publicly identified themselves with the cause in the absence of this pressure.

The sale-by-the-drink proposition, on the other hand, was a political orphan. Candidates and public officials generally viewed it as a vote-losing issue and so remained silent or came out against it. It can fairly be said that it had the open and public support of only a small percentage of even those who favored it in the privacy of the voting booth.

28

Tribune's Crusading Role

DURING THE FIRST FORTY years of its life *The Tribune* was a crusading newspaper. It attacked its enemies and defended its friends with single-minded zeal and enthusiasm. It performed, in a remarkably competent way in view of the facilities it had, the function of communicating information and straight news to its readers. Simultaneously, it expended extraordinary energy in ferreting out causes to support and causes to combat. Its fervor in these pursuits was often more conspicuous than its discrimination.

Up until the end of 1910 its central targets were the economic, political and social aims and practices of the Mormon Church. Throughout this period it was crusading on scores of issues which were peripheral but pertinent to the main targets.

During the following sixty-year span of its life it has not been a crusading newspaper in the sense usually implied by that term. That does not mean that it abdicated its responsibility of keeping a critical eye on governmental affairs; of speaking out on policies and practices it deemed contrary to the public interest or of supporting those it deemed in the public interest; of campaigning for civic improvements; of expressing its views and the reason for its views on controversial alternative courses of action; of initiating and supporting changes which it believed would be constructive or of opposing those it believed would be destructive; and of providing a means for conflicting viewpoints to be heard.

In brief the policy of *The Tribune* for the past sixty years has been to accept the responsibilities of public watchdog but to avoid the role of public gadfly.

In the era of the "irrepressible conflict" *The Tribune* supplemented its crusading assaults on polygamy and Mormon Church influence on economics and politics with campaigns for street paving and lighting, improvement of water supply, construction of public facilities and improvement of the school system. It belabored the city government for alleged inefficiencies and discriminations when the People's Party was in control and as vigorously defended the conduct of city government during the few occasions when the Liberal, or its successor American Party, were in control. In a period of extreme partisanship in almost every area of community activity, it sought to be a champion of its friends and the scourge of its enemies. In this it did not differ from other publications, except perhaps in skill.

After the Mormon-gentile conflict had been stilled, *The Tribune's* campaigns were directed at specific issues related to the public welfare. At times the causes taken up by the newspaper brought it into conflict with its oldest surviving journalistic rival, the *Deseret News*. However, both newspapers were frequently aligned on the same side.

A notable example of issues other than liquor on which *The Tribune* and the *News* took opposite positions was one involving the state's junior colleges. In 1954 two referendum propositions were submitted to the voters. One provided for the discontinuance of Dixie, Snow and Weber Colleges as state institutions and transfer of their properties and facilities to the Mormon Church, which had originally founded them. The other provided for the discontinuance of Carbon College. *The Tribune* opposed the propositions and so did a substantial majority of the voters.

In that same election *The Tribune* vigorously opposed and the *News* supported a proposed constitutional amendment to reapportion the State Legislature by making each county a senatorial district to be represented by a single senator. The effect of the amendment would have been to reduce Salt Lake County from seven senators to one and to give as many as five senators to five-county districts then represented by one. *The Tribune* favored reapportionment in the opposite direction — that of giving more representation to the populous urban centers. Had the editors been able to peer into the future they would have seen themselves as Don Quixotes waging mock battle over an issue the United States Supreme Court would decide in a way which completely undermined the *News* position and went somewhat beyond the position of *The Tribune*. For within a few years, the court began handing down decisions which established the one-man-one-vote principle as the sole criterion for apportionment. No one around *The Tribune* even dreamed in 1954 that a court created by a Constitution which allocated two senators to each state, no matter how small the population, a minimum of one representative to each state regardless of population, and one spokesman in the House for territories before they attained statehood, would find as it did that Utah's Constitution was in conflict with the federal Constitution because it deviated from the population criterion only to the extent that each county was allocated one representative in the House.

While *The Tribune* forsook the flamboyance which characterized its early crusades, it did not lose its tenacity in pressing the causes it undertook to promote. In the early 1930's, for example, it initiated a campaign for a grand jury to investigate rumored irregularities in Salt Lake City government. The grand jury was eventually called and some city officials were indicted and convicted. Because of the political pressures exerted against the investigation, Fitzpatrick decided that the state's grand jury system needed to be made more flexible. Accordingly, *The Tribune* undertook a campaign to accomplish this. It first commissioned and paid for a study by a legal firm to determine what constitutional amendments would be required. These were drafted but were not submitted to the electorate and approved until 1948. Up to this point, the issue had been free of political partisanship. However, when the State Legislature undertook to implement the constitutional amendment liberalizing grand juries, political overtones developed. It was not a Democratic versus Republican conflict but an "ins" versus the "outs" conflict. The party in power tended to look with suspicion and disfavor on the proposed legislation and the party out of power tended to favor it. When the status of the parties changed, their position on the grand jury legislation changed. The apparent reason was a fear that the proposed legislation was politically motivated and had as its target some incumbent officials. So far as *The Tribune* was concerned, this fear was wholly imaginary. For the newspaper continued to press for the legislation through both Democratic and Republican administrations. It was not until 1967 that the implementing legislation was completed and *The Tribune* could regard as accomplished the objectives of this long campaign. The newspaper campaigned almost as long for a state medical examiner act which was enacted in 1965.

Another area in which *The Tribune* has tenaciously but unsuccessfully advocated change is the form of Salt Lake City government. On several occasions the newspaper has initiated, or supported other initiating groups, in efforts to change the government from the commission form adopted in 1912 to some other form. But as *The Tribune* approached its 100th anniversary, the commission form was still firmly entrenched.

Areas of *Tribune* campaigning in which repeated frustrations were finally crowned with success include the Salt Palace, a $19-million arena-convention center located in downtown Salt Lake which was opened in 1969; a new $2.5-million library completed in 1964; a $6-million Metropolitan Hall of Justice completed in 1965 and a $10-million sewage treatment plant completed in 1966. Prior to the successful effort to win public approval of a $17-million bond issue to finance the Salt Palace, *The*

Tribune had initiated over a period of thirty years several campaigns to build a civic auditorium. These efforts foundered in the early stages, primarily because of the divisive issue of site. This hazard was avoided in the campaign for the Salt Palace by deferring until after the bond election the selection of a site.

Throughout its life *The Tribune* has devoted much effort and space to the development and conservation of water supplies; equalization and improvement of educational opportunities and a wide range of other civic and beautification projects. In most of these campaigns it has been but one of several supporting voices and no inference is intended that *The Tribune* was solely responsible for the improvements. It has been, however, the initiator of some. One of its notable defeats was an effort to win public approval of an urban renewal project in Salt Lake City in an election held on August 17, 1965. The proposal had the support of virtually all communications media in the city but the voters rejected it by a ratio of six to one. A similar proposition submitted to the voters of Provo was rejected but a little less emphatically.

One of the longest editorial and informational campaigns waged by *The Tribune* was in behalf of silver. Oriented toward mining when it was founded, the newspaper crusaded vigorously to prevent the demonetization of silver; and when that "crime" (in *The Tribune's* terminology) was committed it continued throughout the late 1880's and through the first third of the twentieth century to campaign for remonetization of the metal. It finally gave up its fifty-year crusade on this subject when a compromise Silver Purchase Act was passed by Congress in 1934.

A recent example of *The Tribune's* public service enterprises was the initiation on November 29, 1970, of a feature called "Common Carrier." Its purpose is to serve as a forum for discussion of political, social and economic issues or problems. Article selection is made by a five-member board of lay editors working outside the editorial direction of the newspaper and without regard to *Tribune* policies.

During the Fitzpatrick regime as publisher he, to an extraordinary degree, was the dictator of *Tribune* policy. This does not mean that he initiated or personally read and approved all policy editorials published in the newspaper, although he did just that with many of them. He was, to a much greater degree than most publishers, a day-to-day participant in the job of getting out a newspaper and determining its content. His editorial writers, through their almost daily contact with him, soon became familiar with his general philosophy and viewpoint on public issues and so could anticipate the editorial course he would want to pursue. But whenever there was a question as to whether *The Tribune* would support or oppose a particular proposition the decision was made by Fitzpatrick. He frequently did seek the opinions of members of his staff and individuals outside the organization whom he considered knowledgeable on the subject under consideration. When he arrived at a decision after examining the pros and cons, that decision became *Tribune* policy and staff members accepted it without argument.

The major editorial writers who carried out his policies were G. B. Heal, Noble Warrum, Sr., who joined *The Tribune* staff in 1934 and was associated with the newspaper until shortly before his death in 1951; Herbert F. Kretchman, who served as editorial writer from 1939 until his retirement in 1967; Ernest Linford, who came to *The Tribune* from the Laramie, Wyoming, *Boomerang* in 1948 and left in 1967 to become head of the journalism department of the University of Wyoming; and Theodore (Ted) Long, a *Tribune* or *Telegram* man his entire working life, who started writing editorials in 1950 and was editor of the editorial page when he retired in 1970. Linford and Kretchman were replaced by Robert C. Blair, who worked in the news department under Fitzpatrick, and Harry E. Fuller, who joined *The Tribune* staff in 1962 after Fitzpatrick's death.

351

The editorial writers were, of course, required to speak for *The Tribune* on a variety of subjects. But they did specialize to the extent permitted by the size of the staff. For several years Heal wrote editorials in virtually all areas, although he did sometimes assign reporters to contribute to the page on their specialties. Warrum wrote most of the editorials dealing with foreign affairs and national politics after he joined the staff. Kretchman specialized in local and state government and civic affairs. Linford's specialty was natural resources and conservation. Long, as editor of the page, wrote on a variety of subjects but specialized in foreign affairs.

Up to 1911 *The Tribune's* direct involvement in partisan politics frequently made it a party or factional mouthpiece and it reflected a feeling of obligation to support the officials it helped to elect to office and to criticize those it sought to defeat. From that point onward, the newspaper asserted its independence to applaud or criticize particular actions or policies of both major political parties. It usually endorsed Republican presidential candidates and in 1940 waged a sustained editorial campaign in support of Wendell L. Willkie, Roosevelt's opponent in his successful third term campaign. These endorsements carried no obligation so far as *The Tribune* was concerned to support all the actions or policies of a successful endorsed candidate. The newspaper, for example, opposed Roosevelt but it editorially supported much of his program. It supported Dwight D. Eisenhower but opposed some of his proposals. Up until 1968 it did not endorse candidates for governor or congressional seats and praised or criticized on a basis of the newspaper's appraisal of positions on specific issues.

Basically, the attitude of *The Tribune* was to provide the voters with information about the candidates and their viewpoints on issues and then to treat the choice of the voters as the head of state government or the state's representative in the United States Senate or House rather than as Republicans or

Democrats. This policy was applied through the eight-year administration of Governor Henry H. Blood, a Democrat; the eight-year administration of Governor Herbert B. Maw, a Democrat; the eight-year administration of Governor J. Bracken Lee, a Republican; the eight-year administration of Governor George D. Clyde, a Republican, and into the administration of Governor Calvin L. Rampton, a Democrat, whom *The Tribune* did endorse in 1968 along with the Republican candidates for president and the congressional seats. The editorial attitude was the same with respect to Senators William H. King, Elbert D. Thomas, Abe Murdock, and Frank E. Moss, Democrats; Arthur V. Watkins, and Wallace F. Bennett, Republicans, as well as members of the House of Representatives.

The Fitzpatrick policy was objectivity in news coverage and non-partisan fairness on the editorial page. In practical application, this meant that *The Tribune's* position on a particular cause was based upon its judgment of the merits and not upon whether it was being advocated by a Republican or a Democrat.

29

War Years

DURING THE THIRD-TERM campaign of Franklin D. Roosevelt in 1940, some *Tribune* readers thought they detected a change in the political policy of the newspaper. Those readers were wrong but there was an understandable reason for their reaction. *The Tribune* did not change its position but for the first time in thirty years it figuratively took off its editorial gloves and really tried to influence its readers to accept its point of view. The editorials took on a more aggressive tone. While it did not wage the sort of slashing, eye-gouging attack on the opposition which was its trademark in an earlier period, it did carry on a sustained and hard-hitting editorial campaign in behalf of Wendell L. Willkie. *The Tribune* had given mild support to the Republican candidate in 1936. But in 1940, while simultaneously defending Roosevelt's preparedness program from attacks of the so-called America First isolationists, it argued with old-time fervor for rejection of the third term bid and for the election of Willkie.

The campaign and the reaction of third-term supporters to its editorials provided an occasion for the newspaper to restate its policy on more than just the current campaign.

A few days before the election *The Tribune* said in a two-column editorial:

> Primarily, *The Tribune* is a newspaper with a mission and a reputation for gathering, printing and

354

disseminating all available legitimate and authentic news of interest or advantage to the reading public. Politically, it has advocated national Republican principles since the division on party lines in Utah.

It was, therefore, something of a surprise as the present campaign gained momentum, to receive a number of reproachful letters and telephone calls from readers protesting editorials setting forth 100 reasons why Willkie and McNary should be elected president and vice-president of the United States.

These angry protests can be regarded as unintended tributes to the uniform fairness of *The Salt Lake Tribune,* which has not indulged in vituperative attacks. . . .Without depending for its support on any class, element or organization, the aim of this newspaper has been to promote the general welfare, to encourage unity in an era of strife, to curb animosities when hatred is consuming civilization and to present all sides of every controversy, while reserving the right of opinion with that of untrammeled expression.

There followed a resume of *The Tribune's* reasons for supporting Willkie against Roosevelt and this concluding paragraph:

The Salt Lake Tribune supports Wendell L. Willkie and Charles L. McNary for president and vice-president of the United States because the country needs a change, the administration needs a vacation, and the federal bureaus need renovation and the public is ready for another deal with a new, unsoiled and unmarked deck of cards. [1]

This was Publisher John F. Fitzpatrick speaking, probably through the pen of Noble Warrum Sr. who always wrote his editorials in long-hand which only a few of the linotype operators could decipher. Warrum, incidentally, was a life-long Democrat.

While *The Tribune's* editorial page was aggressively pro-Willkie, no one but an unreasonable partisan could detect a political bias in the news columns. The newspaper was running signed articles of columnists and letters of readers who almost worshipfully supported and who bitterly attacked Roosevelt. The newspaper's political editor, on the basis of a voter survey, wrote in a front page article that while Roosevelt's 1936 margin of seventy percent of the Utah vote appeared to be diminishing, he was still so strong that Republicans could have no reasonable expectation of carrying the state for president or for congressional candidates. It suggested that the contest between Herbert B. Maw and former Congressman Don B. Colton for governor would be close but predicted that Maw would win. In the election Roosevelt carried the state by 60,000 and Maw by 12,000.

On the morning after the election, with the count incomplete but the results certain, *The Tribune* said editorially: "Whoever is elected president of the republic or governor of the state is to be our president and our governor. Let us follow a course that true Americans have followed, with one or two regrettable exceptions through the history of our government."[2] *The Tribune* proceeded to follow its own advice.

During the period of the 1940 campaign, and thereafter, international events, as reported in *The Tribune*, made it appear almost certain that the country was heading into direct involvement in World War II. It was already deeply involved as an economic ally of the powers under German attack. *The Tribune* almost every day carried such headlines as: "Robinson Says Utah Holds Favorable Spot in Defense;" "Auto Industry Chalks Up Best October;" "Private Building Awards Soar to 10-Year Peak;"

356

"Only War Can Stop Japan, Consular Aide Says in Salt Lake;"
"Nipponese Mass Troops, New Push Perils Moscow." [3]

In the bitter and nationally divisive conflict which developed during this period over the issue of intervention or nonintervention in the war, *The Tribune* was outspokenly on the side of the administration it had opposed on some domestic policies. On December 1, 1941 it said in an editorial carrying the caption "Keep 'Em Flying Until the World Gains Peace":

> Since the early days of this ruinous European conflict it has been apparent that an invincible air force is as necessary to this nation as a musket was to the early settlers of America. Airplanes and pilots have become real sinews of war and whether America builds planes to be sent abroad to fight Hitler or to equip our own fliers in readiness to repel rash foreign foes, they are recognized as constituting our most effective and indispensable weapon. [4]

The national schism over intervention was suddenly and shockingly closed a week later, on December 7, by the Japanese attack on Pearl Harbor. From that point on until 1945 war news dominated the pages of newspapers all over the world.

It was during these war years that *The Tribune* experienced its first and only strike. For more than half a century the newspaper had negotiated contracts with the printing craft unions. There had been disputes over terms from time to time but never a work stoppage. But on November 25, 1943, Salt Lake Typographical Union No. 115 called a strike when the negotiators for the publisher rejected a demand that terms as submitted by the union be accepted. The necessarily curtailed edition of *The Tribune* for the following morning indicated that there was no intention of trying to continue publication. A pub-

357

lished announcement from E. F. Baldwin, then circulation manager, requested circulation distributors and carriers to be prepared to deliver their papers the "first day that regular publication is resumed" and informed them that they would be alerted by special radio announcement.[5] Another announcement informed readers that *The Tribune* and *Telegram* would provide them with the latest news over the various radio stations until publication could be resumed.

But overnight, Arthur C. Deck, then managing editor of the *Telegram*, got an idea. The photo-engravers, stereotypers and the pressmen unions had not struck. Why not paste up newspaper pages of typed copy and pictures, photograph the pages and by-pass the typesetting operation? He suggested the plan to Gallivan, who discussed it with Fitzpatrick and A. L. Fish, general manager. By mid-day a decision had been reached to continue publication if the non-striking craftsmen would continue to work. They would, and next morning a strange looking, four-page *Tribune* appeared on schedule. For ten days both *The Tribune* and *Telegram* were published by this method, thereby keeping intact *The Tribune's* long record of unbroken publication. The work stoppage ceased on December 5, 1943, and normal publication was resumed the following day. *The Tribune's* ingenuity in avoiding a suspension of publication attracted so much attention within the industry that a detailed description of the emergency operation was prepared and mailed to those who made inquiries. Some years later the *Chicago Tribune*, caught in the same kind of strike, expanded and elaborated *The Tribune's* technique and published a virtually full-sized newspaper for months by the same method.

It was something more than coincidence that the idea for continuing publication came from Deck. Educated in engineering, he had an aptitude for newspaper production procedures not common to editorial employes. He started working for the *Telegram* in 1928 and, except for a year with the United Press, has been associated with *The Tribune* or the *Telegram* throughout his working life. He was managing editor of the *Telegram* when it was absorbed by the *Deseret News* and then became executive editor of *The Tribune,* the position he holds as the newspaper enters its centennial year.

A good one-word characterization of Deck as a newspaperman is "competence." He acquired the skills which enabled him to do anything people working under him were called upon to do, and do them all well. Additionally, he was exceptionally knowledgeable, for a news-editorial man, in the areas of newspaper publishing in which he was not directly involved. Flexible and adjustable, he would have been a competent editor on a *New York Times,* a *Christian Science Monitor,* a *New York Daily News* or a *Chicago Tribune.* He has served as managing editor or executive editor under publishers Fitzpatrick and Gallivan and under general managers A. L. Fish and Eugene MacKinnon of the *Tribune-Telegram.* MacKinnon came to *The Tribune* in 1947 from the *Philadelphia Evening Bulletin,* where he was assistant general manager, to succeed Fish as general manager of *The Tribune-Telegram,* continuing in that position until shortly before his death on August 9, 1951.

The fact the Deck could work with four such disparate personalities, holding the confidence and approbation of each one, was a testimonial to his flexibility. For, with the exception of Gallivan, all of them had complex personalities which were sometimes difficult to fathom and to appease.

The war and postwar years of the 1940's posed a new set of problems for *The Tribune.* During the depression years a major concern was to keep shrinking circulation and advertising volume from pushing the enterprise into deficits. In the succeeding decade the ills of inflation replaced those of deflation. Advertising volume boomed and people had money to subscribe to the newspaper. But production costs closely followed the upward spiral of revenues and *The Tribune-Telegram* was handicapped

359

in the expansion of its circulation and advertising by a paper shortage which brought about newsprint rationing. In a brief historical sketch of *The Tribune* written for its seventy-fifth anniversary in 1946 the writer pointed out that under Fitzpatrick's business management and editorial direction *The Tribune's* circulation had almost doubled to 80,000 daily and 120,000 Sunday by mid-1943.[6] At this point the paper shortage forced an arbitrary reduction in circulation and rationing of advertising. The newspaper went through a painful process of withdrawing from fringe areas which had been cultivated with much effort and cost in expanding its territory. It was confronted with a choice of shrinking its territory at the edges or of diminishing the density of its coverage closer to the center.

A particularly painful part of the circulation curtailment was the discontinuance of subscriptions going to long-time *Tribune* readers living far outside *The Tribune's* territory. The newspaper had long prided itself upon the loyalty of readers who, moving to major cities outside the Intermountain area, still wanted *The Tribune* because it had become part of their daily lives and because it represented to them what a newspaper should be. In California alone more than 700 such subscribers were affected by the forced cuts.

With the termination of the war in Europe in May, 1945, and in the Pacific in September of the same year, *The Tribune* organization, along with everyone else, could hopefully look forward to a gradual return to normalcy — whatever that might turn out to be. But, for *The Tribune* the next several years were to be anything but normal; for the newspaper was heading into one of the major crises of its long crises-filled life — a bruising, five-year battle with its old rival, the *Deseret News*. It was not a revival of the old multi-fanged "irrepressible conflict" but rather a reaction to the economic facts of newspaper publishing which had been pressing with increasing intensity on the industry since the turn of the century. By determined effort, *The Tribune's* competitor sought to stem mounting monetary losses and the necessity for increasing subsidies from non-newspaper sources. In so doing, the *Deseret News* hoped to solve an economic problem which subsequent events demonstrated was insolvable without a change in the city's then existing newspaper structure — three papers published from two separate plants. In the restricted area of economic competition the ensuing battle equaled or surpassed in intensity any of the prior confrontations between the two newspapers.

30

Economic Struggle Again

AT THE BEGINNING of Utah's centennial year of 1947 *The Salt Lake Tribune,* along with its sister newspaper, the evening *Telegram,* was riding high. It had had its ups and downs during the booming twenties, the depression thirties and the war-dominated forties. But its general direction had been up from the time of the muffling of the "irrepressible conflict" beginning in 1911. At that point it had been kept alive and fighting for a decade by infusions of money from the non-newspaper income of Thomas Kearns. It was poorly housed, poorly equipped and meagerly staffed; hated by Mormons for its long fight against various church policies; and scorned, immediately after the accommodation, by the more-hard-nosed gentiles who considered it cowardly for giving up the fight.

By 1947 it had a modern, efficient plant, ownership concentrated in a single family, a publisher of extraordinary ability, and a competent staff. It was read and respected by Mormons and gentiles, and its public acceptance indicated that the Intermountain residents regarded it as one of the country's great newspapers. It had from the beginning enjoyed prestige, even when its editorial policy restricted its general public acceptance. One thing the newspaper lacked was financial reserves or a flow of non-publishing income to tide it over periods of deficits should they return. It had been making a good profit since the worst of the depression years and was at its peak in earnings as it entered the state's centennial year. These earnings had been reinvested in the business or used to pay death taxes so that ownership could be kept in the family corporation. A large investment had been made in 1937 to purchase the newspapers a new home — the present Tribune Building,[1] which had been owned by the Ezra Thompson estate. Substantial expenditures were being made throughout the period to expand and improve physical facilities and equipment. On January 24, 1936, Edmond J. Kearns, one of Thomas Kearns' three children, died and substantial sums were needed to pay taxes. Subsequently his widow wanted to sell part of her interest and more money was needed to buy the stock for the Kearns Corporation. On July 4, 1943, Helen Kearns Brophy, daughter of Thomas Kearns, died, and more money was needed for taxes. Less than three months later, on September 21, Mrs. Jennie J. Kearns, Thomas Kearns' widow, died and still more money had to be raised for taxes.

The abnormal profits of the war years had been skimmed off by the excess profits tax. The non-publishing enterprises of the Kearns family corporation were at this time a drag on *The Tribune* rather than a source of income to pay newspaper deficits as mining had been in the past. A profitable investment had been made in potentially competitive radio in the form of an interest of slightly less than one-fourth in radio station KSL. But *The Tribune* management was in process of selling this to acquire a one-half interest in radio station KALL. So radio, while representing a valuable asset, was a drain on and not a contributor to cash assets. In short, *The Tribune* was at this time the breadwinner of the family corporation and not a luxury to be supported, if necessary, with other income.

At this point, the beginning of 1947, *The Tribune-Telegram* held a dominant position in every county of Utah and every county of Idaho, Nevada and Wyoming within what was classified as the Salt Lake market. *The Tribune's* daily circulation was 84,895, more than twice the *Deseret News* circulation of 40,147.

In Salt Lake City proper *The Tribune* ranked first with 28,619 circulation, the *Telegram* second with 20,290 and the *News* third with 12,583. *The Tribune-Telegram* was capturing approximately eighty percent of each dollar spent in Salt Lake newspaper advertising. [2]

The Tribune-Telegram management had been aware for months that something big was stirring at the *Deseret News*. It received second-hand reports that substantial sums had been earmarked by the church to launch a drive to make the *News* the number one newspaper of the area. On July 1, 1947, the *News* published a 174-page centennial issue in which its expansion plans were publicly disclosed. As related in Wendell H. Ashton's history of the *Deseret News, Voice in the West:*

> It was at this time that the management of the *Deseret News* decided to unwrap a surprise birthday gift of its own for the people. It was really a present the *News* had planned for its friends before, but the war had come in the way. There was no better time than the present — the Mountain West's centenary — to deliver it.
> The gift: a vastly expanded newspaper, a greater *Deseret News*. [3]

On May 24, 1948, *Newsweek* published an article on the expansion of the *Deseret News* under the caption "Mormon Spruce-Up." Staff members of *The Tribune-Telegram* were disposed to regard the big push up the street as just another promotion drive which would die out in a few weeks or a few months. But they soon began hearing that they could increase their salaries if they moved to the *News*, as some of them did. Fitzpatrick, who was frequently far ahead of his reporters in gathering information, had been aware for months that a sleeping giant had awakened; that *The Tribune-Telegram*, a pygmy in financial resources by comparison with its competitor, was going to have to fight as it had never fought before for economic survival.

During the next five years the *News* waged one of the most aggressive and effective campaigns for circulation and advertising in the history of American newspapers. The battle was quite unlike the bitter conflicts which *The Tribune* and *News* had fought in the now distant days of the "irrepressible conflict." Readers of the newspapers were not given a blow-by-blow account of the conflict in the combatant newspapers, as they had been in the old days; but they were made aware that something unusual was going on by an outburst of telephone and door calls from circulation solicitors and a flood of premium offers. In toe-to-toe competition between the two newspapers, there had never been anything like it in the past.

Both combatants had some obvious advantages at the outset of the competition. Among those possessed by the *News*, the most important was the ability to out-spend *The Tribune* by as much and for as long as its ownership chose. Through its church ownership, it had an established promotional organization which was far beyond *The Tribune's* ability to match. And it had newsprint for a massive expansion at a time when *The Tribune* was being forced by the paper shortage to arbitrarily curtail circulation and size of paper. The *News* acquired its extra paper from the Finnish paper association and through an investment (with the *Los Angeles Times*) for a twenty-four and one-half percent interest in a paper company in Oregon City, Oregon, which was valued at about $8,500,000.[4] *The Tribune*, incidentally, had an opportunity to participate in the purchase but lacked the necessary cash at the time. The investment proved to be very profitable for those who did participate.

The obvious advantages of *The Tribune-Telegram* were dominance by a wide margin in both circulation and advertising; long-established prestige in the advertising business as an especially effective medium; a deep-rooted acceptance and preference among its readers which could not easily be weaned away by premium inducements; and an established and profitable Sunday paper.

The *News* sought to counter the Sunday paper advantage by launching one of its own on May 16, 1948.

The *News* drive on the circulation front was begun in the spring of 1947 with an offer to Mormon wards of a library of church books worth from $15 to $125 for from fifteen to 100 carrier delivered subscriptions. *The Tribune* circulation department was astounded. Its cost for starts gained through standard carrier contests ranged from 19 to 30 cents. Yet here was the *News* offering from $1.00 to $1.25 per order and this was only a beginning. During the next four years the *News* kept up a steady bombardment of premium offers for subscriptions — carving sets, pots and pans, thimbledrome racers (scale model racing cars), radios, bicycles, watches and motion picture projectors. This was supplemented with telephone campaigns by professional telephone solicitors and intensification of efforts of the regular carrier organization. In addition to the premiums, the *News* solicitors enjoyed a price advantage as the monthly rate of $1.30 for the six-day paper was continued after the Sunday issue was started. The rate for *The Tribune* or the *Telegram* with the Sunday *Tribune* was $1.50 per month.

Audit Bureau of Circulation (ABC) reports for the five-year period 1947-1951 show that the subscription starts obtained by the *Deseret News* through these extraordinary promotions totaled 255,728. This total does not include subscriptions obtained by carriers or full-time payroll solicitors. *The Tribune-Telegram* circulation department could only guess at the cost but it was certainly far in excess of what the Kearns Corporation could have spent, even if it had been disposed to compete in the spending spree. To counter the *News* drive *The Tribune-Telegram* pushed its carrier organizations to the limit and inaugurated some special reader contests designed to bring in new subscription starts. Other types of campaigns were considered but rejected because of excessive cost or because the management believed that what they gained in circulation would be more than offset in loss of goodwill.

Most of the new starts obtained through gifts and high pressure sales tactics evaporated at the first renewal period. But enough of them stuck to give the *News* an audited circulation of 87,421 for the twelve months prior to June 30, 1951. This was more than double its 1947 circulation. Its unaudited circulation undoubtedly reached higher levels in surges resulting from the campaigns and the week before Christmas in 1951 the *News* informed advertisers by telegram that its circulation exceeded 103,000, which was well ahead of *The Tribune,* and that it had the circulation leadership in the city, county and "all other" zones.

Circulation was only one front of the competitive war. An equally important and costly one was advertising. The *News* greatly expanded its advertising staff and launched expensive direct mail and trade magazine advertising campaigns. The fact that the *News* was owned by the Mormon Church was a competitive factor more difficult to counter in the advertising than in circulation. In 1949, *The Tribune's* largest single advertiser, Z.C.M.I., withdrew from *The Tribune* and *Telegram* for thirteen weeks, and the *News* began circulating for the department store an eight- to twelve-page throw-away to virtually every home in the city. The most vulnerable spot for *The Tribune* in the battle for advertising was the evening *Telegram.* Under the impact of the intensive drive of the *News,* retailers began giving more space to the *News* and less to the *Telegram. Tribune-Telegram* salesmen, trying to counter this trend, were told, in effect: "The town doesn't need the *Telegram.* We could best be served if only *The Tribune* and *Deseret News* existed."

While *Tribune-Telegram* salesmen and executives did not concede it at the time, the advertisers were making a valid point and time was sure to vindicate their position. What they were talking about were the economic facts of life which decreed at an earlier date that either *The Tribune* or the morning *Herald* had to die because the market would not support two newspapers in the morning field. The clear message now was that the market would not support two newspapers in the afternoon field; that either the *News* or the *Telegram* must die. No one among the advertisers or in *The Tribune-Telegram* organization had even a fleeting thought that the casualty would be the *News*.

It is probable that Fitzpatrick had read the message before anyone else and that this set him to thinking about and planning a solution which would satisfy the economics of newspaper publishing in the Salt Lake area.

During the period of the competitive confrontation other problems arose to harass *Tribune-Telegram* management and shake staff morale. Rumors began sprouting like toadstools after a spring rain that *The Tribune* had been sold. One day the buyer was the *Philadelphia Bulletin;* a few days later it was the *Chicago Tribune* or the Hearst newspapers, or Scripps-Howard or any other publisher who happened to register at the Hotel Utah. Had *The Tribune* been a public corporation, required to issue financial reports, the rumors would have been strengthened. For such a report would have shown that *Tribune-Telegram* profits had dwindled to less than one-fifth the 1947 level. It would have further shown that a continuation of the trend from 1947 would have, within a very few years, plunged the newspapers into deficits which the owners would be unable to meet.

The rumor that really shook the city erupted in the summer of 1950 — *The Tribune* had been sold to the Mormon Church. This one at least made economic sense. For at this point it is doubtful, had *The Tribune* decided to "throw in the sponge," that any third publisher would want to pick it up and thereby buy a fight which a competent management had decided was already lost. But a purchase by the *News*, viewed from the standpoint of economics alone, would have been a master coup. It would have been in keeping with what was happening, and what would continue to happen, in other cities — establishment of a monopoly by purchase. This would have stopped the massively uneconomic competitive fight and place in the hands of the single owner an impressive array of cost-reducing opportunities.

This rumor did not quickly die. It cropped up in various forms. One version was that a completely reliable person had seen the conveyance document on the desk of a banker, who incidentally was a close personal friend of Fitzpatrick. The Retail Trades Association, representing major advertisers of the city, planned a meeting to consider what position they should take. *The Tribune-Telegram* was deluged with telephone calls demanding to know if the story were true. Columnist Drew Pearson reported in his column that a reliable source close to the Mormon hierarchy had confirmed the purchase by the church. The *Telegram* at that time ordinarily carried the Pearson column, but knowing that in this instance what it reported was untrue, it was withheld from publication. This only served to "confirm" the report for some who received clippings of the column from relatives, friends or business associates. Whether publication of the column, with a denial, would have quashed the rumor was a subject of post-mortem debate around *The Tribune*.

The rumored sales of *The Tribune,* incidentally, were not entirely without factual foundation. When Mrs. Kearns placed her trust in Fitzpatrick to manage the family corporation and selected Gallivan to be educated and trained as his successor, she had presumably concluded that her own children would not be disposed to shoulder the responsibility of publishing a newspaper.

Edmond J. Kearns and Helen Kearns Brophy had pursued their own interests, left management of their inheritances wholly to Fitzpatrick and passed their interests on to heirs upon their deaths. Thomas F. Kearns, however, had participated to a greater degree than the other children in the family business affairs and, through some inter-family transactions, had acquired an interest of approximately forty percent. At this critical point he decided he wanted to sell to obtain funds for other business enterprises.

To anyone less dedicated to the perpetuation of the newspaper than were Fitzpatrick and Gallivan, it was an understandable decision. *The Tribune's* profits had been reduced close to the vanishing point by the economic encounter with the *News;* the future looked bleak and the newspapers were undoubtedly shrinking in value. To Fitzpatrick the sale of *The Tribune* was unthinkable and he worked feverishly to prevent it. It is probable that he already had in mind a plan to keep *The Tribune* ownership in the family corporation — a plan which involved a sale to the Mormon Church but not of his beloved *Tribune.*

During this period A. L. Fish and T. J. Mullin, general manager and business manager, respectively, were forced to retire for reasons of health. Their replacement from the outside strengthened the rumors of a sale and intensified apprehension among staff members. This in turn strengthened an organizational drive by the American Newspaper Guild because some staff members who did not want the guild under the existing management felt they might want it under different ownership. Thus, when an election was held in the spring of 1951, the guild was able to establish bargaining units for the editorial and the circulation departments. Subsequent negotiations resulted in the filing of unfair labor practices against the newspaper, which were dismissed following hearings. Another off-shoot of the negotiations was the filing of a half-million dollar suit against *The Tribune* for purportedly libelous statements against the guild by the general manager. The guild soon died a natural death from lack of interest on the part of the employes.

A particularly menacing cloud for *The Tribune* then appeared a few thousand miles away. The United States Department of Justice filed charges in the Federal District Court of New Orleans attacking as a monopolistic practice the combined advertising rates of the New Orleans *Times-Picayune* and its sister paper, the *States.* The system of combined advertising and circulation rates used by the New Orleans newspapers was identical to that used by *The Tribune-Telegram.* It was the understanding of *The Tribune* management that the New Orleans action was taken at the insistence of the *Item,* a third New Orleans newspaper that was in the same competitive position as the *Deseret News.* If the New Orleans action were successful the *News* could bring a similar action against *The Tribune-Telegram.* The seriousness of this threat can be indicated by a few advertising linage figures. Even with the power and prestige of *The Tribune* pushing advertising into the *Telegram* at a very low cost to the advertiser for the additional circulation, the *Deseret News* was clearly winning the battle with its free-spending sales program and its low-cost price for space. In 1947 the retail advertising volume in the *Telegram* was 337,463 inches compared with 288,352 for the *News.* For 1951 the *Telegram* total was 499,354 inches compared with 515,167 for the *News.*[5] A continuation of this trend for very long would surely kill the *Telegram,* even with the combination rate. Without the combination rate it probably would have expired some time earlier as a viable economic enterprise. Without the *Telegram* to "run interference" in the afternoon field, *The Tribune's* economic position would have been weakened at a time when it was already being pushed to the

371

brink of the deficit grave into which so many of its contemporaries had disappeared.

At this juncture a light appeared. Massive losses by the *Deseret News* and disappearing profits, with prospects of insupportable losses, for *The Tribune* had at long last brought about discussion between the managements of the newspapers of possible solutions. One satisfactory to both parties was found in what was known as a newspaper agency operation.

The plan involved the sale of the *Telegram* to the *Deseret News* for merger into a single afternoon newspaper, something Fitzpatrick had advocated twenty years earlier when *The Tribune* had reacquired the failing *Telegram;* and the transfer of business and production operations of the surviving *Tribune* and *Deseret News* to a non-profit, jointly-owned agency corporation. As this solution developed, the money obtained from the sale of the *Telegram*, along with borrowed funds, enabled Fitzpatrick to purchase the interest of Thomas F. Kearns and thereby keep *Tribune* ownership within the family corporation.

31

Birth of NAC

SOON AFTER THE fiscal blood-letting between *The Tribune* and *Deseret News* was ended by the establishment of a joint operating agency, John W. Gallivan, then assistant to Fitzpatrick and secretary of The Tribune Publishing Company, was asked, "Why did it happen — why was Newspaper Agency Corporation formed?" His response was, "Why didn't it happen sooner?"[1] This pointedly reflected the reaction of *The Tribune* management and owners, and presumably that of the *Deseret News* management and owners, toward the new cooperative arrangement.

On *The Tribune* side, only Fitzpatrick knew such details as who first thought of this particular solution? Who first proposed it? Did one side have to "sell" it to the other? Fitzpatrick never answered such questions in writing or verbally to anyone in *The Tribune* organization now alive. The first inkling to reach anyone that such a plan was under consideration by the publisher came to Gallivan in the form of a question. Fitzpatrick, in a rather routine manner, asked his chief assistant what he thought of an agency solution to the deepening problem of newspaper survival. Gallivan responded that it would be ideal but added what appeared to him to be the obvious: "But, of course, it would be impossible." Fitzpatrick remarked that he thought something might be worked out and dropped the subject for the time being.[2]

It can be presumed from Fitzpatrick's question and from subsequent developments that some exploratory discussions had taken place between Fitzpatrick and representatives of the *Deseret News*. Fitzpatrick had enjoyed a personal friendship with George Albert Smith, president of the Mormon Church, which had not been disrupted by the competition between the newspapers. In fact, when President Smith died in April, 1951, Fitzpatrick, with his strong aversion to public platforms, surprised close associates by complying with a wish of the family that he appear as one of the speakers at the funeral.

It should be recalled at this point that in 1907 when the feud between *The Tribune* and *Deseret News* was in one of its bitterest phases, *The Tribune* had exempted David O. McKay (Smith's successor as president of the Mormon Church) and Anthony W. Ivins from its attacks on the church leadership. A close friendship existed between A. N. McKay, *The Tribune's* general manager from 1911 to 1924, and David O. McKay. (These two McKays were not related.) Fitzpatrick continued this warm relationship.

An incident in the early 1940's, seemingly inconsequential at the time but of real importance to the close personal relations of Fitzpatrick and McKay, was the acceptance by Fitzpatrick of an appointment to the executive committee of the Utah Centennial Commission which was created to plan for the state's centennial observance in 1947. Fitzpatrick was not reluctant to participate in and lend the support of *The Tribune* to public enterprises. Since he preferred to make his contributions of work or money anonymously, he was really making an exception in this instance by accepting a title. The chairman of the commission was David O. McKay. During the planning and performance of the centennial observance, the friendship between McKay and Fitzpatrick deepened into a mutual trust which would later help make agreement between the two newspapers possible. There were, then, no insuperable personal reasons why a new accommodation could not be reached in the journalistic field. Agreement between the two papers seemed unlikely or impossible to some only because of memories of past animosities.

374

Regardless of when the first exploratory conversations might have taken place, or who initiated them, discussions between Fitzpatrick and representatives of the *Deseret News* relating to the deepening financial crisis in the city's newspaper publishing business did occur during the spring and summer of 1952. It can reasonably be assumed that various solutions were considered in the process of reaching an agreement on the Newspaper Agency Corporation plan.

There were compelling reasons why both parties were anxious to quickly agree on some plan. *The Tribune-Telegram,* as a joint operation was not actually losing money at the time, but by 1952 profits had declined to less than one-fourth of the 1947 level. The *Telegram* had already failed financially as an independent business enterprise back in 1930 and had been taken again under the wing of *The Tribune.* Economic forces had so depleted *Telegram* advertising and circulation by 1952 that it was surviving only because of the fiscal umbrella provided by *The Tribune.*

The financial plight of the *Deseret News,* as a business enterprise, was summed up in testimony presented by its legal counsel, George L. Nelson, to the Subcommittee on Antitrust and Monopoly of the Senate Judiciary Committee during hearings on the Failing Newspaper Act (a forerunner of the subsequently enacted Newspaper Preservation Act) from July 27 through August 15, 1967. Substance of that testimony was contained in this paragraph:

> Because it was losing circulation and advertising revenue the *Deseret News* in 1947 commenced aggressive action to build its circulation in order to achieve and maintain essential advertising revenues, and simultaneously took active steps which greatly improved its quality as a newspaper. This effort, which continued for five years, entailed high

cost, and resulted in substantial annual financial losses to the company. Indeed, in 1952, it was apparent that such losses could not be continued. The agency operation was then suggested as a possible solution, and by mutual agreement with the owners of *The Salt Lake Tribune*, the Newspaper Agency Corporation came into being on August 12, 1952.[3]

Briefly then, the pre-agency financial situation in Salt Lake City was this: one losing newspaper, one being kept alive by the economic strength of a third, and *The Tribune* showing such a steep profit decline that it would have been plunged into losses in a very few years if the existing situation continued unabated.

One of the first, if not the first person, other than the publishing company officers and their legal counsel to be advised of the agreement was Gus P. Backman, who was chosen as the fifth or "swing" member of the board of directors of the proposed agency. Backman, who in 1930 had resigned as manager of the Z.C.M.I. to become secretary of the Salt Lake Chamber of Commerce, was a friend and a confidant of both Fitzpatrick and President McKay. The three had been meeting every Tuesday morning since the creation of the 1947 Centennial Commission to discuss community problems so it was a simple matter to add problems arising from the agency agreement to the agenda of the breakfast meetings. These meetings were continued until Fitzpatrick's death.

Backman recalls that he was recuperating from an illness in a hospital when the church president and *The Tribune* publisher walked unannounced into his room. They outlined the plan to him, asked if he would serve and he willingly accepted the assignment. He does not recollect that he was informed at that time as to negotiations leading to the agreement but it was his impression that both President McKay and Fitzpatrick were pleased with the arrangement and that neither had found it difficult to convince the other of the wisdom of such a solution. [4]

On every count, it appeared to the managements of both newspapers that the agency plan — providing for joint business, production and distribution operations with separate ownerships and independent editorial voices — was the best solution for Salt Lake. Single ownership of both newspapers had been established in many cities and the number of such mergers was constantly growing. But the notion that Salt Lake was different still had some validity. It is conceivable at least that a Lord Thompson of Fleet Street, London, or a Newhouse of the U.S.A. could acquire a newspaper monopoly in a market and still maintain two editorial voices by leaving editorial policy strictly to local management. But it is hardly conceivable that a church — Mormon, Catholic or Protestant — could own two newspapers and permit them to take opposing positions on issues like prohibition, prohibition repeal, sale of liquor by the drink, or horse racing and parimutuel betting without discrediting both positions and both newspapers.

Aside from the conviction of managements of both newspapers that a solution which would continue two editorial voices in the area would be best for the area, there was a legal reason for adopting the agency concept. Soon after the plan was proposed Athol Rawlins, counsel for *The Tribune,* and Paul H. Ray, counsel for the *Deseret News* and a close personal friend of Fitzpatrick, made a study of the proposal in relation to antitrust laws. Their conclusion, as reported to Fitzpatrick, was that it would not violate antitrust laws and that it would, in fact, preserve rather than weaken competition.

Having agreed that the agency plan was the most suitable for Salt Lake, representatives of *The Tribune* and *News* began laying the groundwork for its establishment. The agency plan was not new. It was then operating in a score or more cities and

377

in all instances had proved satisfactory to the participants. The depression had given it birth, and it had matured in a post-depression era of booming prosperity for the nation but, in many instances, pseudo-prosperity for newspapers. Costs had been rising even faster than circulation and advertising revenues. Newsprint became so costly that many papers were encountering diminishing profits and actual losses while publishing huge editions crammed with advertising. Publishers in markets larger than Salt Lake had already found it necessary to reduce costs by establishment of joint operations either under a single ownership or under an agency plan.

Representatives of *The Tribune* and *News* visited many of the agency cities to study the operations. Almost all the major agency agreements were carefully studied. Legal opinions as to possible antitrust problems were obtained from specialists in Chicago, San Francisco and Salt Lake City. Tax ramifications were anticipated and "cleared" with appropriate agencies. After some nine months of work there emerged a draft of a Newspaper Agency Corporation plan acceptable to both publishers and their legal counsel. In brief outline, the plan provided that the jointly owned agency would handle production, circulation and advertising for both newspapers. It would collect all revenues derived from advertising and circulation and pay all expenses (other than editorial) for both publishers and distribute what was left to *The Tribune* and the *News* according to an agreed formula. The NAC was to have as its president the publisher of *The Tribune*. He would be one of five members constituting the board of directors. *The Tribune* would also name the treasurer, and the *Deseret News* would select the vice-president and secretary. The fifth or "neutral" member of the board was the already selected Gus P. Backman. *The Tribune* would publish seven mornings weekly and the *News* six afternoons weekly. The agreement spelled out the guarantees of the editorial independence of each newspaper.

378

Fitzpatrick, perhaps better than anyone else involved in newspaper publishing in the Salt Lake market, had an awareness of the cost-reducing potentials of the agency plan. He had observed the results of joint publication of *The Tribune* and *Telegram* as compared with separate publication in two plants. He could now look forward to a period of easing financial pressures. For in addition to the economic benefits offered by the agency arrangement in operational costs, it had come along at an opportune time to remove a threat to family ownership of *The Tribune*. During the period of the fierce competitive battle between the rival newspapers, Thomas F. Kearns, owner of the largest single interest in *The Tribune-Telegram*, posed a new complication. He had never really liked the newspaper business and wanted to use his capital in some enterprise of his own. He reached a decision to sell and discussed the matter with prospective purchasers. Results of these discussions leaked out from time to time and served to give substance to the rumors that *The Tribune* had been sold. By sale of the *Telegram* to the *Deseret News* as part of the agency arrangement, and by borrowing on real estate, Fitzpatrick was able to raise sufficient cash to buy the Thomas F. Kearns interest for the Kearns Corporation, thereby nailing down, hopefully for another generation or more, the family ownership of the newspaper.

The creation of NAC marked for the longtime journalistic rivals a pinnacle of accommodation which had been in the making for more than eighty years. In form it probably went beyond any expectations of the combative Fred Lockley or the caustic and scholarly C. C. Goodwin. It was, in effect, a realization of the accommodation which Lockley and Goodwin said could take place if certain economic, political, social and ecclesiastical aims and practices were revised. In substance, if not in form, it achieved the goal Thomas Kearns had set when he employed A. N. McKay as *The Tribune's* general manager in late 1910. It was the accommodation John F. Fitzpatrick had affirmatively sought throughout his career with *The Tribune,* and it came in a form which even he probably could not have visualized until a year or two before it was achieved.

The NAC agreement was formally signed and publicly announced on August 30, 1952. Stockholders of the Kearns Corporation drew a sigh of relief. Newspaper publishers across the country telephoned and wired congratulations. Some added an expression of envy. Others, who had some knowledge of the past history and current state of journalism in Salt Lake City, admitted amazement. Like Gallivan, they viewed the plan as an ideal but impossible solution. The newspaper readers of the Intermountain area were astounded. To some the announced plan of joint publication by the rival newspapers was simply unbelievable. Some preferred to accept as factual, a rumor which was more unbelievable than the fact—that the *Deseret News* had purchased *The Tribune.* A few accepted the most unbelievable version of all—that *The Tribune* had purchased the *Deseret News.*

After the agency agreement had been operating for about eighteen months to the satisfaction of the parties a threatening cloud reappeared on the horizon. In March, 1954, counsel for the two newspapers and the agency corporation learned that the attorney general's office had initiated a detailed investigation of the operation of the newspapers and the joint agency. The investigation, under the direction of Lyle L. Jones of the San Francisco office, continued through 1954, all of 1955 and into 1956.

In October, 1955, representatives of the *Deseret News* and *The Tribune* met with the Justice Department investigators for the purpose of seeking an agreement which would permit continued operation of the agency. But a few days after this session the department served upon the newspaper publishers a complaint charging violation of the antitrust laws and seeking an injunction against further carrying out of the contract. Actual filing of the complaint, however, was withheld to permit further discussion and negotiations prompted by a form of consent decree presented by the Department of Justice for adoption and acceptance by defendants. The proposed consent decree and a revised draft were discussed at meetings in Salt Lake City and San Francisco and on December 5, 1955, representatives of all the defendants were summoned to Washington to meet with Assistant Attorney General Stanley N. Barnes and the Justice Department investigators. This conference led, in January of 1956, to a demand for additional material, all of which was supplied. No further requests for information were made and no complaint was filed. The agency continued to function in accordance with the contract and the parties assumed that the department had concluded that the arrangement was not in violation of antitrust laws.

Except for the burden of supplying massive bundles of documents, accounts and contracts required by the Justice Department and participating in conferences with the investigators, Fitzpatrick had an eight-year respite from pressing financial harassments during which he could concentrate on improving the quality of *The Tribune* and operation of the agency. He had suffered a mild heart attack and was under medical orders to diminish the heavy work-load he had carried from the time he became the indispensable secretary and assistant of Thomas Kearns in 1913.

The Tribune, under his guidance, had established an excellent reputation within the newspaper publishing industry within its service area, for comprehensive and objective news coverage; for typographical excellence; for recognition of its public responsibilities; and especially for its local news coverage. And for *The Tribune*, "local" meant an area of more than 208,000 square miles in four states in which some 200 correspondents were deployed to keep the home-office editorial force "on top of things."

381

A typical example of the readiness of *The Tribune* news organization to respond occurred on June 30, 1956, when two commercial airliners (UAL and TWA) collided over the Grand Canyon in northern Arizona, killing all 128 persons aboard. For its coverage of this commercial air tragedy, *The Tribune* was awarded the Pulitzer Prize for 1957 for "local reporting under the pressure of edition time." As the citation said:

> This was a team job that surmounted great difficulties in distance, time and terrain. . . . The accident occurred in one of the most inaccessible places in the U.S. Although individual reporters and photographers performed in an outstanding fashion, the results of their work were made possible because of the complete coordination of editors, rewrite men, laboratory photographers and technicians.[5]

The really unusual aspect of this coverage of a disaster was that it won a Pulitzer Prize. The extraordinary circumstances of an airliner collision in such a remote area and the number of persons killed naturally attracted world-wide attention. But *The Tribune's* coverage was what its readers could expect. Airplane crashes was a field in which *The Tribune* staff had acquired special proficiency through experience. With a scarcity of major newspapers in the Intermountain area, *The Tribune's* "beat" covered a huge territory encompassing large parts of five states. Because of this geographical fact, the news of so many air accidents had been distributed under a Salt Lake City dateline that the city was often referred to, much to the distress of the Chamber of Commerce, as "the graveyard of aviation." As chamber officials feared, the appellation no doubt served to give the Salt Lake area an undeservedly bad image among those readers who failed to recognize the immensity of the graveyard.

During this period Fitzpatrick delegated more and more responsibilities to his chief assistant and prospective successor,

Gallivan. He spent more time playing golf, his favorite sport; and he genuinely tried to reduce the stresses of his tension-filled life. This was prompted in part by entreaties of his associates. For by this time no one around the newspaper could imagine what *The Tribune* would be like without "J. F." No one wanted to think or talk about it. But it is part of a newspaper's business to anticipate the death of prominent individuals, at least to the extent of preparing what is known in the newsroom as an advance obituary. Fitzpatrick himself would have been scathingly critical of an editor who, notified of a highly newsworthy death just before a deadline, had nothing in the files ready for publication after insertion of a short lead on time, place and circumstances of death.

An advance obituary on Fitzpatrick posed a touchy problem for *The Tribune* management and staff. No one wanted to broach the subject to him, and those who knew him well realized that it would not be easy to write anything even approaching adequacy which he would approve. Someone finally did convince him he should sit down with a reporter and at least provide some background information for use upon his death. The reporter assigned to the job arranged an appointment in the publisher's office but found him too busy to cooperate that day. Fitzpatrick, however, did take time to indicate what he desired. It was characteristically Fitzpatrick. One of the phrases he commonly used for emphasis was: "in no way." On this day he informed the reporter that anything published in *The Tribune* upon his death should "in no way" suggest or create an impression that *The Tribune* was going to be adversely affected by his demise. Above all, he did not want his obituary to be over-written or over-played, for this would create the impression he wanted to avoid. He reiterated the point several times, using over and over the phrase "in no way." The reporter came away with the impression that, so far as the publisher was concerned, his death would not matter — only *The Tribune* mattered.

Several more appointments were made but each time Fitzpatrick found a reason to postpone the interview. Thus, when he returned to his home on the evening of Sept. 11, 1960, after watching the Utah Open Golf Tournament at Salt Lake Country Club and unexpectedly died from a heart attack, *The Tribune* was faced with a deadline a few hours away and no obituary. It is doubtful any other person in the city of comparable importance and prominence could have suddenly died and caught the newspaper so ill-prepared to record the event. The files contained only a few modest clippings relating to the conferring of honorary degrees upon him by the University of Utah and Brigham Young University, a papal appointment as a Knight of St. Gregory in 1948, and his activities in support of education, college athletics and the Salt Lake Country Club. Any additional information about his background had to be obtained quickly, and under the difficult circumstances posed by sudden death, from members of his family and close personal friends. So the account of his death was not over-written or over-played in *The Tribune* as he feared it would be; but had he been in his office next morning to read it, he would almost certainly have chastized the editor for offending on both counts.

A sentence from a statement sent to *The Tribune* by the late Harry Chandler, then president of the Los Angeles Times-Mirror Company, summed up an evaluation by his fellow publishers: ". . . He was one of the grandest men in our profession and one of the most conscientious publishers that it has ever been my privilege and good fortune to know." [6]

Time magazine, which sometimes strives for impertinence, struck a pertinent note with this comment on his death: "On Fitzpatrick's death *The Tribune,* in open defiance of the old man's longstanding order, ran his picture on Page One, thereby providing many subscribers with their first glimpse of the ungregarious Irishman who had greatly altered and immeasurably improved Utah's journalistic landscape." [7]

Bishop Robert J. Dwyer accurately characterized him for his associates on *The Tribune* in a eulogy delivered at a Pontifical High Mass in the Cathedral of the Madeleine:

> If we seek the keynote of his life, the 'leit motiv,'
> there is only one term that is adequate and inevita-
> ble — stewardship.
>
> . . . He was a man admirable for his grasp of real-
> ity, his application of the virtue of prudence. He
> may never have cared to put a name to it, but we
> recognize it as his inner strength, as the strong
> fibre of his personality.
>
> We may not always have agreed with his inter-
> pretation of reality, but we were always sure that
> he was seeking, at the top of his bent, to find it and
> act in accordance with its dictates. Sometimes he
> gave an impression of hardness, almost ruthless-
> ness, for the search for reality, the encompassing of
> it, not infrequently requires this of us.
>
> Yet in his heart of hearts he was wonderfully ten-
> der, utterly self-effacing, wholly dedicated to his
> ideals. . . .[8]

For members of *The Tribune* organization the inevitable
which they had not liked to contemplate was now a present reality. Fitzpatrick was no longer there to "see around corners" and
chart the newspaper's course accordingly. They could all be
thankful that it hadn't happened ten years sooner. For that
would have been an appallingly bad time to lose the seasoned
and confidence-inspiring skipper. But in 1960 the newspaper
was prosperous and growing. Newspaper Agency Corporation
was firmly established and fulfilling the hopes which brought it
into being. *The Tribune* was facing no extraordinary problems
and the outlook was for clear and untroubled sailing ahead. Not
even Fitzpatrick, however, could have negotiated shoals before
they appeared. A rather menacing one was soon to confront the
new publisher.

32

Diversification
Program Initiated

EXCEPT FOR TIMING, the death of John F. Fitzpatrick occurred precisely as he would have planned it had he possessed the power to dictate the manner of his exit. For he had more than a normal horror of becoming incapacitated and living on. Thus, a nine-hole round of golf in the morning, an afternoon watching the finish of the Utah Open Tournament and greeting golfing friends, a return to his home in the evening for dinner and a sudden lapse into the oblivion of death was the perfect script for the kind of exit he would have preferred. But it was a disconcerting and shocking experience for his family and associates. His successor, John W. Gallivan, was in San Francisco taking care of a business assignment delegated to him by Fitzpatrick. The parting instruction to Gallivan the morning of his departure had been a jocular expression of a serious idea. Fitzpatrick had on several occasions expressed the conviction that a newspaper based upon *The Tribune* formula would succeed in the San Francisco market. So, as Gallivan was walking to a car to go to the airport, Fitzpatrick called out: "Hey, Jack, buy the *Chronicle* while you are down there." [1]

It was the last contact Gallivan ever had with John F. Fitzpatrick. On Sunday evening, September 11, 1960, a telephone call from Fitzpatrick's son Joe, informed him of the sudden and unexpected death. By getting a plane to delay take-off fifteen minutes, *The Tribune's* new publisher was able to get back

386

to the newspaper's editorial rooms in time to assist with late edition revisions in the Fitzpatrick obituary. Next day he convened a meeting of the directors of the Kearns-Tribune Corporation who formally elected him president of the corporation and publisher of *The Tribune*. Members of the First Presidency of the Mormon Church, David O. McKay, J. Reuben Clark, Jr., and Henry D. Moyle, indicated their satisfaction with Newspaper Agency Corporation's operations under Fitzpatrick by endorsing Gallivan as his successor in the position of NAC president. So the agency continued, without interruption, to function according to plan.

When Gallivan assumed Kearns-Tribune Corporation responsibilities which Fitzpatrick had carried for more than forty years he inherited an organization which fortified his confidence that he could carry on without serious transitional upsets. Arthur C. Deck, executive editor, was in direct charge of *The Tribune's* editorial and news departments, and he had been trained in the same school as Gallivan. Other key personnel included George F. Egan, controller of the Kearns-Tribune Corporation who had set up NAC's accounting system when it was established, and A. F. (Tony) Peterson, who had come to *The Tribune-Telegram* from the Portland *Oregon Journal* in 1951 and who became business manager of NAC when it was activated.

At this juncture the new publisher could have relaxed and set his sights on just keeping things going as well as they had been going for the prior eight years. The NAC was functioning in accord with expectations; *The Tribune* was profitable and growing with its territory; other interests of the family corporation were being capably managed and were in good shape; and at long last fiscal pressures had receded to a normal level. Maintenance of the status quo would not have looked like failure. Neither would it have looked like success to Gallivan's eyes. He concluded that the stewardship which had been transferred to his shoulders called not only for preservation of existing tangible and intangible assets but a positive contribution of additional sources of income. In pursuit of his self-imposed challenge he sought and received from the owners of the family corporation authority to initiate a long-range program of expansion and diversification of economic interests. *The Tribune* had undoubtedly been saved from extinction on more than one occasion by infusions of capital from non-newspaper sources and it might sometime in the future need another "Silver King" mine or its equivalent to survive. Fitzpatrick frequently emphasized this point by quoting Senator Kearns: "It takes a great mine to publish a newspaper."

One obvious opportunity for expansion was in the field of electronic communications. Both Fitzpatrick and Gallivan had long been convinced that any newspaper publisher who ignored changing methods of news delivery might one day wake up to find his paper's delivery obsolete. To quote Gallivan on this point:

> I am one of those who believe that we are approaching the day of electronic delivery of the newspaper to the home, and I believe in what I have preached across the land—that a publisher is remiss in his duty if he does not prepare for that day. I further believe that electronic delivery by cable or broadcast signal is the only possible hope for one day reducing publishing costs sufficiently to make new entries in the metropolitan newspaper publishing field again possible.

The Tribune's first venture into the new-fangled methods of communication had been a modest $1,050 investment in Utah Radio Corporation (the corporate parent of Salt Lake City Station KSL) in July, 1925. Fitzpatrick subsequently financed the founder of the station (the late Earl J. Glade who served a record four terms as Salt Lake City mayor and who was reelected to one

388

term without an opposing candidate in the field) over the pioneering hump and thereby acquired an interest of approximately one-fourth in the station. This was in a period when many were convinced that radio was a novelty with no commercial future.

The prevailing attitude was reflected by A. L. Fish, publisher of the *Telegram,* who contracted for a special circulation campaign in which crystal receiving sets were offered as premiums for six-months subscriptions. To make the receiving sets attractive he arranged to broadcast news bulletins, phonograph music and volunteer live entertainment; but neglected to acquire a federal license until a friend reminded him that he would be in violation of the law if he proceeded without a license. He applied for one during the morning in a telegram to Senator Reed Smoot and later in the same day was advised in a telegram from Senator Smoot to: "Go ahead, license has been granted."

Soon after the circulation campaign had ended Fish offered to sell the broadcasting license to some members of the *Telegram* staff, but there were no takers. The license was subsequently sold to Sidney S. Fox who utilized it to establish Radio Station KDYL and then Television Station KDYL-TV, now KCPX-TV, Channel 4.

The interest *The Tribune's* corporate owner acquired in KSL for financing Glade's project from novelty to commercial enterprise led to its first business partnership with the Mormon Church, which eventually acquired 100 percent ownership of the station. This partnership was terminated in 1947 when *The Tribune* sold its stock after acquiring an interest in another Salt Lake station. Federal Communications Commission regulations permit ownership interest in only one such license in the same market area. In 1946 *The Tribune* purchased a fifty percent interest in radio station KALL from Mr. and Mrs. George C. Hatch and Mr. and Mrs. Robert H. Hinckley who had founded that station the previous year. This interest in turn was sold in

389

1954 to permit the Kearns-Tribune Corporation to apply for a Channel 2 television license in a fifty-fifty partnership with Frank C. Carman and associates. In 1956 the Carman group sold its interest to A. L. Glasmann for the *Ogden Standard-Examiner* and his son-in-law and daughter, George and Gene Hatch. In the reorganization, the Kearns-Tribune Corporation retained a thirty-five percent interest in the station until December of 1970. In a transaction completed on December 28 and announced the following day by Gallivan, the corporation which owns *The Tribune* re-acquired forty percent of its outstanding shares from two stockholders in exchange principally for its interest in the television station and two downtown Salt Lake City office buildings—the Kearns Building and the Tribune Building. The stockholders were Mrs. Sheila McCarthey Wood of Hillsborough, California, and John P. Brophy of Del Mar, California, both children of the late Helen Kearns Brophy, one of the three children of the late Senator Kearns.

Effect of the exchange was to concentrate in the hands of the other grandchildren and great-grandchildren of the late Senator Kearns all of the stock of the Kearns-Tribune Corporation except eight percent which is owned by the heirs of the late publisher, John F. Fitzpatrick, and the management which succeeded him.

An incidental effect of the transaction was to leave the corporation which owns *The Tribune* without an interest in a Salt Lake City television or radio broadcasting station for the first time since 1925. A factor which influenced the decision to relinquish the ownership interest in the television station was the possibility that such a step might be forced in the future by legislation or an often threatened Federal Communications Commission ruling prohibiting the cross-ownership of newspapers and television or radio broadcasting stations in the same market area.

From the time Gallivan advanced from chores in the news and promotion departments of *The Tribune* into the publisher's office he had been directly involved in the corporation's radio and television interests. Fitzpatrick's first love was the newspaper, and it remained first in his affection and interest until his death. He recognized the potential of the new media both as a competitor of and supplement to the printed word but he never acquired the enthusiasm for radio and television which came quite naturally to his young assistant.

As a consequence he delegated management of electronic interests, except investment decisions, to Gallivan. Because of Gallivan's direct involvement in this field, he was in the vanguard of those who saw a future in cable television. It was Gallivan's confidence in CATV which induced a skeptical Fitzpatrick to authorize a modest investment by the Kearns-Tribune Corporation to establish a cable system in Elko, Nevada, in partnership with Glasmann in 1956.

The project was essentially Gallivan's "baby" and there were times when it looked like it might become Gallivan's folly. It took twice as much money, twice as much time and several times as much effort as Gallivan had estimated to get the system into operation. But Fitzpatrick lived long enough to see the venture operating at a profit.

The Elko system received Salt Lake City TV pictures via a 240-mile microwave link established by Gallivan, Glasmann, Hatch and associates. It was described at the time as the longest microwave route of its kind in the country.

By 1962, there were three cable systems in the group with the addition of CATVs at Lake Tahoe, California, and Carson City, Nevada, and the company, called TV Pix, Inc., was a thriving little business in a burgeoning industry.

In early 1964 a merger of TV Pix into a new entity called Community Television, Inc., gave Kearns-Tribune a substantial interest in ten cable systems, six of them in Montana, one at Vernal, Utah, and the TV Pix three.

It also brought Kearns-Tribune in touch with Bob Magness, an astute, affable former cotton seed salesman from Oklahoma who visualized the cable TV potential as early as 1950 and pioneered systems in Texas and Montana. Magness, now equally proficient in business and electronics, Gallivan, the energetic George C. Hatch and A. L. Glasmann made a successful and compatible team and Community Television, Inc., began to move. By 1970, Kearns-Tribune's modest CATV and microwave venture in Nevada had grown to a fifteen percent interest in Tele-Communications, Inc., which owns and operates microwave transmission systems along with seventy-two cable systems serving 140,000 subscribers in twenty-one states, extending geographically from California to Pennsylvania and from Montana to Texas and Georgia. The company's 10,000-mile microwave system had by late 1970 become second in length only to the Bell System's.

Publisher Gallivan's program of expansion and diversification of the Kearns-Tribune Corporation's economic base has been steadily enlarged through a process of one thing leading to another. For example, the job of getting television station KUTV into operation in Salt Lake City was responsible for a chance meeting that led Gallivan and his associates in electronics into a notably successful manufacturing business.

This sequence of events started in August of 1954 when the partners were struggling to get the TV station on the air by the September 10 target date. Odds were heavily against them, mostly because of unavailability or slow delivery of essential transmitter parts. As the odds lengthened, an itinerant equipment salesman named Lyle Oscar Keys from Wibaux, Montana, dropped by to get acquainted. He got acquainted first with the station's problems. From his travels, Keys not only knew where KUTV could find the parts in a hurry, but he would personally go get them and help with the installation. His offer was promptly accepted, Keys went into action and the station made it on September 10 as scheduled.

Impressed and grateful, Gallivan offered Lyle Keys a job on the spot. But Keys was single, liked his life on the road and decided he did not want to settle down in Salt Lake City or elsewhere. "If you get tired traveling," Gallivan told him, "be sure to come back and see me. We need you here."

Two years later things did change. Keys got married, called Gallivan and accepted the offer of a job as a KUTV engineer. Keys and his talents started Gallivan and other KUTV executives thinking about the opportunities offered by the burgeoning electronic sales business and in late 1962 they organized Electronic Sales Corporation (ELSCO). They installed Keys as president and went into business on January 1, 1963, in a room at the Kearns Building. With Gallivan, Glasmann and Hatch as officers and directors, the company, under Keys' direction, moved quickly. Within eight years, the company, which had been incorporated as TeleMation, had 420 employes producing and marketing 156 products for the television industry with annual sales of more than $10 million. It had become the nation's largest supplier of closed circuit TV systems and had developed scores of proprietory items for cable television, industrial, educational and commercial TV.

Keys, like Fitzpatrick and Gallivan in their own areas of responsibility, possessed a driving urge to know every aspect of the business he was directing. As a result he has personally "dreamed up" many of the firm's products, helped engineer them, produced millions of dollars in sales, developed budgets, conducted financial negotiations and has even written TeleMation's news releases and advertising copy. And it was Keys who laid out the blueprint for the company's new production and administration complex — a three-building development with 84,000 square feet of floor space in southwest Salt Lake County's Technological Park. The Kearns-Tribune Corporation interest in this publicly owned enterprise as of early 1971 was twenty-four and one-half percent.

In 1951 the Kearns-Tribune Corporation sold all its Park City mining interests and thereby withdrew from activity in natural resources development. Gallivan, deeming it prudent to seek some diversification outside the communications field, turned once more to natural resources and specifically to the Great Salt Lake, which had long been recognized as a potential source of vast mineral wealth.

At that time James E. Hogle, whose family had in an earlier period been associated with the Kearns family in enterprises to develop Utah and Salt Lake City, was actively interested in brine research work then being conducted by James G. Macey, a Salt Lake City chemist. Gallivan and Hogle decided to renew the business relationships of the families and organized H-K Company to test, at a cost of approximately $100,000, a magnesium recovery process developed by Macey. To H-K, the process proved to be commercially uneconomic.

Additional research work for H-K Company by James Ivers, Jr., whose father and grandfather had been associated with Kearns in mining ventures, Sherman B. Hinckley, representing Hogle, and Lockwood Ferris, resulted in another process which permits commercial recovery of valuable minerals from lake brines. Ferris was a chemist with an international reputation for his knowledge of extraction of minerals from brines, one of his achievements being the development of the process used in the Wendover, Utah, potash extraction project. At this point the Hogle-Gallivan venture, known as the Magnesium Project, called not only for a process but for capital investment which H-K Company could not provide, and a search was started among major chemical companies for a partner with adequate capital resources. The search ended when National Lead Company, looking for a magnesium source, approached H-K. National

Lead, in 1964, took an eighty percent interest in the project. Four years later National Lead announced plans to proceed with a seventy-million dollar production facility on the west shore of Great Salt Lake and H-K Company exchanged its interest in the venture for National Lead stock.

The experimental work seeking processes to extract mineral values from Great Salt Lake brines led to a contact with Forrest Brayshaw, an inventive scientist with an idea for solving a moisture removal problem by use of ionized gas plasma. This contact led in turn to the formation of Hogle-Kearns International to engage in plasma research. The first product of this venture was the plasma scalpel, a surgical instrument which permits blood-free surgery. Continuing research work in this and other ventures is directed to the application of plasma and electrochemical processes to mineral recovery and metal spraying.

To assist in the management of the growing diversification interest of the family corporation, Gallivan in 1963 employed as assistant to the president Paul J. (Jerry) O'Brien, whose experience as a bureau chief of the Associated Press paralleled the needs of the Kearns-Tribune Corporation.

The assignment Gallivan requested and received from the owners of the Kearns family corporation in 1960 has progressed during the first decade of his stewardship far beyond his or their expectations at the time the program was initiated. More importantly, the diversification ventures are in fields which have bright prospects for future growth and which, by their innovative nature, promise to continue the pattern of one thing leading to another.

Changes in *The Tribune* since Gallivan succeeded Fitzpatrick as publisher have been more pronounced in style than in basic policies. Some of the rigidities which developed during the Fitzpatrick regime, or which were carried over from the A. N. McKay era, have been relaxed; some taboos of the past have been abandoned; and certain unmentionables have become mention-able. Editorially, the newspaper is somewhat more aggressive in support of things it is for and in opposition to things it is against than it was under Fitzpatrick. Editorial style is not so formal as it was between 1911 and 1960; but neither is it so uninhibited as it was prior to 1911.

A break with what, since 1911, had become a *Tribune* tradition in political editorializing occurred in 1968. In that campaign *The Tribune* followed tradition at the national level by endorsing Richard M. Nixon, the Republican candidate for president. But it broke with tradition at the state level by editorially supporting candidates for congressional and state offices. It endorsed Senator Wallace F. Bennett, Republican, for reelection to the Senate and Representative Laurence J. Burton and Sherman P. Lloyd, both Republicans, for reelection to the House. *The Tribune* gave two principal reasons for its support of these candidates; first, if its choice for president were elected the interests of the country would be best served by the election of a Congress which would be politically obligated to support rather than oppose him; and, second, all three had, in the opinion of *The Tribune,* established records which entitled them to reelection.

For governor of the state *The Tribune* supported Calvin L. Rampton, a Democrat, for reelection. It supported also the Democratic candidates for secretary of state and attorney general because of the fact that these two officials, along with the governor, comprise the State Board of Examiners which can exercise control over some important executive functions. *The Tribune's* position was that without the cooperation of that board a governor might be deprived of powers which a chief executive should wield if he is to be held fully accountable for his administration.

Another stylistic, as distinguished from substantive, change which has been reflected in *The Tribune* since Gallivan became publisher is in the mode of approaching activist functions. The newspaper's involvement in public affairs is more direct than it was under Fitzpatrick's guidance and the public exposure of the publisher as an individual is consequently greater. Gallivan, for example, does not share Fitzpatrick's horror of public speaking; he has no compulsive aversion to personal involvement in controversial issues taken up by the newspaper, as did Fitzpatrick; and his natural bent leads to direct rather than circuitous action.

A concrete example of this change in *The Tribune* was its campaign for sale of liquor by the drink. Support and advocacy of liberalization of the liquor laws was in conformity with a long-established position of the newspaper. But the degree to which *The Tribune* assumed leadership in the 1968 campaign and the extent of the publisher's involvement represented a break with tradition which has become quite firmly established during the second half-century of the newspaper's life.

The Tribune position in the campaign to change Utah's liquor laws was consistent with its traditional efforts to develop the economy of the state. The newspaper argued in this case that Utah's greatest "industry" could be the tourist business, that the state is blessed with fabulous natural wonders that offer enormous potential but that visitors don't come because there are so few facilities to accommodate them. And there aren't, *The Tribune* suggested, because resort developers won't build in states where they are deprived of the vital revenue from the sale of alcoholic beverages. *The Tribune* noted that there were more tourist beds in the resort area of Aspen, Colorado, than in the entire state of Utah.

Both sides in the controversial campaign of 1968 agreed that Utah's current liquor laws needed revising. *The Tribune* supported the view that liquor-by-the-drink was an economic issue, not a moral one; that Utah was already awash with booze under a state monopoly system that permitted people to carry around open fifths in brown bags and pour the stiffest drinks in America, and that a change would not only encourage more moderate drinking but also put profits into the hands of developers who would build the facilities to attract the tourists, thus creating a great new industry with many new jobs and a broader tax base.

More than 50,000 Utahns signed the controversial petition to qualify the question for the general election ballot in November, 1968. Voters were not asked simply if they approved of liquor-by-the-drink or not, but whether they approved a specific bill drafted in advance to effect it. By law, the issue had to be presented that way. Amid a flood of argument about morals, economics and, at the end, the merits of some specifics in the proposed bill, the issue was defeated almost two to one.

Another example of *Tribune* involvement in a less controversial area was its crusade for the Salt Palace. For more than a quarter of a century *The Tribune* had been advocating the construction of a large public auditorium complex or convention center. In the successful campaign for the Salt Palace the newspaper and its publisher played a much more direct role in such controversial tangential issues as financing, site and components of the complex.

Still another example, which in the eyes of some *Tribune* readers represented a more fundamental deviation from long-established policy, grew out of the participation of *The Tribune* publisher's and the Kearns family corporation in the promotion of the Great Salt Lake Magnesium Project. Publisher Gallivan and his associates worked directly and energetically for enactment of the so-called relicted land bills which serve to make valid the leases of H-K Company on disputed areas of the Great Salt Lake as well as the leases of others attracted to the lake by National Lead's announced interest in it. Had Fitzpatrick been alive he might well have viewed this activity as being inconsistent with *Tribune* policy on newspaper publisher "lobbying." When economic studies of the proposed magnesium project led to the conclusion that it could not be commercially feasible without a supply of electric power at rates substantially lower than any then available, one of the financial backers, Hooker Chemical,

398

withdrew and National Lead's executive committee concluded that it could not recommend it to its board unless cheaper power could be obtained.

At this point Gallivan, as an officer of H-K Company, took a step which did represent a departure from the position *The Tribune* had theretofore taken on the issue of private versus public power. H-K Company became a supporter of a petition of the Raft River Rural Electric Cooperative to bring Bonneville Power Administration public power into the area to sell to industries at a price which backers of the Magnesium Project did regard as satisfactory and Gallivan appeared personally before the Utah Public Service Commission to urge certification.

Although Gallivan refrained from editorial comment or editorial support of the petition in *The Tribune,* he did recognize that he could not totally separate his roles as president of H-K Company and publisher of *The Tribune.* Accordingly, when he appeared before the Utah Public Service Commission as president of H-K Company, he testified also as publisher of *The Tribune.* A few excerpts from his testimony defines his position in both roles:

> Traditionally, he said, *The Tribune* has been a strong advocate of private power and in many instances through the years has defended [private power] when a conflict developed between it and public power. . . . Through the years *The Tribune* has, by continuing conviction, argued that public power must not prevail except when private power is unwilling or unable to do the job.

He conceded in that particular instance private power was obviously willing to provide the power at a price which would permit the project to proceed but was unable to do so. Continuing, he said:

Seven years ago . . . James E. Hogle and I organized for the business interests we represent the H-K Company, a joint venture to research and hopefully develop the commercial potential of the Great Salt Lake in the light of today's knowledge of brine chemistry. This was done with a profit in mind, certainly, but with the same love of and faith in Utah that has motivated generations of Hogles and Kearns-Tribune owners to plow back into Utah profits made in Utah. The Great Salt Lake venture was undertaken in the same spirit which Pro-Utah was later organized principally by Mr. Hogle and myself and with promotional expenses entirely borne by the companies we represent. [2]

Gallivan might have appropriately and accurately added that the Salt Palace campaign had been undertaken and the liquor by the drink campaign was then being undertaken in the same spirit which the privately financed Pro-Utah, Inc., was organized — to promote and encourage the development of the economic resources of the state.

Happily, the power cost problem of the proposed Great Salt Lake Magnesium Project was resolved by a plan for providing private power on an interruptible basis which was worked out and preferred by the area's private power supplier, Utah Power and Light Company.

When Gallivan became *The Tribune's* publisher in late 1960 it appeared that he could reasonably look forward to a period of relative tranquility and prosperity for the newspaper; a period in which he could concentrate his energies on diversification and expansion of the economic base of the family corporation which owned it. But the rosy outlook was soon clouded by the revival of an old problem in reverse. The long-sought and finally achieved rationalization of the Salt Lake newspaper business was shortly threatened by an antitrust action filed against an agency arrangement in Tucson, Arizona. The clear message which emerged from the action and the resultant court decisions was that what appeared to the managements of *The Tribune* and *Deseret News* to be the most sensible and acceptable (to the reading public) solution of an economic problem looked like over-accommodation between *The Tribune* and *Deseret News* to the Antitrust Division of the United States Department of Justice.

33

Antitrust Episode

IN SUMMARY, the hundred-year life-span of *The Salt Lake Tribune* can be divided roughly into seven periods, each of which posed its own peculiar problems and editorial responses which management deemed appropriate for their solution.

One problem common to all the periods was generating from circulation and advertising enough revenue to pay costs of publishing plus a margin of profit or of raising money from other sources to cover deficits. *The Tribune* passed through periods of profitable and of deficit operations but throughout both strove to publish a product which would merit and attract the public acceptance required to achieve profitability. There were, no doubt, periods when its owners deliberately and knowingly pursued editorial policies which they could anticipate would produce deficits. In those instances it can be fairly assumed that they either thought the deficits would in the long run turn into profits or they were imbued with a conviction that the newspaper had a public obligation of higher priority than short-run profits for themselves. For the mission *The Tribune* had undertaken — to serve as the other voice in a bitterly divided society — demanded that it take positions which would be deeply resented by a large part of the citizenry within its circulation territory. Had it sacrificed principle and its moral concern on the crucial issues of the times it surely would have expired long before changing attitudes and policies cleared the way to an accommodation.

For the schismatic Mormon elders who founded the newspaper, the problem peculiar to their period was how to effectively challenge economic and political policies of the church without becoming embroiled in an ecclesiastical confrontation. They found the problem to be insolvable because too many partisans on both sides of the controversy either could not or would not draw the distinction they sought to establish. Brigham Young, for one, regarded opposition to church economic or political policies as proof of ecclesiastical disloyalty. So he reacted to the economic-political challenge with an ecclesiastical weapon — excommunication. This, of course, branded *The Tribune* founders as anti-Mormons in the eyes of loyal, orthodox members; and their frequent protestations that they were not attacking theological beliefs served to make them suspect among the anti-Mormon gentiles. They thus reaped hostility or indifference from both worlds and shrank their base of potential support to a small third world. This condemned their publishing venture to economic failure from the outset.

Fred Lockley and his fellow "border ruffians" were confronted with essentially the same situation and, after a few attempts to separate religion from the other issues, resolved their problem by attacking the church on all fronts — economic, political, ecclesiastical and social. This approach served to solidify their support on the anti-Mormon side of the conflict.

During the Lannan-Goodwin period an effort was again made, with partial success, to pin-point the "irrepressible conflict" on economic and political differences. But the unrestrained use by *The Tribune* and its allies of their most effective weapon — polygamy — inevitably turned it once more into an ecclesiastical conflict as well. Nevertheless, some progress toward an accommodation was achieved and this was temporarily accelerated during the first few years of the Kearns-Keith ownership of the newspaper.

403

The American Party period (1905 to 1911) can be characterized as a reversion of the simplified approach of Lockley — attack on all fronts.

During the A. N. McKay period under Kearns-Keith ownership the objective of *The Tribune* became disengagement from the "irrepressible conflict" and reactivation of the heretofore stop-and-go gropings toward an accommodation. Marked progress toward this goal was achieved, although the old fight continued to erupt for a few more years on the political front. *The Tribune* and its allies were not yet quite ready to forget their feud with Senator Smoot and his political organization; and this hangover from the gradually subsiding conflict served to keep some religious animosities alive. It might have been possible to attack Apostle-Senator Smoot without reviving the ecclesiastical frictions had *The Tribune* been willing to stop goading Smoot as the political puppet of Joseph F. Smith. But so long as the president of the church was kept under fire as the power-behind-the-scenes in the political arena the odor of religious conflict was bound to continue to permeate the state and Salt Lake City journalism. This odor did continue in slowly diminishing strength until the Fitzpatrick period when *The Tribune* embarked upon an irreversible policy of seeking to relegate the "irrepressible conflict" in all of its aspects to history and to establish a lasting accommodation by erasure of ecclesiastical divisions in non-ecclesiastical matters. The capstone of the success of this policy in the journalistic area was the creation of Newspaper Agency Corporation.

An economic problem peculiar to the current Gallivan period has been to preserve this two-voice newspaper accommodation from disruption by the federal government.

As has been pointed out earlier, the agency solution to the newspaper problem in Salt Lake City was in part a reaction to a costly competitive struggle during the five years preceding its creation. Beyond that it was also a recognition of the inexorable economic forces within the newspaper publishing industry which

404

had already forced agency or single ownership solutions in scores of cities across the land. The five-year competitive confrontation between Salt Lake's two newspaper publishers had only hastened a solution which was bound to come anyway in one form or another. For while Salt Lake City has some unique aspects, it was subject to the same economic factors which, since the turn of the century, had reduced newspaper publication to one plant in ninety-seven percent of the cities and towns of the United States. [1]

As of February, 1968, 231 cities had two or more metropolitan daily newspapers. In 169 of these cities both newspapers were in single ownership; in twenty-two cities two newspapers were separately owned but operated under an agency agreement in one plant; in thirty-five cities two newspapers, separately owned, were being published in separate plants; and in five cities more than two newspapers were being published in two or more plants. In a large majority of the forty cities with more than one plant, one or more of the newspapers were being published at a loss or were subsidized in one form or another. [2]

As noted earlier, the joint agency solution adopted was not the only one available. But the parties were in agreement that it was the best for Salt Lake City.

Up to that time neither the agency or single ownership solutions had been challenged in the courts. The irony of the subsequent developments was that the solution which the Salt Lake publishers had every reason to believe would be most palatable to the public and which would preserve news and editorial competition was the one picked out for attack. The victim was an agency agreement entered into by *Tucson Arizona Star* and the *Tucson Daily Citizen* in 1940, twelve years before the Salt Lake City agency was established. A common-sense question suggested by the action was why Tucson was singled out for Antitrust Department attack rather than neighboring Phoenix, a much larger newspaper market where a single ownership solution had

405

evolved. The answer to the question, as the Tucson case disclosed, was legalistic.

Upshot of the Tucson case was a U. S. District Court decision that the agency agreement was in violation of antitrust laws[3] and a seven to one U. S. Supreme Court decision upholding the trial court.[4] Inasmuch as the case directly involved only the agency type arrangement, it cannot be said that the total merger solution to the competitive dilemma would not have been held in violation of antitrust laws had one of those been attacked. But the fact that single ownership solutions had gone unchallenged and that an agency agreement was selected for attack suggests that the single ownership solution could have been adopted in Salt Lake City in 1952 without raising an antitrust eyebrow, then or since.

This presumption is strengthened by certain aspects of the Tucson case. For example, the court decision held that a key legal doctrine which could be used to justify a total merger was not available in the defense of an agency agreement. Justice Potter Stewart, in a partially dissenting opinion, in response to a question as the availability of the "failing company" doctrine had the Tucson newspapers been totally merged, responded:

> I think if the *Star* had acquired all of *Citizen's* assets and gave stock to the owners of *Citizen,* it [the failing company doctrine] probably would be available. I would say that the Government wouldn't have much chance in this particular case of attacking that acquisition.[5]

The question of whether the public interest would be better served by two entities competitively collecting and disseminating news and expressing separate editorial viewpoints than by one entity exercising a monopoly of all business, news and editorial functions apparently was not recognized as part of the case.

However correct that might have been legally, there surely is a valid common-sense viewpoint that that question should have been the heart of the case.

It was this viewpoint which impelled *The Tribune*, along with other participants in and supporters of the agency concept, to start preparing soon after the Tucson case was initiated to carry their case to the legislative branch of government in the event of a decision adverse to the agency plan. One of the most persistent activists in this enterprise was Gallivan. For five years he devoted a substantial portion of his time and energies to preparing and helping to mobilize support for the 1970 legislation which became known as the Newspaper Preservation Act. He served as treasurer of the group of agency publishers who pressed the campaign for the legislation and was a member of a three-man committee which implemented the strategy largely formulated by Washington counsel Morris W. Levin. The other members were Byron V. Boone, publisher of the *Tulsa World*, and Amon Carter Evans, publisher of the *Nashville Tennessean*. An important contributor to the immense amount of legal work involved in drafting, revising and amending the numerous proposals which eventually emerged as the Newspaper Preservation Act was Donald W. Holbrook, member of the Salt Lake City firm which serves as general counsel for the Kearns-Tribune Corporation.

Although the legislation was approved by large majorities in both houses of Congress, it was stubbornly fought by its opponents at every stage of the legislative process. Governmental departments were divided. The Department of Justice, understandably, opposed the bill but the Department of Commerce, representing the administration, supported it. However, all the pros and cons submitted by proponents and opponents in committee hearings really boiled down to a few simple points of disagreement. Opponents maintained that the Tucson decision did not bar joint activities necessary for survival of two newspapers and was therefore unnecessary; and that the proposed legislation would give forty-four agency newspapers a special and permanent monopoly in twenty-two cities. The case of the proponents rested on the contentions that the Tucson decision did bar joint activities necessary for survival of two newspapers; that of the two alternatives, the agency plan should be given equality if not preference over single ownership; that the proposed legislation would do no more than place agency agreements on economic equal footing under antitrust laws with single ownerships.

As one Washington, D.C., newspaper reported with a seeming implication of shocked disapproval, Gallivan did openly lobby for the bill. He did so with the conviction that in this instance the interests of the community and *The Tribune* were not merely compatible but reciprocal. His position was summed up in this paragraph of testimony presented to the Antitrust and Monopoly Subcommittee of the Senate Judiciary Committee in August, 1967:

> We wish to preserve this editorial competition [that is provided by an agency agreement] in Salt Lake City. On a basis of closest association with the Salt Lake newspaper market since 1937, I can say without qualification that the only alternative in my community was and is single ownership — an alternative that neither party to the present arrangement seeks or wants. *The Tribune* and the *Deseret News* have been traditional balancing factors in our particular society for nearly a century and it seems obvious that the public interest is best served when they continue to be.[6]

Whatever the merits of the conflicting viewpoints concerning the Newspaper Preservation Act, its enactment into law surely strengthened for the foreseeable future the 1952 agency agreement which permitted the continuation of two newspapers and two editorial voices in Salt Lake City and enhanced the prospects of *The Tribune's* continuing into its second century the role it has played since its birth.

34

Tribune Personalities

BECAUSE OF FREQUENT changes in ownership up to the turn of the century and the proclivity of publishers thereafter for anonymity, the prestige of *The Salt Lake Tribune* has always been focused on the newspaper as an institution rather than on the individuals who created it. There are, for example, no counterparts in its history of a Joseph Pulitzer of the *St. Louis Post-Dispatch* and *New York World,* or a Colonel Henry Watterson of the Louisville *Courier-Journal,* or a Charles Dana of the *New York Sun,* or a Horace Greeley of the *New York Tribune,* or a F. G. Bonfils and H. H. Tammen of the *Denver Post,* or a William Allen White of the *Emporia Gazette.*

The subordination of personal prominence to institutional advancement, which was particularly pronounced after John F. Fitzpatrick became the dominant influence in policy-making, was not just an incidental reflection of a publisher who disliked personal glorification. It was rather the result of a deliberate and sustained effort to give *The Tribune* an institutional personality of its own; an effort which encompassed a wide range of services and programs to bring the newspaper into intimate contact with the people it served in areas other than its primary function of gathering and disseminating news and information.

Offshoots of this policy are numerous, occur at a one-a-week pace and are geared to the masses as well as the individual.

The policy is reflected in the open-door information department (library or "morgue") to serve not just the members of the newspaper staff but individuals seeking answers to questions ("How long is an elephant pregnant?" "Can you tell me of any significant events that have taken place the past year that affected the lives of persons living in Utah?"). This office receives more than 250,000 inquiries a year and maintains photographs on nearly 100,000 individuals, an extensive newspaper clipping file, microfilm of all *Tribune* editions, and houses the Home Service Bureau.

A "Sub-for-Santa" program, started during the depression of the 1930's, has brightened Christmas for more than 80,000 youngsters in the Salt Lake Valley. With *The Tribune* providing the office personnel and publicity, the more fortunate public annually assists its needy neighbors through the family-to-family program. A community Christmas Tree project, started in 1945, has established the huge decorated tree in front of The Tribune Building as an expected feature of the city's holiday season. This project prompted the inauguration in 1960 of a *Tribune* Arbor Day observance in which more than 200 spruce seedlings are re-planted annually in its Christmas Tree Grove at the Mt. Dell Golf Course in Parleys Canyon. This grove, an example of long-range planning, is expected to supply the newspaper's community Christmas Tree beginning in the year 2000. But probably more important, the annual project focuses the attention of *Tribune* readers on the need of protecting the environment and importance of tree-planting.

Programs to encourage physical fitness include the annual No Champs Tennis Tournament which attracts about 2,000 registrants, handicaps the better player and gives the average athlete a good opportunity of winning—thus its No Champs name. Another such program is the annual Ski Classic, which brings the region's top young skiers to the nearby ski slopes for a race each spring which helps keep the sport before the public.

A *Tribune*-sponsored spring garden festival, started in the old *Tribune* auditorium, has drawn thousands of spectators since it was moved to the Salt Palace. This event attempts to encourage plantings and home improvements. A state-wide Civic Beautification Awards program annually honors individuals and communities for their beautification efforts in another ecological-related event.

Largest one-day event in the newspaper's community services calendar is its old-fashioned Fourth of July celebration which attracts about 40,000 participants to view horseless carriages on parade, pie- and watermelon-eating contest, aerial acts and skylighting fireworks.

The Inquiring Editor, started in 1943 as a traveling radio program, now spotlights Utah high school students and their knowledge of current events in a half-hour television program. The news-quiz is based on the news of the week and the students' ability to recall the events.

Law enforcement officers are given individual recognition for community services by awards for the Salt Lake County Deputy of the Month and the Salt Lake City Policeman of the Month.

Youth-oriented projects include the Teen-Age Safety Conference which stresses highway safety and the high school student's ideas on the topic, high school and junior high school poetry and short story contests, a jazz festival, and numerous award presentations for outstanding journalistic, art, and athletic talent. Fund-raising drives and animal-naming contests sponsored by *The Tribune* have brought Salt Lake City's Hogle Zoological Gardens into public view often.

In addition, a Newspaper in the Classroom program, started in 1960, finds Intermountain area students receiving their own copy of *The Tribune* to get a first-hand view of the numerous topics covered by a newspaper daily.

The Tribune's weekly section "In" is devoted to news of junior high, high school and college students and their activities.

Many of the articles in this section are written by the students who participated in the news events.

In 1970 *The Tribune* launched one of its major community service projects when it undertook the sponsorship of an organ donor drive for the Intermountain Organ Bank of the University of Utah Medical Center. A six-week mass appeal and educational effort on human tissue transplantation resulted in more than 10,000 residents of the area registering to become potential organ donors to the bank upon their deaths.

The Tribune personality who achieved the greatest personal fame was undoubtedly C. C. Goodwin, who both dictated and implemented editorial policy from 1880 until the end of the century. But his personal fame rested upon the prestige of *The Tribune* rather than the other way around. However, the fact that *The Salt Lake Tribune* was always more prestigious than its owners or editors does not mean that it lacked strong and dominant personalities. Fred Lockley was one such individual and so were P. H. Lannan, Thomas Kearns and A. N. McKay. And it would be difficult to imagine any owner-publisher or editor exerting a stronger and more pervasive influence upon any newspaper than John F. Fitzpatrick did upon *The Tribune* during the period he was publisher.

The influence, public acceptance and status of *The Salt Lake Tribune,* like every other newspaper, are products of the collective effort of an entire organization. Many individuals who have made important contributions to the creation, survival and growth of *The Tribune* go unmentioned in this account of the newspaper's first hundred years, not because they do not merit identification but because of their large number or because their names are unknown to people now living.

By-lines were a rarity in *The Tribune* up until the 1940's. So the names of the early writers, however prominent they might have been among their contemporaries, have disappeared into the void of anonymity unless they were controversial enough to

413

draw attacks from rival publications. A few have been saved from historical oblivion because of the enemies they made.

Important contributors to the success of *The Tribune* in more recent years who did not hold management or policy-making powers have acquired a public identity through the use of by-lines. One such person, whose initials were better known than his name, was J.C.D. (John C. Derks), a *Tribune* man from 1909 until his death in 1944 and sports editor and columnist for all but a few of those years. If there is such a thing as an "authority" on baseball, J.C.D. was one. He was not only a superb sports writer but a dedicated supporter of athletic programs from the vacant lot to professional levels. He was instrumental in the organization of four baseball leagues in which Salt Lake City held memberships and the city honored him for his contributions in sports generally and baseball in particular by naming the community baseball park Derks Field.

J.C.D.'s sports stories and columns were notable for writing skill and humor as well as technical accuracy. Some of his most avidly read humor appeared in accounts of wrestling matches when that sport was evolving from athletic competition into entertaining exhibitionism. Many readers who had never seen a wrestling match, and who had no desire to see one, were faithful readers of J.C.D.'s wrestling stories. He gave Tony Lazzeri, famous baseball star, a permanent nickname with one of his headlines: "The crowd yelled poosh 'em up Tony, and Tony, he poosh." He was almost as knowledgeable and as entertaining in the role of book and drama critic as sports writer and frequently contributed to the book and theater sections of *The Tribune.* One of his most quoted drama reviews, which typified his writing style but not his usual kindly tolerance of efforts which did not quite come off, consisted of the identification of a certain play in the old Salt Lake Theater and a critical appraisal compressed into ten words: "It could have been worse. It could have been longer."[1]

414

Derks' successor as sports editor, after a brief lapse during which the post was occupied by individuals who proved unsatisfactory or who decided they did not want the responsibility, was John Mooney, a gregarious Irishman who came from the *Chicago Tribune* to the *Telegram* sports department in 1939. He subsequently served as sports editor of the *Telegram* and then moved to *The Tribune* to fill Derks' shoes. He never quite filled them with respect to baseball, football being his favorite sport. But he did share the Derks commitment to quality writing on the sports pages. A testimonial to his success in maintaining that aspect of the Derks tradition was the fact that one of his most faithful readers and admirers was the late Professor B. Roland Lewis of the University of Utah who won renown in this country and England as a Shakespeare scholar.

Among the specialists who have contributed notably to the quality of *The Tribune's* sports section since Mooney became editor are William (Bill) Coltrin, who has been associated with *The Tribune* or *Telegram* since 1940, and Don C. Brooks, a *Tribune* man since 1934. Coltrin, since 1942, has specialized in high school sports and is the author of a book *Twenty-five Years of Utah Sports* which accentuates the attitude he reflected in his day-to-day reportorial work — that covering the activities of youth is a responsibility, not a mere job. Brooks, after an apprenticeship as police beat and general assignment reporter, became *The Tribune's* specialist in fishing, hunting and wildlife management and conservation.

The Tribune-Telegram's closest approach to the fictionalized tough and ulcer-ridden city editor was Frank A. Hunt, who held that position on the *Telegram* for several years before and after it was reacquired by *The Tribune* in 1930. Except for an occasional lapse, he was an aggressive, competent chief of the city news staff who could cover a fast-breaking news story with speed and thoroughness. His occasional lapses were caused by overreaction. A specific example which will long be remembered in

The Tribune news room, involved a major prison break at the old Utah State Penitentiary near Sugar House. City Editor Hunt, determined to outdo the afternoon competition and to leave no uncovered angles for the morning *Tribune*, deployed his entire reportorial force on information gathering duties. When the telephones started jangling with incoming calls he found himself with no rewrite men in the office to take the calls and write something in time to meet a deadline only minutes away. A *Tribune* reporter who had come into the office early, found him frantically running around his desk and shouting for someone to get on the phone. *The Tribune* man, whose competitive instinct was weaker than Hunt's, came to the rescue and filled in on a rewrite desk until some *Telegram* reporters could be recalled to the office.

Proud of his image as a tough, demanding and adder-tongued city editor, Hunt sometimes left written reminders of future chastizing duties. An assistant, thumbing through his assignments or date book, noted a Thursday notation to "give Williams hell." Curious, he went through the book and found the same notation for several succeeding Thursdays. The Williams who got hell every Thursday was Clarence (Scoop) Williams, a veteran reporter on the *Telegram* and later *The Tribune* who survived many city editors and who was well-known to several generations of city and county officials.

The Tribune's prestige had been enhanced over the years in various areas by outstanding reporters who specialized in particular subjects. One such example was N. Lamont Wilson, a member of the newspaper's staff from 1920 to 1935 and subsequently secretary to Governor Henry H. Blood and a member of the State Tax Commission staff. Wilson specialized in state government and water development. His specialty within a specialty was Utah Lake water rights, long a prolific source of litigation and news in Utah and Salt Lake counties. Water experts in the legal profession and in administrative positions accepted

416

Wilson as one of themselves and read his articles not only as news reports on their own views and activities but as contributions to expansion of knowledge on the subject. Among *Tribune* editors, Wilson was known as the reporter whose frequently over-long articles could not be cut a single sentence without leaving a gaping hole and who could solve calculus problems over the telephone for his college sons at a time when many newspaper reporters did not know whether calculus referred to mathematics or astrology.

Another *Tribune* specialist-reporter who contributed significantly to the status of the newspaper in the medical profession and among scientists was William C. Patrick, who joined the staff in 1924 and retired in 1969. He began specializing in medicine and science in 1946, thereby becoming one of the pioneers in the expansion and popularization of news in these areas by the American press generally. Aside from formal, organizational recognitions for excellence in these news fields, Patrick brought to *The Tribune* many letters from medical authorities and scientists stating that they regarded *The Tribune's* coverage of these subjects as fine as could be found anywhere in the general press and much superior to that found in most newspapers.

In the early years of the twentieth century *The Tribune* served as the launching pad for some extraordinary careers in art and literary pursuits. Mahonri Young, who attained international recognition as an artist, especially in the fields of etchings and sculpture, was a *Tribune* artist who did line drawings of famous and infamous people for reproduction in the newspaper. Jack Sears, a prominent western artist who worked for newspapers and magazines throughout the country, got his professional start on *The Tribune.*

A pair of "cubs" who started working for *The Tribune* about 1906 moved onward into careers which seemed to suggest some sort of commentary on sophistication if one could only put his finger on the right comment. The two boys first met at West High

417

School in Salt Lake City and worked together on the school newspaper, the *Red and Black*. One was John Held, Jr., son of a locally famous band leader, and the other was Harold Ross, son of a mining technician who moved from Colorado to Salt Lake City to work for a smelting company. Held, who drew a regular cartoon for *The Tribune*, later created a distinctive style in newspaper and magazine art work with his "flapper" girls and woodcuts of Victorian and "gay nineties" scenes and characters. Ross, a high school dropout after his freshman year, began hanging around *The Tribune-Telegram* editorial department (both papers were published from the same plant at that time) after his friend John Held got a job. Finally, Ross caught on himself as a messenger boy for the *Telegram* sports editor. He soon was given a promotion to cub reporter at fourteen and from this experience "fell overwhelmingly and faithfully in love with the profession."[2] He soon left *The Tribune* to become a tramp newspaperman and this in turn led to the editorship of the *Stars and Stripes* in Europe during World War I and the role of founding editor of *The New Yorker*. It is possible that Ross' puritanical attitude toward sex and his valiant efforts to keep this "incident," as he called sex, from intruding into *The New Yorker* or its offices stemmed in part from his experiences on *The Tribune*. One of his duties as a sports desk messenger was to seek out fighters and wrestlers wanted for interviews and he usually found them in one of the bawdy houses on Commercial Street near *The Tribune* plant. One of his first assignments as a reporter was to interview a madam. As *The New Yorker* cartoonist-writer James Thurber recounts in his book *The Years With Ross,* the young reporter, who classified all women into "good" and "fallen," started the interview with the question: "And how many fallen women do you have?"[3]

Ross and Held renewed their *Tribune* days friendship when both were famous as editor and artist in New York. Ross would not buy Held's flapper girls because so many of them were appearing in other magazines. But he did frequently buy his friend's old-fashioned, melodramatic engravings or woodcuts, a style which Held had picked up from his father who, in addition to conducting his band, owned a fountain pen repair business.

It must have been a source of wonderment and amusement to the ex-*Tribune* cubs to reflect upon careers which had established as synonyms for sophistication among the "sophisticates" of New York the names of two youngsters who came from such an unsophisticated background.

The artist with the longest service record with *The Tribune-Telegram* was Chris Jensen, a native of Ephraim, Utah. Jensen was associated with *The Tribune* or *Telegram,* either as an employe or as a member of an artist partnership whose chief client was *The Tribune,* from 1924 until 1970 when he retired as a full-time employe. His trademark character, Sheepherder Sam, was a *Tribune* feature for more than eighteen years.

The Tribune's first female general assignment reporter turned out to be a national celebrity in sensational journalism. A redhead who came to Salt Lake City from a Wyoming ranch, her name was Florabel Muir.[4] She started her newspaper career with the *Salt Lake Herald* but, regarding *The Tribune* as the leading newspaper of the area, she hounded city editor Forest Lowry for a job until he finally let down the sex bar and put her to work as a general assignment reporter. Theretofore the proper place for women on *The Tribune* had been in such genteel departments as society, art and literature. Florabel made it clear to the city editor that she was not interested in society or club news but wanted to run with the men on the rough and tough assignments. And she did exactly that throughout her professional career. She soon won unqualified acceptance among the men covering the execution of a murderer in a case which she had covered from the outset. At first the sheriff in charge of the execution refused to permit her to attend the execution by firing squad on the grounds that the state law limited witnesses to males. She

419

appealed to her friend Dan Shields, who was then attorney general, and he ruled that under such circumstances she was a newspaper reporter rather than a woman. City editor Lowry, who apparently had some misgivings about assigning a girl to such an event, sent another reporter, William T. Iglehart, as a backup in case Florabel couldn't cope. But it was Iglehart who got ill and almost fainted while Florabel marched into the death compound, watched the execution and wrote an account of it which drew the praises of city and managing editors. The experience left her with a strong feeling against capital punishment for the rest of her violence-studded career of covering murders, gang wars, executions and sensational trials. Thereafter her name became a trade-mark for sensational reporting to readers of Hearst newspapers, the *New York Daily News* and various syndicates and magazines which featured such events as the escapades of Errol Flynn, the Charlie Chaplin trials, the Ruth Snyder-Judd Gray murder, and the activities of Mickey Cohen, Willie Bioff and Bugsy Siegel.

A *Tribune* "character" who was unique in several respects was Walter G. (Walt) King, member of a prominent Salt Lake Chinese family who started working for the newspaper as an office boy in the early nineteen hundreds and was one of its personnel fixtures until his death in 1954. He left from time to time in his youth to do a little newspaper "tramping" around the country but *The Tribune* was always his home base. Soft-spoken, suave and naturally endowed with a remarkable capacity for remembering names, faces and facts, he built up over the years an extraordinary network of information sources and obliging friends, as well as some enemies. He frequently amazed colleagues with his ability to penetrate supposedly closed sources of information in government, politics, business or the underworld. In fact, one of his chief assets was directing fellow reporters to sources of hard-to-get information, without involving himself to a degree which might in the future close the sources.

It was not at all unusual for Walt to get a long distance telephone call from St. Louis, San Francisco or Las Vegas informing him that some bank robbers had left for another point via Salt Lake City and might be planning a holdup in Salt Lake. After meetings of the State Board of Pardons it was normal procedure for some of those receiving paroles or termination of sentences to show up at Walt's desk to get a few dollars for a new start. King's charities were numerous and some gifts or loans were no doubt prompted by the thought that the receiver might be helpful in the future, as well as by purely charitable impulses.

King's closest political friendship at the national level was with James A. Farley, Democratic national chairman who guided Franklin D. Roosevelt to his first two presidential victories. The friendship started in 1932 when the Roosevelt campaign entourage paused in Salt Lake City over a weekend. Farley's reputation for lavish use of long distance telephone had preceded him and *The Tribune* political editor, thinking this might provide an interesting sidelight story, assigned King to check the number and the destination of all of Farley's calls during the visit. King, a master at the art of ingratiation, decided that in this instance the direct approach might be the most productive so he explained to Farley the nature of the assignment. Farley was intrigued with the idea and gave complete cooperation, even inviting King to monitor the conversation when an extension telephone was available. By the time the campaign train pulled out for Butte, Montana, and points west, King had a friend and source of information at the top of the Democratic national organization and Farley had a friend and trusted informant in Utah. Thereafter, when Farley wanted information on Utah politics he included King of *The Tribune* in his list of calls and whenever he visited Salt Lake one of the first, and frequently the first, of his contacts was with Walter King. This relationship continued up until King's death.

Although King was frequently a friend in need to members of the city's Chinese community, he was thoroughly Americanized. Once, when a "tong war" erupted in San Francisco, the news dispatches mentioned that repercussions might be felt in Salt Lake City, among other places. A reporter who contacted a prominent Chinese businessman to check on the report suggested that perhaps he (the businessman) would prefer to talk to King, who would have been sent on the assignment had he been available. "Oh, that is all right," the Chinese gentleman responded. "You are more Chinese than Walter. He is all American."

The Tribune's most durable local columnists over the past half century have been Hamilton G. Park, whose "Senator From Sandpit" column appeared on the editorial page from 1929 until shortly before his death in 1965, and Dan Valentine, whose "Nothing Serious" column has been featured on the local page since 1948.

Park, a native of Salt Lake City, became a columnist without serving a newspaper apprenticeship. Graduating from the old West High School with an ambition to become a concert or operatic baritone, he spent several years with musical comedy troupes, married a singer-actress and then turned to vaudeville. But because of the difficulties of getting joint bookings for himself and wife, he decided to quit show business and become a traveling salesman. But he soon found an opportunity to appease his theatrical urge on radio. He identified himself on his radio program as the "Senator From Sandpit" and his specialty was a commentary on current affairs and philosophical observations in Scandinavian dialect. This led to invitations to serve as master of ceremonies and on one of these appearances he was heard by the publisher of *The Tribune.* Fitzpatrick decided that the Senator had something which would brighten the editorial page of *The Tribune* and offered him a job as a columnist. Thus Park, quite by accident, found himself a permanent job as columnist.

Park's column, a mixture of low-keyed humor, aphoristic philosophy, personal reminiscences, and verse, always retained a theatrical quality which no doubt assuaged a thwarted ambition. Despite his lack of background in writing, his prose was generally both graceful and structurally polished. Some of his paragraphs, which he worked over with painstaking care, were journalistic gems. His ear for and appreciation of poetry enabled him to recruit a following of verse writing contributors who enriched his column in an era when anything that scanned or rhymed was regarded by most newspapermen as something suitable only for the poetry magazines.

Every reader of a column carrying a by-line has his or her own appraisal of the columnist. It may not coincide with anyone else's appraisal. Thus "versatility" is offered as a one-word characterization of Dan Valentine by one reader of his "Nothing Serious" column. He might, on any given day, turn up as an impish humorist, satirist, sentimentalist, philosophical ideologist or just plain clown. He is better in some of those roles than in others but entertaining in all of them most of the time. He can illuminate and exaggerate an absurdity in one paragraph, thrust a non-venomous shive in the next and gracefully pass out an ingratiating "valentine" in the next. It is no doubt this knack for change of pace which gives his column the high readership it attracts.

Although primarily as a humorist, some of his best columns are the product of the sentimentalist in him. His most widely reprinted *Tribune* column, for example, was one entitled "Dear World" which expressed the reflections, the apprehensions and the hopes of a father when a son leaves for his first day at school.

A recent addition to *The Tribune's* local columnist personalities is Harold Schindler, who has been writing a television column since 1967 and who earlier had filled in for Valentine during one of his brief absences from the newspaper. Schindler started with *The Tribune* as an office boy in 1945 and, except for a stint in the military service, has been associated with the newspaper since in various capacities, including police beat reporter. His chief claim to special distinction, however, is his interest in and knowledge of western history, and Utah history in particular. His major contribution to date in that field is a thoroughly researched biography of an intriguing and notorious character in Mormon history, Orrin Porter Rockwell, which carries the title: *Man of God, Son of Thunder.*

A by-line familiar to *Tribune* readers for more than thirty years was that of Harry J. Brown, the newspaper's Washington, D.C., correspondent from 1918 until his death in 1949. Brown was something more than a *Tribune* reporter and columnist covering the national beat. He was guide and adviser to thousands of Intermountain residents traveling to Washington to seek redress or favors from or understandings with government bureaus and officials. He was often a friend in time of need for freshmen members of Congress from the western states in the process of "learning the ropes" in the bureaucratic jumble of the national capital. His expertise in such subjects as reclamation, Indian affairs, mining and forestry and his knowledge of whom to see, how to get to them and how to proceed made him a sort of institution within an institution for *Tribune* territory groups and individuals with federal government problems. Within his profession he was both popular and respected and was honored with the presidency of the Gridiron Club in 1928. He was one of the founders of the National Press Club which was organized in 1908. Since Brown's death his role has been capably filled by Frank Hewlett, a native of Pocatello, Idaho.

Former *Tribune* employes still living in 1971 whose connection with the newspaper goes farthest back into the past are A. G. Mackenzie and Eva Hollis. Mackenzie, now 94 and a resident of Salt Lake City, started working in the business office in 1898. After a tour of military service in the Spanish-American War he returned to the newspaper to work in the editorial department and soon became city editor. A few years later he was lured to the *Herald* by the offer of his own column. He was prominent for many years in the area as secretary and manager of the Utah Mining Association.

Miss Hollis began her career on *The Tribune* in 1911, performing secretarial duties for general manager A. N. McKay and editor-in-chief William Nelson. She later became books and art editor, a position she held until her retirement in 1948. She resides in Santa Monica, California, and will reach her 100th birthday eight months after *The Tribune's* centennial.

The individual still connected with the newspaper whose service spans the longest period is C. W. McGillis, street sales manager. He was employed in 1909 by owner Thomas Kearns on recommendations from the *Denver Post* where he had demonstrated the hard-nosed, tough qualifications needed for supervision of street sales in that period. Charlie's avocation was boxing and prize fight promotions. For many years, Christmas and Thanksgiving parties for newsboys sponsored by McGillis and Russel L. Tracy, founder of Tracy Bank & Trust Company, rated institutional status in the city. After Tracy's death, the late Joe Dupler, onetime Denver newsboy, furrier and mink rancher, became the newsboys' Santa Claus.

Advertising department personalities who were probably known to the largest number of newspaper advertisers over the longest periods of time were Albert A. (Ace) Campbell and James S. (Jim) Perry. Campbell started working for the *Herald-Republican* in 1910, moved to the *Telegram* when that newspaper expired and came to *The Tribune* along with the *Telegram* in 1930. He was display advertising manager for *The Tribune* until the formation of Newspaper Agency Corporation in 1952 and held an executive position in the agency's advertising department until his retirement in 1962. He died in 1964.

425

Perry started working as an advertising salesman for the *Telegram* in 1922, came to *The Tribune* by the same route as Campbell and served for many years as feature advertising manager. As salesman for advertising in special editions, such as the Scenic Edition, he acquired a wide personal acquaintance with municipal and county officials, civic organization leaders and advertisers throughout *The Tribune's* large territory. He retired in 1962 and died in 1963.

The Tribune, over the past century has, of course, had on its staff a normal quota of newspaper tramps of the competent and incompetent varieties as well as a sprinkling of scamps who are best left unidentified and unsung.

Those employes given special mention in this chapter are but a sampling of the many individuals who, without top-level management or policy-making responsibilities, have nevertheless made significant contributions to the newspaper's success. Others, equally worthy of identification, have moved on to achieve distinction with other publications or in other businesses and professions; and some are still in process of making their contributions and, hopefully, will continue to do so in the second century of *The Tribune's* life.

Footnotes Section

CHAPTER 1
The Irrepressible Conflict

1. Edward W. Tullidge, *History of Salt Lake City* (Salt Lake City, 1886), 296.
2. *Ibid.,* Appendix, 13.
3. *The Salt Lake Tribune,* September 10, 1873.
4. Tullidge, *op.cit.,* 7-8.
5. *Deseret News,* November 27, 1867.
6. *The Utah Magazine,* October 16, 1869, 376-378.
7. J. Cecil Alter, *Early Utah Journalism* (Salt Lake City, 1938), 378.
8. *The Utah Magazine,* October 2, 1869, 342.
9. Alter, *op.cit.,* 379.
10. Tullidge, *op.cit.,* 400-401.
11. *Ibid.,* 387.
12. *Ibid.,* 387-388.
13. Leonard J. Arrington, *Great Basin Kingdom* (Cambridge, Mass., 1958), 301-302.
14. T. B. H. Stenhouse, *The Rocky Mountain Saints* (New York, 1873), 623-624.
15. Arrington, *op.cit.,* 306-307. Arrington is quoting here from "Merchants and Miners of Utah: Biographies of the Walker Brothers," p. 3 ms. Bancroft Library; H. H. Bancroft, *History of Utah,* 654.
16. *Ibid.,* 307.
17. From a prospectus distributed December 24, 1870: "New Daily Paper, The Daily Tribune and Utah Mining Gazette."

CHAPTER 2
Schism Within a Schism

1. Tullidge, *History of Salt Lake,* 589.
2. *Ibid.,* 296. A Civil War expression, "irrepressible conflict" gained Utah currency because of Harding's speech applying it to the polygamy controversy.
3. Cardinal Goodwin, *John Charles Fremont: An Explanation of His Career* (Stanford, Calif., 1930), 199.
4. Tullidge, *op.cit.,* 469.
5. *Ibid.,* 481.
6. *Ibid.,* 507-508.

7. *Ibid.*, 479.
8. Arrington, *Basin Kingdom,* 503.
9. Tullidge, *op.cit.,* 590.
10. Arrington, *op.cit.,* 243.

CHAPTER 3
"The Border Ruffians"

1. *The Salt Lake Tribune,* July 24, 1873.
2. *Ibid.,* July 27, 1873.
3. *Ibid.,* September 10, 1873.
4. Tullidge, *History of Salt Lake,* 623.
5. *Ibid.,* 537-538.
6. Charles Dickens, *The Complete Works of Charles Dickens: Great Expectations and The Uncommercial Traveller* (Philadelphia, The Bibliophilist Society [n.d.]), 528.
7. Howard Stansbury, *Exploration and Survey of the Valley of the Great Salt Lake of Utah* (Philadelphia, 1852), 120-150. See also: J. W. Gunnison, *The Mormons or Latter-day Saints in the Valley of the Great Salt Lake* (Philadelphia, 1852).
8. For a full treatment of this subject see: Thomas G. Alexander, "An Experiment in Progressive Legislation: The Granting of Woman Suffrage in Utah in 1870," *Utah Historical Quarterly,* 38 (Winter, 1970), 20-30.
9. *The Salt Lake Tribune,* August 10, 1873.
10. *Ibid.,* August 21, 1873.
11. *Ibid.*
12. *Ibid.,* August 1, 1873.
13. *Ibid.,* October 6, 1873.
14. *Ibid.,* January 4, 1880.
15. *Deseret News,* March 31, 1880.
16. *The Salt Lake Tribune,* May 2, 1880.

CHAPTER 4
End of a Dynasty

1. *The Salt Lake Tribune,* August 28, 1877.
2. *Ibid.,* August 29, 1877.
3. *Ibid.,* August 30, 1877.
4. *Ibid.,* September 1, 1877.
5. Quotations from various newspapers on the death of Brigham Young were republished in *The Salt Lake Tribune,* September 2-7, 1877.

6. Tullidge, *History of Salt Lake,* 624.
7. *The Salt Lake Tribune,* September 15, 1877.
8. *Ibid.,* October 7, 1877.
9. *Ibid.,* September 22, 1877.

CHAPTER 5
"My Friend, the Enemy"

1. Tullidge, *History of Salt Lake,* Appendix, 13.
2. Minutes of meetings from private corporate records of *The Tribune.*
3. *The Salt Lake Tribune,* May 23, 1880.
4. Wendell J. Ashton, *Voice in the West: Biography of a Pioneer Newspaper* (New York, 1950) 187.
5. Orson F. Whitney, *History of Utah* (Salt Lake City, 1882-1904) vol. 3, 135.
6. *Ibid.,* 134.
7. *Ibid.,* 137.
8. *Ibid.,* 146.
9. *Deseret News,* September 22, 1881.
10. *The Salt Lake Tribune,* September 23, 1881.
11. Whitney, *op.cit.,* 173.
12. *Ibid.,* 161.
13. *Ibid.,* 154
14. *Ibid.,* 191.
15. Arrington, *Basin Kingdom,* 356.

CHAPTER 6
New Owners Take Over

1. Whitney, *History of Utah,* 243.
2. Tullidge, *History of Salt Lake,* 849-850.
3. *Ibid.,* 842.
4. *Ibid.,* 842-843.
5. *Ibid.,* 845-847.
6. *The Salt Lake Tribune,* October 13, 1883.
7. Whitney, *op.cit.,* 274.
8. *Ibid.,* 271.
9. *The Salt Lake Tribune,* October 23, 1883.
10. *Ibid.,* January 1, 1884.
11. *Ibid., August 9, 1893.*

CHAPTER 7
Polygamy Crusade

1. *The Salt Lake Tribune,* November 7, 1884.
2. *Deseret News,* November 7, 1884.

3. Whitney, *History of Utah,* 420.
4. *The Salt Lake Tribune,* October 26, 1884.
5. Whitney, *op.cit.,* 308.
6. *Ibid.,* 309.
7. *Ibid.,* 311.
8. *Ibid.,* 317-318.
9. *Ibid.,* 318-319.
10. *Ibid.,* 443.
11. *Ibid.,* 464.
12. *Ibid.,* 470-472.
13. *Ibid.,* 397-398.
14. *Ibid.,* 398.
15. *Ibid.,* 358.
16. *Ibid.,* 359.
17. *Ibid.,* 420.
18. *Ibid.,* 422.
19. *The Salt Lake Tribune,* September 19, 1885.
20. Whitney, *op.cit.,* 422-423.
21. *The Salt Lake Tribune,* January 21, 1886.

CHAPTER 8
"The Madam"

1. Whitney, *History of Utah,* 433-444.
2. *Ibid.,* 447.
3. *The Salt Lake Tribune,* February 17, 1886.
4. *Ibid.,* February 18, 1886.
5. Whitney, *op.cit.,* 498.
6. *Ibid.,* 511-512.
7. *Ibid.,* 514.
8. *The Salt Lake Tribune,* August 6, 1887.
9. *Ibid.,* May 8, 1886.
10. The author found this *Deseret News* quote in an old scrapbook but was unable to fix the exact May, 1886, date from available microfilm records at the Utah Historical Society, the newspapers of May 6 through 11 being missing.
11. *The Salt Lake Tribune,* May 1, 1886.

CHAPTER 9
The Raid

1. Arrington, *Basin Kingdom,* 361.
2. Whitney, *History of Utah,* 547-548.
3. *The Salt Lake Tribune,* June 23, 1887.
4. *Ibid.,* June 26, 1887.

5. *Deseret News,* July 8, 1885.
6. *The Salt Lake Tribune,* August 2, 1887.
7. *Ibid.,* July 27, 1887.
8. *Ibid.,* August 6, 1887.
9. Arrington, *op.cit.,* 371.
10. *Ibid.,* 360.
11. *The Salt Lake Tribune,* April 26, 1887.

CHAPTER 10
Year of Political Ferment

1. Whitney, *History of Utah,* 619-620.
2. *Ibid.,* 635.
3. *Ibid.,* 665.
4. *Ibid.,* 668-670.
5. *Ibid.,* 670.
6. *The Salt Lake Tribune,* February 13, 1889.
7. *Ibid.,* February 15, 1889.
8. *Ibid.,* August 6, 1889.
9. *Ibid.*
10. Whitney, *op.cit.,* 682.
11. *The Salt Lake Tribune,* November 3, 1899.
12. Whitney, *op.cit.,* 689.
13. *Ibid.,* 737-738.

CHAPTER 11
End of Church Sanctioned Polygamy

1. *The Salt Lake Tribune,* September 25, 1890.
2. *Ibid.,* September 26, 1890.
3. *Ibid.,* October 7, 1890.
4. Arrington, *Basin Kingdom,* 377.
5. *Ibid.,* 372.
6. *Ibid.,* 378.
7. Gordon B. Hinckley, *James Henry Moyle: The Story of a Distinguished American and an Honored Churchman.* (Salt Lake City, 1951) 213.
8. *Ibid.,* 214.
9. *Ibid.*
10. *The Salt Lake Tribune,* November 5, 1893.
11. *Ibid.,* November 10, 1893.
12. *Deseret News,* November 18, 1893.
13. Alter, *Utah Journalism,* 358.
14. Hinckley, *op.cit.,* 219.

15. *Ibid.*, 219-222.
16. *The Salt Lake Tribune*, November 10, 1883.
17. *Ibid.*, November 17, 1893.

CHAPTER 12
A New State Is Born

1. B. H. Roberts, *A Comprehensive History of The Church of Jesus Christ of Latter-day Saints, Century I*, 6 vols. (Salt Lake City, 1930) vol. 6, 317.
2. Hinckley, *Moyle*, 224-225.
3. Roberts, *op.cit.*, 316.
4. *Ibid.*, 317-319.
5. *Utah Historical Quarterly* (Salt Lake City, 1957) vol. xxv, 114.
6. *Official Report of the Proceedings and Debates of the Convention Assembled at Salt Lake City on the Fourth Day of March, 1895, to Adopt a Constitution for the State of Utah*, 2 vols. (Salt Lake City, 1898) vol. 2, 1164.
7. *Ibid.*, 1878.
8. *Ibid.*
9. *Ibid.*, vol. 1, 4.
10. *Ibid.*
11. *Ibid.*, vol. 2, 1736-1749.
12. Roberts, *op.cit.*, 327.
13. *Ibid.*, 334.
14. *The Salt Lake Tribune*, January 5, 1896.
15. *Ibid.*, January 7, 1896.
16. *Ibid.*, January 1, 1896.

CHAPTER 13
Senatorial Fiasco

1. *The Salt Lake Tribune*, January 2, 1896.
2. *Ibid.*, January 5, 1896.
3. *Ibid.*, January 15, 1896.
4. Roberts, *History of The Church*, 342.
5. *Ibid.*, 343.
6. *Ibid.*
7. *Ibid.*, 344.
8. There appears to have been some confusion as to McCune's church membership, but newspaper articles of the time do not indicate whether this issue was raised in the Legislature or whether it contributed to his failure to get a two-thirds majority. B. H. Roberts, who was certainly well informed in political and Mormon church af-

fairs, stated in his church history that McCune was "not a Mormon, though friendly to the Church" (vol. 6, 344). Descendants of McCune affirm, however, that he was a Mormon. Church records confirm his baptism in 1857, eight years after his birth in Calcutta, India; his marriage to Elizabeth Ann Claridge in the Endowment House in 1872; and his baptism by proxy on March 3, 1969, at which time "all previous Church blessings were reconfirmed and ratified in the confirmation ordinances."

9. Hinckley, *Moyle,* 236-237.
10. *Ibid.,* 234.
11. *The Salt Lake Tribune,* September 3, 1898.
12. Roberts, *op.cit.,* 350.
13. Leonard J. Arrington, who read a typescript of this history prior to publication, provided some additional information on the religious background of Sutherland. In a letter to Harold Schindler of *The Tribune,* he wrote that Sutherland "was the son of Mormon convert-immigrants, was almost certainly baptized into the Church (LDS) and went to Brigham Young Academy at Provo. . . . It is true that he was a Protestant and therefore a non-Mormon theologically. But culturally, he was a Mormon and on excellent relationships with some Mormon leaders. . . ."
14. Hinckley, *op.cit.,* 242.

CHAPTER 14
Thomas Kearns

1. Biographical material relating to Thomas Kearns was culled from articles published in *The Salt Lake Tribune, Park Record* (Park City, Utah), and other newspapers of the period, various histories, *"The Life of Thomas Kearns,"* a thesis submitted to the University of Utah for a Master of Arts degree in the Department of History by Kent Sheldon Larsen, and from recollections of friends and associates of Kearns, notably James Ivers, a close personal friend and business associate.
2. *Salt Lake Herald,* January 29, 1901.
3. *The Salt Lake Tribune,* January 20, 1901.
4. Interview with James Ivers.
5. *The Salt Lake Tribune,* January 25, 1901.
6. *Ibid.,* January 27, 1901.
7. *Ibid.,* January 24, 1901.
8. *Salt Lake Herald,* January 25, 1901.
9. *Bingham Bulletin,* January 25, 1901.
10. Roberts, *History of The Church,* 384-385.
11. Interview with James Ivers.

CHAPTER 15
Goodwin Out—Kearns In

1. *Salt Lake Herald,* January 29, 1901.
2. *The Salt Lake Tribune,* January 29, 1901.
3. *Ibid.,* February 15, 1901.
4. *Ibid.,* February 24, 1901.
5. *Truth* (a weekly published in Salt Lake City), October 5, 1901.
6. The author is indebted to Leonard J. Arrington for a diary entry of Brigham Young Jr., relating to Snow's preference for Kearns over Smoot. In the original diary of Young for years 1900 to 1902, now in the New York Public Library Manuscripts Division, Young wrote under the date of December 29,1900:
   Saw Pres. Snow, asked him privately if he could find it in his heart to send that man (pointing to R. S. [Reed Smoot] who sat at a table writing J. F. S. Jno. H. S. sitting close by). He answered 'No, No,' I said Amen though every fibre in my body said, Reed is the man for the Senate.

   This comment could be interpreted in a variety of ways, but, in the light of the circumstances existing at the time, a plausible conclusion is that Young agreed with Snow's decision not to support Smoot, despite his conviction that "Reed is the man;" that Snow might have had the same high regard for Smoot but was turning to a non-Mormon simply because he felt it would be unwise to send an apostle to the Senate; that it might (as it subsequently did) provoke an unwanted revival of the polygamy controversy.
7. *Salt Lake Herald,* May 17, 1901.
8. *The Salt Lake Tribune,* May 17, 1901.
9. *Ibid.,* September 7, 1901.
10. *Ibid.,* October 19, 1901.
11. *Ibid.,* November 7, 1901.

CHAPTER 16
The Silver Queen

1. *Challis Messenger* (Idaho), October 29, 1901.
2. *Truth,* November 2, 1901.
3. *Deseret News,* January 8, 1902.
4. *Salt Lake Herald,* November 20, 1901.
5. *Intermountain Catholic,* November 23, 1901.
6. *The Salt Lake Tribune,* November 29, 1901.
7. *Lehi Banner,* January 9, 1902.
8. *Castle Dale Progress,* January 11, 1902.
9. *Washington Star,* January 10, 1902.

10. Information about Utah's "Silver Queen" was taken from interviews given the author by Mrs. Susanna Bransford Emery Holmes Delitch Engalitcheff for a projected biographical sketch.
11. *Salt Lake Herald,* January 13, 1902.
12. *Deseret News,* January 16, 1902.
13. *Salt Lake Telegram, January 30, 1902.*
14. *Park Record,* May 16, 1896.

CHAPTER 17
Polygamy Issue Revived

1. *Baltimore Herald,* July 22, 1902.
2. *Salt Lake Herald,* January 9, 1902.
3. *The Salt Lake Tribune,* January 9, 1903.
4. *Truth,* March 11, 1905.
5. *Intermountain Catholic,* August 2, 1902.
6. Roberts, *History of The Church,* 409.
7. *Salt Lake Herald,* May 16, 1902.
8. Roberts, *op.cit.,* 393.
9. *The Salt Lake Tribune,* January 12, 1903.
10. *Ibid.,* January 12, 1903.
11. *Ibid.,* January 21, 1903.
12. *Ibid.,* January 22, 1903.
13. Roberts, *op.cit.,* 394.
14. *Colliers Weekly,* April 15, 1911.
15. This delightful sidelight on the Smoot controversy was a frequently told story at *The Tribune* when the author first joined the staff. He could not trace it to any printed source.
16. Roberts, *op.cit.,* 400-401.

CHAPTER 18
A Redeclaration of War

1. *Deseret News,* March 22, 1902.
2. Roberts, *History of The Church,* 407.
3. *The Salt Lake Tribune,* September 11, 1904.
4. *Ibid.,* July 1, 1904.
5. *Ibid.,* September 16, 1904.
6. *Ibid.,* November 2, 1904.
7. The speech will be found in full in the *Congressional Record* for the Fifth-eighth Congress, vol. 39, part iv, 3608-3613.
8. Roberts, *op.cit.,* 407
9. *Deseret News,* March 1, 1905.
10. *Salt Lake Herald,* March 1, 1905.

11. *Goodwin's Weekly,* March 4, 1905.
12. *The Salt Lake Tribune,* March 1, 1905.
13. *Ogden Standard,* March 1, 1905.
14. Roberts, *op.cit.,* 408.
15. Recollection of Georgius Y. Cannon, youngest brother of Frank J. Cannon.

CHAPTER 19

Give 'Em Hell Politics Again

1. Whitney, *History of Utah,* 23-27.
2. *The Salt Lake Tribune,* October 27, 1913.
3. *Ibid.,* October 28, 1913.
4. *Ibid.,* November 3, 1905.
5. Roberts, *History of The Church,* 409-410.
6. *The Salt Lake Tribune,* November 1, 1905.
7. *Ibid.,* November 5, 1905.
8. *Ibid.,* November 6, 1905.
9. *Ibid.*
10. *Ibid.,* November 8, 1905.
11. Roberts, *op.cit.,* 410.
12. *The Salt Lake Tribune,* November 8, 1905.
13. *Deseret News,* October 30-November 6, 1911.
14. *Herald-Republican,* October 30-November 6, 1911.
15. *The Salt Lake Tribune,* November 5, 1911.
16. Source of information on this agreement is unpublished historical notes left by Noble Warrum, Sr., an associate editor of *The Tribune* for many years. Warrum was a close friend and confidant of A. N. McKay and, like McKay, he had close personal ties with influential individuals on both sides of the conflict. Also, like McKay, he was one of the gentile "bridges" to an accommodation. Although not an employe of *The Tribune* at this time, Warrum was occasionally called upon by McKay to write *Tribune* editorials designed to advance the cause of accommodation.
17. *The Salt Lake Tribune,* January 1, 1911.
18. *Ibid.*
19. See note 16 above.

CHAPTER 20

Toward Accommodation

1. From an interview with James Ivers.
2. See note 16, Chapter 19.
3. *The Salt Lake Tribune,* November 1, 1912.
4. *Ibid.,* November 5, 1912.

5. *Ibid.*, November 6, 1912.
6. Hinckley, *Moyle*, 243.
7. *Ibid.*, 277.
8. *The Salt Lake Tribune*, November 1, 1914.
9. *Ibid.*, November 5, 1914.

CHAPTER 21
"Mr. Tribune" Appears

1. Material for this chapter was drawn largely from observations and recollections of relatives, friends and associates of J. F. Fitzpatrick, notably: W. J. Fitzpatrick, a brother; Willis W. Cassidy, chairman of the board of Sweet Candy Co. and a close personal friend; Gus P. Backman of the Chamber of Commerce and the Newspaper Agency Corp. board of directors; James Ivers; and J. W. Gallivan, Arthur C. Deck, Theodore Long and O. N. Malmquist, all of *The Tribune*.
2. Letter in the files of *The Tribune*.
3. Despite the reluctance of some, the editorial employes organized a unit of the American Newspaper Guild after enactment of the Wagner Labor Relations Act by the federal government and the "Little Wagner Act" by the state. Before the unit became operative, however, defections killed it. Some withdrew because they had never really had their hearts in it. Some pulled out because they did not want to identify with an organization that presumed to tell the world where they stood on political questions such as the Spanish Civil War or on other ideological issues which seemed unrelated to wages and working conditions at *The Tribune*. A subsequent attempt to revive the organization failed, but in 1951 guild supporters succeeded in organizing a unit covering the circulation, editorial and news departments. Contracts were negotiated for 1951-1953 but again defections and attrition set in and the organization died a natural death when no one showed up to negotiate a renewal contract.
4. From the 1956 commencement program of Brigham Young University.
5. For all practical purposes, Fitzpatrick functioned as publisher from the time of Thomas Kearns' death, although he did not assume the title of publisher until the death of A. N. McKay in 1924.

CHAPTER 22
Journalistic Brawl Revived

1. *Harper's Weekly*, April 4, 1913.
2. *Fourth Estate* (a newspaper trade publication), December 6, 1913.

3. *Ibid.*
4. *The Salt Lake Tribune,* August 30, 1914.
5. *Herald-Republican,* August 31, 1914.
6. *Ibid.,* February 28, 1918.
7. *Ibid.,* July 9, 1918.
8. *Salt Lake Herald,* July 18, 1920.
9. *Deseret News,* July 4, 1918.
10. *The Salt Lake Tribune,* July 6, 1918.
11. *Deseret News,* July 6, 1918.
12. *The Salt Lake Tribune,* November 1, 1916.
13. *Ibid.,* November 9, 1916.

CHAPTER 23
Deaths Temper Conflict

1. From many food advertisements published in *The Salt Lake Tribune* the week prior to Thanksgiving Day, November, 1918.
2. *The Salt Lake Tribune,* November 11, 1918.
3. *Ibid.,* November 12, 1918.
4. Unpublished historical notes of Noble Warrum, Sr., in the possession of *The Tribune.*
5. Author's interview with Heber J. Grant.
6. *Deseret News,* November 19, 1918.
7. *The Salt Lake Tribune,* October 20, 1918.
8. *Ibid.,* November 8, 1918.
9. *Ibid.,* October 5, 1918.

CHAPTER 24
From Brimstone to Soothing Syrup

1. Alter, *Utah Journalism,* 360.
2. Sworn statements of circulation and ownership published twice each year. (These figures are at variance with Alter's for the same dates.)
3. *The Salt Lake Tribune,* November 2, 1920.
4. *Ibid.,* October 31, 1924.
5. *Ibid.,* October 8, 1924.
6. *Ibid.,* November 8, 1924.
7. *Ibid.,* October 7, 1907
8. *Ibid.*
9. *Ibid.,* October 13, 1907.
10. *Ibid.,* October 15, 1907.
11. *Ibid.*
12. *Ibid.,* October 17, 1907.

13. The author heard this story from colleagues at *The Tribune* where it is one of the "classic tales" handed down on the sports desk. Several hours diligent squinting at the microfilm viewer failed to locate the exact September, 1934, date.
14. *The Salt Lake Tribune,* September 25, 1934.

CHAPTER 25
"J. F." Takes Over

1. As we enter the contemporary period, historical sources are necessarily limited. In this chapter, especially, the author draws from his own experience and observations as a *Tribune* employe and assumes the traditional reporter's responsibility for the accurate interpretation of events and conversations to which he was a witness.

CHAPTER 26
A Declaration of Voter Independence

1. Corporate records of *The Salt Lake Tribune.*
2. Sworn statements of circulation and ownership published twice each year.
3. *The Salt Lake Tribune,* November 4, 1932. (On October 30, 1932, the First Presidency of the Mormon Church had issued a statement denying rumors that they had aided or opposed any candidates.)
4. *Ibid.,* November 6, 1932.
5. *Ibid.,* November 1, 1936.
6. *Deseret News,* October 31, 1936.

CHAPTER 27
Prohibition: Sale by Drink

1. *Salt Lake Evening Democrat,* April 29, 1886.
2. *The Salt Lake Tribune,* July 14, 1908.
3. *Ibid.,* December 18, 1918.
4. *Ibid.,* October 18, 1933.
5. *Ibid.,* October 7, 1933.
6. *Ibid.,* October 29, 1933.
7. *Ibid.,* October 10, 1933.
8. *Ibid.,* November 1, 1933.
9. *Ibid.,* October 28, 1933.
10. *Ibid.,* October 10, 1933.

CHAPTER 28
Tribune's Crusading Role

CHAPTER 29
War Years

1. *The Salt Lake Tribune,* November 3, 1940.
2. *Ibid.,* November 6, 1940.
3. *Ibid.,* headlines gleaned from a number of issues published during the final months of 1940.
4. *Ibid.,* December 1, 1941.
5. *Ibid.,* November 26, 1943.
6. *Ibid.,* April 15, 1946.

CHAPTER 30
Economic Struggle Again

1. During its first 100 years, *The Tribune* has been issued from eight different locations in Salt Lake City: (1) April 15 to July 25, 1871, south side of First South Street, a quarter block west of Main Street. (2) July 25, 1871, to July 17, 1874, 34 E. Temple (Main Street)* between South Temple and First South on the east side of the street. This was the site of the old Western Union Telegraph office. (3) July 17, 1874, to January 17, 1880, 30 East Second South, the south side of the street, "nearly opposite the Foot of Commercial." (4) January 17, 1880, to July 5, 1887, 22-24 West Second South, north side of the street. (5) June 5, 1887, to January 1, 1891, 80 West Second South, the northeast corner of West Temple and Second South streets. (6) January 2, 1891, to October 17, 1906, 133 South West Temple, the east side of the street between First and Second South streets. (7) October 17, 1906, to June, 1938, 145 South Main Street. (8) From June, 1938, to present, 143 South Main Street.

*In later years the Salt Lake street numbering system was revised, thus 34 East Temple was on the east side of Main, where in 1970, that number is located on the west side of the street.

2. Advertising figures calculated by *Tribune* auditors.
3. Ashton, *Voice in the West,* 325.
4. *Ibid.,* 326-330.
5. Lineage figures calculated by *Tribune* auditors.

CHAPTER 31
Birth of NAC

1. From the private files of *The Tribune*.
2. Gallivan's recollection of events as related to the author.
3. Testimony presented by George L. Nelson at Senate Subcommittee hearing in 1967.
4. From an interview with Gus P. Backman.
5. From the Pulitzer Prize citation issued in 1957.
6. *The Salt Lake Tribune,* September 12, 1960.
7. *Time,* September 26, 1960.
8. *The Salt Lake Tribune,* September 15, 1960.

CHAPTER 32
Diversification Program Initiated

1. This recollection and subsequent information attributed to Gallivan was obtained by the author in an interview.
2. Testimony delivered by Gallivan at a Utah Public Service Commission hearing February 6, 1968.

CHAPTER 33
Antitrust Episode

1. Information gathered by Gallivan from many trade sources to use in his testimony before the Antitrust and Monopoly Subcommittee of the Senate Judiciary Committee in August, 1967.
2. See footnote 1 above.
3. *United States vs. Citizen Publishing Company et al.* (This case was entered in U.S. District Court of Arizona on September 7, 1965; came to trial April 5, 1966; judgment handed down January 31, 1968, and appealed by the defendants.)
4. *United States vs. Citizen Publishing Company et al.* (No. 243, U.S. Supreme Court, October Term, 1968. Opinion handed down March 10, 1969.)
5. *Ibid.* (The failing company doctrine is a judicially created defense to antitrust violation charges which permits acquisitions that would otherwise be illegal if it can be shown that the acquired company is failing and that there are no other available purchasers.)
6. From Gallivan's testimony before the Antitrust and Monopoly Subcommittee of the Senate Judiciary Committee in August, 1967.

CHAPTER 34
Tribune Personalities

1. Stories handed down in *Tribune* lore.
2. Dale Kramer, *Ross and The New Yorker* (New York City, 1952), 7.
3. James Thurber, *The Years with Ross* (New York City, 1957), 9-10.
4. Florabel Muir, *Headline Happy* (New York City, 1950), 3-32.

Index

C

CATV, 391-392.

Caine, John T., 69-70, 115, 128, 142-143, 145.

Callister, E. H., 231, 281, 283.

Campbell, Albert A. (Ace), 425.

Campbell, Allen G., 69, 214; 1880 election, 58-63.

Cannon, Angus, 42.

Cannon, Frank J., 145-147, 153, 194, 237; U.S. Senator, 168-172; *Tribune* editorial writer, 236-237, 241-244, 249, 257.

Cannon, George Q., 10, 92-94, 106, 108-109, 114, 118, 140, 143-145, 149, 153, 168-169, 172; 1880 election, 58; his election protested, 60-63; polygamy arrest, 97-102; polygamy sentence, 127-128; death, 190-191.

Cannon, Georgius Y., 190.

Cannon, Hugh J., 100, 242-243.

Cannon, Mrs. Hugh J., 100.

Carlson, A. W., 125.

Carman, Frank C., 390.

Castle Dale Progress, 210.

Chamber of Commerce, 136, 152, 295, 382; founding of Salt Lake group, 115-117, 123, 125; rejects municipal fusion ticket, 126; Backman named to NAC board, 376.

Chambers, R. C., 211-212, 214.

Chandler, Harry, 384.

Chaplin, Charlie, 420.

Chicago Tribune, The, 206, 332, 334, 358, 359, 368.

Chislett, John, 27.

Choate, Rufus, 241.

Christensen, Elayne, 317.

Christian Science Monitor, 359.

Churchill, Winston, 308.

Church of Jesus Christ of Latter-day Saints, The, tithing, 39-40; presiding authorities, 50; end of internal reform movement, 81; disincorporation, 110, 112; federal property "raid," 113, 120-123, 141-142; statehood drive, 128; political influence, 143-145, 148-150, 153, 155-157, 161-163, 167, 185-189, 199, 250, 261, 327-331, 342, 347; employment in Mormon-owned firms, 249-250; in business, 324, 389; opposes repeal, 339. See also, Brigham Young, John Taylor, Wilford Woodruff, Lorenzo Snow, George Q. Cannon, Joseph F. Smith, Heber J. Grant, David O. McKay, Polygamy, Irrepressible Conflict, Accommodation, New Movement, Z.C.M.I.

Citizen's Party, 146, 254.

Clark, John, 125.

Clark, J. Reuben, Jr., *Telegram* stockholder, 282; LDS First Presidency, 387.

Clark, W. A., Montana Senator, 173, 183, 189, 196, 209, 215; recommends Fitzpatrick, 267.

Clawson, Rudger, polygamy trial, 82-86, 94.

Clay, Henry, 241.

Clayton, N. W., 282.

Cleveland, Grover, President, 63, 102, 113, 116, 128-129, 151, 163, 209, 226, 234.

Clinton, Jeter, Dr., false imprisonment suit, 245-246.

Clyde, George D., 353.

Codman, John, 51.

Cohen, Mickey, 420.

Colfax, Schuyler, 23.

Colliers Weekly, 228.

Colton, Don B., 307, 356.

Coltrin, William, 334, 415.

Community Television, Inc., 391-392.

Connor, Patrick, E., Liberal Party founder, 133, 135.

Coolidge, Calvin, 307.

Courier-Journal (Louisville, Ky.), 410.

Cowley, M. F., resigns as Mormon apostle, 229.

Crawford, Eleanor F. (Mrs. John F. Fitzpatrick), 267.

Critchlow, Edward B., 225, 236.

Crouch, George W., *Tribune* associate editor, 19, 27.

Crusaders, back repeal, 341.

Cullom, Shelby M., 23.

Cullom-Struble Bill, 136-137.

Cutler, John C., 235, 237.

444

447

N

Nashville Tennessean, 407.
National Lead Company, 394, 398.
National Press Club, 424.
Nelson, George L., 375.
Nelson, William, Col., *Tribune* editor, 244-245; biographical data, 245-246.
Newell, Henry, 182, 214.
Newhouse, ( ), 377.
Newhouse, Samuel, 214.
Newman, J. P., polygamy debate, 25-26.
New Movement, 2, 6-7, 29; birth of, 12-14; support of, 21; *Tribune* as spokesman for, 17, 19-20, 27; attitude toward polygamy, 24-25. See also entries under William Godbe, Edward Tullidge, Brigham Young.
Newspaper Agency Corporation (NAC), 385, 404, 425; origins, 372-378; structure, 378; aids accommodation, 379; formal agreement signed, 380; antitrust investigation, 380, 400-401, 405, 407-409; Gallivan president, 387.
Newspaper Preservation Act, 375, 407-409.
Newsweek, 364.
New Orleans *Item,* 371.
New Orleans *States,* 371.
New Orleans *Times-Picayune,* 371.
New York Daily News, 318, 359, 420.
New Yorker, The, 418.
New York Herald, 20, 25-26, 36.
New York Post, 47.
New York Sun, 410.
New York Times, The, 153, 359.
New York Tribune, 410.
New York World, 410.
Nibley, Charles W., 283, 324.
Nibley Company, The, *Telegram* owners surrender stock to, 323-324.
Nixon, Richard M., 396.
Notre Dame University, 332-334.

O

O'Brien, Paul J. (Jerry), 395.
Ogden Standard, 241.

Ogden Standard-Examiner, 316, 390.
Olson, Ray L., 341.
Omaha Herald, 48.
Omaha Republican, 48.
Oregon Journal, 387.

P

Packard, John Q., 214.
Paden, William, 225.
Park, Hamilton G., 422-423.
Park Record, 215.
Park, Samuel C., 254.
Patrick, William C., 417.
Pearson, Drew, 369.
Peep O'Day, 9.
Peery, D. H., 214.
Penrose, Boies, 229.
Penrose, C. W., 2; *Deseret News* editor, 42, 237, 254-255; rivalry with Goodwin, 57, 61-64, 66; denounces polygamy, 299-300.
People's Party, 62, 128, 142-145, 247, 347; 1882 platform, 69; plans Constitutional Convention, 114-115; municipal fusion ticket, 125-126; election of 1890, 133-136.
Perris, Fred T., *Tribune* general manager, 28, 31.
Perry, James S., 425-426.
Peters, George S., 121
Peterson, A. F. (Tony), NAC business manager, 387.
Philadelphia Evening Bulletin, 359, 368.
Platt, Thomas C., 201.
Political developments, Mormon church political influence, 143-145, 148-150, 153, 155-157, 161-163, 167, 185-189, 199, 250, 261, 327-331, 342, 347; national parties organized in Utah, 142-149, 151, 152. See also entries under American, Citizens, Democratic, Liberal, People's and Republican parties; Statehood; Elections; *Salt Lake Tribune; Salt Lake Herald; Deseret News.*
Polygamy, 6-7, 9, 21-24, 73, 80-81, 88, 90, 94-95, 102, 110-111, 113-114, 122, 127-129, 152, 204, 217, 295, 310-311, 319, 347; Tabernacle de-

bate, 25-26; women's suffrage, 38; practice declines, 39; federal legislation against, 63-65, 69-70, 72; Idaho test oath, 136; Manifesto, 138-143; Utah Constitution bans, 160-161; Smoot election revives issue, 225-226, 228-229, 238-240; Mormon conference denounces, 299-300. See also entries under Irrepressible conflict, Rudger Clawson, Lorenzo Snow, Wilford Woodruff, Edmunds Act, Edmunds-Tucker Act.

Portland Oregonian, 222-223.

Powers, Orlando W., judge, 89, 133, 154, 236, 336-337.

Pratt, Orson, 10; polygamy debate, 25-26.

Prescott, George F., 7; *Tribune* owner, 31, 44, 54-55.

Preston, George D., 339.

Priest, Joel L., 196.

Priest, Joel L., Jr., 196.

Prohibition, 298-299; repeal, 336-345; sale by drink, 342-345. See also Simon Bamberger, Liquor.

Prohibition National Party, 337-338.

Pro-Utah, Inc., 400.

Pulitzer, Joseph, 410.

Pyper, George D., 125.

R

Raft River Rural Electric Cooperative, 399.

Raleigh, A. H., 2.

Rampton, Calvin L., 396.

Ransohoff, N. S., and Company, 15.

Rawlins, Athol, 377.

Rawlins, Joseph L., 145-146, 148, 151, 153, 171, 188, 194, 210.

Rawlins, J. R., 126.

Raybould, Benjamin, 27.

Ray, Paul H., 377.

Red and Black, 418.

Reed, George W., 55.

Republican Party, 161, 166, 172, 184, 197, 231, 234-237, 247, 254, 266, 281; opposes polygamy, 22; organized in Utah, 142-149, 151-152; first U.S. Senate election, 167-170; 1902 Senate election, 218, 226-227; na-

tional parties firmly established, 253; 1920 election victory, 306-307; 1924 election, 307; 1932 defeat, 329.

Reynolds, George, 43.

Rice, Windsor V., 182-183.

Richards, Franklin S., 100, 133, 143.

Riter, Franklin, 341.

Riter, William W., 125.

Roberts, B. H., historian, 2-3, 154, 161-162, 170-171, 173-174, 191, 228, 232, 240; resigns as *Herald* editor, 215-216; opinion of *Tribune,* 223-224, 248-249, 252; aversion to Frank J. Cannon, 241-242.

Roberts, Bolivar, 125.

Robinson, Homer F., *Tribune* business manager, 295, 304-305; initiates Sub-for-Santa, 305.

Robinson, J. W., 329.

Rockwell, Orrin Porter, 424.

Rogers, Will, 327.

Roosevelt, Franklin D., 277, 352, 421; 1932 election victory, 327-329; 1936 election, 330-331; pledges prohibition repeal, 337, 345; 1940 election, 354-356.

Roosevelt, Theodore, 201-202, 209, 213, 217, 231; position on Smoot, 219-220, 226-228, 234-235; Bull Moose, 261-262.

Ross, Harold, 417-419.

Rossiter, William A., 116-117.

Rouche, Thomas F., 117.

S

Sagebrush Democratic Party, 128.

St. Louis Post-Dispatch, 410.

St. Louis Republican, 48.

Salisbury, O. J., 185, 207.

Salt Lake Evening Democrat, 335.

Salt Lake Herald, 66, 69-70, 77, 98, 112, 132, 142, 150, 153, 157, 166, 173, 185, 189, 192, 196, 198, 200, 209, 210, 214, 248-249, 255, 308, 323, 325, 368, 419; founding, 34; *Tribune* opponent, 42; editorial policy, 215; merges with *Inter-Mountain Republican,* 215, 253, 280, 285; attacks Kearns, 221-222, 233; Democratic spokesman, 221, 224, 281; position on Smoot, 224-

451

Smoot, Reed, 186, 193, 198, 205, 237, 252, 254, 289-291, 389; Smoot-Kearns feud, 218-220, 233, 240, 282, 295, 321, 404; senatorial candidate, 224; wins U.S. Senate seat, 225, 227; his seating is opposed, 225-235, 244; *Herald* owner, 253, 261, 281-283; third term, 262-265; fourth term, 306; 1932 election defeat, 327-329.

Snow, Lorenzo, polygamy arrest, 87-90, 95, 103-105; Mormon president, 174, 176; supports Kearns, 186-187, 196, 198-199, 220, 234, 239; death, 190-191.

Snyder, Ruth, 420.

Snyder, Willard F., 236.

Socialist Party, 247.

Solomon, Alfred, 125.

Sowles, M. B., 125.

Spencer, Lydia, 83.

Spiers, Adam, 95.

Spry, William H., 253, 262, 291.

Stansbury, Howard, 37.

Stars and Stripes, 418.

Statehood, 8, 70, 109, 142, 148, 157, 225, 238; opposition to, 35, 113-114, 128-129; Mormons back, 128; enabling act, 151, 153, 158; Constitutional Convention, 153, 158-161, 177; forty-fifth state, 163-164; first U.S. Senate election, 167.

Stenhouse, T. B. H., historian, 12, 17.

Sunday Herald-Republican-Telegram, 286.

Sutherland, George, 175, 210, 219-221, 225, 281; U.S. Senator, 238, 289-290.

Sweet Candy Company, 250.

T

Taft, William Howard, 261.

Tammen, H. H., 410.

Taylor, John, 25, 50, 72, 92, 98, 102, 106, 108, 114, 140; death, 117-120.

Taylor, John W., resigns as apostle, 229.

Taylor, ( ), city sexton, 42.

Taylor, W. H., *Tribune* owner, 55.

Teasdale, George, Mormon apostle, 311.

Teasdel, Samuel P., 125.

Tele-Communications, Inc., 392.

Telegram, see *Salt Lake Telegram, The.*

TeleMation, 393.

Thatcher, Moses V., 125, 162, 171, 234, 239.

Thomas, Arthur L., 129, 136.

Thomas, Elbert D., 329, 353.

Thompson, Ezra, 247, 251, 363.

Thompson, ( ), Lord, 377.

Thurber, James, 418.

Thurman, Samuel R., 128.

Time, 384.

Toohy, Dennis J., 24.

Tracy Collins Bank and Trust Co., 425.

Tracy, Russel L., 425.

Tribune, see *Salt Lake Tribune, The.*

Tribune Building, 312, 314, 333, 363, 390.

Truth, 197-198, 206-207, 221, 233.

Tullidge, Edward W., historian, 1-2, 7, 49-50, 67; *Tribune* founder, 1-2; New Movement, 2; excommunication, 2; *The Utah Magazine*, 9, 11-12; *Mormon Tribune*, 17; *The Salt Lake Tribune*, 19-21, 27-29, 38-39.

Tullidge, John, 9.

Tulsa World, 407.

Tucson Arizona Star, 405-406.

Tucson Daily Citizen, 405-406.

TV Pix, Inc., 391.

Twenty-five Years of Utah Sports, 415.

U

University of Utah, 273.

Utah Centennial Commission, 374, 376.

Utah Historical Quarterly, 158.

Utah Magazine, The, 164; founding, 9; Mormon ban, 10-11, 17.

Utah Public Service Commission, 399.

Utah Radio Corporation, 388.

Utica *Herald*, 47.

V

Valentine, Dan, 422-423.

Vandercook, Oscar C., 95, 97.

Van Zile, Philip T., 69-70.

Looking west at Park City in 1880s.